W9-CLJ-753

Organizations and
Nation-States

Robert L. Kahn
Mayer N. Zald
Editors

ORGANIZATIONS AND NATION-STATES

New Perspectives on Conflict and Cooperation

Jossey-Bass Publishers

San Francisco • Oxford • 1990

ORGANIZATIONS AND NATION-STATES
New Perspectives on Conflict and Cooperation
Robert L. Kahn and Mayer N. Zald, Editors

Copyright © 1990 by: Jossey-Bass Inc., Publishers
350 Sansome Street
San Francisco, California 94104
&
Jossey-Bass Limited
Headington Hill Hall
Oxford OX3 0BW

Library of Congress Cataloging-in-Publication Data

Organizations and nation-states : new perspectives on conflict and
cooperation / Robert L. Kahn, Mayer N. Zald, editors—1st ed.
p. cm.—(The Jossey-Bass management series)
Includes bibliographical references and index.
ISBN 1-55542-291-8 (alk. paper)
1. International relations. 2. Security, International.
3. International cooperation. I. Kahn, Robert Louis, date.
II. Zald, Mayer N. III. Series. IV. Series: The Jossey-Bass social
and behavioral science series.
JX1391.069   1990
327.1—dc20   90-43454
                                                            CIP

Manufactured in the United States of America

The paper in this book meets the guidelines for
permanence and durability of the Committee on
Production Guidelines for Book Longevity of the
Council on Library Resources.

JACKET DESIGN BY WILLI BAUM

FIRST EDITION

Code 9094

A joint publication in
The Jossey-Bass
Management Series
and
The Jossey-Bass
Social and Behavioral Science Series

Contents

ix

Preface

Organizations and Nation-States is based on the proposition that organizational theory and research can contribute substantially to understanding and thereby improving international relations. Some years ago, when the ideas for the book were beginning to take form, the importance of organizational issues for international affairs might have seemed debatable. Recent events in the Soviet Union, Eastern Europe, the two Germanys, and the European Community have shifted the focus on organizational issues to the forefront of international relations. The main new fact in international affairs, as exemplified by these events, can be expressed in a single phrase: the decision to cooperate. What was not obvious before that decision was made has since become startlingly clear: when parties in conflict make the momentous decision to cooperate, the key question shifts from *whether* to *how* to do so.

The change in language is simple, but the implied change in thinking is profound. International affairs have been dominated by a point of view that is explicitly or implicitly Hobbesian; that is, relationships among nations are assumed to tend toward anarchy, and the potentiality of "each against all" is presumably relieved only when a dominant nation enforces peace or when potential enemies are so nearly equal in power that neither dares initiate open conflict. The decision to cooperate rests on a different set of assumptions, chief among them the assumption of unavoidable and increasing interdependence among nations. Especially for nations possessing nuclear weapons, achieving national security means learning to manage interdependence and to create organizational structures that can sustain cooperation under changing conditions.

The management of interdependence from the interpersonal to the interorganizational is what organizations and organizational theory are all about. The invention of organizational forms that enable cooperation among diverse groups has been accomplished, at least in part, in the simpler arenas of corporate, university, and government life. Most such organizations function without being torn apart by conflicts between departments or divisions, despite differences in their subcultures and competition among them for scarce organizational resources. Moreover, the solutions that work within organizations have to some extent been studied and codified through organizational research. This is the basis of our claim that organizational theory and research can offer some guidance in the search for appropriate forms of international cooperation.

Each chapter of *Organizations and Nation-States* attempts to validate that claim by addressing the key question of how to cooperate in a specific problem area—treaties and joint ventures, deterrence and nuclear security, escalation and de-escalation, and others. The uses of organizational research described in these chapters are numerous, but two themes are dominant throughout—the organizational embeddedness of actors on the international scene and the appropriateness of using organizations as models for nation-states.

Overview of the Contents

The book's eleven chapters, aside from the introduction (Chapter One) and the conclusion (Chapter Eleven), are grouped into three main sections. Part One deals with the formal and informal arrangements that have been developed to manage and prevent conflict between organizations and between nations. Chapter Two analyzes the strengths and weaknesses of three such structures: contracts, treaties, and joint ventures. Chapter Three, on cooperative security regimes, considers the costs and benefits of a less formalized structure, one that is more recognized in international than in interorganizational affairs. Such regimes have at times been remarkably successful in preventing international conflict; the problem is how they can best be developed and maintained given the unique circumstances of nuclear armament.

In Part Two, the emphasis shifts from the structure to the dynamics of international and interorganizational relations. Chapters Four and Five deal with escalation and de-escalation, respectively. Escalation of conflict between organizations and between nations has been studied extensively. At the international level, de-escalation has received much less attention than has escalation; but organizational studies of de-escalation, usually described as conflict management, are numerous. Accordingly, Chapter Four begins with models of escalation at the international level and adds to them the findings of organizational research. Chapter Five draws mainly on experimental and organizational research to analyze the process of de-escalation in terms that are relevant for initiating that process between nations as well as between organizations. Chapter Six discusses two other processes—deterrence and negotiation—in which conflict and cooperation are intermingled. Chapter Seven, the final chapter in Part Two, describes a process that has become increasingly important in international affairs: impression management, or spin control as it is called in the media. This is the process by which organizations or nations, during and immediately after a significant episode of conflict or negotiation, attempt to persuade their constituencies that their leaders acted wisely and that the outcomes were favorable to their interests.

Part Three addresses the continuing question for decision makers of how to make major decisions under conditions of uncertainty and crisis while minimizing avoidable errors. Chapter Eight answers this question by proposing a theoretical framework and a set of procedures for vigilant problem solving derived from an analysis of crucial decisions in the recent history of the United States. Chapter Nine addresses the related question of how decisions by organized groups, from committees to international legislatures, are shaped, often in unintended ways, by the group's formal rules and procedures.

Finally, in Chapter Eleven, the concluding chapter, we return to the analogy on which the book is built—the similarities between large-scale organizations and nation-states—and reevaluate it in light of the theoretical content and empirical findings of the preceding chapters.

Intended Audience

The readers we hope to reach comprise three rather separate groups. The first consists of scholars and research workers in the field of organizational studies; we hope they may be led to share our excitement about the international uses of organizational research and to shape their own work in ways that will address international problems. The second group consists of scholars in the field of international relations, most of whom have yet to explore the overlapping territory of organizational phenomena. Finally, we have tried to write in a way that will be useful to international specialists concerned more with practice and policy than with research. Although the organizational aspects of international relations are more researchable than researched, enough research has been done to warrant the attention of practitioners who face decisions that cannot wait for further research.

Genesis of the Book

Our book had its immediate origins in a year-long seminar at the Center for Advanced Study in the Behavioral Sciences. Kahn and Zald were scheduled to spend the 1986-87 academic year at the center, and Kahn planned to use that year to explore the implications of organizational research for international relations. Gardner Lindzey, then director of the center, proposed that the topic might be appropriate for a group project rather than a solitary effort. We agreed to form such a group, and Robert Sutton, also a prospective center fellow, joined us. The enthusiastic response of other fellows to our plan soon led us to enlarge the group substantially and to adopt the seminar format. Most members of the seminar are also authors of this volume. Robert Boruch, Carl Kaysen, and Gail Lapidus are not authors, but they were valued members of the seminar group. We hope their contributions are well reflected in our joint product.

The seminar itself was a project of the Center for Advanced Study in the Behavioral Sciences, and most of its members were center fellows for the 1986-87 academic year. Two members of the Stanford University faculty also joined us: Roderick Kramer and Leonard

Greenhalgh, a visiting professor from Dartmouth. Irving Janis, a former center fellow already working along similar lines, joined our group later. Gerald Davis, then a doctoral student at Stanford, joined us as a research assistant and quickly became a colleague. Richard N. Lebow of Cornell University was not a member of our group but allowed us to reprint his chapter on nuclear command and control, which we had relied on in our discussion of that topic.

Although the main content of this book was generated in the uniquely stimulating and nurturant environment of the Center for Advanced Study, it was completed under more familiar and less facilitative circumstances—by dispersed authors coping with competing demands. We are grateful to our chapter authors, who persisted in their work, and to our colleagues at the University of Michigan, Sue Meyer and Beth Waltz, who did so much to bring it to publication.

It remains for us to offer our appreciation to others who made possible the initiation and completion of this enterprise. The Carnegie Corporation and the William and Flora Hewlett Foundation supported our work from the beginning through grants to the Center for Adanced Study. We are grateful for that support and for the continuing interest of David Hamburg and Frederic Mosher at Carnegie and of Roger Heyns and Robert Barrett at the Hewlett Foundation.

Ann Arbor, Michigan   Robert L. Kahn
September 1990   Mayer N. Zald

The Authors

Gerald F. Davis is currently an assistant professor in the Graduate School of Business at Northwestern University. He received his A.B. degree (1984) in philosophy and psychology from the University of Michigan and his A.M. degree (1987) in sociology from Stanford University. He received his Ph.D. degree (1990) in business (organizational behavior) from Stanford University. In addition to applications of organization theory to areas of security studies, his current research focuses on large corporate takeovers and their implications for organization theory.

Leonard Greenhalgh is professor of management at the Amos Tuck School of Business Administration and adjunct professor of psychology at Dartmouth College. He received his B.S. degree (1968) in biology and his M.B.A. (1972) degree, both from the University of Rhode Island. He received his Ph.D. degree (1979) from Cornell University. He is cofounder of the Power, Negotiation, and Conflict Management Interest group of the Academy of Management. His primary research interest is in the psychological experience of conflict in interpersonal relationships, and much of his teaching and executive education is in this area.

Irving L. Janis received his Ph.D. degree (1948) in psychology from Columbia University. He is professor emeritus of psychology at Yale University and currently is adjunct professor of psychology at the University of California, Berkeley. He has long been a contributor to research on stress, attitude change, and decision making. During the past decade he has been carrying out social-psychological studies of crisis management, foreign policy decisions, and fiascos (reported in his books *Groupthink* [1982] and *Crucial Decisions* [1989]). He received the Distinguished Scientific Contributions Award from the American Psychological Association in 1981, the Kurt Lewin Memorial Award from the Society for the Psychological Study of Social Issues in 1985, and the Stanford Award for Distinguished Professional Contributions to Political Psychology from the International Society of Political Psychology in 1990. His chapter in this book is based on research that was supported by the National Science Foundation and the Carnegie Foundation of New York.

Robert L. Kahn is professor emeritus of psychology and of public health and research scientist in the Institute for Social Research at the University of Michigan. He received his B.A. (1939), M.A. (1940), and Ph.D. (1952) degrees in social psychology from the University of Michigan. He also holds an honorary Ph.D. degree from the University of Amsterdam. Kahn was a Fellow at the Netherlands Institute for Advanced Study in 1976–77 and at the Center for Advanced Study in Behavioral Sciences (Palo Alto) in 1986–87. He received a Distinguished Faculty Achievement Award from the University of Michigan in 1985, a Scholarly Contributions Award from the Academy of Management in 1987, and the Kurt Lewin Memorial Award from the Society for the Psychological Study of Social Issues (American Psychological Association) in 1988. Books of which Kahn is author or coauthor include *The Dynamics of Interviewing* (1957, with C. F. Cannell), *Organizational Stress* (1964, with D. W. Wolfe, R. P. Quinn, J. D. Snoek, and R. A. Rosenthal), *The Social Psychology of Organizations* (1966 and 1978, with D. Katz), *Surveys by Telephone: A National Comparison with Personal Interview* (1979, with R. Groves), *The Study of Organizations: Findings from the Field and Laboratory* (1980, with D. Katz and S. Adams), and *Work and Health* (1981).

Roderick M. Kramer is associate professor of organizational behavior at the Stanford University Graduate School of Business. He received his B.A. degree (1977) in experimental psychology from California State University, Los Angeles, and his Ph.D. degree (1985) in social psychology from the University of California, Los

Angeles. His current research interests include organizational conflict and cooperation, organizational learning, social dilemmas, psychological aspects of the arms race, and negotiation behavior.

Richard N. Lebow is director of the peace studies program and professor of government at Cornell University. He was previously professor of strategy of the National War College and scholar-in-residence in the Central Intelligence Agency. He received his Ph.D. degree (1968) in political science from City University of New York. Lebow's most recent book is *Nuclear Crisis Management: A Dangerous Illusion* (1987). A coauthored study of superpower crisis prevention and management, based on case studies of the Cuban missile and 1973 Middle East crises, is forthcoming.

David R. Mares is associate professor of political science at the University of California, San Diego. He received his Ph.D. degree (1982) in political science from Harvard University and has taught in Mexico and Chile. His current interests revolve around the security conceptions and policies of middle-level powers. He has published *Penetrating the International Market* (1987) as well as articles in *International Organization, International Studies Quarterly, Third World Quarterly, Latin American Research Review,* and in Spanish and Chinese publications.

Walter W. Powell is associate professor of sociology at the University of Arizona. He has also been a member of the faculty at M.I.T. and at Yale University. He received his Ph.D. (1978) in sociology from SUNY at Stony Brook. He is coeditor of *The New Institutionalism in Organizational Analysis* (forthcoming), editor of and contributor to *The Nonprofit Sector: A Research Handbook* (1967), author of *Getting into Print: The Decision Making Process in Scholarly Publishing* (1985), and coauthor of *Books: The Culture and Commerce of Publishing* (1982, with L. A. Coser and C. Kadushin).

Fritz W. Scharpf is codirector of the Max-Planck Research Institute in Koln, Germany. Before assuming that position, he was a fellow and director of the International Institute of Management,

Wissenschaftszentrum, in Berlin. He has also been a faculty member in the Department of Political Science at Konstanz and in the Yale Law School. He received his LL.M. degree (1961) from Yale University and his Dr.Jur. degree (1964) from the University of Freiburg. Scharpf's research interests are in the broad domain of political economy. Within that area, he is particularly concerned with the formal political structures within which major policy decisions are made and the ways in which those structures shape and constrain policy decisions.

Robert I. Sutton is associate professor of organizational behavior in the Department of Industrial Engineering and Engineering Management at Stanford University and associate director of the Stanford Center for Organizations Research. He received his Ph.D. degree (1984) in organizational psychology from the University of Michigan. Sutton's primary research interests are in organizational decline and death and in the role that emotion plays in the behavior of individuals and organizations. His other interests include impression management, cognition, job stress, and institutional theory.

Mayer N. Zald is professor of sociology, social work, and business administration at the University of Michigan. He received his Ph.D. degree (1961) in social psychology from the University of Michigan. He has published widely on complex organizations, social welfare, and social movements. In 1986-87 he was vice-president of the American Sociological Association. Recently, he edited *Social Movements in an Organizational Society: Collected Essays* (with J. D. McCarthy). Currently, he is engaged in studies of the intersection of history and organizational theory. He is also involved in foundational work on the relationship of the social sciences to the humanities.

Organizations and Nation-States

Chapter 1

Organizational Theory and International Relations
Mutually Informing Paradigms

Robert L. Kahn

The academic domain usually labeled, with uncharacteristic scholarly optimism, *international security* is an area of increasing activity if one can judge from the volume of published material. This fact reflects the importance of the topics addressed rather than any sudden scientific success, predictive or explanatory. The obvious examples to be cited in support of this dual assertion are the dramatic changes in domestic affairs and foreign policies of the Soviet Union that began with Gorbachev's election as general secretary in 1986. Scholars did not predict these developments before the fact; nor were they able to agree thereafter about their immediate implications for international relations, let alone the course of future events.

Experts in organizational behavior have reason to sympathize with such difficulties. Changes in the corporate structure of the United States in recent years have been great enough to require a whole new descriptive vocabulary—junk bonds, leveraged buyouts, poison-pill defenses, white-knight rescues, and the like—but they were not well predicted. In organizational affairs as in international relations, events in the real world have set a pace that scholarship has yet to match. No single paradigm comprehends the complexities of relations between nations or between organizations, and

1

research workers are in need of adding to their theoretical scaffolding as well as to their empirical data.

It is the purpose of this book to propose organizational theory and research as a source of such contributions to the field of international relations, as well as to illustrate some of the ways in which work at the international level can inform organizational theory. Contributions of both kinds are more potential than actual, however. Except for the specialty areas usually designated by the abbreviation C^3I—communication, command, control, and intelligence—the literature of international affairs contains little that draws on mainstream organizational research and theory. And organizational scholars, except for occasional ventures into the special problems of multinational corporations, have ignored the domain of international relations and security.

We believe that the separation is unfortunate, primarily because we believe organizational research and theory can contribute to an understanding of international affairs. The contribution can come in part from improved prediction and explanation of the behavior of individual actors on the international scene, actors who are necessarily behaving in organizational roles and responding to the expectations and influence attempts characteristics of those roles. A further contribution, however, can come from the utilization of organizations as models for nation-states. They are, of course, imperfect models because they are much simpler in structure and much more limited in function than nations. Yet these two kinds of social systems, nations and organizations, share many characteristics, and the organizational microcosms offer the research advantages of large numbers and relative accessibility to observation, measurement, and even occasional experimentation.

We do not imply that the benefits of scholarly convergence would be totally asymmetrical. Organizational researchers could learn a great deal from international specialists, for example, about the negotiation of conflicts, the formation of coalitions, and the potentiality of informal accords (regimes) for introducing order into anarchic situations.

This book is organized around substantive areas in which the promise of exchange between organizational and international research seems especially great. Each of these areas is the subject of a chapter, and each chapter thus becomes an essay on an issue of relevance for both organizations and nations. Each also discusses research at the organizational level in ways that shed light on the international.

In the remainder of this introductory chapter, we will consider the frames of reference that have been influential in organizational research, their relationship to international affairs, and the management of interdependence as an integrative theme in organizational and international relations. These lead to the final section of the chapter, which consists of a brief description of the substantive topics around which the research chapters, or essays, are grouped.

Frames of Reference in Organizational Research

The brief history of organizational theory has been shaped by two frames of reference. The first regards organizations as producing units and defines the prime task of organizational research as discovering factors that determine organizational effectiveness or productivity. The second frame of reference regards organizations as sets of individuals whose well-being is affected by the terms of organizational membership and whose motivation to continue that membership depends on their assessment of its comparative contribution to their well-being.

These two frames of reference are not so much oppositional as complementary. The second, which came later, has enlarged the first rather than replaced it, and the combination has been beneficial. We regard the use of organizational theory and research in the international context as implying a third frame of reference, which we propose to make explicit.

Organizations as Producing Units. The dominant frame of reference in organizational theory and research treats organizations as producing units and tends to disregard their other characteristics. It is an old and persisting point of view. Even the more recent treatment of organizations as natural systems, which Scott (1981, 1987) has called a major shift in the types of theoretical models that guide organizational investigations, continues the emphasis on productivity and efficiency, although these are taken as markers for organizational survival, which is the ultimate criterion of success in the natural systems view.

The emphasis on productivity or efficiency as the key variable in organizational assessment and the prime justification for organizational designs and technological choices is very old. Adam Smith, in his historic description of the division of labor, wrote in 1776 that the transformation of pin making from a single skilled trade to eighteen unskilled tasks coordinated by a supervisor brought about tremendous increases in productivity. The result of this "proper division and combination of their separate operation," Smith ([1776] 1978, p. 5) asserted, was to increase productivity by a factor of 240!

The link to human well-being in such theories is almost entirely via increased productivity and consequent increases in levels of consumption. Smith was explicit about such matters: "It is the great multiplication of the productions of all the different arts, in consequence of the division of labor, which occasions, in a well-governed society, that universal opulence which extends itself to the lowest ranks of people" (p. 8).

One hundred and fifty years later, Frederick Taylor's ([1916] 1978, p. 12) description of the benefits of "scientific management" echoed Adam Smith, both in its claim for increased productivity and in its faith that those increases would be widely shared: "This increasing of output per individual in the trade results, of course, in cheapening the product; it results, therefore, in larger profits usually to the owners of the business; it results also, in many cases, in a lowering of the selling price, although that has not come to the extent it will later. In the end the public gets the good."

More basic organizational theorists, of whom Weber is the prototype, were less concerned with the engineering aspects of machine technology and more concerned with the bureaucratic form of social organization that seemed to be the natural concomitant of that technology. Weber was primarily an analyst and critic—not, as is so often assumed, an uncritical admirer—of bureaucracy, but he had no doubt about its functional superiority with respect to product output. His reference to the "efficiency of Caesarism" expresses in a phrase both his criticism and his grudging admiration (Weber, 1947, quoted in Shafritz and Whitbeck, 1978, p. 41). The application of Weberian concepts to public administration begun by Gulick and Urwick (1937) retained the admiration but not the criticism of the original.

In short, organizational theory, basic and applied, acquired an early preoccupation with productivity, and it remains the dominant frame of reference within which human organizations are assessed. At their simplest, and perhaps their most influential, organizational theories and applications that take this frame of reference offer universalistic prescriptions for maximizing organizational performance. This is what Smith did in advocating the division of labor into small fragments, and this is what Taylor, Gilbreth, Bedeaux, and their modern time-and-motion heirs have attempted to do.

Their substantial success should be acknowledged, even by their critics. Modern productive technology and the invention of social organization for its efficient use have developed together, although the technological partner has almost always sung the lead part in this long historical duet.

Organizations as Sources of Worker Well-Being. Human organizations are sets of people engaged in recurrent cycles of behavior, using tools of greater or lesser complexity, coordinating their actions in ways that produce a particular good or service. The performance of organizationally designated acts at a time, place, and pace that are also organizationally designated has direct effects on the well-being of organizational members. Some of these effects are physiological, some psychological; some of them are positive, some negative. In combination they suggest an alternative frame of reference for understanding and assessing organizations: the well-being of their members.

It can be argued that even the earliest machine technology made positive contributions to employee well-being. The steam engines of the industrial revolution freed men and women from some of the most brutalizing and monotonous manual tasks—pumping, dragging, and repetitive heavy lifting—but the demands of the early machine technology and the social arrangements for its use were scarcely less onerous. And in any case, the primary justification for those organizational innovations was their productive efficiency, not their side benefits to employees.

Most of the constraints that were subsequently enacted for the sake of worker well-being—limitations in hours of machine work, elimination of child labor, installation of safety devices, and the like—were regarded by management as additional costs of production and were initially opposed on that basis. They were advocated on humanitarian grounds, at first by trade unions and voluntary associations and ultimately by legislators who made them law.

In organizational research, the evaluation of work organizations in terms of employee well-being is usually said to have begun with the human relations school of research, which in turn had its beginnings with Elton Mayo and his colleagues in the 1930s. That assertion is true, but one should not conclude that employee well-being was immediately proposed as an alternative criterion to productivity. Mayo (1933) and his co-workers did not contest the dominance of the productivity frame of reference or use job satisfaction and other social-psychological variables as criteria in their own right. Rather, as Roethlisberger and Dickson's (1939) classic work made clear, social-psychological variables were introduced to explain unanticipated patterns of productivity that emerged during experimental changes in illumination and other physical conditions.

In short, when worker satisfaction began to command the attention of organizational researchers, it was as a predictor of productivity, either through its main effects or its interactions with other factors, rather than as a criterion variable in its own right. Even the early Tavistock work on organizations as sociotechnical systems urged the "composite system"—a simple formal structure with complex work roles rather than the reverse—on the grounds of superiority over the conventional in terms of production and costs (Emery and Trist, 1960).

Not until the 1960s do we find the developments that have made research on employee well-being the important second theme in organizational scholarship: (1) the enlargement of well-being measures from job satisfaction to an array of affective, behavioral, and physiological variables that assess the quality of individual life on and off the job, (2) the serious study of such outcomes as they are affected by characteristics of the work situation, and (3) the insistence that these outcomes, no less than productivity and profitability, should become factors in organizational assessment, design, and management.

Developments along these lines took place more or less concomitantly in a number of countries, including England, Norway, Sweden, Holland, and the United States. In more recent years, research on work-related stress has become a theme of great importance in the organizational domain. It involves biomedical as well as social-psychological research workers, and it has established employee well-being as a complementary frame of reference to the familiar criteria of productivity and efficiency.

Organizational Factors in International Relations

We now propose a third frame of reference for understanding and evaluating human organizations. It continues the theme of well-being, but carries it beyond the populations of owners and managers, consumers and producers. It involves the effects of organizations, positive and negative, at community, national, and global levels.

The ramifications of using this frame of reference are numerous. It directs our attention to what is probably the most important organizational change in our time, the tendency toward organizational combinations of various kinds, national and international. It calls attention to the effects, intended and unintended, of organizations on populations far beyond their own boundaries. More directly to the purpose of this book, inquiry into the effects of organizational actions on international relations leads us to consider two specific research connections between the organizational and international levels: the study of international relations as organizational behaviors, and the use of organizations as models for the behaviors of nations themselves.

International Relations as Organizational Behaviors. The interdependence of individuals and of nations has always been greater than our comprehension of it, and it has been mediated by organizations to a greater extent than is generally acknowledged. Industrial development has greatly increased that interdependence, and multinational organizations have made it increasingly visible. Most important of all, the existence and proliferation of nuclear weapons have made the management of interdependence between nations a matter of species survival.

That task, the management of interdependence, is what organizations and organizational theory are about, at levels ranging from the interpersonal to the international. The recognition of interdependence between individuals at the level of the work group was central to the early work of the human relations school (Argyris, 1957; McGregor, 1960; Likert, 1961), which treated the management of that interdependence as the central task of supervision. Emery and Trist (1973) proposed an analogous argument at the level of interdependence between organizations. In their initial exposition of the sociotechnical concept of organizations, they asserted: "Similarly, the primary task in managing the enterprise as a whole is to relate the total system to its environment and is not an internal regulation per se" (Emery and Trist, 1973, p. 220).

The argument is no less valid with respect to international relations. The survival of every nation and the quality of life within each depends in great degree on its relations with others. Moreover, the behaviors that express and determine such relationships are organizational. Diplomats and other governmental figures act not as free agents but as individuals in organizational roles. They are responsible to organized constituencies within their governments and polities, and they speak with the force of organizational resources— military, economic, and political. The signing of treaties, the conclusion of trade agreements, and even the making of war are expressions of organizational decisions.

It would be highly appropriate, therefore, for organizational scholars to deal with such matters, to develop concepts and measures that refer to international relations and global outcomes, and thus to provide a third frame of reference for the assessment and evaluation of human organizations. They have not done so, however. Organizational theory and research, with few exceptions, have been peculiarly and inappropriately silent about international relations. In complementary fashion, research that deals with international relations has tended to neglect the organizational level and the research literature of organizations.

Recent years have seen some change in the latter tendency. Scholars like Allison (1971) and Kevles (personal communication, 1986) have utilized organizational explanations for the dynamics of the arms race. In the area of concentrated scholarship C^3I, as we have said, specialists in government have made some use of organizational concepts in their analyses of military capacity, vulnerability, and risk of accidental war. (See, for example, Blair, 1985, and Bracken, 1983.) We now urge a complementary effort on the part of organizational research scholars.

Organizations as Models for Nation-States. There is a second and different respect in which organizational research and theory are potentially relevant to an understanding of international relations. Organizations can serve as models, in the biomedical sense of the term, for the interaction of nations.

In the life sciences, investigators put great emphasis on such models, that is, on the discovery and appropriate use of readily accessible and relatively simple organisms that exhibit behaviors and pathologies relevant for understanding the same phenomena in human populations. Most social psychologists interested in conflict processes have apparently considered organizations too complex for their purposes and have utilized the simpler model of the two-person game. Axelrod (1984, p. 28) asserts that the prisoner's dilemma "has become the E. coli. of social psychology."

We do not suggest an end to such work; the trade-off between experimental control and external validity is unavoidable and implies complementary work in the laboratory and in the field. We do propose that organizations themselves can serve as models for certain behaviors of nation-states. The unfriendly takeovers, the resisted mergers, and the mutually chosen alliances of organizations, for example, have obvious counterparts at the international level. Particularly relevant for peaceful international relations are the recent interorganizational phenomena usually referred to as joint ventures.

According to Scott (1981, p. 196), "an organizational joint venture occurs when two or more firms create a new organization to pursue some common purpose. Joint ventures differ from mergers in that they entail only limited pooling of resources by the participating organizations." Joint ventures thus constitute a special category of organizational combinations: the combining is voluntary; it is partial, and the "parent" organizations do not lose their separate identities.

The creation of the NUMMI organization by General Motors and

Toyota, for the purpose of manufacturing and marketing in the United States a Japanese-engineered automobile using Toyota components, is a corporate joint venture. The European Community is also a joint venture, although it is a tremendously more complex example of the phenomenon. The Standing Consultative Commission, a body of delegates from the United States and the Soviet Union that was created to resolve questions arising subsequent to the signing of the Anti-Ballistic Missile Treaty (sometimes called ABM or SALT I), is yet another joint organizational venture. It is, however, a joint venture of a special type, in which a new organization is created to maintain a less intensive but extremely important effort at international cooperation by treaty agreement. Even the United Nations can be regarded as a joint venture, and its recurrent difficulties reflect in part our imperfect understanding of what formal structures and what processes make for the success of joint ventures, as well as the inherent complexities of international federations.

The Management of Interdependence

No single theoretical framework is available to guide the formulation of organizational research relevant for international relations. We believe, however, that the integrating theme should be the management of interdependence. Interdependence of some kind is a precondition for conflict and an inevitable part of cooperation, both interorganizational and international. Without some degree of interdependence with respect to resource acquisition, territorial boundaries, and the like, there would be no incentive to assume the risks and costs of conflict or to explore the potentialities for cooperation.

The persisting question for every organization and nation is how best to manage existing interdependencies. Let us begin with the organizational case and assume that the elimination of an existing interdependency is impossible. We can then imagine a hypothetical continuum in which the identifiable scale points represent specific structural arrangements for the management of interdependence. Arranged in order of increasing proportions of managed as compared to "unmanaged" interdependence, we then have a scale anchored at one end by total combination (conquest, merger, takeover) and at the other by no-holds-barred conflict.

When two organizations combine, the content of their interorganizational relationship becomes intraorganizational. Problems of coordination are not eliminated, but they are moved inside the organizational boundary and made subject to the authority structure of the organization. They become, in that sense, managed. The other extreme, interorganizational conflict without constraint, is not encountered in civil society. The social norms and the laws of the land limit the forms in which interorganizational conflict can be expressed, so that the more common situation is that of the market, in which the expression of conflict is constrained by some sociolegal factors and protected by others—antitrust legislation and laws against collusion, for example.

Figure 1.1 represents the continuum of organizational interdependence just described. Each of the structural arrangements for organizations has its counterpart at the international level. Organizational mergers and hostile takeovers resemble international conquest and absorption. Organizational joint ventures have many international counterparts, from bilateral single-purpose arrangements like the U.S.-USSR Antarctic expeditions to the multination and multipurpose European Community or the United Nations itself. Organizational contracts resemble international treaties, and so on to the unmanaged end state of open organizational conflict and international war.

**Figure 1.1. Hypothetical Continuum of Managed Interdependence
Between Organizations.**

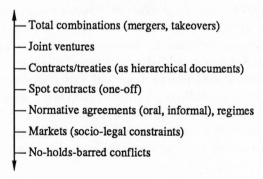

— Total combinations (mergers, takeovers)

— Joint ventures

— Contracts/treaties (as hierarchical documents)

— Spot contracts (one-off)

— Normative agreements (oral, informal), regimes

— Markets (socio-legal constraints)

— No-holds-barred conflicts

These structural arrangements between organizations are linked
by interorganizational processes. Organizations—and nations—
move toward or away from open conflict by processes of escalation
or de-escalation that have their own dynamics and causal laws. And
macroprocesses like escalation and de-escalation are themselves outcomes of more specific exchanges, including negotiation and bargaining around particular issues and the projection of particular
impressions, threats, and promises.

Moreover, these interorganizational structures and processes are
linked to intraorganizational factors, both structural and proces-
sual, although neither empirical research nor theoretical development enables us to specify one-to-one correspondences between
structure and process or between inter- and intraorganizational
phenomena.

Organization of the Book

The concept of interdependence and its ramifications for organizations and nations constitute the integrating theme for this book.
Our extrapolation from the organizational to the national level is
thus concerned with interorganizational and international relationships, along with the internal processes that affect such relationships. This emphasis is reflected in the content of the individual
chapters and in the three main clusters that they form: structures of
interdependence, processes of conflict, and the internal characteristics of decision and control.

Structures of Interdependence. The first section of the book,
Chapters Two and Three, deals directly with issues of interorganizational and international structure. Contracts, treaties, joint ventures, and regimes are structural solutions to the problem of
interdependence. Each has its advantages and its costs. Chapter
Two (Davis, Kahn, and Zald) develops more fully the continuum of
managed interdependence proposed in this introduction, distinguishing between conflicts of interest that arise between market
competitors and those that arise between purchasing and supplying
organizations. The framework developed to deal with these issues
is applied to the international level by analyzing a particular inter-

national joint venture, the United States and USSR Standing
Consultative Commission, which was established by the Strategic
Arms Limitation Treaty (SALT) of 1971 as a means for implement-
ing and maintaining that agreement.

Chapter Three (Mares and Powell) concentrates on the nature
and origins of regimes, a term used by political scientists to desig-
nate international agreements that are less formal than treaties or
joint ventures but that nevertheless have the ability to manage conflicts of interest and prevent conflicts of arms between nations. The
origin of such regimes is analyzed as a learning process, and research on organizational learning is invoked as a basis for the
analysis.

Processes of Conflict. The second section of the book, Chapters
Four through Seven, addresses four processes central to understanding organizational and international conflict. Chapters Four (Davis
and Powell) and Five (Kahn and Kramer) deal with the macroprocesses of escalation and de-escalation, the former a topic long emphasized in international affairs and the latter persistently neglected. It
is approached here in terms of the motivational forces toward reducing conflict and the social-psychological barriers to doing so.

Chapters Six and Seven discuss two processes that are linked
more closely to individual as well as institutional behavior: negotiation and impression management. In Chapter Six (Greenhalgh
and Kramer) three forms of negotiation—distributive bargaining,
integrative bargaining, and deterrence—are compared with respect
to their probable payoff to both parties at conflict and with respect
to the conditions for their success in practice. Chapter Seven (Sutton and Kramer) utilizes an analysis of the Iceland arms control
talks between the United States and the USSR to illuminate an
aspect of negotiation not included in current theories—impression
management or, in the language of political journalism, "spin control." This case study reminds us of the dual nature of organizational and international negotiation: the necessity of the negotiators
to reach agreement both with their opponents and with their constituencies. Moreover, the process of satisfying the constituency involves more than responsiveness; it has come to involve as well the
active and sometimes elaborate effort to impose an interpretation of

events that preserves or enhances the position of the negotiators and their hierarchical superiors.

Decision and Control. Conflict between organizations and between nations is usually regarded as purposeful, even if it is also judged to be misguided or malevolent. Such approaches necessarily involve the assumptions that the decisions of leaders are shaped by a kind of rationality and that control by leaders ensures that decisions, once made, will be carried out. Chapters Eight, Nine, and Ten show the weakness of these assumptions and the consequences for conflict and conflict management.

Chapter Eight (Janis) is concerned with the quality of the decisions themselves, especially under conditions of crisis, when the time pressures are great and the stakes are extremely high. A model, the constraints model, is proposed for analyzing situational demands, sources of decision error, and quality of decisions. Chapter Nine (Scharpf) is also concerned with the quality of decisions, and it uses the framework of game theory and the examples of four mixed-motive games to examine the determinants of decision quality. Two main classes of determinants are proposed: decision rules, which are expressed as payoff matrices in the four games, and decision styles, which consist of the cognitive and normative factors that shape the definition of interests and the framing of issues used by each of the parties at conflict.

Chapter Ten (Lebow and Zald) addresses issues that are temporally subsequent to the making of decisions. It deals mainly with decision implementation and treats it as a problem of control and loss of control. Such problems are analyzed as they emerge in the most vital area of superpower relations: detection of and response to nuclear threat.

Finally, Chapter Eleven (Zald) reinvokes the analogy between organizational and international relations and begins the development of a research agenda that utilizes it.

References

Allison, G. T. *Essence of Decision: Explaining the Cuban Missile Crisis.* Boston: Little, Brown, 1971.

Argyris, C. *Personality and Organization.* New York: Harper & Row, 1957.

Axelrod, R. *The Evolution of Cooperation.* New York: Basic Books, 1984.

Blair, B. G. *Strategic Command and Control: Redefining the Nuclear Threat.* Washington, D.C.: Brookings Institution, 1985.

Bracken, P. *The Command and Control of Nuclear Forces.* New Haven, Conn.: Yale University Press, 1983.

Emery, F. E., and Trist, E. L. "Socio-Technical Systems." In *Management Science Models and Techniques.* Vol. 2. Elmsford, N.Y.: Pergamon Press, 1960.

Emery, F. E., and Trist, E. L. *Toward a Social Ecology.* New York: Plenum, 1973.

Gulick, L., and Urwick, L. (eds.). *Papers on the Science of Administration.* New York: Institute of Public Administration, 1937.

Likert, R. *New Patterns of Management.* New York: McGraw-Hill, 1961.

McGregor, D. *The Human Side of Enterprise.* New York: McGraw-Hill, 1960.

Mayo, E. *The Human Problems of an Industrial Civilization.* New York: Macmillan, 1933.

Roethlisberger, F. J., and Dickson, W. J. *Management and the Worker.* Cambridge, Mass.: Harvard University Press, 1939.

Scott, W. R. *Organizations: Rational, Natural, and Open Systems.* Englewood Cliffs, N.J.: Prentice-Hall, 1981.

Scott, W. R. *Organizations: Rational, Natural, and Open Systems.* (2nd ed.) Englewood Cliffs, N.J.: Prentice-Hall, 1987.

Shafritz, J. M., and Whitbeck, P. H. (eds). *Classics of Organization Theory.* Oak Park, Ill.: Moore, 1978.

Smith, A. *The Wealth of Nations.* In J. M. Shafritz and P. H. Whitbeck (eds.), *Classics of Organization Theory.* Oak Park, Ill.: Moore, 1978. (Originally published 1776.)

Taylor, F. W. "The Principles of Scientific Management." *Bulletin of the Taylor Society,* Dec. 1916. Reprinted in J. M. Shafritz and P. H. Whitbeck (eds.), *Classics of Organization Theory.* Oak Park, Ill.: Moore, 1978.

Weber, M. *The Theory of Social and Economic Organizations.* (A. M. Henderson and T. Parsons, trans.) New York: Free Press, 1947.

PART 1

Structures of
Interdependence

Chapter 2

Contracts, Treaties, and Joint Ventures

Gerald F. Davis
Robert L. Kahn
Mayer N. Zald

There is a formal similarity to the conduct of international relations and the conduct of interorganizational relations. Nation-states compete, conflict, and cooperate with each other, as do organizations. Nations enter into treaties with each other, operate joint ventures, enter into long-term negotiations and contracts, and merge with each other. Similarly, organizations engage in hostile and friendly takeovers, enter into formal and informal alliances, set up joint ventures, and enter into long-term contracts.

In the last two decades the analysis of interorganizational relations has been a "hot" topic. Both theory and research have mushroomed. At the same time, current events in the world of organizations forcefully draw our attention to these topics. When General Motors and Toyota enter into joint ventures, when computer firms set up joint research ventures, when investment bankers and corporate raiders initiate takeover proposals, it is hard to ignore the relevance of interorganizational fields, of environmental turbulence, to the functioning of organizations. This chapter reflects our first cut at drawing out the implications of this literature and interest for thinking about joint ventures and contracts in international relations.

As noted in the introduction to this volume, we believe that there is a relatively robust analogy between organizations and nations and between interorganizational relations and international relations (Kahn, 1985; Zald, 1975). Our first task is to lay out explicitly the structure of this analogy and argue for its relevance. Second, we will contend that by examining some of the institutions that have evolved to structure cooperative relations among organizations, we can gain insight into some of the problems in attaining cooperation among nations and their potential solutions, with a particular focus on superpower relations and the threat of nuclear conflict. Finally, we will illustrate the value of this approach by applying it to the problems of a particular case, the Standing Consultative Commission (SCC). The SCC is a joint organization that was established by the United States and the USSR during the Strategic Arms Limitation Treaty (SALT) talks to deal with issues related to compliance with and implementation of arms control agreements.

Organizations and Nations: The Structure of the Analogy

Studies of political processes in organizations have often relied implicitly and, occasionally, explicitly on an analogy between organizations and nations. This analogy underlies much of the work done since the early 1960s that examines issues of power, authority, and conflict within organizations. March (1962; Cyert and March, 1963) used pluralist democratic imagery to characterize the firm in terms of coalitions of actors pressing their policy and other interests. Selznick (1969) finds one of the results of collective bargaining to be the constitution of the worker as an "industrial citizen" with attendant rights and responsibilities, a characterization upon which Burawoy (1979) builds in describing the "internal state" created within organizations to maintain worker consent. Zald and Berger (1978) find processes comparable to those of social movements in states within organizations. One aspect of our task is to be very explicit in exploiting the analogy between nation and organization. Moreover, there is a structural similarity in the dynamics of relations *between* these corporate actors that has not received the attention it deserves.

The Problem of Order. The problem faced by interdependent nations, like that faced by interdependent organizations, is a special case of the "problem of order": how can actors with conflicting short-term interests be coordinated so as to serve long-term interests? This is, of course, the problem Hobbes ([1651] 1962) ascribed to individuals in a presocietal "state of nature," where no single actor was powerful enough to enforce a mutually beneficial normative order. Instead, anarchy reigned, with each actor short-sightedly pursuing its immediate self-interest. This came at the expense of long-term interests, which could only be served via the cooperation that a normative order could support. From the point of view of the theorist, the problem of order for organizations and for nations is complicated by an order of magnitude by the fact that the relevant units are collective actors, not individuals: the potentially conflicting interests both within and between collectives must be taken into account. As we shall see, conflicting interests of constituents and conflicting definitions of collective interest are critical to an understanding of the fate of the Standing Consultative Commission in the first half of the 1980s. They are no less important for understanding the imperative need for creating such institutions and using them constructively.

The most obvious case of organizations in conflict is that of those that compete in markets, either for factors of production, such as capital, raw materials, and labor, or in product markets. Even between buyer and seller, however, there is a potential for conflict when both organizations are strongly vested in this particular relationship, as in a situation of "bilateral supply" (Williamson, 1985). Under this condition, both have an interest in maintaining the relation into the future, yet each can gain by cheating on any particular exchange because of the high cost the other would face if the relation were severed. Ideally, each organization would like to take maximum advantage of the existing relationship up to the point of rupturing it; the danger, of course, is in crossing beyond that point of rupture, where the potential loss outweighs the short-term gain of cheating.

In the case of nation-states, the conflicts are perhaps more obvious. Rather than the diffuse and anonymous competition among firms in perfect markets, direct conflict among a small number of parties is more likely to be the case. Nations compete, to varying extents, in the economic realm, for territory, and over ideology. The generalized struggle of East and West over "areas of influence," to the extent that it occurs, contains elements of all three types of conflict—economic, territorial, and ideological. The potential losses that a rupture in this relationship can cause are catastrophic, and the potential for conflicts in this relationship are extreme. Thus, organizations and nations both find themselves in situations of largely unavoidable interdependence with other collective actors, and this interdependence is characterized by varying degrees of conflicting interests.

Under conditions of heightened interdependence where one party cannot easily vanquish the other, organizations and states often stand to benefit from avoiding overt conflict and managing their interdependence by cooperating.[1] One case in which this seems unequivocally true is that of the nuclear superpowers, which are locked into the most precarious form of interdependence. Yet recognizing the benefits of cooperation is not always sufficient to sustain cooperative relations: actors face temptations to "defect" from the norm of cooperation to reap short-term gains, and they know their partners are similarly tempted. Exploiting the trust of a partner in a relation of interdependence is often appealing even when the short-term benefits are outweighed by the long-term costs. Organizations seek gains in product demand through price cuts, yet these can be more than offset by the price wars that can result. States erect trade barriers to protect threatened local industries, but retaliation in kind may be even more severe; nuclear weapons procured to attain a marginal advantage in security are overcompensated for, resulting in even less security in the end.

Perhaps even more damaging is the knowledge that one's partner is also tempted to defect. As Jervis (1978, p. 171) states the problem of cooperation outlined here, "It would be in the interest of each actor to have others deprived of the power to defect; each would be willing to sacrifice this ability if others were similarly restrained. But if the others are not, then it is in the actor's interest to retain the power to defect." Thus, even if actors recognize their long-term interest in cooperation and restraint in these situations, the risks of trusting the other actor may be too great.

In the situations described here there is a commonality, namely, a conflict between each actor's short-term and long-term interests. This situation parallels the famous indefinitely iterated Prisoner's

Dilemma game, a two-actor game in which the dominant or "rational" strategy on each round is to exploit the other player and defect; yet in the long run both players maximize their individual outcomes by cooperating.[2] In each case the long-term good of the individual is identical to the long-term good of the collective, namely, the maintenance of cooperation; yet the individual's self-interest is best served in the short run by violating the collective order. It is in the hope of resolving this problem that various social institutions for managing conflict are created.

Several institutional responses to the problem of order have been proposed. Hobbes's[3] solution to this dilemma was for a superordinate actor such as the state to punish individual defection and maintain order. (Interestingly, the problem of maintaining the Smithian world is the opposite. The maintenance of perfect competition implies that organizations are not allowed to cooperate.) This essentially alters the set of payoffs available such that the benefits of defection are reduced or eliminated; short-term and long-term interests are made to coincide for the individual actor. A second answer emerges from the social psychological literature, where it is suggested that superordinate goals can take the place of superordinate actors in producing cooperation even among groups with a history of mutual hostility (Sherif and others, 1961). It is worth noting that in the famous Robber's Cave experiment in which this was demonstrated, however, the superordinate goal was imposed by the experimenters, who in some sense thereby took the place of Hobbes's superordinate actor. It is in the construction of mutually agreeable superordinate goals by actors with competing interests that most of the interesting problems arise. Goals imposed unilaterally via threats or promises on the part of parties to negotiations are not as effective as goals imposed by the situation itself (Ross, 1987). Moreover, in the absence of such imposed goals, rational cooperation does not usually emerge in experimental studies. As Brewer and Kramer note, "When members of distinct social categories or subgroups are placed in situations involving interdependence—such as shared access to a common resource pool—[the] tendency to seek relative advantage for the in-group persistently interferes with achievement of maximum collective outcomes for the group as a whole, even when cooperative goals have been made salient" (1985, pp. 226–227).

Perhaps even more interesting than either of the foregoing solutions to the problem of order is the outcome yielded by Axelrod's (1984) study, *The Evolution of Cooperation*. Axelrod found that Hobbes's pessimistic prognosis was incorrect when the relationship among actors had the potential to be long term, that is, when the actors expected that they might meet again. In this situation where interdependence is unavoidable, exploitation now can have costs later. Thus, Axelrod found that cooperation among self-interested egoists could be maintained even in the absence of external compulsion and that the strategy of cooperation was the most profitable (and therefore "rational") one overall. More generally, Axelrod (1984) and others suggest a number of factors that can mitigate the paradox of conflicting short- and long-term interests, indicating that neither superordinate enforcers nor shared goals are strictly necessary for cooperation to evolve among actors with conflicting short-term interests. These mitigating factors will be treated below.

Several features of interactions in the real world make the Prisoner's Dilemma (and its multiactor counterparts) imperfectly transferable as a prototype of social interaction. First is the fact that information about the actions of one's counterparts is rarely as unambiguous as the two-option case of the Prisoner's Dilemma. Actions taken in social situations are inherently ambiguous and open to multiple interpretations by others. In the international case this is particularly acute, as Jervis (1978) has pointed out in his explication of the "security dilemma": "[M]any of the means by which a state tries to increase its security decrease the security of others" (p. 169). Thus, even beyond the purely perceptual or cognitive ambiguity inherent in social action, there is the additional problem that some actions are objectively interest threatening regardless of their intent, as in zero-sum games. Armies raised to ward off potential invaders can be used to threaten innocuous neighbors. Moreover, the lack of recognition of this dilemma leads to "failures of empathy" between partners in interdependence: the neighbor sees the actions taken as belligerent, while the actor sees them as precautions taken to preserve the status quo and takes the neighbor's objections as evidence of hostility.

Not only is the intent of action open to multiple interpretations, but actors involved in situations of interdependence may not perceive themselves as facing the same "payoff matrix" for actions taken. American policymakers tend to misperceive what the Soviets see as the expected outcomes of their actions as well as what the Soviets think the United States expects from its actions, and Soviet leaders suffer a similar ignorance (Plous, 1985).

Finally, unlike the situation in the prisoner's dilemma, communication is usually possible among actors. We can make threats, promises, and commitments to our fellow players (Pruitt and Rubin, 1986), as well as constructing and selling accounts or interpretations (Sutton and Kramer, Chapter Seven of this volume). Norms can be established and reaffirmed. However, communication is not an unequivocal good; given the generalized ambiguity and "noisiness" of information about social action, it is frequently possible to misrepresent intentions and give false accounts of past actions, making possible ongoing exploitation.

Given all of these complexities, how is order established and maintained? How is it possible for actors with competing long- and short-term interests, in a situation characterized by ambiguous information about each other's actions and the mixed blessing of communication, to avoid exploiting each other long enough to reap the long-term gains of cooperation?

Modes of Managing Interdependence. We distinguish three broad classes of institutions for maintaining order and cooperation among corporate actors such as organizations and states, characterized roughly by increasing levels of formality. The first and least formalized of these is an interorganizational network or informal regime; the second is a long-term formal agreement, such as a contract or treaty; and the third is a formal organization, such as a trade association, joint venture, or intergovernmental organization.

International regimes are defined as "sets of implicit or explicit principles, norms, rules, and decision-making procedures around which actors' expectations converge in a given area of international relations" (Krasner, 1983, p. 2). These rules and procedures may be constructed initially by a powerful central actor or "hegemon" who can ensure that the normative order is maintained. Such a case might be the United States in the postwar world political economy

(Keohane, 1984). This solution to the problem of order corresponds to Hobbes's expected outcome of the struggles in the primordial state of nature. It has its analog in class-based research on interorganizational networks (for example, Mintz and Schwartz, 1981, 1985), where financial institutions are the central actors in the network, coordinating the actions of the other actors largely via interlocking boards of directors as well as through intercorporate and institutional stockholding and lending relationships. It also has an analogy in the role of the dominant firm in a cartel or oligopoly. These hegemonic actors are able to maintain a form of cooperation by subordinating the interests of the individual firms in the network to those of the network as a whole. The corresponding international case may be the Soviet (or American) "sphere of influence," where local elites act as agents of the hegemon rather than their own nation, making possible a high degree of coordination of the activities of these states.

Without a hegemon or formalized structure, the regime or network becomes problematic as a device for maintaining order. Cartels, for example, are inherently unstable in the absence of a superordinate authority to uphold the principles and procedures that make up the normative order, and the short-run tendency to defect typically becomes irresistible. Nevertheless, it seems that regimes can survive without a hegemon. The Concert of Europe in the nineteenth century was a relatively long-lived regime in which elites within several European nations displayed a surprising level of trust toward each other, interpreted ambiguous actions charitably, and took pains to maintain the status quo (Jervis, 1982). Keohane (1984), in examining the world political economy in the wake of the decline of America's power as a hegemon, maintains that regimes may continue to function even in the absence of such a superordinate actor. Similarly, there are instances of organizations in oligopolistic industries maintaining implicit collusive agreements in the absence of coercion; although these cases are for obvious reasons somewhat less well documented, the large electric generator case of the early 1960s seems to be such a case. The study of interorganizational networks as devices for maintaining a type of stability is a highly promising and relatively new area of organizational research that deserves much attention. "Regime theory," the comparable area in international relations, has already received a great deal of attention from political scientists (see Mares and Powell in Chapter Three of this volume). Therefore, for the purposes of this chapter, we will focus on the other two formal types of institutions.

Contracts and treaties represent formalized agreements that are meant to be legally binding on the parties involved. A treaty is defined as "an agreement between two or more subjects of international law" that is "governed by international law" (Henkin, Pugh, Schachter, and Smit, 1980, pp. 583–584). Subjects of international law include states and international organizations; whether an agreement among these parties is governed by international law, and therefore counts as a treaty, is determined by the intention of the parties as well as whether any municipal law applies. Contracts are a more general category of agreements and subsume treaties. Contracts are less well defined, and the term *contract* is used rather loosely. Thompson (1967, p. 35) defines contracting as "the negotiation of an agreement for the exchange of performances in the future," while Williamson (1985, p. 17) more broadly maintains that contracting is pervasive in economic life and that a great variety of transactions can be considered as contracting problems: "Every exchange relation qualifies. Many other issues which at the outset appear to lack a contracting aspect turn out, upon scrutiny, to have an implicit contracting quality. (The cartel problem is an example.)"

Under this broader conception, then, all of the specialized structures considered here that are designed to maintain cooperation would count as different modes of contracting. Following the definition of treaty above, however, we will restrict our consideration to those agreements that are explicitly intended as legally binding.

Despite the stated intention of legal commitment in formal contracts and treaties, both are much more flexible in practice than they are popularly thought to be. Relatively rarely are contract violations brought to litigation, because such appeal to higher authority tends to have corrosive effects on the relationship and is typically costly. Rather, as Macaulay (1963) notes, such disputes are more often resolved by private ordering than by appeal to courts. This supports a subtler interpretation of the function served by contracts, that is, that of a normative framework: "[T]he major importance of legal contract is to provide a framework for well nigh every type of group organization and for well nigh every type of passing or permanent relation between individuals and groups . . . a framework highly adjustable, a framework which almost never accurately indicates real working relations, but which affords a rough indication around which such relations vary, an occasional guide in cases of doubt, and a norm of ultimate appeal when the relations cease in fact to work" (Llewellyn, 1931, pp. 736-737, quoted in Williamson, 1985, p. 5).

This characterization of a contract as a framework for relations, coupled with the fact that superordinate authorities are rarely invoked to resolve disputes among economic actors such as unions and firms, serves to bolster the analogy between organizations and nations: parties to contracts and treaties both are loathe to escalate disputes when resolution through appeal to a shared formal norm is possible and when the alternative (litigation or war) is costly. The absence of a superordinate enforcer in the case of nations is paralleled in the organizational case by the extreme aversion that parties have to using the option of court resolution.

One of the modes by which contracting organizations are able to avert or to resolve disputes without appeal to the courts is by the use of hierarchical contracting (Stinchcombe, 1985). This involves embedding into the contract clauses for resolving potential difficulties that may arise in executing or interpreting the contract. Often, this may involve interpenetrating the authority structures of two organizations, as in the case of American defense contractors cited in Stinchcombe (1985), where the U.S. Department of Defense demands authority (for inspection of facilities, hiring, and so on) normally reserved to the organization itself. One aspect of hierarchical contracting that is quite popular is the use of built-in clauses for arbitrating disputes. As Gould (1986) notes, approximately 95 percent of collective bargaining agreements in the United States include such clauses. These modes of nonstandard contracting provide "ways to construct social structures that work like hierarchies out of contracts between legally equal corporate bargaining agents in a market" (Stinchcombe, 1985, p. 122). Thus, they provide a model for similar arrangements among states.

The most formal mode of governance used to maintain order among corporate actors is the formal organization. Among organizations, such supraorganizational entities have taken a variety of forms over the course of corporate history, including trusts and trade associations (Fligstein, 1990) as well as mergers, which involve the dissolution of the separate organizations' legal boundaries. Trade associations and other supraorganizations can be classified under the broader rubric of joint venture, a formal organization that occurs "when two or more firms create a new organization to pursue some common purpose. Joint ventures differ from mergers . . . in that they entail only a limited pooling of resources by the participating organizations" (Scott, 1987, p. 189). Joint ventures may be designed with a variety of formally stated purposes in mind; regardless of the stated intent of the parent organizations, however, it is asserted by some (for example, Pfeffer and Nowak, 1976) that joint ventures are used primarily to manage organizational interdependence, with collusion being a special case of this.

International organizations include a variety of cultural, economic, and political institutions designed to facilitate exchanges of various types and to promote cooperative relations in all of these spheres. Of particular concern to us are intergovernmental organizations, or IGOs (see Jacobson, 1984); these include the United Nations and the European Economic Community. As with some of the above cases, these organizations have the stated intention of maintaining cooperative relations among collective actors with more or less competing interests.

Aggregating Preferences and Principal-Agent Relations. Because they are "collective actors," organizations and nations share a variety of points of congruence in addition to their common "problem of order." Two are relevant to our analysis.

One of the classic issues confronted by political scientists, economists, and organizational scholars is the question of how constituent preferences are aggregated and represented in the goals of the collective. The goals that are pursued with the resources of the collective and the interests that are served are largely determined by this prior basic question. Political models of organizations that focus upon dominant coalitions, power structures, and political process (Cyert and March, 1963; Zald, 1970) almost always treat the choice of organizational goals as a problematic and political process in which powerful stakeholders and constituents register preferences, and the study of domestic politics can be described as the examination of "who gets what" and how institutional structures affect this. Thus, within both organizations and states there are structures of power and decision making that to a greater or lesser extent represent constituent interests. These structures form a "constitutional order," and they give different groups access and control of collective decisions.

The same issues are raised at the level of the supraorganization for both organizations and states. Creating mechanisms for setting collective goals, such as voting procedures, when the organization's constituents are actors with rather different levels of power is problematic for both trade associations and other joint ventures, as well as international organizations such as the United Nations (McIntyre, 1954; Russett, 1955; see also Scharpf, Chapter Nine in this volume).

The second issue is the question of agency: how can it be ensured that individuals delegated to represent the collective carry out this role adequately? Issues of incentive structures in principal-agent problems are one area of research that has received some thoughtful work under the rubric of "agency theory" (see, for example, Jensen and Meckling, 1976), and questions of delegated bargaining are relevant to negotiators in both types of context, that is, state and organization. However, an agent of the collective cannot be presumed to represent a single, coherent set of interests, as is typically assumed in principal-agent problems (but see Bernheim and Whinston, 1986): the constituency of the collective may contain multiple relevant "principals" with potentially conflicting interests. For example, contract and arms control negotiators may be simultaneously responsible to these conflicting interests as well as having parochial interests of their own, yet "they speak with the force of organizational resources." Thus, agents of collectives may represent multiple and conflicting principals within the polity, yet they often have the authority of the whole behind them.

In sum, the basic problems of collective action are common to organizations and states. Both corporate actors can be characterized by their constitutional arrangements, or basic purposes and decision-making procedures, and the degree to which these are "captured" by elites; in joining forces with other such actors for "second-order collective action" (that is, collective action by collective actors), in particular through supraorganizations, both may face difficulties in aggregating their preferences in a mutually satisfactory manner; and agents of both types of collective are frequently responsible to multiple, often conflicting constituents.

Limits to the Analogy. Despite the relatively strong analogy drawn between organizations and nations, there are significant differences that place limits on the degree to which relations among nations can be examined usefully in light of organizational theory. First, organizations operate largely in a national context. They are governed by law and the state, which has a monopoly on the lawful use of force. The state thus provides a framework for ordered action in organizational life as it does for individual action. In international relations, however, and particularly in security relations among the superpowers, no party can enforce agreements unilaterally. To the extent that the presence of a superordinate enforcer is a crucial factor in interorganizational relations, the organization-nation analogy is weakened. This is not a fatal difficulty. As we have seen, organizations tied by mutual interdependence generally find appeal to the courts costly in the short term and corrosive to their relationship in the long term. Our focus is on the issues surrounding institutions voluntarily constructed by interdependent corporate actors with a recognized interest in cooperation: networks and regimes, contracts and treaties, joint ventures and intergovernmental organizations.[3] Nevertheless, this difference must be noted.

The types of interdependence involved are largely different between organizations and nations, in particular as regards security relations among nations. In the economic realm of international relations, as with the relations among organizations, the games played may be zero-sum or otherwise, but they rarely involve costs with no positive reward available. In the realm of security, however, the interdependence is largely negative—the expenditure of resources to avoid the infliction of still greater costs.[4] In this case both the stakes of the conflict and the modes of conflict are considerably more eventful: while competition among firms with conflicting interests may cause each party economic damage, with the winner perhaps gaining market share and the loser perhaps dissolving itself as a collective actor, the carnage that results from such conflict is of course relatively minimal. Nations create ideologies of nationalism and commitment to the state far beyond loyalties to organizations. Nations are part of peoplehood and can command sacrifices rarely found among the members of organizations. Further points of disanalogy have been noted by Zald and Berger (1978, p. 856): "Nation-states are relatively large in territory, whereas organizations are more concentrated geographically. Nation-states can present great obstacles to mobility (that is, entry and exit), whereas in most organizations, except for coercive types, entry and exit are comparatively easy. Finally, the cleavages and structure of nation-states endure for generations and are transmitted through families and the class system, while the cleavages of organizations have a less enduring base."

While all of these points raise important issues that must be kept in mind as we proceed with our analysis, we are confident that the strength of the analogy is sufficient to warrant its extended consideration.

Bridging Strategies Between Formal Organizations

Accepting the analogy in the section, we will elaborate an account of the use of formal agreements and formal organizations as "bridging strategies" (Scott, 1987), techniques for constructing relatively long-term cooperative ties between organizations, without discussing full-scale mergers. First, we will analyze the main dimensions of interdependence relevant to collective actors. Then we will describe a number of institutional forms that have emerged historically to structure cooperative relations among interdependent organizations, hypothesize determinants of the use of each form, and examine how each serves to resolve some of the issues associated with the problem of order.

It is important to note two things about this analysis. First, it is based on the American case, which may tend to limit its generality. For example, the United States has a strong tradition of inhospitality to trusts, cartels, and other forms of corporate organization that limit competition. This differs from Germany, among others, where such corporate forms historically were tolerated and even encouraged by the national government. Thus, it is not surprising that the organizational forms and interorganizational behaviors that are found here are not universal. This must be kept in mind when considering the applicability to other cases of the institutions that evolved here to structure cooperative relations among organizations. Second, the "disorganized" market holds a peculiar place in our analysis. Our interest is in institutions voluntarily constructed by organizations to foster cooperative relations among themselves; the prototypical market, on the other hand, contains no such cooperation, and indeed cooperation is illegal in some instances because it is thought to inhibit the workings of the free market. The market, then, should be thought of as a reference point in our analysis, beyond the substantive thrust of this chapter.

Types of Interdependence Among Organizations

Interdependence among actors exists when the actions or outcomes of one affect the actions or outcomes of the other. Interdependence is at the heart of the problem of order, as well as politics and economics. In Chapter One we introduced a continuum of interdependence that distinguished among levels but not type. In this chapter, we require an additional distinction between two broad typological categories of interdependence: symbiotic and competitive. *Symbiotic interdependence* exists "when two or more organizations that are differentiated from one another exchange resources" (Scott, 1987, p. 186), with the primary case being the buyer-seller relationship. This type of relation has been analyzed in terms of the "efficient boundaries" or "make-or-buy" decision facing organizational decision makers (for example, Williamson, 1975). What is the more efficient arrangement for maintaining supplies of a particular factor of production—to buy it ready-made in the market or to acquire an internal supply, such as through vertical integration of a supplier? The dichotomy implicit in this analysis, however, is artificial. A frontier or continuum of arrangements is available between "make" (or vertical acquisition) and "buy," including most notably the option of hierarchical contracting (Stinchcombe, 1985). Such a continuum is shown in Figure 2.1. The determinants of the

Figure 2.1. Modes of Symbiotic Interdependence Management.

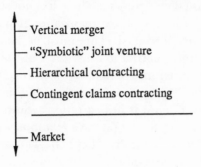

outcome of make-or-buy decisions identified by Williamson (1975) and others provide a first step in specifying the conditions that lead to choices among the options on this continuum.[5]

The second type of interdependence among organizations, *competitive interdependence,* "occurs when two or more similar organizations compete for the resources of another party" (Scott, 1987, p. 186). This situation might be described in terms of the "compete-or-cooperate" choice that faces organizations under such conditions: which benefits the organization more, to compete against those facing the same markets or to band together with them for mutual coordination? Competition is often favored in the short term, but long-term interests are typically served by cooperation. Again, competition and cooperation present a simplistic dichotomy; a variety of institutional arrangements can and have been used over the course of industrial history to attain order or at least to reduce the disorder imposed by all-out competition (see, for example, Fligstein, 1990). This continuum is presented in Figure 2.2.

Symbiotic interdependence is often thought to generate cooperative relations more easily than does competitive interdependence. Symbiotic interdependence requires interaction, and repeated interaction is facilitated by trust and common feeling. On the other hand, competitive interdependence does not require interaction (the interdependence is indirect, filtered through the choices of third parties), and repeated competition is likely to promote rivalry and distrust. Yet, depending upon the structure of the situation, competitors may actually have more to gain from cooperation than

Figure 2.2. Modes of Competitive Interdependence Management.

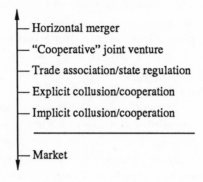

— Horizontal merger

— "Cooperative" joint venture

— Trade association/state regulation

— Explicit collusion/cooperation

— Implicit collusion/cooperation

— Market

those in a symbiotic relation. For instance, competitors may band together to petition the government for tariffs on a product, say, semiconductors, which is against the interests of the purchasing computer companies. To some extent American distaste for cooperation among competitors stems from our populist heritage and the inhospitality tradition of antitrust ideology. Many of the dimensions of interdependence are relevant to both types identified here. We will first describe some of these dimensions and then discuss how they relate to the outcomes of make-or-buy and compete-or-cooperate decisions, that is, to the arrangements arrived at for managing this interdependence.

Determinants and Components of Interdependence

A number of factors shape the amount, intensity, and duration of interdependence. Interdependence has long been a theme in organization theory, and social science (compare Axelrod, 1984; Burt, 1980; Emerson, 1962; George, 1988; March and Simon, 1958; Pfeffer and Salancik, 1978; Thompson, 1967; Williamson, 1975). We can cluster the determinants and components of interdependence into several categories: structural, informational, time, cultural, and individual.[6]

Structural Determinants. Structural determinants are dimensions that describe the density of the industries or sectors with which an organization is interdependent and affect power-dependence relations. An organization that faces a small number of alternative suppliers for its inputs or consumers for its outputs is highly dependent on these respective actors; conversely, they have power over the organization. The concentration within an industry also affects an organization's freedom of response, both with suppliers and consumers and with competitors. (The theory of monopoly and oligopoly is relevant here.)

Information. Two types of information are relevant: information about the future and information about present behavior. There are three levels of knowledge about the future: certainty, risk, and uncertainty. Under *certainty*, the outcomes of any relevant course of behavior are known in advance. *Risk* occurs when the outcomes of actions are only known probabilistically, as in throwing dice. *Uncertainty* is the inability to assign specific probabilities to outcomes, as in fair elections. Because of "bounded rationality," some risky situations contain so many possible outcomes that it is too costly or time-consuming to consider each, and so for all practical purposes they can be considered uncertain. The ability to know what one's partner in interdependence is doing is another relevant dimension. *Information impactedness* describes situations in which it is impossible or costly to monitor whether one's partner is complying with an agreement. For example, if you hire someone to walk your dog while you are out of town or if a nation signs agreements limiting certain types of weapons research, it may be difficult in either case to tell whether the agreement is being upheld.

Time. The anticipated time horizon of a relationship in its current state and the frequency of contact between interdependent parties are both related to interdependence, as is the "discount rate on the future" that each party holds. In contracting, an agreement may be one off, short term, long term, or indefinite. Changes in an industry's environment may also shift the time horizon of competitive relationships, as when legislation limiting imports is passed or when technological breakthroughs presage the entrance of new competitors. In addition, contact may be continuous, as in joint ventures, or discrete with varying frequency, as with monthly deliveries or annual contract negotiation.

Finally, the *discount rate* describes the value of future outcomes in the present. If prevailing interest rates are 20 percent, then $120 one year from now is worth only $100 today. The same concept applies to other outcomes: organizational leaders are more likely to close plants in a community if they are relatively unconcerned about the organization's future ability to attract workers and consumers in that community.

Culture. The ability to empathize and the ability to communicate effectively both affect interdependence and its management, and both of these may be considered cultural factors. Empathy is promoted by facing a common situation and sharing a common interpretation of history. To the extent that another's behavior, attitudes, and expectations seem inexplicable, cooperation is problematic. Communication is affected by language, culture, and norms. The inability to communicate effectively can hinder the management of interdependence even when both parties recognize a common interest in cooperation.

Individual Factors. Characteristics of individual organizations also affect their degree of interdependence. The value an organization places on a particular relationship is a defining characteristic of interdependence. An organization is highly interdependent with a supplier of a particularly crucial input, making this a valued relationship for the focal organization. The discretion an organization has over its contribution to another's actions or outcomes also affects the degree of its interdependence and that of its partner. Although an entire region may depend on a single utility for its power, the fact that this organization is highly regulated limits the degree to which other organizations in the region may be said to be dependent on it.

While all of the dimensions just described are analytically distinct, they of course covary among themselves empirically. Frequency of contact is likely to make communication easier over time; having a large number of alternative suppliers is likely to reduce the discretion a supplier has and thus limit the areas of uncertainty associated with this relationship. Nevertheless, it is useful to keep these dimensions distinct. The important point is that analysis of cases of interdependence must take these factors into account.

Managing Symbiotic Interdependence: Make, Buy, or Something Else?

The use of nonstandard contracting, that is, governance structures such as hierarchical contracts and formal organizations as a means to manage symbiotic interdependence, has been analyzed by Williamson (1975, 1985) through so-called "transaction costs analysis" of the make-or-buy decision. This account has also been refined by Stinchcombe (1985) in his analysis of the use of contracts as hierarchical documents. The transaction costs approach focuses on the costs associated with negotiating contracts and seeing to their fulfillment under various conditions of interdependence. We can briefly summarize the factors that lead to the use of each of the types of institution depicted in Figure 2.1 by building on this account.

Underlying the continuum from market to merger in Figure 2.1 is a tension between sovereignty and costs. We assume that managers highly value the sovereignty of their organization, that is, autonomy in action and freedom from external interference. Nonetheless, the uncertainty that accompanies autonomy can be noxious (Thompson, 1967), and the pursuit of growth, profitability, and even survival often conflicts with autonomy. The managerial task, then, is to balance sovereignty on the one hand with greater certainty, efficiency, and stability, as depicted in Figure 2.1. These institutional structures form a virtual Guttman scale, with the forms on the right implying the relinquishing of sovereignty and greater interpenetration and permanency of organizational coordination.

Under conditions of risk we expect to see "contingent claims contracting," in which all relevant future contingencies and the appropriate responses are specified in advance at the time of contract negotiation. If the future is uncertain (including cases where there are "so many contingencies that it is too expensive to give alterations of contract performances for all of them in advance" [Stinchcombe, 1985, p. 137]) or information impactedness is high, then "hierarchical contracting" is appropriate. This involves some interpenetration of the governance structures of the contracting organizations, including the specification of conditions under which third-party arbitration will be invoked. If the previous conditions hold and the relationship between the contracting organizations involves frequently repeated and/or relatively prolonged contracting, the use of "symbiotic joint ventures" is the appropriate management strategy. For instance, a supplier and a buyer may set up product development teams or even jointly owned production facilities or solely owned facilities dedicated to the other party on the basis of long-term contracts.

Finally, if all of the previous conditions hold and the relationship has an indefinite time horizon, then vertical merger, which involves the dissolution of the legal boundaries of the two organizations, will be observed. This involves the relationship being brought within a single organizational boundary, and will be used only when it is demanded by the organization's environment or when the trade-offs of sovereignty for growth, certainty, or stability merit it.

Managing Competitive Interdependence: Compete, Cooperate, or Merge?

The compete-or-cooperate continuum in Figure 2.2, like the make-or-buy continuum, is anchored on one end by market, which again is beyond our analysis, and the other by merger, but the latter pole is horizontal rather than vertical merger. This continuum is also characterized by increasing centralization of governance (or, alternatively, decreasing organizational sovereignty) from bottom to top. We continue to assume that managers have a taste for sovereignty but that this is often overridden by a taste for certainty or profitability. The organizations here are those in more or less "structurally equivalent" positions—their actions and outcomes are tied with each other to a greater or lesser extent. The degree to which the outcomes of any two such organizations are interdependent is in part determined by their industry concentration, that is, the number of other structurally equivalent organizations. As argued earlier in the chapter, actors in such positions generally have an interest in maintaining cooperation and avoiding competition. In addition to this interest in avoiding competition, organizations also may be driven by a "need" for growth, which would also push them toward arrangements at the top of the continuum. A strong force mediating against this movement in the United States is state regulation against various types of cooperation/collusion and antitrust law violations. State regulation, of course, is analogous to a hegemon.

Following Fligstein (1990), we can identify at least five types of arrangement between the competitive market and horizontal merger. Implicit cooperation/collusion typically takes the form of price leadership by a dominant firm in an industry. This is most feasible in oligopolistic industries, where the state is typically vigilant against more explicit forms of cooperation/collusion and merger is legally forbidden. Explicit cooperation/collusion includes arrangements such as cartels or cooperative "regimes." Trade associations are "organizations created to represent business interests within specific domains, mobilizing firms within their domain so that collective action can be taken on common problems" (Aldrich and Staber, 1988, p. 111). One type observed in the past is the "open price trade association" (Fligstein, 1990), in which members funded the association in order to find out how others in the industry were setting their prices, typically the decision variable through which firms compete. This eliminates "information impactedness" and thereby eliminates the incentive to defect from the collective order by giving prices just a little less than the prevailing standard, as this action would be found out and taken into account by competitors through the association's publication of recent prices of all industry members.

Cooperative joint ventures are those that involve not only increased interpenetration of governance (in particular over pricing decisions), as was the case for trade associations and collusive arrangements, but also joint production to a greater or lesser extent; the NUMMI joint venture involving GM and Toyota is an example of such an arrangement. While such arrangements are not explicitly collusive, this may well be their de facto function in some cases (Pfeffer and Nowak, 1976).

Finally, horizontal merger involves the more or less complete interpenetration of governance and production. Horizontal mergers are motivated by a different set of factors than drive vertical mergers. A desire to increase market share or, in industries with slack capacity and a mature market, a desire to reduce industry capacity may drive horizontal mergers. Sometimes the horizontal merger allows for the consolidation and rationalization of industry facilities, thus leading to scale economies, in the face of foreign competition. It should be remembered that in the American antitrust climate, horizontal mergers have at times been quite suspect, certainly more so than vertical mergers.

State regulation is a nonobvious mode of competition avoidance but corresponds to the invocation of a superordinate actor. This strategy is only effective, of course, if the regulating committee can be "captured" to a significant degree, as happened in the late nineteenth century in the case of the Interstate Commerce Commission, which imposed a mutually beneficial order upon the railroads.

Much of our discussion of the forms of interorganizational relations and governance of those relations has been colored by an assumption that the organizations exist in a competitive market system. But many of the same issues occur in any system in which separate organizations have some autonomy in negotiating their relations to other organizations. Hospitals, universities, and social service agencies of all kinds may enter into alliances, contract for long-term exchange relations, operate joint ventures, join trade associations, and/or merge with one another (Litwak and Hylton, 1962). In all such cases we would suspect that an analysis of resource and informational dependencies, the costs and benefits of autonomy and/or different forms of interorganizational governance, and the constraint of the external environment (third parties, antitrust law, and so on) go far to explain the patterns that emerge. Whether comparable mechanisms and factors are present in the case of states is of course problematic; however, as we will see below, a variety of dimensions of interdependence relevant to organizations are also relevant to states, making arrangements that have proven functional for dealing with the various problems of interdependence at the organization level useful candidates for similar arrangements dealing with similar problems among states.

Superpower Security Interdependence and the SCC

The nation-state system has developed a variety of mechanisms for dealing with interstate relations. The whole system of international diplomatic relations operates as a set of generalized mechanisms for the coordination of communications and more substantive interactions between governments. Moreover, a host of legal mechanisms operate to coordinate economic exchange across national boundaries. A wide variety of mechanisms and agencies exist for the conduct of general (for example, United Nations) and specific (International Air Traffic Agreement) international ventures. In addition, nations conduct joint military ventures, create organizations such as the International Monetary Fund, and operate a host of compacts such as international postal service and phone services that share the organizational properties of interorganizational relations discussed above. Rather than taking on the general case, in this section we will first indicate the types of interdependence relevant for the case of the nuclear superpowers and then analyze the Standing Consultative Commission (SCC), an institution designed to facilitate cooperative behavior between the two superpowers, from the perspective outlined above. Earlier we treated contracts and treaties as separate from joint ventures, but of course they may be intertwined. Here we deal with a joint venture, the SCC, nested with a treaty.

The situation facing the United States and the USSR in the nuclear age is not adequately captured by either of the two types of interdependence we have described (symbiotic or competitive). Rather, dimensions of each type of interdependence are relevant for describing this case. Perhaps the most salient feature of the nuclear situation, apart from the incomparably high stakes involved, is the level of uncertainty each side faces in trying to "manage" this interdependence. In drafting treaties and monitoring their compliance, there is high uncertainty regarding both immediate impact and longer-range effects. The ability to monitor compliance is problematic (for example, neither side has had the authority to inspect fully the facilities of the other side, and each is able to maintain a fair deal of secrecy about many of its activities relevant to the treaty involved). Thus, this is a situation of high information impactedness. In addition, the complexity of the technologies involved and the pace of development of these technologies make any contract between the two parties vulnerable to becoming obsolete: treaties that outlaw one type of technological development can have the effect of directing weapons research and development to new areas not covered by the original treaty. Such new developments cannot be specified fully at the time the contract is negotiated, implying the need for ongoing negotiation and adaptation.

An additional set of problems in "managing nuclear interdependence" comes from the lack of "empathy" that generally characterizes the leadership of the two nations. American and Soviet elites have rather different views of their situation, and each may fail to grasp how the other sees the situation (Plous, 1985). This supports Jervis's (1978) notion that the "security dilemma" leads to "failures of empathy" on the part of the actors involved. Additionally, in trying to work through agreements, problems of "culture clash" are inevitable. This may be realized in part through differing interpretations of what the contract implies.

Finally, the security relationship between the two superpowers in its current mode is characterized by an indefinite time horizon. Barring total disarmament, there is every reason to think that a nuclear attack initiated by one side would lead inexorably to a total war that would annihilate the species. This situation is likely to continue throughout the foreseeable future. Thus, as a result of the capacities for destruction that the possession of nuclear weapons implies, the United States and USSR are locked inescapably into the most extreme form of interdependence, with an undeniable mutual interest in its "management."

If states were exactly homologous with organizations, then given the extremely high levels of information impactedness and uncertainty and the indefinite time horizon that characterize the relationship between the two major nuclear powers, our analysis above would lead us to expect them to merge as the most "efficient" solution. Such a theoretical outcome is severely constrained by the overarching importance of sovereignty: after all, it is presumably the maintenance of sovereignty that motivates the arms race in the first place. This "taste for sovereignty" in the case of nations, unlike that of organizations, is likely to be absolute. Thus, the tension identified in the make-or-buy decision between efficiency and sovereignty reaches a peak in the case of U.S.-Soviet relations. All of the factors that favor joining the two parties into a single overarching organization exist in tandem with the absolute opposition to this "solution" by both parties. This relationship is thus *sui generis*, stretching the boundaries of existing organization theory. Not surprisingly, the two states have attempted to balance their interest in maintaining minimally cooperative relations with respect to nuclear war with their mutual distaste for arrangements that limit their individual authority and discretion through the use of an intermediate contractual solution: arms control treaties with an embedded formal organization to provide regular contact for discussing issues and exchanging information. This organization, the Standing Consultative Commission, is discussed below.

SALT and the Standing Consultative Commission. The need for a formal body to help maintain the viability of written agreements was recognized early in the process of negotiation for arms control. The ambiguity and lack of precision that almost inevitably characterize the language of technical treaties and the virtual certainty of differing interpretations that this implies, as well as the high rate of technological change in the realm of nuclear weapons, led the governments involved with SALT I to include Article XIII of the ABM Treaty, creating the Standing Consultative Commission, which was formally established in December 1972. Although the mandate of the SCC is rather broad, it "has concerned itself primarily with implementation and compliance questions for the SALT accords" (Graybeal and Krepon, 1985, p. 185). Like the ABM Treaty with which it was established, the SCC is of unlimited duration.[7]

The document that established the SCC lays down a simple basic structure. "Each side is represented by a Commissioner, a Deputy Commissioner, an Executive Officer, and members of the delegation," who are mandated to meet together at least twice each year, usually in the spring and fall in Geneva; sessions typically last about two months (Graybeal and Krepon, 1985, pp. 184–185). Also by mandate, the proceedings of the SCC are kept secret, and even the products of its deliberations are not widely known to the public. This stipulation was suggested by the Soviets as a way to make the SCC more effective by shielding it from public scrutiny and thereby enabling both parties to compromise without losing face. Unfortunately, this requirement for secrecy makes study of the internal workings of the SCC essentially impossible; even the texts of most agreements reached within the SCC have never been made public.

Thus, analysis of this organization must be based largely on indirect evidence.

The SCC is not an independent third-party arbitrator, and it has no authority with respect to enforcement; rather, it is a forum in which the two parties can meet to work out ambiguities stemming from the implementation of arms control treaties. Dalton (1988) notes two types of ambiguities, either of which may be present: ambiguities in the activities of the parties and ambiguities in the treaty language. This points up the relevance of our characterization of contracts as *normative frameworks* rather than rigid and perfectly specified documents. Graybeal and Krepon (1985, p. 191) point out that "an arms control agreement, like the American Constitution, is a living document. It requires constant interpretation in order to remain viable under unforeseen circumstances or to meet unanticipated events."[8] Through the 1970s, the SCC was a useful mechanism for keeping the SALT agreement viable by allowing a forum for discussing problems and exchanging data. The types of issues raised include Soviet concealment measures, the location of Soviet ABM radar outside the limits prescribed in the ABM Treaty, the propriety of shelters covering American Minutemen missile silos, and the status of various efforts at dismantling equipment, among others (Buchheim and Farley, 1988, p. 260). While its past work is veiled in secrecy, the SCC's role in resolving the issue of the Soviet SA-5 radar is public knowledge and provides an example of how the SCC functioned in the 1970s.

The Anti-Ballistic Missile Treaty negotiated during the Nixon administration banned the testing of non-ABM air-defense-system radar "in an ABM mode." The intention of this rather vague phrase was to close off the possibility of upgrading new or existing air defenses to defend against strategic ballistic missiles, that is, to rule out their use for ABM purposes. The United States came to suspect that intermittent Soviet tests of the SA-5 radar in 1973–1974 may have been a violation of this ban. Dalton (1988, p. 21) states that "the problem in the SA-5 case was ambiguous treaty language which the Soviets exploited to justify actions which were also ambiguous, that is, not clearly prohibited by the agreement." After American intelligence had gained a clear picture of this practice, the United States raised this issue during the SCC's February 1975 meetings, and "[a]ccording to [former secretary of state] Kissinger, seventeen days after the U.S. raised the issue . . . this activity stopped, and was not resumed" (Graybeal and Krepon, 1985, p. 190). Further deliberations led to an agreed statement arrived at by the SCC in 1978. This statement supplemented the basic principle in the treaty with a number of applications related to ABM testing and the use of non-ABM radars at ABM test ranges.

The case of the SA-5 radar is taken by SCC supporters as evidence of the SCC's effectiveness as a tool for maintaining compliance by providing an ongoing forum for raising and dealing with concerns, and as an instrument for constructing workable and mutually agreeable interpretations of arms control agreements. Critics such as Reagan's former Assistant Secretary of Defense Richard Perle saw the case otherwise, however. They saw the SCC as a failure that survived on the goodwill of arms control enthusiasts, who had a desire not to face the harsh realities of Soviet noncompliance. Such critics had the upper hand during most of the Reagan administration. The next section examines some of the reasons for the apparent turnaround in the effective use of the SCC during most of the Reagan years.

SCC Success and Failure. Several causes of the decline of the SCC are unsurprising in light of the analysis above. Dalton (1988) has described this breakdown in terms of the movement from problem solving to public diplomacy as the dominant administration strategy with respect to arms control implementation. He contrasts several dimensions on which the Nixon, Ford, and Carter administrations differed from the Reagan administration in their approaches to arms control and how these were reflected in the role of the SCC. The SCC "worked" under previous administrations in large part because of the commitment of the principals to arms control: Nixon, Ford, and Carter all were personally and politically invested in the success of arms control and thus had an interest in using the SCC to facilitate the implementation of arms control agreements. Reagan, on the other hand, had been hostile to arms control, arguing that the Evil Empire could not be trusted to uphold its end of the bargain and initially holding the position that there would be no future arms agreements with the Soviets. (This hostility was realized in the United States abrogation of the SALT II treaty in

November 1986.) As in the case of Axelrod's (1984) prisoners, the expectation of future contracting made for incentives to cooperate, chiefly within the SCC; the Senate's shelving of SALT II in 1979 and the election of Reagan in 1980 put the future of U.S.-Soviet arms control agreements in grave doubt, eliminating this incentive for the Soviets. By 1985, Soviet behavior suggested that "they may have concluded that arms control is doomed," according to Paul Warnke, chief U.S. negotiator for SALT II (Smith, 1985a, p. 1181).

The support of the principals relates to the issue of trust in negotiation. A normative agreement such as a contract or regime often depends first on the expectation of future contracting, noted above, and second on some level of trust. In the absence of some level of trust (or in some cases a sufficient mechanism for enforcement), no agreement can hold up. "Numerous roads can lead to success when both parties wish to maintain the viability of existing agreements. Conversely, when each side questions the other's intentions, even brilliant tactical decisions are unlikely to produce satisfactory results" (Graybeal and Krepon, 1985, p. 192). Again, the general mistrust of the Soviets that pervaded the Reagan administration implied serious problems in maintaining arms control agreements, even if they were seen as desirable. Thus, whereas Secretary of Defense James Schlesinger in the Ford administration characterized problems with Soviet compliance as "ambiguities which needed to be resolved" within the SCC rather than as "violations," Assistant Secretary of Defense Richard Perle in the Reagan administration was unwilling to give such a benefit of the doubt; in his estimation, "serious compliance problems [on the part of the Soviets] have generally not been resolved by the SCC or in any other manner" (quoted in Graybeal and Krepon, 1985, p. 187). In a 1985 report, Perle and Secretary of Defense Caspar Weinberger went even further, charging that the SCC is "a languid, confidential and ineffective forum . . . , an Orwellian memory-hole into which our concerns have been dumped like yesterday's trash" and recommending that the president abandon its use (quoted in Buchheim and Farley, 1988, p. 261). If an administration is hostile to the very enterprise of arms control, then those elements of the executive branch that support the work of the SCC are likely to be overridden.

At the beginning of the 1990s hopeful trends are emerging in arms control. The INF treaty has received an unprecedented level of support both within the Bush administration and in the international community, and there are gestures toward further progress in arms control. This would seem to mark a reversal in the Reagan administration's earlier attitude toward the desirability and feasibility of agreements with the Soviets on nuclear weapons. Previously, the Reagan administration had resorted to a policy of making public charges of treaty violations in an attempt to use public opinion to control Soviet arms behavior (Dalton, 1988), thus bypassing the SCC. Whether the new round of arms control agreements will help to revive the SCC as an effective tool has yet to be seen. On the one hand, the United States abrogated SALT II in 1986 and therefore abandoned efforts to resolve compliance issues related to this agreement through the SCC. On the other, the Soviets have shown a greatly increased willingness to make concessions, as well as a new level of openness to rigorous verification standards; and within the SCC itself, two new common understandings were worked out in June 1985, indicating that its usefulness was not completely destroyed during the earlier years of the Reagan administration (Buchheim and Farley, 1988). Thus, there is clearly a place for an organization such as the SCC given the current arms control climate.

It is worth reiterating that the forum represented by the SCC depends upon the prior goodwill of the principals outside the organization itself; as a Reagan administration official was quoted as saying in a *Science* article, "In the end, [the SCC] will only be as successful as the overall political relationship" between the United States and the USSR (Smith, 1985b, p. 536). While the SCC could operate as a mechanism to reduce ambiguities about specific performances of both parties, prior commitment to arms control relates to domestic politics and the ideologies of national elites in both countries. In that sense, the joint organization is hostage to its founding partners, unlike some other international ventures, such as the United Nations or the International Monetary Fund, that take on some autonomy from their constituent elements.

Conclusions

At the core of our chapter is a fundamental belief that organizational theory ought to be of use in thinking about the relations among the superpowers and the conditions surrounding war and peace. We have argued that interorganizational relations provide a robust analogy to international relations and that theories developed to deal with the former ought to have applicability to the latter. Indeed, since we sometimes use the language of the theory of games, it is clear that at base a general theory of interaction is being invoked. However, a general theory of interaction is less useful, we think, than interorganizational theory, because it tends to ignore constituency effects and conflicts within collectivities that are seamlessly invoked in interorganizational theory. We went to some lengths to establish the strengths and weaknesses of the analogy. We then turned to a discussion of the conditions for different types of interorganizational ventures, using as prototypes various forms of organizational alliances, joint ventures, and mergers. Of course, it is not enough to argue for the analogy. And we tried to demonstrate, however briefly, the value of thinking about a specific international joint organization, the SCC, within our framework. While that discussion is necessarily brief, we believe we can point the way to a rich research agenda, one that may be consequential for all of us.

Notes

1. Note that cooperation does not imply altruism or even a fundamental harmony of interests; rather, cooperation involves adhering to a more or less elaborated set of principles or normative order. Alexander George (1988, p. 642) argues that, although it takes on special meaning, "cooperation" between adversaries is entirely possible and does not necessarily eliminate competition; in fact, it can involve "an agreement, quite useful to both sides, that changes the ground rules and channels, rather than eliminates, continuing competition, in a particular security issue area."

2. For a concise description of this game, see Axelrod (1984, pp. 7-12).

3. For the problems the superpowers face in recognizing this interest in cooperation, see Chapter Three. Our discussion assumes that this prior problem has been solved and that the issue is the construction of institutions for structuring operation.

4. Keohane and Nye (1977) distinguish between "sensitivity,"

where A's actions affect B, and "vulnerability," where it is costly for B to adjust to A's actions. Problems in international security are more often ones of vulnerability.

5. Although perfect markets impose a type of order on interdependent organizations, order here is an emergent property of the system, not the intended product of continuing cooperative relations. Thus, such markets are beyond our analysis here and are represented in the figure only to remind the reader of the relations of markets to more permanent and extensive forms of organizational interaction.

6. George (1988) uses an alternative conceptualization to the one presented here, considering different components of the United States–USSR security relationship separately as to the "tightness" or "looseness" of the mutual dependence experienced (that is, the degree to which each can inflict damage to the other's interests in that security area) and the degree of "centrality" of the issue for fundamental security interests. Our schematization, based primarily on previous organizational theory, is complementary to this framework.

7. Buchheim and Farley (1988, p. 257) noted that "while the SCC is the most specific and continuing device for assessing and reinforcing the viability of strategic arms agreements, it is not the only one. Others are the provisions in the ABM Treaty for treaty review every five years and the amendment procedure (Article XIV); and the ongoing SALT/START negotiations themselves, which are explicitly recognized in the SALT I and SALT II accords as essential to the viability of the offensive arms agreements. The first two five-year reviews of the AMB Treaty, in 1977 and 1982, were considered by some to be little more than pro forma, and were conducted in the SCC."

8. Indeed, Buchheim and Farley (1988) argue that it is neither necessary nor even desirable in the general case to spell out all commitments in detail at the time arms control treaties are negotiated.

References

Abelson, R. P., and Levi, A. "Decision Making and Decision Theory." In G. Lindzey and E. Aronson (eds.), *Handbook of Social Psychology.* (3rd ed.) New York: Random House, 1985.

Aldrich, H., and Staber, U.H. "Organizing Business Interests: Patterns of Trade Association Foundings, Transformations, and Deaths." In G. Carroll (ed.), *Ecological Models of Organizations.* Cambridge, Mass.: Ballinger, 1988.

Axelrod, R. *The Evolution of Cooperation.* New York: Basic Books, 1984.

Bernheim, B. D., and Whinston, M. D. "Common Agency." *Econometrica,* 1986, *54,* 923–942.

Bracken, P. *The Command and Control of Nuclear Forces.* New Haven, Conn.: Yale University Press, 1983.

Brewer, M. B., and Kramer, R. M. "The Psychology of Intergroup Attitudes and Behavior." *Annual Review of Psychology,* 1985, *36,* 219–243.

Buchheim, R., and Farley, P. J. "The US-Soviet Standing Consultative Commission." In A. L. George, P. J. Farley, and A. Dallin (eds.), *US-Soviet Security Cooperation: Achievements, Failures, Lessons.* New York: Oxford University Press, 1988.

Bueno de Mesquita, B. "The Contributions of Expected Utility Theory to the Study of International Conflict." Unpublished manuscript, Stanford University, 1987.

Burawoy, M. *Manufacturing Consent: Changes in the Labor Process Under Monopoly Capitalism.* Chicago: University of Chicago Press, 1979.

Burt, R. "Autonomy in a Social Topology." *American Journal of Sociology,* 1980, *85,* 892–925.

Cyert, R. M., and March, J. G. *A Behavioral Theory of the Firm.* Englewood Cliffs, N.J.: Prentice-Hall, 1963.

Dalton, G. "The Standing Consultative Commission: From Problem Solving to Public Diplomacy." In G. Duffy (ed.), *Compliance and the Future of Arms Control.* Cambridge, Mass.: Ballinger, 1988.

Duffy, G. "Administration Redefines Soviet 'Violations.'" *Bulletin of the Atomic Scientists,* Feb. 1986, pp. 13–17.

Emerson, R. M. "Power-Dependence Relations." *American Sociological Review,* 1962, *27,* 31–40.

Fligstein, N. *The Transformation of Corporate Control.* Cambridge, Mass.: Harvard University Press, 1990.

George, A. L. "Incentives for U.S.-Soviet Security Cooperation and

Mutual Adjustment." In A. L. George, P. J. Farley, and A. Dallin (eds.), *U.S.-Soviet Security Cooperation: Achievements, Failures, Lessons.* New York: Oxford University Press, 1988.

Gould, W. B., IV. *A Primer on American Labor Law.* (2nd ed.) Cambridge, Mass.: MIT Press, 1986.

Graybeal, S. N., and Krepon, M. "Making Better Use of the Standing Consultative Commission." *International Security,* 1985, *10,* 183-199.

Henkin, L., Pugh, R. C., Schachter, O., and Smit, H. *International Law: Cases and Materials.* St. Paul, Minn.: West, 1980.

Hobbes, T. *Leviathan: Or the Matter, Forme, and Power of a Commonwealth Ecclesiasticall and Civil.* New York: Collier, 1962. (Originally published 1651.)

Jacobson, H. K. *Networks of Interdependence: International Organizations and the Global Political System.* (2nd ed.) New York: Knopf, 1984.

Jensen, M. C., and Meckling, W. "Theory of the Firm: Managerial Behavior, Agency Costs, and Ownership Structure." *Journal of Financial Economics,* 1976, *3,* 305-360.

Jervis, R. "Cooperation Under the Security Dilemma." *World Politics,* 1978, *30,* 167-214.

Jervis, R. "Security Regimes." *International Organization,* 1982, *36,* 357-378.

Kahn, R. L. "Organizations and Well-Being: The Great Convergence." Paper presented at the annual meetings of the Academy of Management on receipt of the Distinguished Scholar Award, San Diego, Calif., 1985.

Kahn, R. L., and others. *Organizational Stress: Studies in Role Conflict and Ambiguity.* New York: Wiley, 1964.

Keohane, R. O. *After Hegemony: Cooperation and Discord in the World Political Economy.* Princeton, N.J.: Princeton University Press, 1984.

Keohane, R. O., and Nye, J. S. *Power and Interdependence: World Politics in Transition.* Boston: Little, Brown, 1977.

Krasner, S. D. "Structural Causes and Regime Consequences: Regimes as Intervening Variables." In S. D. Krasner (ed.), *International Regimes.* Ithaca, N.Y.: Cornell University Press, 1983.

Litwak, E., and Hylton, L. F. "Interorganizational Analysis: A Hypothesis on Coordinating Agencies." *Administrative Science Quarterly*, 1962, *6*, 395–420.

Llewellyn, K. N. "What Price Contract? An Essay in Perspective." *Yale Law Journal*, May 1931, *40*, 704–750.

Luce, R. D., and Raiffa, H. *Games and Decisions: Introduction and Critical Survey*. New York: Wiley, 1957.

Macaulay, S. "Non-Contractual Relations in Business: A Preliminary Study." *American Sociological Review*, 1963, *28*, 55–69.

McIntyre, E. "Weighted Voting in International Organizations." *International Organization*, 1954, *8*, 484–497.

March, J. G. "The Business Firm as a Political Coalition." *Journal of Politics*, 1962, *24*, 662–678.

March, J. G., and Simon, H. A. *Organizations*. New York: Wiley, 1958.

Mintz, B., and Schwartz, M. "The Structure of Intercorporate Unity in American Business." *Social Problems*, 1981, *29*, 87–103.

Mintz, B., and Schwartz, M. *The Power Structure of American Business*. Chicago: University of Chicago Press, 1985.

Pfeffer, J., and Nowak, P. "Joint Ventures and Interorganizational Interdependence." *Administrative Science Quarterly*, 1976, *21*, 398–418.

Pfeffer, J., and Salancik, G. *The External Control of Organizations: A Resource Dependence Perspective*. New York: Harper & Row, 1978.

Plous, S. "Perceptual Illusions and Military Realities: The Nuclear Arms Race." *Journal of Conflict Resolution*, 1985, *29*, 363–389.

Pruitt, D. G., and Rubin, J. Z. *Social Conflict: Escalation, Stalemate, and Settlement*. New York: Random House, 1986.

Ross, L. "Notes on Conflict and Conflict Resolution." Unpublished manuscript, Stanford University, 1987.

Russett, A. de. "Large and Small States in International Organization: The Need for a New Approach to the Question of Weighting Votes in the General Assembly." *International Affairs*, 1955, *31*, 192–202.

Scott, W. R. *Organizations: Rational, Natural, and Open Systems*. (2nd ed.) Englewood Cliffs, N.J.: Prentice-Hall, 1987.

Selznick, P. *Law, Society, and Industrial Justice*. New York: Russell Sage Foundation, 1969.

Sherif, M., Harvey, O. J., White, B. J., Hood, W. R., and Sherif, C. W. *Intergroup Conflict and Cooperation: The Robbers' Cave Experiment*. Norman: University of Oklahoma Press, 1961.

Smith, R. J. "Allegations of Cheating Endanger Arms Talks." *Science*, 1985a, *227*, 1180–1181.

Smith, R. J. "Arms Agreement Breathes New Life into the SCC." *Science*, 1985b, *229*, 535–536.

Stinchcombe, A. L. "Contracts as Hierarchical Documents." In A. L. Stinchcombe and C. A. Heimner (eds.), *Organization Theory and Project Management: Administering Uncertainty in Norwegian Offshore Oil*. Oslo: Norwegian University Press, 1985.

Thompson, J. D. *Organizations in Action*. New York: McGraw-Hill, 1967.

Williamson, O. E. *Markets and Hierarchies: Analysis and Antitrust Implications*. New York: Free Press, 1975.

Williamson, O. E. *The Economic Institutions of Capitalism: Firms, Markets, and Relational Contracting*. New York: Free Press, 1985.

Zald, M. N. "Political Economy: A Framework for Comparative Analysis." In M. N. Zald (ed.), *Power in Organizations*. Nashville, Tenn.: Vanderbilt University Press, 1970.

Zald, M. N. "Interorganizational Relations as Foreign Relations: The Use of Analogy and Metaphor." Paper presented at the annual meetings of the American Sociological Association, San Francisco, 1975.

Zald, M. N., and Berger, M. A. "Social Movements in Organizations: Coup d'Etat, Insurgency, and Mass Movements." *American Journal of Sociology*, 1978, *83*, 823–861.

Chapter 3

Cooperative Security Regimes

Preventing International Conflicts

David R. Mares
Walter W. Powell

Recent developments, notably the dismantling of the Soviet empire in Eastern Europe and the decline in Soviet defense spending and military modernization, offer an unparalleled window of opportunity for significant reshaping of superpower relations. For more than forty years, American military doctrine and foreign policy were firmly based on the assumption that a possible Soviet invasion of Western Europe represented the gravest threat to U.S. security. Suddenly, the threat of Soviet aggression has receded. At the same time, however, the tumbling of the Berlin Wall and the unraveling of the military structure of the Warsaw Pact have quite possibly expanded the number of factors that could trigger inadvertent war. The Soviet threat may well have weakened and grown more ambiguous, but in its place there is great uncertainty—the rebirth of nationalism, virulent territorial disputes, instability in Eastern Europe and the Third World, and the prospect of nuclear weapons in the hands of terrorist groups, to name only a few examples.

In our view, it is an opportune time for a reassessment of the core tenets of American foreign policy, which have long been guided by what has come to be known as the realist tradition. We draw upon regime theory in political science and organizational analysis to fashion what is an admittedly speculative (but we hope suggestive and creative) account of how new procedures and institutional arrangements might contribute to the development of a cooperative security regime.[1] Such a regime, we argue, could help prevent unintended military escalation through the misreading of events and might well enable the superpowers to respond collectively to the challenges and uncertainty posed by social changes in the less developed world.

Creating such an international regime requires profound innovation. But nations, like organizations, are typically inertia driven and hostile to innovations that go deep, especially those that involve vexing issues of authority, autonomy, and sovereignty. No stable bilateral institutions currently exist. There is no regular pattern of summitry, no routinized joint military exercises, no carefully worked out procedures for responding to crises. Nor are we yet able to offer detailed prescriptions for what such a security regime might entail. Instead, we adopt a conservative approach. We explore how both the threat of nuclear war and the thawing of East-West hostilities might lead the superpowers to a new era of cooperation, and we reflect on how military strategy and organizations might respond to these changes.

A Road Map

The study of international politics in the nuclear age has been dominated by the realist tradition. Although realists differ about whether the dynamics of their models derive from human nature (Morgenthau, 1975) or the structure of the international system (Waltz, 1979), they agree that in the absence of an effective international authority (for example, an agency above individual states with the authority and power to make laws and settle disputes), conflict is inherent in the relations among states. Even among those who reject the inevitability of conflict among independent states and focus instead on the particular governmental forms that are alleged to create aggressive states (for example, the Communist system), there is general agreement that the relationship between "good" and "bad" states should be guided by realist tenets until "bad" states are eliminated from the world polity.

Critiques of the realist tradition abound, but historically they have made few inroads into the chambers in which foreign policy, especially concerning security, is made (Waltz, 1959). In the contemporary era, these criticisms seem to have taken on a new urgency because of the risks of reliance on nuclear weapons as instruments of policy, even if only as diplomatic tools. Unfortunately, these commentaries have little impact because security analysts and policymakers find it easy to dismiss analyses that merely assume away the problems of security in an anarchic world (Hardin and others, 1985; Kaplan, 1957, 1979; Waltz, 1979; Jervis, 1982).

Regime theory (Krasner, 1983; Keohane, 1984), the assertion that stable, semiformal international agreements and institutions are both feasible and (sometimes) effective, is the main theoretical challenge to realism. This view stresses how interaction among states can lead to the development of cooperative norms and institutions. Realists, of course, do not deny that nations can respond to changes in the international political order. But realists have little to say about how a nation's self-interest might be altered by political change. As Nye (1987, p. 373) observes, "to say that states act in their self-interest is merely tautological unless we can account for how such interests are perceived and redefined." Regime theorists, on the other hand, suggest that changes at the international level that foster cooperation among states can shape domestic politics in a manner that leads to a new perception of interests and promotes new domestic coalitions and policies.

Yet little work in the regime literature has focused on how cooperation might develop in the absence of a dominant power, or hegemon, that is willing to "underwrite" the costs of a regime. We suggest that recent work in organizational theory focusing on learning can help one understand how a security regime might develop.

Our argument is developed in three parts. In the first part, the concept of nuclear weapons as an instrument to enhance security is examined *in terms of the realist paradigm itself*. Of central concern here is the development of the knowledge base from which learning and a security regime might draw. In the second part, the concept of a regime and its potential contribution to the regulation of international conflict are examined. Here we argue that a regime could decrease the possibility of armed conflict between nuclear powers and that the criticisms that realists frequently make of regime theory can be fruitfully addressed by an examination of how organizations learn. The third part reconsiders the view that the military as an organization constitutes an implacable obstacle to any change in defense strategy that might be entailed by the creation of a nuclear security regime. Here we argue that advances in organizational theory call into serious question important work done by international relations scholars (Posen, 1984; Snyder, 1984) on the military's interests and roles in grand strategy.

In the conclusion we suggest specific topics for further research that emerge from our review of realism, regime theory, and research on organizational learning. In particular, we offer several hypotheses about the effect of organizational learning upon the dynamics of regime creation and possible decay.

The Logic of Realism, and the Challenge Posed by Nuclear War

We divide our treatment of the realist paradigm into three subsections. In the first subsection the realist perspective that dominates security policy is examined in its pure form. This allows us to highlight the underlying logic of security studies. Since few policymakers are dogmatic realists, in the second subsection we examine the national versions of security policy in both the United States and the Soviet Union to illustrate how the basic tenets of realism shape policy-making. In the third subsection we examine the challenge that the nuclear revolution has posed to realist thinking. This last point leads to the discussion in the second part, in which the subjective nature of a security regime forms the core of the discussion.

Realism. Realism begins with two fundamental assumptions: the international system is anarchic (it lacks an authority recognized by all the major units) and is populated by sovereign states. Though other actors exist in the system, states are the major ones and structures are defined by the major actors (Waltz, 1979). The defining character of a realist analysis is that the anarchic nature of the international system imposes severe constraints on the behavior of states that desire to remain independent. Because of the absence of an overarching general authority, the sovereignty of peace-loving states is constantly at risk by aggressor states. Given shifts in domestic politics, even today's friend might become tomorrow's foe. Thus a self-help system develops in which each state prepares for war *in order to survive*. As a result, relative gain predominates over absolute gain, turning security issues into a zero-sum game.

The goal of states in this realist world is not peace; any state can have international peace by merely surrendering to the aggressor. The goal is rather the maintenance of sovereignty. In this struggle to survive, war becomes an instrument, a signal that systemic imperatives are being addressed, not a sign of the breakdown of the system. Indeed, for realists, the key question is not why war occurs, but why war does not occur more often than it does.

The realists tell us, then, that conflict is endemic to international politics as long as anarchy exists and states wish to survive as independent units (that is, have sovereignty). The challenge for the realist is thus to find ways to regulate, not eliminate, that conflict. The cooperation that emerges in this realist paradigm is purely short-run oriented. Statesmen survey the system and respond to either power imbalances or threats by forming alliances with other states who identify the same potential aggressor (Waltz, 1979; Walt, 1987). A fundamental insight of realist thinking is that whether or not statesmen initially intend such an outcome, balances of power will form. The purpose of the balance of power is not to avoid war but to prevent the creation of a world empire. War is thus an acceptable means to a desired end, sovereignty.

One of the major complications that a realist world presents for the management of conflict is the existence of a "security dilemma" (Jervis, 1978, pp. 167–214). In a self-help system, states take action designed to increase their own individual security. Unfortunately, many of the means pursued in this quest for security decrease the security of others. Under conditions of anarchy, states cannot trust each other and it is the *capability* of weapons, not the (always unreliable) *intent* of policymakers, that matters. The security dilemma is greatest when offensive weapons have the advantage over defensive ones and an offensive posture is not distinguishable from a defensive one.

While realism is the dominant paradigm in security studies and policy-making, it is not without its shortcomings. Chief among them is its conception of the nation-state. Although much of the criticism of realism revolves around its assumption of the state as a rational unitary actor, for analytic purposes this is not an unreasonable first step. In terms of the realist perspective itself, a more important issue is why the nation-state and its conception of sovereignty are taken as a given and a constant. This organizational actor and its values did not always exist; they really are a product of the modern world. Yet war is much, much older than the modern state system, and there is no reason to expect the peculiar form and values of the modern nation-state to continue indefinitely. But realists are at a loss to explain past changes in their chief analytic variables (Ruggie, 1982-83) or to predict future change. Realism turns out to be a rather static account, lacking insight into how changes in the world system occur.

Waltz (1979, pp. 118-119) offers a functional explanation for the primacy of the nation-state as his core concept: states are the most efficient actors in an international system; therefore, other states imitate their structure and behavior of the most powerful actors. But as organizational scholars point out, there is no reason to expect that such a process leads to optimal outcomes (DiMaggio and Powell, 1983; Hannan and Freeman, 1977). To be sure, within organizational populations, we often find a process of homogenization whereby key organizational units come to resemble one another. This process of isomorphism (that is, a constraining process that forces one unit in a population to resemble other units that face the same set of environmental conditions), however, may result in the selection of nonoptimal organizational arrangements as well as more adaptive ones. From an organizational point of view, then, a different set of questions is posed: (1) why did the modern nation-state arise at a particular point in time, and (2) what factors account for the persistence of this institutional arrangement? These questions express a more dynamic, process-oriented view of the nation-state as a central actor in the world polity than the standard account offered by realist approaches.

Realism and Nationalist Security Policy. The chief theoretical contribution of realism to the study of international politics is its emphasis upon systemic influences. Statesmen and most citizens, nevertheless, are reluctant to accept that their "just" foreign policy is roughly equivalent to that of a potential aggressor. Hence, much of foreign policy is rhetorically couched in terms of differences between one's own political and economic systems and those of rival nations. A true realist would maintain that this focus on national attributes makes little difference to whether balances of power form. But the level of tension between alliances, and thus the possibilities for managing conflict, will be affected by these subsystemic elements. Discussion of conflict management schemes thus leads to an examination of how the United States and the Soviets blend realism with national self-righteousness.

In the United States, grand strategy after World War II was oriented toward a view of the Soviet Union that emphasized both its historical and ideological propensity to expand its domination (Kennan, 1947). While the British had thought it possible to meet Soviet great power aspirations and security needs by organizing world politics into spheres of influence, U.S. presidents Franklin D. Roosevelt and Harry Truman rejected such an approach. For the United States, notwithstanding its own sphere of influence in Latin America, such divisions merely perpetuated conflict among nations. U.S. policymakers saw European history as proof of this maxim and regarded U.S. participation in international conflict (for example, World War I) as one of the negative consequences of balance of power politics.

Instead, the United States offered a world order based upon norms and principles that would bring peace and prosperity to all. Economic "laws" and the U.S. historical experience (with the Pan-American Union and the Reciprocal Trade Agreements Act of 1934) were believed to provide proof of the correctness of this approach to world politics. Those who opposed these norms and principles, including at times even those who disagreed merely with the manner of implementing them (Block, 1977),[2] were perceived to be short-sighted nationalists. In the late 1940s, Soviet rejection of the norms and principles advocated by the United States galvanized the containment logic of U.S. grand strategy; but we also need to remember that the United States even opposed its own allies (Britain and France) when they acted in a manner contrary to the decolonization principle during the Suez crisis of 1956.

Soviet opposition to the U.S. worldview rendered the USSR illegitimate in U.S. eyes. U.S. political and military strategy developed as a means to keep the Soviets from upsetting the international status quo. Atomic and nuclear arsenals were justified as necessary deterrent mechanisms. Military doctrine changed in response to the credibility of the deterrent (from massive retaliation to flexible response as the Soviets gained the ability to inflict massive destruction upon the U.S. homeland) and not to changes in evaluations of the Soviet Union itself.

Soviet progress in attaining strategic nuclear parity raised important questions about the manner in which the Soviets could be contained. The preclusion of "meaningful superiority" and a realization that unilateral security measures could heighten the security dilemma ultimately led the United States to pursue arms control with the Soviets in the 1960s (Rice, 1988, p. 294) and to begin a broader process of détente in the early 1970s. But the USSR was still perceived as an illegitimate revolutionary power, and the United States as the only nation capable of restraining its expansion (Hoffman, 1978). The caution exercised by the second Reagan administration and the Bush administration in responding to changes in Soviet international and domestic behavior under Gorbachev reflects this mixture of realism (as a major power, they cannot be ignored, especially in a nuclear world) and the U.S. worldview (because they are still communist, they remain a threat).

In the Soviet Union, until recently, grand military strategy has stressed the need to be able to fight a conventional war and, if necessary, a limited nuclear war. The explanation for this view lies first in the Russian/Soviet historical experiences of invasion (Denmark, Poland, France, Germany twice, an international capitalist alliance, and an attack by Japan). An ideology that postulated an inevitable opposition between socialist and capitalist economic systems also contributed to a perception of national self-righteousness and of the untrustworthy nature of enemies.

This historical experience, combined with ideological beliefs, contributed to Soviet rejection of the logic of mutually assured destruction, which is the core concept in the arguments about a "nuclear revolution" in international politics. Soviet doctrine that emphasizes the ability to fight a nuclear war or find other ways to defeat the United States if war breaks out might be defensive in intent, but it heightens the security dilemma between the Soviet Union and the United States (Jervis, 1978).

Nevertheless, history and ideology do not act in a determinate manner. At different times they have been interpreted in ways that support recognition of the interdependence of security. In the early 1960s, before any official recognition of Soviet-U.S. mutual interest in arms control, the USSR argued to the more adventuresome Chinese communists that "nuclear weapons do not observe the class principle" (Nye, 1987, pp. 386–387). Recently, the underpinnings of security doctrine in the Soviet Union have begun to change: territorial expansion is recognized as expensive and an inaccurate measure of power and security; the costs of isolation from the West are understood to be steep; international security is perceived as a positive non-zero–sum game in at least some issue areas; and the Soviets seek to be recognized as legitimate and major players in a stable international system (Dallin, 1988).

Realism and the Nuclear Revolution. Since Einstein, many concerned citizens have called for the abandonment of "prenuclear" thinking. The nuclear revolution is alleged to have made old ways of thinking about war both obsolete and dangerous. The horrors of nuclear war, however, tend to put antirealists and realists on separate paths to security policy. Antirealists have been so convinced of the folly of nuclear war that until recently they have made little effort to engage realists in any dialogue (Jervis, 1984; Halperin, 1987). Realist thinking, however, firmly dominates political and military offices. Hence it is necessary to stress how nuclear weapons differ from other forms of weaponry and to emphasize how these differences render realist thinking implausible.

Three elements make nuclear weapons significantly different from other weapons that the human race has known. The most obvious and perhaps the least interesting difference is their destructive capacity per se. A second item is the inability to ensure command and control over the use of these weapons by political authorities because of the possibility of decapitation strikes as well as technological changes that threaten to force decentralization of launch authority.[3] Perhaps the most fundamentally different feature of nuclear weapons resides in the ability of the "defeated" nation to destroy the "victor" (Jervis, 1984).

For these reasons, nuclear war is not likely to be "the continuation of politics by other means." Nuclear war cannot serve the purpose of ensuring the survival of a state once political negotiations break down. Although policymakers have not really wrestled with this fact (Bundy, 1984, pp. 42–54), it represents a fundamental challenge to the realist logic and therefore to foreign policy made under its auspices.

What specifically does the nuclear capacity challenge in realist thinking? First, the link between anarchy and aggression among the Great Powers is dramatically weakened. In the absence of a higher international authority, the strong possibility that nuclear confrontation will mean the destruction of the aggressor state will tend to create in the Great Powers a powerful incentive for maintaining the status quo. The threat of hegemonic domination, which a balance of power tends to attenuate, is thus greatly minimized. Second, nuclear states no longer find themselves in a self-help system. Given the existence of a second-strike capability,[4] defined as the ability to inflict unacceptable damage on an aggressor even after sustaining a first strike, the security of a nuclear power can only be furthered through cooperation with other nuclear powers. Finally, if security is enhanced only through cooperation, then we are no longer in a zero-sum prisoner's dilemma situation.

Despite the plausibility of these potent challenges to realist thinking and the enormous costs of ignoring them if they are correct, civil and military authorities (as well as much of the U.S. public) continue to live in a realist world modified by national righteousness. This mentality has been labeled the "conventionalization of nuclear strategy" (Jervis, 1984, pp. 56–63). An explanation of the continued predominance of this view and the possibilities for reform takes us into a discussion of a nuclear security regime.

A Nuclear Security Regime

In this section we introduce the concept of a regime, the problems that analysts confront in explaining the creation of regimes, and the potential contribution of this line of work to the management of conflict among nuclear powers. We conclude with a discussion of the possible features and utility of a nuclear security regime.

Regimes. The concept of regime was developed to explain cooperative behavior among nation-states, which appeared at odds with the realists' emphasis on a self-help zero-sum game. Realists recognize that all states might be better off if they cooperated on security issues (that is, that security is a collective good), but since the realist conceives of international politics as a one-shot prisoner's dilemma game, security cooperation among competing states is perceived as an irrational policy from the perspective of individual sovereign states.

Regime analysts argue that international regimes can provide a way out of the prisoner's dilemma, that it is not necessary to assume either a harmony of interests or the lack of anarchy in order to have international cooperation (Oye, 1986). "International regimes neither enforce hierarchical rules on governments nor substitute their own rules for autonomous calculation; instead, they provide rules of thumb in place of those that governments would otherwise adopt" (Keohane, 1984, pp. 115–116). Regime theorists, therefore, attempt a critique of the realist world on its own terms.

Regimes are formal or informal social mechanisms that produce recognizable patterns of behavior. They consist of implicit or explicit principles, norms, rules, and decision-making procedures. In the language of regime theory, principles are beliefs of fact, causation, and rectitude. Norms are standards of behavior defined in terms of rights and obligations. Rules are specific prescriptions or proscriptions for action. Decision-making procedures are prevailing practices for making and implementing collective choice. The first two components, principles and norms, constitute the core of a regime; a change in them will constitute a change of the regime itself. Changes in rules and decision-making procedures can be accommodated under the same norms and principles and thus represent a change within a regime (Krasner, 1982, p. 186; Aggarwal, 1985; Keohane, 1984). Regimes are created to regulate behavior in an "issue-area," that is, "a recognized cluster of concerns involving interdependence not only among the parties but among the issues themselves" (Haas, 1980, pp. 358, 365).

The core argument of regime analysis is that members of the regime can develop a convergence of expectations about each other's behavior (Young, 1980). A regime, therefore, has a fundamental subjective component: members cooperate in addressing common problems because each perceives that the others will reciprocate rather than exploit. In other words, those who cooperate will not be stuck with the "sucker payoff" in a prisoners' dilemma game. Because regimes postulate a normative rather than a power-based explanation of international cooperation, the regime paradigm is a contentious issue in the study of international politics (Strange, 1982, pp. 479–496).

The regime approach to world politics raises an important objection to the realist's zero-sum world. But this argument is justifiable only if the regime has an impact independent of the distribution of political power among its members. Otherwise, cooperation would occur only as the result of states acting in their own short-run interests. Cooperation under these circumstances would be limited and consonant with the realist world. Jervis (1982) has argued that the links between superpowers' restraint and their own self-interest (in survival) are too direct to warrant invoking the regime concept.

Regime analysts are quite aware of these objections and have attempted to respond to them. Because the most durable and important regimes (for example, the Bretton Woods monetary agreements or the liberal trade regime) were essentially the product of a dominant power's actions, whether by forcing adherence to the regime or by underwriting its costs, regime theorists acknowledge that major regimes are usually created by power disparities in accordance with the realists' view, but they argue that cooperation comes to be valued in its own right by all participants (Keohane, 1984). Thus, cooperation takes on a life of its own and can transform self-interest. Still other regime analysts use game theory to reveal the conditions under which interstate cooperation can occur and become stable, and functional approaches specify when demand for a regime will occur (Haggard and Simmons, 1987).

Nevertheless, these explanations of the development of regimes are in some respects lacking. States are postulated to learn the benefits of cooperation from their experience with cooperation that is underwritten by a hegemonic power, but these regime analysts offer no theory of learning. A primary reason for this failure was the need to develop "a structural analysis of constraints and a functional understanding of regimes . . . [as] necessary to put the phenomenon of actor cognition into its proper political context" (Keohane, 1984, p. 132). Another problem for our purposes is that since both the United States and the USSR are superpowers, the creation of a nuclear security regime as a result of hegemonic imposition (that is, by a coercive hegemon) or subsidy (by a benevolent hegemon), from which actors can learn that cooperation pays, is precluded.

The utility of regime analysis for the development of a nuclear security regime is therefore greatly limited unless we can explain how relevant actors would learn that cooperation pays. There is a cognitive approach to regime creation and transformation that stresses learning and ideology (Haggard and Simmons, 1987). But this work has centered on demonstrating that knowledge and ideology affect behavior without clearly specifying how states learn to value and create regimes.

Organizational theory may be helpful in addressing this gap in the regime literature. Much of the research in political science on organizational processes stresses that organizations and their leaders typically pursue positions that maximize short-run interests. Security analysts, in particular, have focused on organizational and bureaucratic factors to explain the answers to such diverse questions as how to deal with nuclear missiles in Cuba and how to fight World War II (Allison, 1971; Posen, 1984, respectively). Regime analysts utilize these insights by postulating that regimes may lead organizations to identify their own interest with the success of the regime (Nye, 1987). While this work may help explain the *success* of a regime, we still need an explanation for why an organization would modify its short-run definition of self-interest to support the *creation* of a regime.

Of course, learning itself is not sufficient. What is learned is crucial and not entirely objective. For example, military and civilian leaders "learned" from the Prussian military experience in the second half of the nineteenth century that the offense had the advantage. This so-called "cult of the offensive" was mistaken, but it helped propel the world into war in 1914 by convincing actors that war was inevitable and that whoever struck first would have the upper hand. From World War I, British (and to a lesser extent French) policymakers "learned" that defense had the advantage, and therefore negotiation rather than confrontation with Hitler was proper (Van Evera, 1985, pp. 58–107; Jervis, 1978, pp. 188–193). The possibility that "mistaken learning," Jervis's phrase, might have been responsible for a war that did not have to be (World War I) and made a necessary war more dangerous than it might have been (World War II) cautions us that learning may sometimes be superstitious and maladaptive (March and Olsen, 1976). Before examining the potential for organizational learning in the military, we turn to the issue of security regimes in order to delineate what factors must be learned in order to facilitate a decrease in tension among the nuclear powers.

Security Regimes. Regimes have been found to exist in numerous international arenas, but the security realm is acknowledged to have enjoyed very few regimes. Four key differences between security and nonsecurity issues account for the paucity of cooperative arrangements in the security arena. The security arena is more competitive than other arenas because the existence of anarchy created a zero-sum game in the prenuclear world. In addition, in matters of security it is difficult to infer motives from behavior: offensive and defensive motives often result in the same behavior. The stakes are higher in the security realm because the independence of nations is in play. Finally, measurement of one's own security and detection of others' security efforts are generally much more difficult than in nonsecurity areas (Jervis, 1982). Despite these difficulties, analysts have identified security regimes at two levels: the level of the overall relationship among great powers and the level of subissues that comprise the overall relationship (Nye, 1987; George, 1988). Regimes at the more general level we will refer to as comprehensive security regimes.

In the modern state system only one comprehensive security regime has existed, and it was relatively short lived (the Concert of Europe, 1815–1823) (Haas, 1983; Jervis, 1982). We currently do not have a nuclear security regime because both the United States and the Soviet Union structure their overall relationship on the basis of their immediate self-interest in avoiding a nuclear holocaust (Haas,

1983; Jervis, 1982). Although the nuclear balance of power has coincided with relative stability in superpower relations since 1945, despite the lack of a comprehensive regime, we believe that the world would be safer (particularly as the nuclear club grows) if collective conflict management among nuclear powers could be institutionalized.

The objective conditions that favor the establishment of a comprehensive security regime exist when "offensive and defensive weapons and policies are distinguishable but the former are cheaper and more effective than the latter, or in which they cannot be told apart but it is easier to defend than to attack" (Jervis, 1982, pp. 360–361). Under these conditions, states that are satisfied with such a status quo would find that war and expansion do not pay and that security would be attainable only through mutual cooperation.

Simply decreasing the objective risks of cooperation under anarchy, however, is not sufficient for the development of a comprehensive security regime. Agreement on the subjective core of a regime is a necessary condition. This subjective core consists of principles and norms. The following principles and norms seem appropriate to a comprehensive security regime:

> *Principles* (beliefs of fact, causation, and rectitude): security in a nuclear world can only be achieved through cooperation; the security dilemma is real; the coexistence of distinct national political systems is possible; the probability of secret deployment in sufficient numbers to constitute first-strike threat is not very high.
>
> *Norms* (standards of behavior defined in terms of rights and obligations): military expansion is not permissible; first-strike weapons are destabilizing; vital interests must be negotiated and respected.

These principles and norms could be congruent with a variety of rules and decision-making procedures. The experience of a number of security agreements at the subissue level suggests that the following are appropriate:

Rules (specific prescriptions or proscriptions for action): verification is necessary.

Decision-making procedures (practices for making and implementing collective choice, such as those utilized by the Standing Consultative Commission discussed in Chapter Two).

How might a comprehensive security regime develop? One critical institution in any such arrangement is the military. In order for cooperative relations between the superpowers to become institutionalized, the armed forces must play a critical role. Both sides would need much more sustained contact and interaction; joint military training exercises or strategy sessions among top military officers would have to become more frequent, and routinized procedures in times of crises would have to be developed. We are still a long way from cooperation of this kind, although a few first steps were made in 1989. The military is commonly thought to represent a barrier to more peaceful international relations. In the next section, we take a critical look at this view and examine what role the military might play in a nuclear security regime.

The Military and a Security Regime: Organizational Learning and Grand Strategy

In both popular and scholarly accounts, military leaders are frequently depicted as advocates of the "conventionalization" of nuclear weapons. In this view, the military is seen as incapable of understanding that its goal (to safeguard the security of the nation) cannot be achieved by its traditional means (war). Because the military is "oversocialized" (Snyder, 1984) to fighting, it responds to security threats by advocating use of the means of destruction that it has at its disposal, for example, "surgical air strikes" against Soviet nuclear missiles in Cuba.

Since Allison's (1971) path-breaking study of the Cuban missile crisis, international relations specialists have often turned to organizational theory for explanations of why military planners and leaders repeatedly choose offensive strategies that depend for their success on conditions that no longer hold, if they ever did. (See, in particular, Posen, 1984; Snyder, 1984.) These studies provide us with a clear message: in the absence of an institutional crisis or military failure, the armed services will resist change at this strategic level and continue to prepare for and advocate fighting in the traditional way. As long as we live in a world of mutually assured destruction, we cannot hope for either crisis or failure of military doctrine, especially of nuclear deterrence. Consequently, the military should be expected to provide a strong pressure group for the "conventionalization" of nuclear weapons.

In our view, however, international relations scholars who use organizational theory have not kept abreast of advances in organizational theory, which suggest that organizations may be less bureaucratically rigid and unreceptive to change than Allison suggested some two decades ago. In brief, we argue that the common usage of organizational theory in international relations has three major shortcomings. First, the perspective on organizations that is utilized, a rational rather than an open system view, is too simple and static to deal with the question of adaptation. Second, there is little appreciation of recent organizational research that suggests the conditions under which learning leads to changes in organizational behavior. (See Leavitt and March, 1988, for a review of this literature.) And third, studies of international relations tend to ignore empirical work showing that the perceptions of organizational leaders cannot be well predicted on the basis of their organizational position or interests alone (March and Olsen, 1976).

Recent advances in organizational theory suggest several approaches to organizational learning that may be quite fruitful for understanding how and when the military innovates, especially at the level of grand strategy, and under what conditions the military may become a force for "deconventionalizing" nuclear weapons. For organizational theorists, such questions are examples of a more general issue: how the past imposes itself on the present in large-scale organizations. This perspective forces us to focus on how traditions and memory operate in organizations and to analyze and illustrate these processes so as to identify useful empirical questions. This knowledge will enable us to make progress in solving two of the thornier problems in organizational analysis: How strong are inertial pressures on organizations? Under what circumstances do organizations display a high degree of adaptability?

We begin this section with a critique of Posen and Snyder, whose work on military doctrine well represents current thinking among scholars of international relations. We then establish a baseline understanding of the uses and liabilities of memory and tradition. A series of general and speculative propositions concerning the force or absence of tradition in different kinds of organizational settings follows. A brief discussion of several important unresolved issues and the shape of a future research agenda concludes the section.

The Military Preference for Offense. Posen's and Snyder's work represents thoughtful, explicit, and systematic efforts to use organizational theory to predict military behavior. Specifically, Posen and Snyder both seek to explain why military organizations across nations tend to choose offensive military doctrines. Posen is particularly concerned with the interplay between military and civilian policy preferences, while Snyder limits his study to military decision making.

Posen compares balance of power theory and organizational theory in his search for a theoretically parsimonious explanation of military strategy. Since balance of power theory is rather limited in both its theoretical development and predictive power (Waltz, 1979; Walt, 1987), Posen's deduction of hypotheses here is rather straightforward and does this perspective no great injustice. But organizational theory presents him with a difficult challenge. In Posen's view, "organizational theory itself is a rather incoherent field." He opts to focus on "solely . . . those insights that may help yield answers to the central questions of this study" (Posen, 1984, p. 42). Unfortunately, his choices lead him to overemphasize the elements of short-sightedness and reluctance to change in organizations in general and military organizations in particular.

Posen begins where many organizational theorists begin: uncertainty threatens the ability of an organization to reach its goals and therefore must be reduced. The chief sources of this uncertainty are found in the behavior of individuals within the organization and in the environment from which the organization must secure resources and pursue its goals. As a result, organizations adopt standard operating procedures (SOPs) designed to reduce uncertainty and safeguard organizational autonomy from the environment. These SOPs interpret demands and opportunities in the environment and suggest appropriate responses from an organization's repertoire of procedures. Effective SOPs constrain individuals' behavior so that they select the standard rather than the idiosyncratic response.

Because of these organizational imperatives, Posen argues, militaries prefer offensive rather than defensive or deterrent doctrines. Offensive military strategies allow the organization to fight with its own SOP, deny adversaries their own SOPs, increase organizational size and wealth, and enhance military autonomy. Consequently, Posen tells us, we should expect only small, incremental change in military doctrine. Thus, he concludes: "Very little of the preceding summary of organizational theory suggests that organizational innovation is either probable or simple. As 'rational' purposeful instruments, organizations place a premium on predictability, stability, and certainty. These values are inimical to innovation. Individuals within organizations develop personal stakes in particular elements of their organizations. They have little interest in change. For these reasons, students of organizational behavior have more frequently addressed incremental change than innovation" (1984, p. 46).

Posen notes that five circumstances may prompt the military to change its doctrines. The two most important sources of such innovation are imposed from outside. Failure of the old doctrine to deliver the organizational goals and pressure from clients force the organization to redesign its SOP. A change in the technology of fighting wars may also be a source of strategic innovation, but only if the new technology favors offensive strategy and has been actually proven in battle, either directly or via the experience of a client state. If the new technology favors the doctrine of defense, Posen believes that it will be misinterpreted because organizational interests dominate the perception of reality (Posen, 1984, pp. 47, 55–56).

In Posen's work, only one factor internal to the organization provides a stimulus to change: the desire to expand. The power of this internal incentive, moreover, seems weak. Drawing on the research of Betts (1977) and Downs (1967), Posen notes that innovation is not necessarily the preferred strategy for expansion and that autonomy is often preferred over wealth. Unfortunately, he omits any discussion of the conditions under which organizations might prefer wealth over autonomy or innovation as a means of expansion. Posen's conclusions about the sources of military doctrine follow quite closely from his particular reading of organizational theory. The military prefer offensive, disintegrated, and stagnant military doctrines. Innovation occurs almost exclusively when imposed upon the military by failure, crisis, or civilian intervention (Posen, 1984).

Snyder (1984) presents a more complex argument about military doctrine. In a very important sense, he picks up the argument where Posen leaves off. For example, in his argument civilian intervention becomes important only when military interests and sound strategy conflict. Strategists act rationally when they choose on the basis of an unbiased evaluation of three factors: national aims, technological and geographic constraints, and the military balance of power. If the rational incentives for a particular doctrine are clear, there will be no military bias in formulating military doctrine.

Of course, misperception is a consistent reality in international politics (Jervis, 1976). Snyder seeks to explain this misperception by incorporating insights from organizational theory. Like Posen, he focuses on the fact that institutions have interests of their own and that the routinization necessary to deal with uncertainty may make the organization ill equipped to deal with a changing environment. He categorizes these two sources of misperception as motivational bias and doctrinal oversimplification. Snyder's analysis of bias differs from Posen's in two fundamental ways. First, Snyder combines organizational and cognitive perspectives to explain the choices of military planners. Thus it is not only the conflict between institutional interests and rational strategy that leads to bias, but also the fact that individuals attempt to deal with the stress produced by such conflicting interests by denying the existence of any conflict. Hence, the individual misperceives the situation (Snyder, 1984).

A second difference between the Posen and Snyder analyses is that the latter sees the offensive bias of the military as contingent, while the former sees it as inherent. In terms of motivational bias, Snyder is not systematic, but he does claim that some sources always favor the offense, while others might favor either offensive or defensive strategies. Doctrinal simplification is treated more analytically. Here we find five sources of bias. Two sources always favor the offense: the oversocialization of military professionals to war and the need to reduce uncertainty. (Posen's discussion of uncertainty encompasses all five of Snyder's sources of bias.) Another two sources intensify the existing bias, whatever it may be: the dogmatization of doctrine and economy of calculation. The direction of bias of the fifth source (formation of doctrine) depends upon the "lessons" perceived in the formative stage of doctrine. Thus, there are no sources that consistently favor defensive doctrines (Snyder, 1984).

Critique and Implications of the Military Preference for Conventionalization. Although Posen and Snyder disagree somewhat about the sources of the preference toward the offensive, they seem to be in substantial agreement about how the nuclear revolution has been incorporated into military doctrine thus far. Posen notes that technological change will usually be assimilated into existing doctrine rather than stimulate change. He claims both theoretical and empirical support for this proposition and attributes it to difficulties in organizational learning, specifically when it comes to operational implications. The strategic implications of a new technology are learned under only two conditions: when client states use the technology in war or when the military organization uses the technology in its own wars (Posen, 1984). Since we have only one instance of the use of atomic weapons in war, and that conformed to our existing military doctrine of attrition, Posen's argument leads us to expect that the military will "conventionalize" nuclear technology.

Another factor in Posen's approach also leads us to expect military advocacy of "conventionalization." Deterrence, which is at the heart of the doctrine of mutual assured destruction (MAD), is allegedly disliked by the military because it requires consideration of an adversary's will to suffer punishment. The military is purportedly trained to think in terms of objective capabilities, and thus its sense of uncertainty is heightened by a doctrine that involves questions of will (Posen, 1984). Moreover, since defense loses credibility in a MAD world, the military is reduced to considering only how to use its nuclear arsenal to defeat a potential aggressor.

Snyder's analysis also supports a "conventionalization" hypothe-

sis, albeit through a more complex process. In the twenty years
before the Soviet achievement of nuclear parity created a MAD
world, rational strategic choice made the U.S. nuclear arsenal seem
appropriate. In line with Snyder's analysis, bias would seem to
come into play in two instances: when we seek to break out of a
MAD world by regaining nuclear superiority and when we attempt
to convince ourselves that conventional and nuclear escalation in a
U.S.-Soviet military confrontation can be managed.

The direction of bias, following Snyder, would seem to be in
favor of conventionalization. First, the military is allegedly oversocialized toward war, viewing international politics as a simplified
zero-sum game. Second, the reduction of uncertainty favors offensive doctrines, so the military plans to use its resources to attack
rather than deter or defend. Since doctrine must utilize those resources available to the military, the military would presumably
want to advocate a strategy that made use of its large investments
in nuclear weaponry. Reduction of uncertainty also favors conventionalization because the focus of uncertainty reduction is on advance planning, not on actions taken during actual battles. Nuclear
weapons are thus likely to be programmed to do a job with less than
appropriate concern over the actual outcome of their use.

Conventionalization seems to follow quite easily from such analyses of organizational interest. Different, though equally plausible, interpretations of Posen's and Snyder's independent variables,
however, suggest that conventionalization of nuclear weapons was
not predetermined and that a basis for military rejection of this
doctrine can be found.

Two items in Posen's analysis are relevant here: wealth and autonomy. Offensive doctrines provide both to the military, but conventionalization actually detracts from the military's wealth and
autonomy. A grand strategy based on nuclear weapons is less expensive and requires less manpower than a strategy based on nonnuclear weapons. Moreover, command and control of nuclear
weapons, precisely because they are unique in destructive power
and speed of delivery, are in the hands of the civilian leaderships
in all of the nuclear powers. A conventionalized nuclear military
doctrine, therefore, institutionalizes nonmilitary involvement and
interference to a far greater degree than previously.

Snyder's analysis also provides elements for disputing the military's interests in conventionalization. For example, offensive doctrine does not appear to be an inevitable outgrowth of the military's oversocialization toward war. The U.S. experience in World War II contradicts Snyder on this point. Civilians, believing this to be a war that could guarantee peace, sought total victory over Germany and Japan and worried about preempting Soviet war-won advantages. The military, schooled in realpolitik, viewed future wars as likely and sought to build a balance of power, irrespective of domestic politics (Huntington, 1957). Thus, the military was willing to end the fighting before civilians were, and the military argued against use of the atomic bomb against Japan (Alperovitz, 1965). This U.S. experience suggests that the military may be conscious of Clausewitz's views about the integration of political and military goals but also that the military, with good reason, may disagree with the political goals pursued by civilians.

The proclivity toward offensive strategies, which is another of Snyder's examples of military bias, may also offer promise of military support for deconventionalizing nuclear weapons. The formative stage of U.S. nuclear doctrine took place in 1945, when we had to decide how, if at all, to use the atomic bomb. If the military's memory of that episode suggests the "lesson" that civilians may try to force the military to use nuclear weapons for political rather than security reasons, the military could have an interest in deconventionalizing nuclear weapons.

In summary, if the analysis that hypothesizes a military predilection for offensive strategies is flawed, the expectation that conventionalization is in the interest of the military is also weakened. Even if the offensive bias were reaffirmed, the link between organizational interests in offense and conventionalization could be broken. Even if we grant that socialization processes, the desire to reduce uncertainty, and the drive for increased wealth and autonomy largely explain military doctrine, the military as an organization could still logically oppose the conventionalization of nuclear weapons.

The implications for our understanding of the determinants of conventionalization are fundamental: political, not military, leaders may be the major obstacle to deconventionalizing nuclear weapons. While it is true that the military has not opposed conventionalization, our reading suggests that if military learning and innovation are possible, the military could become an advocate for a nuclear security regime.

Military Learning and Innovation. Although analyses have emphasized that the military is likely to act on the basis of narrow and short-sighted interests, as well as doggedly to pursue continuity in military strategy, there are numerous examples of military learning in the absence of strategic failure or institutional crisis. We turn now to a discussion of organizational sources of military innovation and to why Posen and Snyder overlooked these developments.

We begin with the organizational models employed by both Posen and Snyder. Both scholars treat the military as a more or less unified entity and argue as if military doctrine overrides interservice differences and rivalries. Clearly, such a view is rather primitive. This unitary-actor model of the military downplays interservice disagreements, bureaucratic struggles, and political coalitions, as well as generational differences within the armed forces. Moreover, because the technology, history, and operational context of the major service branches are quite different, it is plausible to expect that they would adopt divergent approaches to the carrying out of military tasks.

We see these differences operating in myriad ways. In the current budgetary wrangling over planned cuts in defense expenditures, the service branches have not responded with a single voice. Some branches are actively trying to shape the evolution of a new security order, while others are fighting desperately to retain pet projects. Similarly, a recent *New York Times* (Trainor, 1990) article on the war colleges describes the disparate educational responses to the lessening of the Soviet threat. At the Naval War College, the key emphasis is now on coping with uncertainty rather than Soviet aggression. As one lieutenant colonel put it, "The Russians are 'out' and the third world is 'in'." But at the Air War College, the curriculum remains driven by enduring concepts, unrelated to current events. Clearly, some of the services want to be at the forefront of any effort to shift the emphasis from superpower conflict to other arenas, such as terrorism and Third World threats, while other branches see much less need for any change in strategic doctrine.

Similarly, the different branches of the armed forces learn from history and experience in varied ways. Krepinevich (1986) has argued that "in spite of its anguish in Vietnam, the army has learned little of value." In his view, the army continues to prepare itself for conventional war, even though we live in a world in which insurgencies and guerilla warfare have become commonplace. Meanwhile, other branches of the services, notably the marines, now focus their planning on dealing with counterinsurgency. Thus, from our vantage point, the military is anything but a unitary rational actor; instead, it is more aptly viewed as a coalition of different units, with goals that at times diverge. These varied subunits possess differential capabilities to draw lessons from history and to adapt to new circumstances.

We are also more comfortable with a view of organizations as complex open systems rather than the machinelike bureaucracies suggested by Posen or Snyder. This open system view offers greater insight into possible sources of change—both internal and external to the organization. Posen and Snyder both treat the military as a sluggish, backward-looking institution. To be sure, there is some merit in this view, as illustrated by the old adage, "when military men don't know what to do, they do what they know." Armies do seem to consistently organize to fight the last war over again. But the military has also been very forward looking, both on matters of resource management and high-level strategy. For example, a very persuasive case could be made that the U.S. armed forces have responded in a more aggressive and positive manner to the issues of racial and gender equality faster than any other major institution in American society.

We are also more sensitive to possible internal sources of change. Take, for example, the matter of organizational routines. As Posen (1984) notes, routines are an internal mechanism to help manage uncertainty that tend to become institutionalized over time. Routines, however, are not merely a mechanical regulator akin to the thermostats of early cybernetic systems analysis. Highlighting the cognitive and social aspects of organizational routines pushes us to conceive of the military as a more complex social organization, as an open system.

An open system model questions the effort to posit a simple

relationship between individual interests and organizational routines. Both Posen and Snyder downplay the role of individuals in stimulating innovation. Posen (1984) presents a narrow view of the interests of the individual in organizations: they are overwhelmingly (if not solely) determined by organizational interests. This view is appropriate to a closed system conceptualization of organizations. But military history provides examples of both insulated and broad-minded leaders. Among the more notable examples that run counter to Posen's view are the Prussian chief strategist in the nineteenth century and the U.S. senior commanders in World War II. As Snyder (1984, p. 122) observes of the Prussian leader, because the elder Moltke was the "creator, not the captive of his doctrines" and "did not implement them in the manner of a narrow technician," he was able to appreciate when the defense had the advantage. Or take World War II, particularly conflict in the Pacific. Pursuing the attrition path to victory in the Pacific during World War II might have reduced uncertainty, provided more military resources, and postponed the inevitable demobilization that would accompany victory; nevertheless, top U.S. military leaders attempted, albeit unsuccessfully, to convince President Truman to pursue a diplomatic rather than a military end to World War II.[5] Clearly, these military leaders rose above narrow standard operating procedures to advocate policies that would meet the larger organizational goal of defending sovereignty.

A second source of Posen's and Snyder's skepticism about military sources of innovation lies in their underdeveloped concept of how organizations learn, remember, and unlearn. Recent research in organizational theory offers a more sophisticated view of how organizations learn, suggesting when organizations are likely to be flexible and responsive, as well as when they are held firmly in the grip of the past.

Of course, intuitively, we recognize that not all kinds of learning are similar. It seems especially important to distinguish between learning that occurs within organizations and learning at the level of the nation-state. Even within organizations, learning can take a variety of forms: learning to choose among and use established routines that are already in an organization's repertoire is quite a different process from reassembling subroutines to produce new responses to changed circumstances. And even more fundamental change is precipitated by the creation of new routines as part of a more profound reinterpretation of an organization's goals and mission. A similar process of learning at the nation-state level might involve the use of new knowledge or a reassessment of current conditions to redefine the notion of national interest. At present, we can only envision the outlines of such a change. At best, we can only suggest how consensual knowledge, cooperative arrangements, and mutually verifiable procedures might lead the superpowers to a better shared understanding of the nuclear threat and a pause or pullback in the weapons race for nuclear supremacy.

Nelson and Winter (1982) suggest that organizational routines are the primary mechanism for organizational memory. Routines include the forms, rules, procedures, conventions, strategies, and technologies around which organizations are constructed and through which they operate (Leavitt and March, 1988). The basic claim is that organizations remember by doing. Organizational memory consists of the results of routines; it is the retention of response patterns for subsequent use. Memory refines and reinforces skills, preserving certain kinds of behavior and creating continuity. The knowledge of an organization is retained in its routines, and the process of adding to those routines or changing them is the process of organizational learning.

.Files, records, bulletin boards, and various means of communication and information storage are all a part of an organization's memory. Indeed, methods of communication play a crucial role in shaping organizations' identities (see Yates, 1989). Internal flows of communication, both horizontal and vertical, contribute to the establishment of a corporate memory independent of specific individuals.

The concept of organizational memory evokes, at least metaphorically, the repertoire of information, skills, and experience that an organization has at its disposal. But the idea of organizational memory is not some kind of aggregate ability or perception; an organization's memory is not typically reducible to the sum of the knowledge and talents of its individual members. Of course, some organizations are little more than extensions of the wills of dominant coalitions or individuals; they have no lives of their own. In most larger and older organizations, however, memory is, in some fashion, independent of the individuals presently employed by or associated with those organizations. It is the embodiment of an organization's historical self-representation, although it comes to life only insofar as it is held by current members at any given time. An organization's memory must be capable of retention as well as transmission to new members of the organization. In this sense, memory both reflects the past and informs the present. It promotes organizational stability despite personnel turnover because it is a means of "recording" critical actions taken at times prior to the arrival of many of the current members of the organization. These patterned behaviors are usually discernible by the members of an organization and its immediate clients; less frequently, traditions are recognizable more widely, and outsiders may come to associate the organization with an identifiable style or manner of doing things.

Some of what an organization "knows" is never written down. Informal, shared experiences produce a wealth of knowledge and skills that cannot always be committed to instruction on paper. Clark (1972) found that some liberal arts colleges had cherished "sagas" that influenced their interpretations of the past as well as their choices of future action. Symbolic vehicles of meaning—rituals, ceremonies, and language—are carriers of organizational *traditions*. They help to perpetuate ongoing social life. The more that these traditions are acted out, the better they are remembered. Traditions are not fixed but are continually being constructed or re-created. In this view, an organization's tradition does not control or dictate specific behavior so much as it enforces limits and defines the range of what is appropriate. As Howard Becker taught us, even people who cooperate to produce a work of art do not decide things afresh. Instead, they rely on conventions, on earlier agreements that have become customary (Becker, 1974). The more fully an organization's traditions encode conventions and expectations, the more is uncertainty brought under control.

Explaining Discontinuity. Posen and Snyder correctly identify the more common circumstances under which tradition loses its force and organizational routines are rendered insufficient. Failures and crises can create the uncertainty necessary to reevaluate standard procedures. Severe deadlines may force abandonment of standard ways of doing things; poor performance may lead to the discovery that practices were superstitious, that is, based on fallacious learning in which the connection between organizational action and environmental response has somehow become severed. Starbuck (1983, p. 100) maintains that crises "bring unlearning when people discover that their beliefs do not explain events, that their behavior programs are producing bad results, that their superiors' expertise is hollow."

But crises may not be sufficient to generate alternatives. Even in crisis situations when time constraints are severe, the burden of proof is commonly placed on those who propose to depart from existing routines. Snyder's analysis of the military mobilization issue in 1914 is a prime example. The danger of war did not deter the Great Powers from following standard procedures for mobilizing. As a consequence, these procedures sent a signal that the nations were preparing for war. This is why Posen emphasizes the role played by actors outside the organization (civilian leaders). But organizational theorists have found several factors internal to the organization that also serve as stimuli to change: stages in an organization's life cycle, rapid growth, the accomplishment of the original stated purpose, and a major transformation in an organization's primary technology.

Key transitions in an organization's life cycle have been demonstrated to weaken traditions and erode memories (for an illustration of this process in the book-publishing industry, see Coser, Kadushin, and Powell, 1982). The departure of an organization's founder represents the loss of an important tradition-sustaining force. Similarly, changes in ownership or legal status may trigger dramatic alterations in an organization's activities. Mergers, acquisitions, and divestitures represent much more than efforts at expansion or reorganization; they frequently result in dramatic changes in an organization's routines and principles. These changes are commonly accompanied by considerable personnel turnover, including the departure of top executives, shifts in product lines and emphases, and new standards regarding what products or services are considered feasible.

It may be fruitful to think of possible parallels in the history of

military organizations. Does it make sense to speak of the life cycle
of an organization like the military, which was founded alongside
the state itself? Certainly military organizations have become identified with specific military leaders who oversaw the military's expansion in a new direction at a critical moment: for example, the
elder Moltke and Mahan. Can we gain understanding of the dynamics of the military's memory by viewing these leaders as organization "founders"? The longer control remains in the hands of a
leader, the more well developed traditions and procedures become,
and the more memory and routines reinforce these traditions. How
does the departure of top military leaders affect tradition and
memory? In short, are there key transition points in military
organizations?

Less dramatic and more gradual changes in an organization's
traditions and memory can occur during periods of rapid growth or
when organizations accomplish their original stated purposes. Militaries historically experience rapid growth as they mobilize for war.
If they are more susceptible to change at such a time, success of
civilian intervention in military doctrine (as described by Posen)
may have an important organizational determinant. Part of a research agenda for analysts of military doctrine would be to evaluate
the impact of the dramatic and rapid expansion of the military
budget of the Reagan administration on military doctrine. In light
of the mass repudiation in Western Europe and the United States
of the idea that nuclear war was "winnable," did the Reagan military expansion ironically facilitate the military's move in the direction of deconventionalization?

Organizational traditions also may not survive a major transformation in an organization's primary technology or a new regime of
competition ushered in by deregulation or large-scale social change.
For the military, the advent of the nuclear age certainly constitutes
a major technological transformation, of the kind one might expect
to challenge many organizational traditions. One such tradition
may be that of intelligence gathering and interpretation as the sole
prerogative of the military. Some analysts have argued that the rise
of the Central Intelligence Agency as a competitor made military
intelligence agencies less dogmatic (Freedman, 1986).

Conclusion: A Research Agenda for the
Military Contribution to a Nuclear Security Regime

This chapter has argued that a reassessment of the core tenets of American foreign policy is particularly pressing in light of both nuclear and political developments occurring today. We suggested that a nuclear security regime could constitute a fundamental pillar in the U.S.-Soviet relationship. And we argued that organizational theory should help us create that security regime. In particular, we focused on the potential contributions and obstacles from the military, highlighting the importance of innovation in the military's approach to security.

A fundamental component of a research agenda oriented toward military sources of innovation should be the specification of the conditions under which organizations possess a well-developed corporate memory and are most heavily influenced by precedent. As we have seen, in addressing this question of what factors strengthen or inhibit the power of organizational traditions, we are dealing also with the still broader question of organizational learning. Such questions become researchable only when they are disaggrevated into more specific components, and we offer five examples, each of which subsumes a number of testable propositions or hypotheses. Their specificity and their propositional form reflect our wish to develop a research agenda rather than to imply that the empirical work has already been done.

1. When do organizations learn? More specifically, under what circumstances do organizational traditions and routines lose force?

Organizational traditions and routines tend to lose force when their use is associated with failure of any of several kinds: poor performance (quality, quantity, market share, profit, and so on), missed deadlines or commitments, inability to explain and interpret significant events in the organization itself and its environment.

Traditions and routines also lose force when major changes in the organizational environment call their relevance into question. Such environmental changes include technological developments that have important implications for the core productive processes of the organization. They also include changes in external control, of the kind implied by merger, acquisition, or legislation.

Finally, traditions and routines lose force when the organization itself moves into a recognizably different stage in its life cycle. Such stage transitions may occur because of growth, especially rapid growth. They may also occur because of the visible accomplishment of the previous organizational purpose or because of a generational change in top leadership. Nye (1987, p. 387) has suggested that the American government has a weak institutional memory because of frequent turnover of political leaders and administrators; hence new leaders may have to relearn old lessons.

2. How do organizations learn?

Organizational learning is a multistage process, a significant part of which is political. More specifically, organizations do not learn as unitary actors; individuals and organizational subunits discover, invent, or learn from external sources new ways of doing things. Whether these innovations become part of the organizational repertoire depends upon the success of an internal political process; the individuals and subunits that have "learned" face the political task of persuasion in order to make their learning dominant. A critical research question is whether political and military organizations have such different organizational characteristics that they are not able to learn similar lessons from new circumstances or new information.

3. What organizational properties either hinder or facilitate learning?

All organizations are not equal in capacity to learn; some are more tradition bound than others. Organizations engaged in the production of goods or services that are essentially "the same" over long periods of time will have a stronger corporate memory than organizations involved in the production and management of unique, one-of-a-kind products or activities. This rather obvious point suggests that the peacetime military will be greatly influenced by tradition. Similarly, when pressures for accountability are great, organizations will be particularly bound by precedent and laden with the memory of past events. In such circumstances, little learning is likely to occur.

But organizational research suggests both external circumstances and internal factors that promote learning. Competition is the enemy of tradition in several respects. A vigorously competitive environment is not conducive to the development of established traditions. New organizations or organizations undergoing rapid change draw on new means of harnessing capital, know-how, and commitment and thus represent a challenge to older forms of organization. This encroachment increases the likelihood that older organizations will abandon their established practices, search for new procedures, or run the risk of redundancy or failure. Merton (1957, 1973) illustrates this process in his work on scientific discovery, showing that competitive social systems have weaker institutional memories than ascriptive ones. Competition drives out some players and brings upstarts to the fore, and with each change in the status order, memory is reshuffled. In contrast, hierarchical systems based on ascribed status will need to recall many reference points in the past.

Several key internal factors facilitate organizational learning: subsystem autonomy, upward communication and influence, lateral communication, and opportunity for outside contacts on relevant matters. Subsystem autonomy facilitates organizational learning because the different subsystems—production, management, sales and procurement, research—have different tasks, deal with different parts of the organizational environment, and thus tend to develop their own way of perceiving the threats and opportunities that confront the organization. To the extent that such differences are tolerated, they become sources of potential learning for the organization as a whole, which can adapt into its organization-wide routines those practices that have proven successful.

The process by which local developments are so adapted, however, requires openness of communication and influence, especially laterally and upward. Many organizational failures to learn are in fact failures of internal communication and influence; solutions to most organizational problems are known somewhere in the organization. Organizational learning is thus a process of internal discovery and acceptance as well as invention or importation from outside.

Outside contacts are nevertheless crucial factors in organizational learning. The lives of organization members are not wholly subsumed by the organization. Members of most organizations have

substantial parts of their lives outside, and the outside environment
is a source of knowledge and potential innovation. Therefore, systematic opportunities for interaction with relevant outsiders enhance
organizational learning, especially when the individuals who have
such opportunities are also influential within the organization. Indeed, to the extent that we view organizations as open systems,
much learning is the result of debate and consultation with critics,
advisers, academic specialists, regulators, political constituencies,
and consultants. In fact, learning in an organization may occur only
after other organizations in its environment have become more innovative or knowledgeable, and that intelligence eventually diffuses
throughout the organizational field (DiMaggio and Powell, 1983).

4. Who is responsible for organizational learning?

The need for change in organizational routines or traditions, that
is, the need for learning, can be felt by any member of the organization or of its external constituencies. And innovative ideas can
be developed at any level in an organization. Nevertheless, the
members of an organization have very different roles in defining
just what is to be remembered or what changes in organizational
routines are to be attempted. Most organizations are hierarchical in
structure, and different levels have different formal responsibilities
and very different amounts of power and discretion for initiating
innovative behavior, regardless of the original source of the
innovation.

More specifically, the lower levels of management (and the rank
and file members, to the extent that they have discretionary power
at all) are typically limited to choosing among existing organizational routines. Middle levels of management may innovate by
reassembling subroutines, a process that may contribute to organizational adaptation but seldom challenges existing traditions or
alters the organizational mission. In hierarchical organizations, the
creation of new routines, procedures, and policies that reinterpret
or otherwise alter the traditional organizational mission and means
of attaining it is thus the prerogative of top levels of management.

5. How do organizations learn to cooperate?

Learning to cooperate, especially with another group or organization that has been a traditional competitor or enemy, is a special
case of the more general questions we have proposed. The foregoing

propositions about organizational learning therefore apply to the domain of cooperation, but research on organizations and groups suggests additional factors that bear on learning to cooperate.

Organizations, as we have said, learn by doing. Learning to cooperate, therefore, can begin with some joint task, not too demanding of ideological change, the accomplishment of which is in the interest of both organizations and requires cooperative effort. Such a task constitutes what social psychologists call a superordinate goal, and the introduction of such tasks was shown long ago to induce profound changes in attitudes and behavior (Sherif, 1958).

In the absence of an experimenter or hegemon to introduce such a task, however, the initial cooperative move must be made by one of the competing organizations. Experimental evidence of the learning that takes place after low-risk initial cooperative moves is persuasive, but such studies await replication at the organizational level (Deutsch, 1973; Axelrod, 1984).

Organizational factors that impede learning to cooperate are clearer, and one can assume tentatively that their opposites would facilitate cooperative learning, but this too remains to be demonstrated. Such factors include the difficulty (or ease) with which the intentions and motives of a competitor can be inferred from its observable behaviors and the rapidity and accuracy of feedback regarding the competitor's behavior and the effects of one's own behavior. The magnitude of previous organizational investment in the noncooperative mode is a further impediment to cooperation; organizations tend to behave irrationally with respect to justifying "sunk costs."

In short, our reading of organizational theory lends indirect support to regime theory, provides some speculations and hypotheses about how a security regime might develop, and identifies some of the organizational factors that facilitate or impede such cooperative developments. The tasks of learning and unlearning are complex; after more than forty years of cold war, it is not easy for governments and their armed forces to adapt to new circumstances and to learn new patterns of interaction. Research can assist these processes, and we look forward to the kinds of collaboration between scholars of international relations and of organizations that will test and improve upon the modest beginnings described in this chapter. Such scholarly collaboration will in itself constitute an example of organizational learning.

Notes

1. We note at the outset that we have found Nye's (1987) paper on nuclear learning and security regimes especially helpful.
2. For example, the U.S. and British delegates to the International Monetary Fund agreed that adjustments needed to be made without major disruptions to international trade but disagreed over the distribution of costs between surplus and deficit countries.
3. A large literature on the problems with command and control of nuclear weapons has recently sprung up. See Lebow and Zald, Chapter Ten of this volume, for a review of this work.
4. It is this second-strike capability that underlies the change brought about by the nuclear revolution. Thus, the realist paradigm is challenged by *living with nuclear weapons,* and not by an ideal nuclear-free world.
5. As early as the spring of 1945, Japanese peace feelers had been received by both civilian and military leaders. The Japanese wished to negotiate a surrender that would include retention of their emperor and constitution. They made clear that unconditional surrender was unacceptable to them, but that war could be halted. President Truman, however, insisted upon unconditional surrender, thereby making continuation of the war necessary (Alperovitz, 1965).

References

Aggarwal, V. K. *Liberal Protectionism.* Berkeley: University of California Press, 1985.

Allison, G. T. *Essence of Decision: Explaining the Cuban Missile Crisis.* Boston: Little, Brown, 1971.

Alperovitz, G. *Atomic Diplomacy.* New York: Vintage Books, 1965.

Art, R. J. "Bureaucratic Politics and American Foreign Policy: A Critique." *Policy Sciences,* 1973, *4,* 467–490.

Art, R. J., and Jervis, R. *International Politics*. (2nd ed.) Boston: Little, Brown, 1985.

Axelrod, R. *The Evolution of Cooperation*. New York: Basic Books, 1984.

Becker, H. "Art as a Collective Action." *American Sociological Review*, 1974, *39*, 767–776.

Betts, R. K. *Soldiers, Statesman, and Cold War Crises*. Cambridge, Mass.: Harvard University Press, 1977.

Block, F. L. *The Origins of International Monetary Disorder: A Study of United States International Monetary Policy from World War II to the Present*. Berkeley: University of California Press, 1977.

Bundy, M. "The Unimpressive Record of Atomic Diplomacy." In G. Prins (ed.), *The Nuclear Crisis Reader*. New York: Vintage Books, 1984.

Clark, B. "The Organizational Saga in Higher Education." *Administrative Science Quarterly*, 1972, *17*, 178–184.

Coser, L. A., Kadushin, C., and Powell, W. W. *Books: The Culture and Commerce of Publishing*. New York: Basic Books, 1982.

Dallin, A. "Soviet Approaches to Superpower Security Relations." In A. George, P. J. Farley, and A. Dallin (eds.), *U.S.-Soviet Security Cooperation: Achievements, Failures, Lessons*. New York: Oxford University Press, 1988.

Deutsch, M. *The Resolution of Conflict: Constructive and Destructive Processes*. New Haven, Conn.: Yale University Press, 1973.

DiMaggio, P. J., and Powell, W. W. "The Iron Cage Revisited: Institutional Isomorphism and Collective Rationality in Organizational Fields." *American Sociological Review*, 1983, *48* (2), 149.

Downs, A. *Inside Bureaucracy*. Boston: Little, Brown, 1967.

Freedman, L. *U.S. Intelligence and the Soviet Strategic Threat*. (2nd ed.) Princeton, N.J.: Princeton University Press, 1986.

George, A. L. "Factors Influencing Security Cooperation." In A. L. George, P. J. Farley, and A. Dallin (eds.), *U.S.-Soviet Security Cooperation*. New York: Oxford University Press, 1988.

Haas, E. B. "Why Collaborate? Issue-Linkage and International Regimes." *World Politics*, 1980, *32*, 358, 365.

Haas, E. B. "Regime Decay: Conflict Management and International Organizations, 1945-1981." *International Organization,* 1983, *37* (2), 189-235.

Haggard, S., and Simmons, B. A. "Theories of International Regimes." *International Organization,* 1987, *41* (3), 491-517.

Halperin, M. H. *Nuclear Fallacy.* Cambridge, Mass.: Ballinger, 1987.

Halperin, M. H., and Kanter, A. "The Bureaucratic Perspective." In M. Halperin and A. Kanter (eds.), *Readings in American Foreign Policy: A Bureaucratic Perspective.* Boston: Little, Brown, 1973.

Hannan, M. T., and Freeman, J. H. "The Population Ecology of Organizations." *American Journal of Sociology,* 1977, *82,* 929-964.

Hardin, R., and others (eds.). *Nuclear Deterrence: Ethics and Strategy.* Chicago: University of Chicago Press, 1985.

Hoffman, S. *Primacy or World Order.* New York: McGraw-Hill, 1978.

Huntington, S. P. *The Soldier and the State.* New York: Vintage Books, 1957.

Jervis, R. *Perception and Misperception in International Politics.* Princeton, N.J.: Princeton University Press, 1976.

Jervis, R. "Cooperation Under the Security Dilemma." *World Politics,* 1978, *30* (2), 167-214.

Jervis, R. "Security Regimes." *International Organization,* 1982, *36* (2), 357-378.

Jervis, R. *The* Illogic *of American Nuclear Strategy.* Ithaca, N.Y.: Cornell University Press, 1984.

Kaplan, M. *System and Process in International Politics.* New York: Wiley, 1957.

Kaplan, M. *Towards Professionalism in International Theory.* New York: Free Press, 1979.

Kennan, G. [Mr. X]. "The Sources of Soviet Conduct." *Foreign Affairs,* 1947, *25,* 566-582.

Keohane, R. O. *After Hegemony: Cooperation and Discord in the World Political Economy.* Princeton, N.J.: Princeton University Press, 1984.

Krasner, S. D. "Structural Causes and Regime Consequences: Regimes as Intervening Variables." *International Organization,* 1982, *36* (2), 185-206.

Krasner, S. D. (ed.). *International Regimes*. Ithaca, N.Y.: Cornell University Press, 1983.

Krepinevich, A. F. *The Army and Vietnam*. Baltimore, Md.: Johns Hopkins University Press, 1986.

Leavitt, B., and March, J. G. Organizational Learning. *Annual Review of Sociology*, 1988, *14*, 319–340.

March, J. G., and Olsen, J. *Ambiguity and Choice in Organizations*. New York: Oxford, 1976.

March, J. G., and Simon, H. A. *Organizations*. New York: Wiley, 1958.

Merton, R. K. "Priorities in Scientific Discovery." *American Sociological Review*, 1957, *22*, 635–659.

Merton, R. K. *The Sociology of Science*. Chicago: University of Chicago Press, 1973.

Morgenthau, H. J. *Politics Among Nations*. New York: Knopf, 1975.

Nelson, R., and Winter, S. *An Evolutionary Theory of Economic Change*. Cambridge: Harvard University Press, 1982.

Nye, J. S. "Nuclear Learning and U.S.-Soviet Security Regimes." *International Organization*, 1987, *41* (3), 386–387.

Oye, K. A. (ed.). *Cooperation Under Anarchy*. Princeton, N.J.: Princeton University Press, 1986.

Posen, B. R. *The Sources of Military Doctrine: France, Britain, and Germany Between the World Wars*. Ithaca, N.Y.: Cornell University Press, 1984.

Rice, C. "SALT and the Search for Security Regime." In A. L. George, P. J. Farley, and A. Dallin (eds.), *US-Soviet Security Cooperation: Achievements, Failures, Lessons*. New York: Oxford University Press, 1988.

Ruggie, J. G. "Continuity and Transformation in the World Polity: Toward a Neorealist Synthesis." *World Politics*, 1982–83, *35* (1), 261–285.

Scott, W. R. *Organizations: Rational, Natural, and Open Systems*. Englewood Cliffs, N.J.: Prentice-Hall, 1981.

Sherif, M. "Superordinate Goals in the Reduction of Intergroup Conflict." *American Journal of Sociology*, 1958, *63*, 349–356.

Snyder, J. *The Ideology of the Offensive: Military Decision Making and the Disasters of 1914*. Ithaca, N.Y.: Cornell University Press, 1984.

Snyder, J. "Civil-Military Relations and the Cult of the Offensive, 1914 and 1984." In S. E. Miller (ed.), *Military Strategy and the Origins of the First World War*. Princeton, N.J.: Princeton University Press, 1985.

Starbuck, W. "Organizations as Action Generators." *American Sociological Review*, 1983, *48*, 91–102.

Strange, S. "Cave! Hic Dragones: A Critique of Regime Analysis." *International Organization*, 1982, *36* (2), 479–496.

Trainor, B. "As Soviet Bloc Changes, So Does Study of War." *New York Times*, Jan. 16, 1990.

Van Evera, S. "The Cult of the Offensive and the Origins of the First World War." In S. E. Miller (ed.), *Military Strategy and the Origins of the First World War*. Princeton, N.J.: Princeton University Press, 1985.

Walt, S. M. *The Origins of Alliances*. Ithaca, N.Y.: Cornell University Press, 1987.

Waltz, K. *Man, the State, the War*. New York: Columbia University Press, 1959.

Waltz, K. *Theory of International Politics*. New York: Random House, 1979.

Yates, J. *Control Through Communication*. Baltimore, Md.: Johns Hopkins University Press, 1989.

Young, O. R. "International Regimes: Problems of Concept Formation." *World Politics*, 1980, *32*, 332.

PART 2

Processes of Conflict and Cooperation

Chapter 4

Accounting for Escalation

Organizations and the Arms Race

Gerald F. Davis
Walter W. Powell

The atomic bombs dropped by the United States on Hiroshima and Nagasaki were equivalent to about 15,000 tons (fifteen kilotons) of TNT. Today explosions of this size would be regarded as tactical rather than strategic, that is, useful on the battlefield but too small for attack on a major city or military installation. Since the fission process of the atomic bomb was superseded by the fusion process of the hydrogen bomb in the early 1950s, explosive yields have greatly increased. Most modern nuclear weapons carry yields of between one and five million tons, or one and five megatons. (There are reports that in 1961 the Soviets tested a bomb that yielded fifty-six megatons—3,700 times as powerful as the Hiroshima bomb—but no rocket was ever constructed to carry such a monstrous load.)

Some foreign policy analysts suggest that "the long peace" since 1945 testifies to the emergence of collective wisdom (Gaddis, 1987). Surely, they say, without the nuclear threat, war between the United States and the Soviet Union would have erupted long ago. The long peace is evidence of a sense of caution, maturity, and responsibility on both sides.

But it is a strange sort of peace. It is a peace in which recurring proxy wars outside the North Atlantic region have proliferated. It is a peace in which the superpowers try to provide security through policies that heavily emphasize military strength and military deterrence.

The United States today has 12,000 strategic nuclear weapons and spends about $70 billion per year preparing for nuclear war (Center for Defense Information, 1987). The Soviet Union possesses about 10,000 strategic nuclear weapons. During a seven-year period (1981–1987), the Pentagon spent a total of $2 trillion on defense, introducing a new strategic bomber (the B-1B) and a potent new nuclear missile (the MX) and increasing the number of cruise missiles from 20 to 2,080 (Center for Defense Information, cited in *New York Times*, Nov. 6, 1987, p. 1). The U.S. annual defense budgets since 1981 have reached constant dollar levels unsurpassed in any postwar year except 1953 (Korea) and 1968 (Vietnam) (Adams, 1987). According to defense analyst Jacques Gansler (1987), the U.S. defense industry is currently responsible for more than one of every ten jobs in manufacturing and more than one of every four in research and development. Defense has also created and/or stimulated a number of industries: jet aircraft, commercial nuclear power, computers, and communications satellites, among others.

But high levels of defense spending and the concomitant militarization of much of the American economy are only a part of the story. This economic escalation has been accompanied by dramatic increases in destructive capability and distant delivery. As Russett (1983) points out, the number of nuclear weapons stockpiled by both sides is far greater than the number of targets to be hit. He notes that the United States has only 2,000 cities with as many as 10,000 people each. Even a "small" Soviet attack with only 300 to 400 warheads would produce forty-five to seventy million casualties and destroy 25 to 35 percent of American industry (Russett, 1983, p. 5).

Equally chilling is the proficiency with which nuclear weapons can be delivered. Since 1960, warheads with high accuracy and swift deployment have replaced big bombs dropped from aircraft that had to fly many hours to reach their targets. The remoteness with which modern war can be fought constitutes a quantum change from earlier wars. The United States completed a successful test of an unarmed ICBM that landed on target at a South Pacific military range

4,200 miles away, a distance covered in a mere thirty minutes. Freedman (1985, p. 85) provides an apt example of the extent to which modern nuclear weapons have grown in destructive power and remote delivery. Consider the Ohio-class ballistic missile–carrying submarines (SSBNs). Each carries twenty-four Trident-I missiles with multiple independently targeted warheads. The eight warheads on each Trident-I have an individual yield of 100 kilotons. Thus one Ohio-class submarine can attack 192 individual targets, each with a warhead that is six to seven times more powerful than the bomb that destroyed Hiroshima. Freedman suggests that a single nuclear submarine represents "barely 1 percent of American strategic power, and this still excludes American intermediate-range forces in Europe."

U.S.-Soviet relations have undergone profound changes in the past several years that have encouraged a widespread perception that the cold war is over. Yet the arms race continues to be run in weapons labs, defense contractors, and the offices of congressional representatives from districts where these organizations are housed. The organizational coalitions that were provided a hospitable climate by the cold war are not anxious to give up a "peace dividend" that comes at their expense, and the limited cuts in U.S. military spending that have thus far accompanied the collapse of the Eastern Bloc suggests that this reluctance may be paying off.

How do we account for this process? What factors explain the origins of new weapons systems and continued high levels of defense spending? What drives successive technological breakthroughs in destructive potential? Not surprisingly, a small academic industry has developed to analyze the arms race. A thicket of theoretical perspectives has been offered. Meyer (1984), in his thorough review of Soviet national security decision making, describes six contending models that seek to explain weapons acquisitions and force structure.[1] Nincic (1982) and Russett (1983) offer similarly comprehensive reviews of the different explanations that have been offered for U.S. military defense policy.

As outsiders to the fields of international security and defense policy, we are struck by how small a role organizations play in the various accounts of the arms race. Indeed, some of the most sophisticated work in the field deemphasizes an organizational point of view. This decline is unfortunate because organizations play a very crucial role in the American defense structure. Morris (1975, p. 113) points out that weapons acquisition takes place over the course of several years and it is rare for any individual to oversee the whole life course of a weapon; thus, "organizations and organizational arrangements decisively structure weapons acquisitions." More broadly, organizations are the core actors in the governmental policy-making process, determining outcomes from the acquisition of particular weapons to the more general foreign policy stance. Increasingly, the U.S. government is an organizational state, and thus its behavior must be understood in terms of its organizational constituencies (Laumann and Knoke, 1987).

Our goal in this chapter is first to review and criticize some of the more influential research programs on the arms race, with a particular focus on issues of the unit and level of analysis. We review three of the best-known models that have been offered to explain the arms race: the action-reaction model, the military Keynesian model, and the bureaucratic politics model. Second, we take some initial steps toward a theory that integrates these models into a broader framework on international security, a framework that puts organizations and the relations among them at the center. We borrow freely from previous research, especially work informed by the bureaucratic politics perspective, but we assign to interorganizational dynamics a theoretically more significant role. Our effort is two-pronged: to offer a new perspective on the arms race firmly rooted in organization theory and to suggest to organization scholars a fertile setting for interorganizational analysis.

The Action-Reaction Process

The notion that defense policy is interactive, that what one side does is a response to a hostile activity by an adversary, is widely assumed in both political and academic circles. The basic supposition is that arms buildups are responses to aggressive acts and increased military expenditures by opponents. A cursory glance at the manner in which the United States and USSR reacted to each other's moves in the cold war era suggests that the label "arms race" is apt. There was an increase in American military spending with the onset of the

Korean War and a sharp upsurge after 1960 in response to the Soviets' launching of the Sputnik missile and the alleged missile gap. The Soviets upped their spending after 1965, possibly in response to the embarrassment of the Cuban missile crisis. Since 1976, and especially since 1981, there has been a manifold increase in American military expenditures. This continuing and at times parallel expansion by both superpowers is considered by many a dangerous rivalry, with each side racing against the other and reacting to each other's responses in an upward spiral. Robert McNamara, the secretary of defense under presidents Kennedy and Johnson and the man who guided the first major buildup of the U.S. nuclear arsenal, illustrates the essential nature of this process: "What is essential to understand here is that the Soviet Union and the U.S. mutually influence one another's strategic plans. Whatever their intentions or our intentions, actions—or even realistically potential actions—on either side relating to the buildup of nuclear forces necessarily trigger reactions on the other side. It is precisely this action-reaction phenomenon that fuels the arms race" (quoted in Allison, 1974, p. 464).

The action-reaction perspective emerged from the work of Lewis Frye Richardson (1960), an English mathematician, physicist, and meteorologist who probed the causes of international conflict. He is best known for a pair of equations that model arms races as feedback-driven phenomena. His model implies that increases in one state's level of armaments result from the threat posed by the level of armaments held by an opposing state. As both states respond to each other's increase in the previous period, the process contains a built-in dynamic of escalation. The escalation process can also extend to political, economic, and ideological hostilities. The process may ultimately lead to war, or it may perhaps be slowed by fatigue, that is, widespread dissatisfaction with the consequences of diverting resources from social needs to arms spending. Richardson's work has triggered an outpouring of investigations into the arms race by political scientists and economists (see Leidy and Staiger, 1985, for one review).

In the nuclear era, this perspective suggests that the fear of a breakthrough in first-strike capability or fail-proof defense has helped fuel an offense-defense duel between the superpowers. This competitive action-reaction model shares many of the assumptions of the realist tradition in international politics (Morgenthau, 1948; Waltz, 1959, 1979). Realist arguments are based on the view that states are, according to Waltz, "unitary actors who, at a minimum, seek their own preservation and, at a maximum, drive for universal domination" (quoted in Keohane, 1986, p. 15). States must defend themselves or face the possibility of extinction. Yet many of the means by which a state attempts to increase its security decrease the security of other nations. Borrowing freely from neoclassical economics, realists contend that states are rational actors, jockeying for position within the competitive realm of world politics. In this setting, states pursue objective national interests, seeking to maximize their standing vis-à-vis competing states. The realists depart from many students of the nuclear arms race, however, in their view that as states contend with one another, an equilibrium or "balance of power" will be reached and that any balance of power, once disrupted, will be restored in some fashion. Thus, whereas Waltz (1964) argues that military bipolarity is remarkably stable, chroniclers of the action-reaction process (Lapp, 1970; York, 1970) see the superpowers as locked into a dangerous escalating rivalry.[2]

The nuclear arms race began in the early 1940s when American and British scientists felt that they were competing against similar research into atomic weapons in Nazi Germany. In the period after the war, the race was spurred by the idea that the atom bomb provided a valuable counter to the Soviet Union's advantage in conventional forces in Europe. By 1949 the Soviets had tested their own atom bomb. By the early 1950s, the United States had a sufficient nuclear arsenal to pose a formidable threat against Soviet territory. It took a half decade longer for the Soviets to be able to threaten the continental United States with long-range bombers. Soon both sides were contending to deploy the first intercontinental ballistic missiles (ICBMs), thereafter followed by submarine-launched missiles. The late 1960s saw the introduction of antiballistic missile (ABM) systems, designed to defend territory against missile attacks. This advance was matched shortly thereafter by the introduction of missiles with multiple warheads, which made the ABM's task considerably more difficult. The United States has now initiated a highly expensive and possibly futile quest for a satellite defense with its

Strategic Defense Initiative program, and evidence suggests that the Soviets are playing catch-up with an early stage program of their own.

Nuclear weapons transformed the nature of war, although it took most military strategists more than a decade to realize this. Only in the late 1950s and early 1960s did the defense community recognize that the balance of terror was a good deal less stable than had hitherto been assumed. (Albert Wohlstetter's 1959 article "The Delicate Balance of Terror" was influential in this recognition.) Military strategists realized that the action-reaction process was a seemingly unending spiral: in solving one problem for the defense, they would create a new one for the offense, the solution to which put new demands on the defense. The Gaither Report, presented to the National Security Council in 1957, captured the anxiety that instead of a strategic balance, we might have an extremely unstable equilibrium. Writing in 1960, Professor Henry Kissinger warned that every country lives with the nightmare that even if it puts forth its best efforts, a technological breakthrough by its opponent may jeopardize its survival. Complementing this fear is the nation's hope that it will be the one to come up with the ultimate weapon that will give it a decisive advantage over its rival, a notion labeled the "fallacy of the last move." Both motivate continued arms racing well beyond what is minimally sufficient.

Despite many analysts' early recognition that buildups by one party to an arms race will be matched by its opposite, the process continued for decades. Fear of Soviet military superiority was in large measure the impetus for the 1980s American buildup—or "spend up," as detractors called it when they pointed to how few tangible improvements were actually made. In part because of CIA estimates suggesting that the Soviets were outspending the United States on their military,[3] the United States embarked on a massive rearmament effort. From 1980 to 1985, the number of people holding jobs related to military contracts grew by 45 percent, to a total of 3.2 million, according to U.S. Department of Labor statistics. Military spending rose from $157.5 billion in fiscal year 1981 to $273.4 billion in fiscal year 1986. Military outlays increased from 5.3 percent of the U.S. gross national production in 1981 to 6.6 percent in 1986, a slightly higher proportion than in the last years of the

Vietnam War (Adams, 1987). Ironically, although it is argued that buildups by one side spur buildups by the other, a ratchet effect seems to prevent a comparable builddown to match the declining threat posed by a "post-cold war" Soviet Union. The action-reaction account would suggest that the Soviets are likely to respond until fatigue prevents further buildup of their own.[4]

Action-reaction models have a number of limitations. They can tell us something about the interaction of superpower arms spending but not about the level of funding at which this interaction takes place. Action-reaction interpretations often confuse the first appearance and deployment of Soviet weapons with weapons conceptualization and development, ignoring the long lead times necessary for nuclear weapons and the fact that many Soviet reactions actually began to take shape concurrent with and sometimes in advance of American developments. As noted by former Secretary McNamara (Allison, 1974), much of the arms race is based on *anticipatory* responses to *potential* threats. Moreover, the baseline for action-reaction assessments is not clear. The U.S. defense increase in the late 1970s and 1980s was based on an estimate of how much Soviet military programs *cost*, not on any revised assessment of their *strength*. More generally, the debate over which side is ahead is fraught with complications, including the thorny issue of quantitative superiority versus qualitative strength (accuracy, detectability) and the question of the readiness and resolve of allies.

Defense analyst Albert Wohlstetter (1974) has argued that the notion of a strategic arms race is "remarkably unclear" for such a central concept of contemporary foreign policy. He disputes whether the concept has any utility in an explanation of U.S defense policy. "Ambiguities and inconsistencies about as to just what is accelerating," and careful analysis of superpower interactions reveals them to be "muffled, lagged, and very complex" (p. 7, p. 8). Wohlstetter shows that there are action-inaction and inaction-reaction sequences. Indeed, researchers have shown that the U.S.-Soviet interaction is not steady but instead moves in fits and starts; the superpowers move sometimes in tandem and more often along independent paths in response to aggressive acts—many of them non-weapons related, such as the invasion of Afghanistan, tensions in the Middle East, or changing alliances with China (Nincic, 1982).

The action-reaction concept fails to explain many of the realities of superpower military policy. Why did the Soviet Union fail to moderate its defense spending after the United States reduced its expenditures in the post–Vietnam War years? Or as Meyer (1984) has asked, why did the Soviets continue to produce some 200 tanks each month when they already possessed a pool of more than 40,000 tanks? This process seems to parallel the irrational "escalation of commitment" by decision makers documented by Barry Staw and his coauthors in a variety of contexts, including most notably the spiraling commitment of resources incurred by British Columbia for the 1986 World's Fair in Vancouver (Ross and Staw, 1986).

There have, of course, been elements of the action-reaction process in East-West relations over the past four and a half decades. But the assessment of adversary intentions and capabilities is only one of a number of factors that influence defense posture. There are political, economic, technological, and organizational factors at work, too, and it often appears that a perceived external threat is little more than an appropriate justification for a process of accumulation driven by these domestic factors. The action-reaction model's conception of states as rational unitary actors omits a host of competing internal political considerations and military needs. Moreover, the technologies involved contain their own developmental dynamics, generating "new and improved" weapons at frequent intervals, and two independent systems will appear to be reactive because of the nature of this developmental logic (Meyer, 1984, pp. 259-260). Kaldor (1983, p. 42) argues that this logic of technological development follows from the imperative for constant innovation embedded in the institutional structure of military research and development in the United States, where primarily private firms in the defense sector are driven by economic need "to design, develop and produce ever larger, more expensive and elaborate 'baroque' weapon systems in order to remain in existence." Thus, technological momentum based in large part on the economic imperatives facing defense organizations can play an autonomous role in fueling the arms race, independent of any external threat. We turn now to another account that also emphasizes the economic imperatives of the arms race and their independence from international hostilities.

Military Keynesianism and the Political Business Cycle

In contrast to the action-reaction account, which sees American participation in the arms race as exogenously driven, both scholars and journalists in the late 1960s and early 1970s looked to internal processes within the "military-industrial complex" to explain the arms race. This complex consists of "groups with economic and institutional interests in cold-war policies and high military expenditures and linked by shared values and beliefs as well as by overlapping or symbiotic positions in the economic, social, and political structure of American society" (Slater and Nardin, 1973, p. 33). This argument, which is offered by both political activists and social scientists, is informed by the notion that American defense expenditures and, to some extent, military doctrine are driven primarily by domestic interests rather than external threat. C. Wright Mills's *The Power Elite* (1956) warned of the increasingly powerful role played by the military within the ruling elite, and this claim was bolstered by a similar warning in President Eisenhower's famous farewell address in 1961. As a result of these warnings, many came to see decision making about national defense as falling out of the control of dispassionate elected officials and into the hands of those vested interests who compose the military-industrial complex. These interest groups include "(1) the professional soldiers, (2) managers and . . . owners of industries heavily engaged in military supply, (3) high government officials whose careers and interests are tied to military expenditure, and (4) legislators whose districts benefit from defense procurement" (Rosen, 1973, p. 2). These groups either consciously or unconsciously overstate the level of external threat, typically in the context of a "cold war ideology," in order to justify high defense budgets. Further, these parochial interest groups are hypothesized to act as a relatively coherent unit in pursuing their mutual interest in such spending, thus militarizing American society in the process.

A great deal of research has been done on the military-industrial complex.[5] Some important findings stand out: Lieberson (1971) confirmed that there were substantial "revolving door" personnel flows between the military services and defense contractors and that the concentration of defense industries in a state is related to the probability of that state's representatives serving on Armed Services Committees in Congress.[6] Kurth (1972) found that the timing of defense contract awards in the aerospace industry (between 1960 and 1971) was conditioned by the "follow-on imperative" (production on one major contract is followed fairly soon by a contract for a structurally similar product, thereby keeping production lines busy) and the "bail-out imperative" (the government awards "rescue" contracts to corporations facing financial difficulties). Despite the useful findings generated by this research, the "theory of the military-industrial complex" is not in fact a theory per se: it is more a catchall label for research on defense procurements with a particular critical stance than a set of propositions that generate positive, testable hypotheses.[7] A variant of this perspective, however, rooted largely in radical theories of the state (see especially O'Connor, 1973), has emerged as an empirically useful account of the arms race.

The "military Keynesian" account characterizes military spending in the United States as driven by two processes internal to the American state. The first and most important process is linked to the role of the state in capitalist society. Because of tendencies toward crises that are assumed to be inherent in capitalist economies, the state must actively intervene to keep the economic system viable. In post–World War II America, this intervention is primarily linked to the "core" or "monopoly capital" sector of the economy, which is made up of large, primarily unionized firms in oligopolistic industries. This sector is seen as the "engine" of the economy, and the state is dependent on it for the economic growth that supports domestic harmony and state expansion (Lindblom, 1977; Block, 1977a). The core in turn is dependent on the state for various functions, including support for expansion into international markets, the financing of expensive research and development projects that provide necessary technological innovations but are too costly for individual corporations to undertake (Albrecht, 1983), and the countercyclical stimulation of demand to help smooth out business cycles and regulate growth. The state is thus seen as a unit actor acting in the *aggregate* interests of the core of the economy: the state does for monopoly capital what monopoly capital cannot do for itself.

This symbiotic relationship between the state, big labor, and large corporations is realized in a policy of "military Keynesianism," that is, "the policy of using the defense budget as a counter-cyclical and economic growth device" (Griffin, Devine, and Wallace, 1982, p. S116). Military spending is especially useful for these purposes because (1) the timing and magnitude of prime contracts for equipment, research and development, and so on are manipulable "even on a quarterly basis" (Nincic, 1982, p. 30), whereas other categories of spending are less open to short-run alterations; (2) military goods typically have a built-in obsolescence, which is exacerbated by rapid technological advance in areas such as nuclear weapons, and this implies a relatively constant or increasing demand for defense production (Reich, 1972); (3) a relatively diffuse "Soviet threat" serves as a readily invoked justification for increased spending on defense; and (4) military spending serves the obvious purpose of maintaining American might in the world, allowing overseas corporate expansion.[8] Thus, according to this account, military spending is linked more to macroeconomic factors, such as the levels of profitability and employment in the core sector of the economy, than to external threats by the Soviets. Seen in this light, escalation in American participation in the arms race could be explained by escalating economic crisis: if capitalist economies are subject to increasingly deeper troughs in the business cycle, as some Marxists argue, then the state should be obliged to devote more and more resources to defense in order to compensate.

The second factor that determines defense spending is linked to the exigencies of American electoral politics. It is part of the folk wisdom of American politics, as well as the empirical wisdom of political science, that Americans "vote their pocketbook," with incumbents preferred in flush times and challengers preferred during economic downswings (see Tufte, 1978). It is argued that incumbents are keenly aware of these preferences and that they attempt to stimulate the economy artificially before elections to enhance their chances at the polls. One of the preferred means of stimulation is the defense budget. Thus, in addition to the macroeconomic factors that link cycles in the monopoly capital sector to cycles in defense spending, the "political business cycle" links electoral cycles to defense spending, with increases implemented before elections to "heat up" the economy and corresponding decreases after elections to "cool down" the inflationary pressures generated in the previous period (Nincic and Cusack, 1979). Higher defense spending is further encouraged by the fact that politicians perceive fewer costs to being labeled defense spendthrifts and many problems associated with a reputation for being stingy with the Pentagon. Political perceptions thus favor escalation rather than de-escalation in most situations. Military spending, therefore, not only plays an important role in regulating the economy but serves the ambitions of incumbent politicians.

Previous Research. Previous research has found support for each of the arguments cited above. Block (1980) notes that the U.S. policy of cold war rearmament started with the Truman administration's approval in 1950 of NSC-68, a document that assessed the global political economy and particularly the structure of U.S.-Soviet conflict at that time and recommended a massive rearmament effort in response. Rearmament was seen as serving both economic and military aims; according to Block (1980, p. 47), the drafters of NSC-68 "were influenced by Keynesian thought and saw military spending as a way to bolster economic activity. For the United States, rearmament could lead to such a great increase in economic activity that it would be possible to have both guns and butter—a continually rising standard of living." This suggests that military Keynesianism was at least initially a deliberate governmental policy, bolstering this account against charges of being a conspiracy theory.

Nincic and Cusack (1979) found that increased military spending is associated with dips in private demand and the timing of elections, and decreases in military spending correspond to rising demand and postelection years. Griffin, Devine, and Wallace (1982; see also Griffin, Wallace, and Devine, 1982) extended these findings in a careful time-series analysis of U.S. defense budgets from 1949 through 1976. Defense spending as a proportion of GNP increased in years after profits in monopoly industries declined and after unemployment in the unionized sector increased; increases in profit and decreases in unionized unemployment, conversely, had the opposite effect on defense spending. Further, years preceding presidential elections were marked by significantly greater defense spending.

While the study by Griffin, Devine, and Wallace (1982) used aggregate military expenditures, a replication that used defense expenditures disaggregated into four major components (procurement, personnel, operations and maintenance, and research and development) found slightly different results: as expected, procurement was related to profitability in the monopoly sector and unionized employment in the previous year, but the stage in the electoral cycle was not found to be related to spending in this category. The electoral cycle was, however, marginally related in the expected direction to spending on personnel and operations and maintenance (Mintz and Hicks, 1984). Mintz and Hicks suggest that this phenomenon indicates a more "efficient" targeting of defense spending by incumbents on Department of Defense personnel.

Critique. Although some evidence supports the military Keynesian account of U.S. military spending patterns, a number of questions remain unanswered. A crucial issue concerns the magnitude of the effects. Although the studies cited find significant relations between macroeconomic factors and defense spending, these factors were certainly not decisive in determining levels of defense spending in any given year;[9] by far the strongest predictors of annual military expenditures were the level of tax revenues available and the amount of nonmilitary expenditures for the year. Moreover, Krell (1981, p. 225) notes that at least before the Reagan administration, "The defense sector [had] declined substantially relative to the economy as a whole and with it its role as a potential 'surplus absorber,'" and that military spending is only one of a wide variety of the tools of fiscal manipulation available to the government.[10] Thus, although procurements may track business cycles to some degree, the amounts involved are small relative to the "crises" such manipulations are meant to help alleviate. Macroeconomic factors may influence the precise timing of some small proportion of the defense contracts that are awarded, but it is not clear that they determine whether or not such contracts will be awarded in the first place.

A second issue concerns the internal linkages presumed to operate between cycles in the economy and the military budget. The econometric models of annual defense expenditures described above are "reduced form" models: changes in the economic climate are assumed in these models to affect defense expenditures directly.

This assumption oversimplifies the complicated process involved in state budgeting. But it is not clear how one could construct a model of the underlying process that mediates between the economy and the actions of the state on the basis of this account. O'Connor (1973) claims that Congress has little real power in the process, suggesting that it is actions within the executive branch that are the critical components. But this account is silent with respect to how the executive branch chooses the weapons systems that it will fund; it merely notes two of the factors taken into account in the timing of contract awards, that is, macroeconomic factors and the electoral cycle. Which organizations and actors are relevant and how they interact to produce the defense budget are unspecified. Thus we must look elsewhere for an account that examines the internal processes that shape American participation in the arms race.

The Bureaucratic Politics Model

Like the military Keynesian model and again in contrast to the action-reaction model, the bureaucratic politics model (BPM) looks to factors internal to the United States to account for American participation in the arms race. Specifically, this model highlights the process of weapons acquisition and how organizational factors can decisively shape it. As Morris (1975, p. 113) points out: "Weapons choices are not made at a single point, as if in buying goods off a supermarket shelf. Instead, important choices about weapons systems are made sequentially over a decade-long process of research and development. Since rarely is any individual involved in the entire developmental life of a single weapons system, organizations and organizational arrangements decisively structure weapons acquisitions." Thus, in contrast to both of the previous accounts, the state is not presumed to behave as a unitary actor but rather as a set of organizations whose actions are not completely coordinated and that in fact may be in conflict. Weapons procurement is viewed as a series of political bargaining games among a set of actors with more or less divergent interests, goals, and strategies. The structure and level of American forces are the aggregate outcome of this process.

The elements of this perspective have been developed at some length elsewhere (see Allison, 1971; Halperin, 1971; Allison and Halperin, 1972; Allison and Morris, 1975); we will only sketch the rudiments that are necessary to explain the escalation of the arms race. As Allison and Halperin (1972, pp. 46–47) suggest, the building blocks of this model "can be arranged as elements in the answers to three central questions: (1) Who plays? [That is, whose interests and behavior have an important effect on the government's decisions and actions?] (2) What determines each player's stand? [What determines his perceptions and interests that lead to a stand?] (3) How are players' stands aggregated to yield governmental decisions and actions?" In answer to the first question, Allison and Morris state, "In the present weapons-development process, *the services and their subunits are the primary actors in weapons development.* Consequently, force posture is shaped by the goals and procedures and especially the missions and weapons systems to which services (and subunits) are committed" (1975, p. 123; emphasis in original). The interests of the services (and organizations more generally) are to have influence and to maintain autonomy, morale, and the organization's missions and "essence" (for example, flying for the air force). Governmental organizations generally have a further interest in maintaining and expanding the organization's budget. These organizational interests determine to a great extent the stands taken in bureaucratic bargaining games by representatives of the organization; an air force chief of staff, for example, is unlikely to suggest cutting back on manned bombers.

The final element of this account is its characterizations of the weapons acquisition process as a five-stage series of bureaucratic decision games. At each of the five stages—research, requirement formulation, design, development, and procurement—decisions are made that determine the life history of any weapon (see Figure 4.1, which is from Allison and Morris, 1975). Each stage has a characteristic decision process, the outcome of which is conditioned by a recurring set of factors. Often these processes are also accompanied by recurring "pathologies," which boost the escalation of the arms race. Thus it is the structure of the decision processes that make up weapons acquisition that feeds escalation. Rather than being an "arms race," the competition between the two superpowers is more general, primarily motivated on the U.S. side by internal factors.[11]

Figure 4.1. Stylized Chronology of Weapons Acquisition.

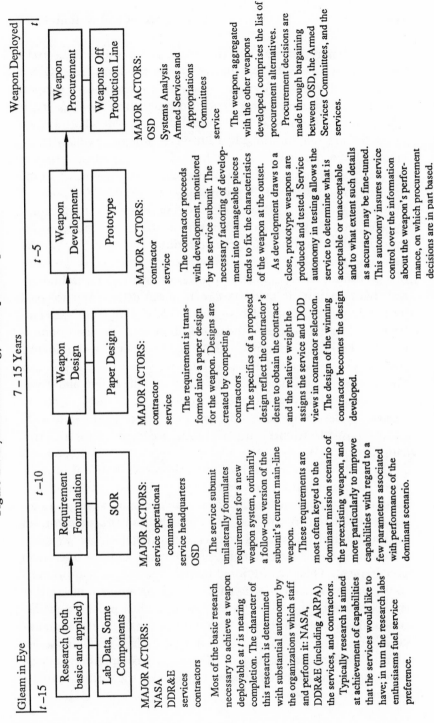

Source: G. T. Allison and F. A. Morris, "Arms Defense Policy and Arms Control," *Daedalus*, 1975, 104 (3), 124. **Reprinted by permission of *Daedalus*, Journal of the American Academy of Arts and Sciences.**

Research plays an extremely important part in this story, as technological advance is the fuel for the "qualitative arms race." Given the long lead time between the initiation of research on a weapon and the point at which procurement decisions can be made (typically seven to fifteen years), the initial decisions on what research to pursue must be informed by cautious estimates of what the Soviets will be capable of in the future. "Consequently, research pursues any technological possibilities that seem promising to the research community, within given budget constraints" (Allison and Morris, 1975, p. 115). These cautious estimates are in turn informed by what our own research community is doing, leading to an *intra*national action-reaction cycle: according to Herbert York, early developments of MIRV and ABM weapons "were largely the result of a continuously reciprocating process consisting of a technological challenge put out by the designers of our defense and accepted by the designers of our offense, then followed by a similar challenge/response sequence in the reverse direction" (Senate Committee on Foreign Relations, 1970, p. 59). The technological possibilities revealed by these research efforts (as well as from other sources such as basic science) "will move into the design and development stage if they meet two of the following three tests: (1) strong interest by the service user; (2) a good chance of working; and (3) relative cost-effectiveness in performing a current mission" (Allison, 1974, p. 474).

Up to this point in the development process, political officials have few opportunities for choice among alternatives. But once a particular weapon reaches the advanced development stage, an alliance of interest groups has developed behind procurement, an alliance typically including the service(s) involved, the weapons contractors, and congressional representatives with an interest in procurement. This "institutional inertia" may be difficult to overcome, and few outside the highest circles of government have either the incentive or the power to overcome it; thus procurement becomes likely. This may be true even if the rationale for the weapon's development has been undermined (for example, a potential Soviet "threat" fails to materialize): at this point, a compelling strategic rationale for the weapon becomes secondary to the various interests procurement will serve.

Finally, the well-known bureaucratic "ratchet effect" prevents de-escalation even when the prevailing doctrine calls for it. According to Allison and Morris (1975, p. 113), "Logically, changes in strategic objectives could require a reduction in forces; rhetorically, such conclusions are occasionally drawn; in fact, the reductions never happen." What is true of forces is equally true of budgets. As John Crecine, a student of defense budgeting, points out, "To cut back on Defense operations . . . means closing bases in someone's congressional district, cutting back on military contracts for some company, putting some workers out of work, killing some officer's pet project, blocking promotions for certain military personnel and the like" (1971, p. 220). All these groups have an incentive to fight against the proposed cutback, but few outsiders have sufficient incentive to fight for it; thus, "mutual noninterference," where each actor seeks indulgences for itself but refrains from opposing indulgences sought by others, is the norm (Lowi, 1964).

Cost overruns are also resistant to containment: military suppliers often "buy in" to contracts (that is, underbid on initial development contracts) in the hope of becoming the sole source contractor and "getting well" (collecting quasi-rents through price increases) on subsequent contract changes and follow-on productions (see Gansler, 1980). The services collude with the contractors, knowing that programs are rarely terminated because of cost, and Congress often acquiesces to overruns, thus giving neither the contractors nor the services reason to change their habits (Burnett, 1987).

Surprisingly, arms control efforts often have the paradoxical effect of reinforcing tendencies toward nuclear escalation. In order to gain support for agreements limiting the increase of weaponry in one area, the executive branch is often obliged by the rules of bureaucratic bargaining games to provide "assurances" to the military in the form of increases outside the affected area. In the case of the ABM treaty, President Nixon was compelled to accelerate the build-up of offensive strategic systems (the B1 and Trident) to get the Joint Chiefs of Staff and the secretary of defense on board. More generally, funds initially intended for an area newly forbidden by an agreement tend to be directed into other areas of military spending rather than eliminated from the budget or spent on civilian needs (George, 1978/1979).

The bureaucratic bargaining games that make up the weapons acquisition process epitomize pork barrel politics, where the distribution of favors breeds coalitions of convenience based on "uncommon interests." Organizations and other actors with little in common join forces for brief periods in the pursuit of self-interest. On this account, escalation that seems irrational at the aggregate or state level can be explained by rational actions on the part of the organizational constituents of the collective. Structurally, where the situation in the action-reaction model mirrors the prisoner's dilemma, the BPM is more akin to the "tragedy of the commons": by virtue of the structure of the weapons acquisition process, each of the organizational actors (including the services, contractors, and congressional representatives) has an incentive to pursue procurement of its own "pet weapon," but none has an incentive to try to stop any of the others, leading to an "irrational" spiraling in the aggregate.

Previous Research. Although the bureaucratic politics model posits an account capable of explaining the arms race per se, previous research informed by this approach has primarily appeared as case studies of particular weapons as they move through the stages and decision points of the acquisition process. Allison (1974), for example, contrasts the action-reaction model explicitly with the BPM in attempting to account for U.S. acquisition of missiles with multiple independently targetable reentry vehicles (MIRV). This case is particularly apt because much of the early public rationale for MIRV was the threat posed by Soviet antiballistic missile (ABM) systems; yet even after the ABM Treaty was signed in 1972, limiting each side to only two ABM-protected areas (later reduced to one), MIRV procurement continued as before, indicating the extent to which strategic rationale is de-coupled from weapons procurement. According to Greenwood (1975, pp. 49–50): "In its formative years, MIRV was a program that contributed to the objectives of all organizations and individual decision-makers that participated in the innovation process. . . . These [organizations'] perspectives were quite different and in some cases opposed. But it mattered little whether the different power centers could agree on underlying policy or priorities as long as they were unanimous in support of initiating and continuing development. That they were." Similarly, deployment served the interests of Secretary of Defense McNamara, the air force, the navy, and the R&D community. This case points up the fact that external threat is neither a necessary nor a sufficient condition for the acquisition of a new weapons system, nor is shared policy interest necessary for coalition formation; rather, even specific actions by the Soviets have their effect only as they are refracted through organizational processes and domestic and bureaucratic politics.

The B1 bomber is perhaps the most famous example of the profound impact of bureaucratic politics on weapons acquisition. Nick Kotz (1988) documents the long history of this "weapons system that would not die." Congress took action on the B1 during each of thirty years prior to 1988, and four presidents (Eisenhower, Kennedy, Johnson, and Carter) considered blocking its development. But with tens of thousands of jobs and contracts with 5,200 companies in forty-eight states hanging in the balance, even vigilant efforts by President Carter to kill a bomber he saw as expensive and unnecessary were not sufficient to halt this juggernaut. Kotz describes how the air force, the contractors, their allies in Congress, and their supporters in the administration waged a "secret war" to save the B1 after Carter prevailed in Congress to cancel its production in 1977. Pentagon officials used their discretionary power with R&D funds to keep the B1's development in process; Rockwell allegedly charged B1 costs to other government contracts; air force brass constructed new strategic rationales for the bomber's use; and efforts were launched to "market" the B1 under different names using different justifications. By 1980, after the Soviet invasion of Afghanistan had helped to create a climate more favorable to military spending, Congress agreed to a plan proposed by Democratic senators Glenn and Cranston to salvage a revised B1 despite Carter's continuing opposition, and in October 1981 President Ronald Reagan ordered the production of 100 B1 bombers. Thus, the "secret war" was ultimately successful in keeping the bomber alive, despite strong opposition from the executive, until the country elected a new president who was willing to fund what has turned out to be the most expensive airplane in history, labeled by some experts a "flying Edsel" (Kotz, 1988).

The acquisition process for nonnuclear weapons has also been studied using some version of a bureaucratic or organizational politics model. Coulam (1977) studied the case of the F-111 tactical fighter, which was to be the first major weapons system jointly developed by two services, the air force and the navy. In 1961, Secretary McNamara directed the two organizations to combine their separate plans for new tactical fighters into a single integrated version, over the strenuous objections of both services. This attempt to reduce costs and rationalize the weapons acquisition process ended disastrously: the navy eventually canceled its program and was allowed to develop its own fighter, the F-14, while the air force ultimately acquired only one-third as many F-111's as it had originally planned, at twice the expected cost. This case highlights the effects of organizational routines on the process of weapons acquisition, in particular how the normal organizational process of factoring problems into subproblems can lead to pathological rigidities even in organizations where flexibility in the face of uncertainty is critical. Thus, "Once the development was under way, the possibilities for modifying the program became increasingly limited and illusory," even in the face of serious design difficulties (Coulam, 1977, p. 340). Organizational processes also severely constrained the type and quality of information available to decision makers such as the secretary of defense. The services and contractors, hardly dispassionate sources, have substantial control over critical information, limiting the power of the secretary of defense to control implementation. All these factors contributed to the ultimate failure of the F-111.

McNaugher (1984) found both organizational ideologies and interorganizational coalitions to be important factors in explaining the controversies surrounding the army's switch from the M14 rifle to the M16 during the 1960s. The M14, developed by the army's Ordnance Department, was the product of a long tradition in the army centering on the importance of marksmanship. This tradition was one aspect of the army's "organizational essence," even though the importance of accurate marksmanship in winning battles had greatly decreased over the course of the twentieth century. Thus there was substantial army resistance to Secretary McNamara's effort to switch the army's principal arm to the commercially developed M16, a lighter and faster though less accurate gun that was seen as more appropriate for the modern battlefield. These organizational forces were sufficient to maintain the M14 as the army's principal small arm until the jungle fighting of Vietnam "spoke to the organization in a clear voice that favored the M16" (McNaugher, 1984, p. 129). This experience, far more than the rational calculations of Secretary McNamara's office, convinced the army to adopt the M16.

A second set of studies, starting at a higher level of aggregation, tries to account for U.S. military spending using a model based in part on bureaucratic politics. Ostrom (1978; Ostrom and Marra, 1986) proposed a "reactive linkage model" to link estimated Soviet arms spending with the annual defense budget for the United States. This model integrates the action-reaction model with a variant of the BPM so that annual U.S. defense expenditures are linked to changes in estimated Soviet expenditures, as well as other important variables in the environments of the relevant organizations, through a set of organizational processes. The reactive linkage model posits simple decision rules by which the president makes his budget request, Congress makes its appropriations decisions, and the Department of Defense makes its expenditures. Using a time-series structural equation model with annual defense spending as the final dependent variable, Ostrom (1978) and Ostrom and Marra (1986) found results that support the reactive linkage model. This work is particularly interesting because the authors include interorganizational linkages explicitly in their structural equations: the decisional output of one organization becomes a primary input of the next organization in the sequence. This work follows in the tradition of Crecine (1971; Crecine and Fischer, 1973) in adapting organizational theory to the budgeting process. One of the limits of this work, however, is that much of the organizational process posited in the theory described above is masked by the highly aggregated nature of the "decisions" accounted for (that is, total budgetary requests and expenditures).

Critique. The virtue of the bureaucratic politics perspective is its insight into how politics can overwhelm strategic decision making.

This model provides a pointed contrast to the image of governmental defense policy-making as a process of rational strategic calculus. Instead, we are presented with an image of organizations and their representatives shortsightedly pursuing parochial interests, forming coalitions, and pulling and hauling in political bargaining games. A number of excellent case studies, including those mentioned above, have given us insight into how bureaucratic processes can shape weapons acquisitions. But although the BPM tells us where to look, that is, at the bargaining games that occur at various points in the acquisition process, it does not give us a clear picture of what determines the outcomes of these games. After all, coalitions favoring procurement of particular weapons do not always win out, and bureaucratic inertia is not always sufficient to hold off cutbacks. Secretary McNamara alone was able to cancel a raft of large defense projects upon taking office, including the air force's B-70 bomber and the Skybolt missile, despite the existence of powerful coalitions favoring them. Thus, the BPM stands in need of revision if we are to have a sufficient model of the defense policy process.

That organizations play a key role in determining the force posture of the United States seems beyond dispute at this point. The bureaucratic politics model is correct in emphasizing the importance of organizations to the arms race and to security affairs more generally. What is necessary, then, is a model that integrates the disparate processes and outcomes described by the previous models while retaining an organizational focus. It is to a first step in this direction that we now turn.

Toward an Interorganizational Model of the Defense Domain

The three models of the arms race we have considered have all looked at different outcomes, and they have posited different processes by which these outcomes are determined. The phenomenon to be explained has ranged from the fate of a particular weapon system to the extent of the GNP accounted for by military spending, and the state has been characterized as a unitary rational actor, a tool of societal elites, and a set of fragmented organizations with more or less conflicting interests. Furthermore, the methods used to analyze the processes involved in the arms race have been rather different, ranging from highly aggregated time-series analyses to detailed case studies. None of these models seems fully adequate on its own to capture the broad range of phenomena that occur in the realm of national security and that provide the basis for escalation. Using previous work in political science and recent organization theory, however, and building on the basic insights of the bureaucratic politics approach, we can integrate the three approaches into a unified interorganizational network model of the defense domain.

In his classic 1964 article in *World Politics,* Theodore Lowi argued that governmental policy processes could be categorized into "arenas of power" according to the expected functional impact of the policy on society. He identified three arenas in domestic politics—distribution, regulation, and redistribution—each of which "tends to develop its own characteristic political structure, political process, elites, and group relations" (Lowi, 1964, pp. 689-690). Distributive issues concern the doling out of "indulgences" (such as public land or defense procurement) that can be disaggregated easily, and they breed a politics of pork barrels, logrolling, mutual noninterference, and coalitions based on "uncommon interests." Regulatory policies cannot be disaggregated in this way, so that in the short run they demand a direct choice as to who will be indulged and who deprived. This leads to a "pluralistic" policy process where coalitions are based on shared interests and the biggest or most powerful coalition generally "wins." These types of issues typically involve outcomes that affect whole sectors of the economy (for example, protectionist legislation for particular industries). Redistributive policies have even broader categories of impact, activating interests along class lines (roughly, the haves and have-nots) and entailing a policy process that is "conflictual elitist" in nature, with the two sides represented by an elite and a counterelite.

Zimmerman (1973) refined the application of Lowi's typology to the foreign policy process by elaborating a fourth arena of power. He argued that when the impact of a foreign policy decision is perceived to be "symmetrical" for the citizens of a society (that is, it is thought that most will be affected in the same way regardless of the choice made) and the political goods at stake are not exclusively tangible resources, the "policy process" does not involve the same types of domestic or bureaucratic politics found in the previous three arenas. In these cases, organizational politicking can be safely ignored, and the "state as unitary actor" model may serve as a fair approximation.[12] Foreign policy events that fall into this category are of two types: those in which the state is profoundly and directly threatened (issues at the "pole of power") and those whose impacts are only minimal (issues at the "pole of indifference"). Thus, crisis decision making and military grand strategy (which both fall on the pole of power) are characterized as highly elitist and "consensual," and the individuals involved generally do not act as mere agents of their organizations; rather, a more rational, purposive process is typical. Between the poles of power and indifference falls the large majority of foreign policy cases, however, including the previous three arenas (distribution, regulation, and redistribution), where domestic and organizational politics have a profound impact on the policy process and thus on state behavior.

This typology provides a useful first step in characterizing the policy processes occurring in the defense domain in the United States. The term *defense domain* conveys an image of cohesion that is belied by the studies we have reviewed above, where it is clear that the processes leading to grand nuclear strategy and those leading to the award of particular defense contracts are very different. Within the broader domain of *defense*, we argue that there are in fact multiple hierarchical levels of cross-cutting issues that correspond roughly to the typology just elaborated.[13] Three of these arenas in turn correspond to the different processes and outcomes described by the bureaucratic politics model, the military Keynesian model, and the action-reaction model.

While the "military-industrial complex" forms a dense interorganizational network encompassing both public and private institutions, not all elements of this network are equally active on all issues. Rather, the extent to which constituent organizations are involved in the policy process is contingent on the arena into which the issue at hand falls. These arenas are organized around three different aspects of defense decision making, corresponding to pivotal foreign policy issues, macroeconomic concerns, and military procurement. Similarly, the policy process—the institutional rules and structures—as well as the social structure linking the members

at each level will differ by issue arena. We will describe the actors
and processes we see as relevant to each of the three arenas below.

Organizations play a crucial role in this story because they are
the key actors in state policy formation (Laumann and Knoke,
1987). Organizations are the basic units of the American polity today, and it is primarily through their actions that interests are articulated and policies formed. This basic insight has been taken to
heart by researchers concerned with relations between organizations
and the state. Research on organizations and environments has increasingly looked to more inclusive units of analysis such as organizational populations, organizational fields, and interorganizational networks. This movement toward larger units has been
accompanied by a move to theory posed at higher levels of analysis.
Along with this greater concern with macro-organizational phenomena has come an increasing awareness of the importance of
relations between organizations and the state. An especially well-
developed model is presented in Laumann and Knoke's *The Organizational State* (1987), which presents an organizationally based
approach to the problem of state policy formation. While this
model is too elaborate to discuss in detail here, we can draw upon
its insights in our discussion of the major issue areas in the defense
domain. More generally, the concepts and methods used in network
analysis of interorganizational fields provide a particularly useful
vocabulary for conceptualizing and analyzing the military-industrial complex.

Organizational actors are linked to each other by a social structure, most importantly including ties of information transmission,
resource transactions, and the interpenetration of organizational
boundaries (for example, through joint ventures, interlocking
boards of directors, coalitions, political action committees, and the
like). This structure conditions the extent to which they are activated on particular issues, the stands they take, and the strategies
they use to pursue their interests (Laumann and Knoke, 1987). As
a consequence, policy-relevant information and politically useful
material resources are passed through interorganizational networks.
Laumann, Knoke, and Kim (1985) found that organizations that
were more prominent in such networks in the health policy domain
were more likely to be active in a diverse range of policy events.

Organizations within political coalitions tend to be related prior to forming the coalition, and whether an individual organization is mobilized is often a function of its prior centrality in a network of resource exchange (Galaskiewicz, 1985). Organizations that operate in the same industry, are geographically proximate, are interdependent in terms of resource flows, and share common relations with financial institutions tend to exhibit similar political behavior (Mizruchi, 1988). All these findings indicate the importance of interorganizational networks in determining the political behavior of organizations. An organization's position in networks of resource and information flows can play an autonomous role in determining its interests, its level of political activation, and its capacities for pressing its perceived interests.

Reframing the Three Models. Previous research that applied network concepts to the energy and health domains worked inductively to uncover clusterings of issues and their distribution, sets of "issue publics" (organizations exhibiting similar patterns of interest levels in domain issues), and relations between them (Laumann and Knoke, 1987). We suggest an a priori principle of categorization that conceives of the defense domain in the United States in terms of multiple hierarchical arenas and multiple overlapping networks.[14] Within each of these arenas the constituent organizations, their placement within the larger network, and the emergent properties of the network as a whole may be characterized along dimensions such as the degree of centralization, hierarchy, and connectivity. A thorough effort at this characterization is beyond the scope of this chapter. We can, however, reframe the three models of the arms race in terms of our synthetic approach.

The orienting questions of the bureaucratic politics model are still the best starting point for analyzing the social structure and policy process within each of the three arenas of the defense domain we are considering. This model was organized around three issues: Who are the actors that have an important impact on the government's policies and actions? What determines each actor's stands on policy issues? And finally, how are these stands aggregated to yield the state's policies and actions? Across the larger domain, the key actors will be those individuals and organizations that are "consequential," that is, those whose intentions and actions are taken into account by other domain participants.[15] By hypothesis, this will vary across arenas within the defense domain. As we have seen, the logic behind the stands taken will be jointly determined by a number of factors, including network position. Finally, the process of aggregation is again dependent on the issue's arena.

The action-reaction process corresponds to the arena of *pivotal foreign policy decision making*. The issues in this arena revolve around America's position in the world political economy and most importantly its stance vis-à-vis the Soviet Union. In the postwar period this stance has been one of mortal enmity, a "cold war" in which the perceived Soviet threat has informed the major policy pronouncements and military grand strategy. It is this basic fact of the cold war environment that sets the general context for the issues falling into the larger defense policy domain. Major concerns have been Soviet intentions and capabilities, American capabilities and obligations, and derivative issues such as arms control. A primary outcome of the policy process in this arena is military posture, broadly construed. This is the arena in which organizations qua organizations have the least impact—it is ideology and "mind-sets" rather than organizationally based interests that underlie policy preferences in the arena of pivotal foreign policy issues (Art, 1973). Following Wolfers (1962) and Zimmerman (1973), we may characterize the policy process in this arena as "consensual elitist," largely divorced from bureaucratic politics. The key actors are the president and other top executive branch decision makers, service elites, and defense intellectuals and think tanks such as RAND. Particularly for crisis foreign policy decisions, presidential preferences are dominant; thus, the state-as-unitary-actor/power-maximizing view is most likely to hold as a useful approximation, and we may look to realist models of state behavior for credible predictions.

The military Keynesian or "power elite" model corresponds to the *macroeconomic policy* arena. The crucial policy outcomes here are summarized by the overall defense budget. The issues falling into the arena concern the aggregate economy, technological progress and industrial development and capacity (especially, but not exclusively, in the defense industries), and the electoral exigencies described by Lindblom (1977), Block (1977a), and Tufte (1978). These issues fall most closely into the redistributive arena in Lowi's

(1964) typology, and thus the policy process corresponds roughly to
the "power elite" model, the central actors being the executive
branch, key congressional committees, and defense trade associations representing the aggregate interests of military contractors.
The policy process in this arena entails stable coalitions based on
common interests. In this case, interests may be based on class and/
or on holding positions of "structural equivalence";[16] for example,
all defense contractors have a mutual interest in increasing the aggregate defense budget independent of any specific procurement
contract. Further, elected representatives are more or less united in
their interest in creating a hospitable business climate to enhance
their chances of reelection and thus are inclined to cast their lot with
the "growth coalitions" that, according to Wolfe (1979), emerge at
each new phase in the cold war.

Finally, the bureaucratic politics model best describes the process
of *contract allocation,* in which the primary issues revolve around
whether weapon systems will be funded and who the prime contrac-
tor(s) will be. The concerns in this subdomain range from contractor suitability to the parochial interests of constituents, follow-on
contracts, and so on. The most significant outcome of this process
is the award of prime contracts. Here the policy process is precisely
that described by Lowi (1964) in the distributive arena: the pork
barrel of military procurement breeds fluid coalitions based on uncommon interests. Bureaucratic bargaining and congressional logrolling are typical processes here, and the norm of mutual noninterference prevails. The key players are the armed services,
congressional committees, congressional representatives with weapons contractors in their districts, the Department of Energy, the
larger defense contractors, and the major R&D labs.

Relating the Three Levels. We argued above that the three arenas
within the larger defense domain revolve around three levels of
issues—pivotal foreign policy questions, macroeconomic concerns,
and military procurement—and that the different types of issues
activate different segments of the larger interorganizational network
that is the military-industrial complex. Two questions arise out of
this characterization: How are issues defined or categorized? How
are the three levels related?

The answer to both questions is *dialectically,* although in two different senses of the word. The definition of an issue depends on the perceptions of the domain participants. In many cases, the definition of an issue area is not given from above but rather is socially constructed and more or less contentious within the larger defense domain. The fact that the policy process and the considerations brought to bear are altered by the "definition of the situation" prevailing around an issue suggests that interested actors will try to define issues to their advantage whenever possible, although the extent to which an issue's arena can be negotiated will differ from event to event. Future research would do well to elaborate the logic behind this type of negotiation.

The process of socially constructing the terms of debate is illustrated nicely by the public discussion surrounding the Strategic Defense Initiative (SDI), or "Star Wars" program. At the level of foreign policy, SDI is touted by higher-level members of the executive branch as a military panacea, or at least as an effective bargaining chip for arms control with the Soviets. At lower levels in the complex, however, SDI is championed more on macroeconomic grounds, as a provider of jobs and a stimulus for American technological advance and economic competitiveness, rather than on strategic grounds. Finally, at the level of specific contract allocations, strategic rationale is almost completely de-coupled from the debate, and parochial interests are the name of the game.

Proponents of Star Wars would like to frame the debate as one of foreign policy and military grand strategy, where a "better safe than sorry" attitude is more likely to prevail. For example, Morrison (1985, p. 32) describes how representatives of the Department of Energy's weapons conglomerate "skillfully parlay promises of tantalizing new nuclear weapons designs and dire predictions of emerging Soviet nuclear design superiority into a political consensus that keeps their production lines running at full capacity." They are aided in this effort by their control of critical and/or confidential information and by the very terms of the debate regarding foreign policy matters. Detractors, on the other hand, see Star Wars as a bottomless pork barrel that invites waste and abuse on the part of contractors. By attempting to frame the issue as an economic one and making salient the trade-offs involved, opponents hope to put themselves on a more supportive framework for negotiation.

For example, Holdren and Green (1986) point out that about $2 billion worth of business went to the top five SDI contractors (General Motors, Lockheed, Boeing, TRW, and McDonnell-Douglas) during fiscal years 1983–1986, and they argue that "such sums are troublesome not merely because of the misdirection of research priorities they represent but also because of the size of the constituency they are creating, in these influential firms, for continuation of the lucrative SDI project regardless of the technical and political merits" (Holdren and Green, 1986, p. 11). Such a reframing of the issue alters the ground rules of debate in a way that brings economic considerations to the forefront and reduces the importance of alleged strategic concerns.

The three levels of issues we have described are related to each other hierarchically, with higher-level issues providing the context or "environment" within which lower-level processes are embedded. This can be described as a relation of "structural limitation." At the highest level, foreign policy processes take place within a context of international events. As a recent example, the military buildup associated with the Reagan years was introduced in large measure as a "show of resolve" in response to Soviet aggression in Afghanistan. Foreign policy and military stance in turn shape the defense budget priorities and size. Thus, Reagan's promise of a buildup to reassert American might in the world led to a "spend up" of estimable proportions. Finally, the overall budget sets implicit criterion levels for contract awards. For example, the Reagan years provided a much more hospitable climate for procurement of the B1 bomber, as we have seen before. Indeed, Gansler (1982) argued early in this era that the embarrassment of riches associated with the Reagan military buildup outstripped the capacity of the defense industry to produce the requested military goods.

The causal relation between the levels of the issue hierarchy is not, however, exclusively from higher to lower. Decisions, policies, and issues at lower levels can also aggregate or redound up to higher levels. There is much evidence to suggest that American foreign policy in the postwar period has been largely driven by macroeconomic concerns, including to some extent the basic cold war stance of hostility toward the Soviet Union. Block (1977b) argues that the Marshall Plan and the military buildup of the 1950s, based on a purposeful exaggeration of cold war tensions, were both the result of the need perceived by elite policy-makers for the continued expansion of the U.S. economy into Europe and the Third World to avoid economic crisis at home. Riddell (1988) also presents evidence that displays of American military power are followed by an increase in the after-tax profit rate of American businesses.

We have also seen how research and development organizations play a relatively autonomous role in the arms race by generating "solutions in search of problems" in a technological "garbage can process" (Cohen, March, and Olsen, 1972). Both public labs such as Lawrence Livermore, Sandia, and Los Alamos and private contractors are driven by organizational self-interest in retaining funding and getting new contracts to push their wares (Morrison, 1985; Kaldor, 1983), and the "gee whiz" character of the products of these labs may prompt key decision makers into a "Wow! Grab it!" response that is divorced from strategic necessity. (See Janis, Chapter Eight of this volume.)[17] Thus, the aggregate result of these intranational processes is to change the nature of processes at the international level. The relation between issues at higher and lower levels, then, is reciprocal, with higher-level policy outputs forming a structure within which lower-level processes are played out, and issues at the lower level aggregating up to the higher level to change this structure.

Conclusion

To summarize, our argument is that the defense domain can be conceived as an interorganizational network in which the constituent organizations are differentially activated depending on the issue at hand. The types of issues or decision-making arenas we have considered can be hierarchically organized into three levels on the basis of the functional impact of their policy outputs on society. These levels correspond to pivotal foreign policy matters (the "politics of interaction"), macroeconomic policy (a "politics of redistribution"), and contract allocation (a "politics of distribution"). Each level or arena has a characteristic policy process, with different institutional rules and network structures linking members, and each activates different elements of the network. Issue definition is more or less contentious, with organizations attempting to set the ground rules of debate in their favor by negotiating the arena into which it falls. Finally, the three levels are related to each other dialectically: the policy outputs from higher levels create the context or structure within which the policy processes at the next lower level are played out, and outcomes and issues from the lower levels in turn aggregate up to the higher levels to alter this structure.

Although our elaboration of this model has been necessarily brief and somewhat speculative, we think our approach has the potential for informing fresh research on the military-industrial complex by suggesting a unique perspective that straddles the boundary between organization theory and political science and builds on important insights regarding the functional character of issues, the organizational character of policy-making domains, and the links between them. The model suggests where research on policy processes in the defense domain should look, that is, at the network structure that links the key actors constituting each arena within the domain, and it also suggests what will be found, that is, different actors, network linkages and structures, and types of interactions, depending on the "level" or functional impact of the issue type. We hope to elaborate, refine, and apply this model in future research, and we hope that others will be similarly inspired.

Notes

1. The different schools of thought include an action-reaction model, a technological dynamic model, a military superiority model, interest group models, a national leadership model, and a military mission model.

2. A similar conception underlies the frequent use of the prisoner's dilemma game as a model of the arms race. In this game, two actors face a situation of unavoidable interdependence where their actions and those of their counterpart combine to determine the "payoff." Both would benefit from cooperation, but usually neither is willing to take the risk. The fact that the other player is likely to confirm one's suspicion by failing to cooperate reinforces one's own strategy of noncooperation. The outcome is that both repeatedly fail to gain the best out-

come available to them. The losses associated with this strategy accumulate over time, much as military buildups accumulate.

3. These estimates were later revised downward; see Ostrom and Marra (1986).

4. It appears however that "fatigue" has set in on the Soviet side. Recent disarmament proposals appear to be directly related to Gorbachev's desire to shift spending from the military to the civilian sector. Similarly, the U.S. Congress and president face a hard budgeting reality: defense spending will have to be curbed if any progress toward a balanced budget is to be made.

5. Pursell (1972), Sarkesian (1972), and Rosen (1973) provide useful anthologies of research on this topic.

6. Lieberson (1971), however, denies the privileged place of the military-industrial complex within the power elite hypothesized by Mills (1956) and his followers; rather, he suggests that special-interest groups in general tend to have particular influence within their own sphere, whether their interest is in defense, education, or any other public policy arena. He also points out that military spending had virtually no impact on total corporate income in the United States during the sample period 1916–1965, whereas nonmilitary spending was highly correlated with total corporate income.

7. Slater and Nardin (1973) offer a telling critique, suggesting that four weaknesses debilitate the theory: (1) reliance on a conspiracy theory as the basis of causal inference, (2) crude economic determinism, (3) inconsistent specification regarding membership in the military-industrial complex, and (4) implausible assumptions about the nature and scope of the power of the complex.

8. Indeed, Riddell (1988), in a time-series analysis, found the exercise of U.S. military power to be significantly and positively related to the after-tax profit rate of U.S. corporations.

9. Griffin, Devine, and Wallace (1982, p. S138) find that about 8 percent of the variation in annual defense spending can be uniquely attributed to their four economic and political variables combined.

10. As late as 1960, military spending was equivalent to 9.5 percent of the U.S. GNP; in 1985, it had fallen to 6.4 percent (Holdren and Green, 1986).

11. Research on Soviet strategic decision making and weapons procurement is for obvious reasons less enlightening on this point, but it has been argued that comparable processes are at work in the USSR as well. See Meyer (1984) and MccGwire (1987) for intelligent discussions of research on Soviet security decision making.

12. Zimmerman (1973) does not advocate using a "state as actor" approach alone, even for studying pivotal foreign policy events; rather, he suggests that such rational policy models should be augmented by a grounding in social psychology. See Janis, Chapter Eight of this volume, for an example of a recent approach to the problem.

13. Following Lowi (1964), we will refer to these levels as arenas (or subdomains).

14. Manigart (1986) applied the "structural analysis" approach to the Belgian defense domain. He identified five broad clusters of issues—general defense policy, budget, operation, manpower, and procurement—finding that these issues indeed attracted distinct groups of organizations and that the basic cleavage was between those strongly interested in manpower issues and those concerned with procurement. However, if the Belgian defense domain were similar to the American one, Manigart's conclusion that this domain was not dominated by a core set of organizations constituting a "power elite" would, if our notion is correct, be an artifact of failing to take into account the hierarchical structure of issues within the domain.

15. Laumann and Knoke (1987) point out that an organization's membership in the domain is not a given. Rather, membership is a continuing social construction by domain actors, and thus whether or not an organization "counts" is the outcome of ongoing negotiations.

16. Holding positions of structural equivalence means sharing common relations with the same set of actors in a network. See Burt (1980) for an explication of this and other network concepts.

17. Such seems to be the case with Star Wars: as Lord Solly Zuckerman points out, "The technical ideas which underlie the SDI concept of a defensive screen over the U.S. were generated not by the president or his chiefs of staff, but by scientists and engineers driven along by the vested interests of the weapons laboratories in which they work" (Zuckerman, 1987, p. 8).

References

Adams, G. "Defense Budget Isn't Economy's Culprit." *San Jose Mercury News*, Oct. 11, 1987, p. 7P.

Albrecht, U. "Military R&D Communities." *International Social Science Journal*, 1983, *35*, 78–93.

Allison, G. T. *Essence of Decision: Explaining the Cuban Missile Crisis*. Boston: Little, Brown, 1971.

Allison, G. T. "The Implications of Arms Control for Doctrine and Forces." In R. L. Pfaltzgraff, Jr., *Contrasting Approaches to Strategic Arms Control*. Lexington, Mass.: Lexington Books, 1974.

Allison, G. T., and Halperin, M. H. "Bureaucratic Politics: A Paradigm and Some Policy Implications." In R. Tanter and R. H. Ullman (eds.), *Theory and Policy in International Relations*. Princeton, N.J.: Princeton University Press, 1972.

Allison, G. T., and Morris, F. A. "Armaments and Arms Control: Exploring the Determinants of Military Weapons." In F. A. Long and G. W. Rathjens (eds.), *Arms, Defense Policy, and Arms Control*. New York: Norton, 1975.

Art, R. J. "Bureaucratic Politics and American Foreign Policy: A Critique." *Policy Sciences*, 1973, *4*, 467–490.

Block, F. L. "The Ruling Class Does Not Rule: Notes on the Marxist Theory of the State." *Socialist Revolution*, 1977a, *7*, 6–28.

Block, F. L. *The Origins of International Economic Disorder: A Study of United States International Monetary Policy from World War II to the Present*. Berkeley: University of California Press, 1977b.

Block, F. L. "Economic Instability and Military Strength: The Paradoxes of the 1950 Rearmament Decision." *Politics and Society*, 1980, *10*, 35–58.

Burnett, W. B. "Competition in the Weapons Acquisition Process: The Case of U.S. Warplanes." *Journal of Policy Analysis and Management,* 1987, *7,* 17-39.

Burt, R. S. "Models of Network Structure." *Annual Review of Sociology,* 1980, *6,* 79-141.

Center for Defense Information. "The Pentagon Prepares for Nuclear War: The 1988 Budget." *Defense Monitor,* 1987, *16* (4).

Cohen, M. D., March, J. G., and Olsen, J. P. "A Garbage Can Model of Organizational Choice." *Administrative Science Quarterly,* 1972, *17,* 1-25.

Coulam, R. F. *Illusions of Choice: The F-111 and the Problem of Weapons Acquisition Reform.* Princeton, N.J.: Princeton University Press, 1977.

Crecine, J. P. "Defense Budgeting: Organizational Adaptation to Environmental Constraints." In R. F. Byrne and others (eds.), *Studies in Budgeting.* Amsterdam: North-Holland, 1971.

Crecine, J. P., and Fischer, G. W. "On Resource Allocation Processes in the U.S. Department of Defense." In C. P. Cotter (ed.), *Political Science Annual.* Vol. 4. Indianapolis, Ind.: Bobbs-Merrill, 1973.

Freedman, L. *Atlas of Global Strategy.* London: Macmillan, 1985.

Gaddis, J. L. *The Long Peace.* New York: Oxford University Press, 1987.

Galaskiewicz, J. "Interorganizational Relations." *Annual Review of Sociology,* 1985, *11,* 281-304.

Gansler, J. S. *The Defense Industry.* Cambridge, Mass.: MIT Press, 1980.

Gansler, J. S. "Can the Defense Industry Respond to the Reagan Initiatives?" *International Security,* 1982, *6* (4), 102-121.

Gansler, J. S. "Needed: A U.S. Defense Industrial Strategy." *International Security,* 1987, *12* (2), 45-62.

George, R. Z. "The Economics of Arms Control." *International Security,* 1978/1979, *3* (3), 94-125.

Greenwood, T. *Making the MIRV: A Study of Defense Decision Making.* Cambridge, Mass.: Ballinger, 1975.

Griffin, L. J., Devine, J. A., and Wallace, M. "Monopoly Capital, Organized Labor, and Military Expenditures in the United

States, 1949-1976." In M. Burawoy and T. Skocpol (eds.), *Marxist Inquiries*. Chicago: University of Chicago Press, 1982.

Griffin, L. J., Wallace, M., and Devine, J. "The Political Economy of Military Spending: Evidence from the United States." *Cambridge Journal of Economics*, 1982, *6*, 1-14.

Halperin, M. H. "Why Bureaucrats Play Games." *Foreign Policy*, 1971, *2*, 70-90.

Holdren, J. P., and Green, F. B. "Military Spending, the SDI, and Government Support of Research and Development: Effects on the Economy and the Health of American Science." *F.A.S. Public Interest Report*, 1986, *39* (7), 1-17.

Kaldor, M. "Military R&D: Cause or Consequence of the Arms Race?" *International Social Science Journal*, 1983, *35*, 25-45.

Keohane, R. O. (ed.). *Neorealism and Its Critics*. New York: Columbia University Press, 1986.

Kissinger, H. "Limited War: Conventional or Nuclear? A Reappraisal." *Daedalus*, 1960, *89* (4), 800-817.

Kotz, N. *Wild, Blue, Yonder: Money, Politics, and the B1 Bomber*. New York: Pantheon, 1988.

Krell, G. "Capitalism and Armaments: Business Cycles and Defense Spending in the United States 1945-1979." *Journal of Peace Research*, 1981, *18*, 221-240.

Kurth, J. R. "The Political Economy of the Weapons Procurement Process: The Follow-on Imperative." *American Economic Review Papers and Proceedings*, 1972, *62* (2), 304-311.

Lapp, R. E. *Arms Beyond Doubt: The Tyranny of Weapons Technology*. New York: Cowles, 1970.

Laumann, E. O., and Knoke, D. *The Organizational State: Social Choice in National Policy Domains*. Madison: University of Wisconsin Press, 1987.

Laumann, E. O., Knoke, D., and Kim, Y. H. "An Organizational Approach to State Policy Formation: A Comparative Study of Energy and Health Domains." *American Sociological Review*, 1985, *50*, 1-19.

Leidy, M. P., and Staiger, R. W. "Economic Issues and Methodology in Arms Race Analysis." *Journal of Conflict Resolution*, 1985, *29*, 503-530.

Lieberson, S. "An Empirical Study of Military-Industrial Link-ages." *American Journal of Sociology*, 1971, *76*, 562–584.

Lindblom, C. E. *Politics and Markets: The World's Political-Economic Systems*. New York: Basic Books, 1977.

Lowi, T. J. "American Business, Public Policy, Case Studies, and Political Theory." *World Politics*, 1964, *16*, 677–715.

MccGwire, M. K. *Military Objectives in Soviet Foreign Policy*. Washington, D.C.: Brookings Institution, 1987.

McNaugher, T. L. *The M16 Controversies: Military Organizations and Weapons Acquisition*. New York: Praeger, 1984.

Manigart, P. "The Belgian Defense Policy Domain in the 1980s." *Armed Forces and Society*, 1986, *13*, 39–56.

Meyer, S. M. "Soviet National Security Decisionmaking: What Do We Know and What Do We Understand?" In J. Valenta and W. C. Potter (eds.), *Soviet Decisionmaking for National Security*. London: Allen & Unwin, 1984.

Mills, C. W. *The Power Elite*. New York: Oxford University Press, 1956.

Mintz, A., and Hicks, A. "Military Keynesianism in the United States , 1949–1976: Disaggregating Military Expenditures and Their Determination." *American Journal of Sociology*, 1984, *90*, 411–417.

Mizruchi, M. S. "Similarity of Political Behavior Among Large American Corporations." Unpublished manuscript, Columbia University, 1988.

Morgenthau, H. J. *Politics Among Nations*. New York: Knopf, 1948.

Morris, F. A. "Acquiring Weapons." In G. T. Allison and others (eds.), *Commission on the Organization of the Government for the Conduct of Foreign Policy*, Vol. 4: *Appendix K: Adequacy of Current Organization: Defense and Arms Control*. Washington, D.C.: U.S. Government Printing Office, 1975.

Morrison, D. C. "Energy Department's Weapons Conglomerate." *Bulletin of the Atomic Scientists*, Apr. 1985, pp. 32–37.

Nincic, M. *The Arms Race: The Political Economy of Military Growth*. New York: Praeger, 1982.

Nincic, M., and Cusack, T. R. "The Political Economy of U.S.

Military Spending." *Journal of Peace Research*, 1979, *10*, 101–115.

O'Connor, J. R. *The Fiscal Crisis of the State*. New York: St. Martin's Press, 1973.

Ostrom, C. W., Jr. "A Reactive Linkage Model of the U.S. Defense Expenditure Policy-Making Process." *American Political Science Review*, 1978, *72*, 941–957.

Ostrom, C. W., Jr., and Marra, R. F. "U.S. Defense Spending and the Soviet Estimate." *American Political Science Review*, 1986, *80*, 819–842.

Pursell, C. W., Jr. (ed.). *The Military-Industrial Complex*. New York: Harper & Row, 1972.

Reich, M. "Does the U.S. Economy Require Military Spending?" *American Economic Review Papers and Proceedings*, 1972, *62* (2), 296–303.

Richardson, L. F. *Arms and Insecurity*. Chicago: Quadrangle, 1960.

Riddell, T. "U.S. Military Power, the Terms of Trade, and the Profit Rate." *American Economic Review Papers and Proceedings*, 1988, *78* (2), 60–65.

Rosen, S. "Testing the Theory of the Military-Industrial Complex." In S. Rosen (ed.), *Testing the Theory of the Military-Industrial Complex*. Lexington, Mass.: Lexington Books, 1973.

Ross, J., and Staw, B. M. "Expo 86: An Escalation Prototype." *Administrative Science Quarterly*, 1986, *31*, 274–297.

Russett, B. *The Prisoners of Insecurity*. New York: W. H. Freeman, 1983.

Sarkesian, S. C. (ed.). *The Military-Industrial Complex: A Reassessment*. Newbury Park, Calif.: Sage, 1972.

Senate Committee on Foreign Relations, Subcommittee on Arms Control, International Law, and Organization. *ABM, MIRV, SALT, and the Nuclear Arms Race*, 91st Cong., 2nd sess., 1970, 59.

Slater, J., and Nardin, T. "The Concept of a Military-Industrial Complex." In S. Rosen (ed.), *Testing the Theory of the Military-Industrial Complex*. Lexington, Mass.: Lexington Books, 1973.

Tufte, E. *The Political Control of the Economy*. Princeton, N.J.: Princeton University Press, 1978.

Waltz, K. N. *Man, the State and War*. New York: Columbia University Press, 1959.

Waltz, K. N. "The Stability of a Bipolar World." *Daedalus*, 1964, *93*, 881–909.

Waltz, K. N. *Theory of International Politics*. Reading, Mass.: Addison-Wesley, 1979.

Wohlstetter, A. "The Delicate Balance of Terror." *Foreign Affairs*, 1959, *37* (2), 211–234.

Wohlstetter, A. "Is There a Strategic Arms Race?" *Foreign Policy*, Summer 1974, *15*, 3–20.

Wolfe, A. *The Rise and Fall of the "Soviet Threat": Domestic Sources of the Cold War Consensus*. Washington, D.C.: Institute for Policy Studies, 1979.

Wolfers, A. *Discord and Collaboration: Essays on International Politics*. Baltimore, Md.: Johns Hopkins University Press, 1962.

York, H. *Race to Oblivion: A Participant's View of the Arms Race*. New York: Simon & Schuster, 1970.

Zimmerman, W. "Issue Area and Foreign-Policy Process: A Research Note in Search of a General Theory." *American Political Science Review*, 1973, *67*, 1204–1212.

Zuckerman, S. "What Price Star Wars?" *New York Review of Books*, Apr. 23, 1987, pp. 8–13.

Chapter 5

Untying the Knot

De-Escalatory Processes
in International Conflict

Robert L. Kahn
Roderick M. Kramer

[T]he harder you and I pull, the tighter this knot [of war]
will become. And a time may come when this knot is tied
so tight that the person who tied it is no longer capable of
untying it.

> Chairman Khrushchev,
> in a letter to President Kennedy
> during the Cuban missile crisis

For at least as long as historical records have existed, conflicts between nations have been a conspicuous feature of the international
landscape. In the twentieth century alone, there have been over 130
international conflicts, which have claimed more than 120 million
lives. Ironically, even those nations that possess massive nuclear and
conventional military superiority over their adversaries have not
been spared such conflict. Nor have they found it easy to use their
seemingly overwhelming advantages to extricate themselves from,
let alone win, those conflicts in which they have been embroiled.
Thus, the United States found itself entrapped in a long and costly
conflict with North Vietnam, as did the Soviet Union in its war
with Afghanistan.

Given both the prevalence of conflict between nations and its importance in shaping international relations, it is not surprising that considerable attention has been directed at understanding the dynamics of international conflict. Much of this literature has focused on detailed examination of specific conflicts (for example, the origins of the First World War or the escalation of the Vietnam War). There have also been numerous attempts at developing general theories or frameworks for conceptualizing the escalation process. These theoretical contributions come from many disciplines, including political science (for example, Jervis, 1976), economics (for example, Boulding, 1966; Schelling, 1960), and psychology (for example, Deutsch, 1973; Pruitt and Rubin, 1986).

In contrast with this robust literature on escalation, relatively little attention has been given to developing theories or models of the *de-escalation* process. As Pruitt and Rubin (1986) cogently note in their assessment of the literature, "We can describe with some precision the processes by which an 'enemy' image is established and empathy toward the 'enemy' is destroyed, but we know little about the steps by which such an image is dissipated and empathy is reestablished. *Indeed, the literature on de-escalation is almost nonexistent*" (p. 184; emphasis added).

Both case studies and personal accounts by participants of major international conflicts such as the Cuban missile crisis (Allison, 1971; Blight and Welch, 1989; Garthoff, 1987; Janis, 1983; Kennedy, 1969), the Vietnam War (Berman, 1989), and the Middle East conflict (Kissinger, 1979; Stein, 1986) have emphasized the central role national leaders and their advisers played in de-escalating these conflicts. They have also drawn attention to the difficulty these decision makers encountered in their de-escalation efforts. Although these accounts suggest that both psychological and organizational factors impeded the ability of decision makers to de-escalate conflict, there has not been systematic discussion of these factors.

Accordingly, the purpose of this chapter is to examine the role psychological and organizational factors play in the de-escalation process. The central question we address is "Why is it so difficult to initiate and sustain a de-escalatory process?" More specifically, "What are the psychological and organizational factors that act as *barriers* or deterrents to de-escalation?"

A systematic examination of factors that prevent de-escalation might prove useful on several accounts. First, it may provide clues to some of the necessary and/or sufficient conditions for de-escalation to occur. Second, it may illuminate the strengths and limitations of the various de-escalation strategies that have been proposed by conflict theorists. Finally, it may facilitate the development of a positive theory of the de-escalation process.

Scope of the Present Chapter

It may be helpful at the outset to say something about the scope of the present chapter and the level of analysis we adopt. In viewing the de-escalation process from the perspective of the principal decision makers involved in a conflict or crisis, we will necessarily examine how psychological processes affect decision making during a conflict. However, we will give equal attention to the impact of the organizational setting or context within which those decisions are made. Many previous studies have examined psychological factors in international conflict (for example, Jervis, 1976), but they have generally given little attention to how the organizational environment shapes behavior (Stein, 1988). As we will attempt to demonstrate, recent research on organizational behavior can help us address this gap in the literature of international relations.

The chapter is organized as follows. In the first part of the chapter we review prior research on escalation and de-escalation. Following this review, we present a general model of the de-escalation process. We use the model to identify psychological and organizational factors that function as barriers to the de-escalation process. We then discuss implications of our analysis for some of the more widely discussed approaches to de-escalation of conflict. We conclude the chapter by considering limitations of our model and proposing some directions for future research.

Overview of Previous Research

Although the topic of de-escalation has received much less attention than escalation, parts of the research literature of conflict are relevant to understanding de-escalatory processes. Political scientists who have studied international conflict have focused on several areas important for understanding de-escalation and conflict containment. These include crisis management or crisis control (George, 1983; Lebow, 1987), the role of negotiation and bargaining to resolve conflict (Fisher, 1964; Snyder and Diesing, 1977), and finally, the use of power-based or coercive techniques such as threats and "nuclear blackmail" (Betts, 1987).

The conflict-oriented literature of experimental social psychology presents a different perspective, as does the organizational research literature. These literatures have focused largely on how to de-escalate interpersonal (Greenhalgh, 1987) and intergroup (Morely, Webb, and Stephenson, 1988) conflicts, often by some form of third-party intervention. The discussions of de-escalation by Osgood (1962), in which he developed a fictional conflict-reducing script between an American president and a Soviet premier, and by Axelrod (1984), who studied the development of cooperation by means of computer tournaments, are almost unique in emphasizing a process of de-escalation that is generated by the protagonists themselves.

Although both the social-psychological and organizational studies of conflict emphasize reduction or resolution by third-party interventions, the interventions are of different kinds. In the organizational literature, the third party is typically a consultant or mediator (for example, Argyris, 1976, and Walton, 1969). In experimental research, the experimenter takes the role of the intervener and, equipped with powers that political scientists would call hegemonic, attempts to reduce conflict by introducing superordinate goals (Sherif, 1958), altering the payoff structure of the conflict (Deutsch, 1973), or using intergroup exercises to break down negative stereotypes and facilitate cooperative exchanges (Blake, Shepard, and Mouton, 1964).

Extrapolation from two-person experimental games and small group simulations to organizations and nation-states is, of course, problematic. Organizations are not unitary actors or decision makers, and nations are even more complex multiorganizational systems. Some experimental researchers are careful to point out the limitations of conflict research at the individual or intergroup level, but there has been little systematic attempt to specify the implications of organizational research for understanding international conflict. Allison's (1971) classic study of the Cuban missile crisis and Snyder's (1984) study of the origins of the First World War are notable exceptions.

In both organizational and international conflicts, the relevant decisions and actions are taken not by individuals acting alone but by individuals and groups operating as units of organizations. De-escalation of a conflict involving the United States, for example, is likely to involve decisions by the president, his cabinet of advisers, members of the Joint Chiefs of Staff, and officials of the State and Defense departments, among others. Accordingly, in the model of de-escalation developed in this chapter, we pay attention to the role psychological factors play in de-escalatory decision making, but in the context of the organizational systems within which those decisions occur or are embedded.

Characteristics of De-Escalation

Students of conflict have tended to be more explicit in defining the process of escalation than de-escalation, leaving us with the implication that the latter is essentially the mirror image of the former. In his extensive review of the literature on organizational conflict, Thomas (1976, p. 905) defines escalation as an increase in the level of a conflict between two parties, characterized by (1) an increase in the number and the size of the issues being disputed, (2) increasing hostility between the parties, (3) increasing competitiveness, (4) the pursuit of increasingly extreme demands or objectives, (5) the use of increasingly coercive tactics, and (6) decreasing trust.

Pruitt and Rubin (1986) describe the escalation of conflict in very similar terms. They propose that as a conflict escalates, there is likely to be a proliferation in the number and magnitude of issues perceived to be at stake in the conflict. In the early stages of a conflict, the issues may be relatively small and specific. Over time, however, the conflict begins to encompass larger and more general issues, including reactivation of past grievances and injuries. Ultimately, the conflict may assume a very diffuse form, whereby the parties can perceive only the irreconcilable differences in their relationship, which seem to preclude even the possibility of peaceful coexistence. Associated with these changes in perceptions, there are likely to be changes in the motivation of the parties. In the early stages of the conflict, the parties may be motivated by a relatively benign form of competition in which each seeks only to excel. As the conflict escalates, however, each party may be increasingly motivated to humiliate, punish, or ultimately to annihilate the other.

Changes associated with the escalation of conflict are manifested not only in terms of the decision makers' perceptions and motives, but they are also expressed in behavioral terms. In the early stages of a conflict, the parties tend to use what Pruitt and Rubin characterize as "light" influence attempts, such as persuasion and ingratiation. As escalation intensifies, they may shift to heavier influence attempts, such as threats, coercion, and direct efforts to incapacitate the other party.

In another major study, Smoke (1986) characterizes escalation in terms of perceptually salient indicators—points of particular significance to the parties involved in the conflict. He proposes that fundamental to an escalatory process is the "crossing of saliencies, which are taken as defining the limits of a conflict. As a war escalates, it moves upward and outward through a pattern of saliences that are provided situationally" (p. 442). Thus, an international conflict might move from private diplomacy to public accusation, from embargo to blockade, and from battlefield to civilian attacks.

These definitions are useful in highlighting several dimensions important for both escalation and de-escalation. First, there is typically a broadening in the scope and complexity of a conflict as it escalates. Second, escalation produces changes in the relationship between the parties that are evident in their perceptions, expectations, motives, and behavior. These characteristics of the escalation process suggest that *de-escalation* entails a *decrease* in the number and size of the issues being disputed, a decrease in the hostility between the parties, and greater use of conciliatory rather than coercive tactics (or at least the willingness to refrain from using coercive or escalatory tactics). These in turn may lead to increased cooperativeness and trust.

By defining de-escalation in this way we do not imply that the process of de-escalation in each case merely reverses a previous sequence of escalatory steps. There may be important asymmetries between escalation and de-escalation. During escalation, for example, *emergent* processes may alter the parties and the relationship between them in fundamental ways (Pondy, 1967; Pruitt and Rubin, 1986). These changes set the conditions under which de-escalation must begin and therefore determine the sequence of steps most likely to be successful.

A Model of Conflict

To organize our discussion of the psychological and organizational factors that affect de-escalatory decision making, we offer a preliminary model (Figure 5.1) that depicts a conflict between two parties, A and B—individuals, organizations, or nations.

The interdependence of the antagonists in a conflict is one of the essential elements that a theory of de-escalation must address. Such interdependence can assume many forms, ranging from tangible and concrete to intangible and symbolic forms. An example of the former is competitive interdependence with respect to crucial resources, such as oil and the control of strategic waterways. Interdependence that is less tangible, although no less important to the parties involved, involves such abstract "goods" as security, status, prestige, or control over the "hearts and minds" of a coveted populace.

On one level, this interdependence reflects the objective state of relationship between the parties, such that the actions, decisions, or goal attainments of one directly affect those of the other. Such effects can be positive or negative, of course. When the effect of one party's actions on the other is negative, that is, when the attempt at goal attainment by one reduces or precludes goal attainment by the other, an objective conflict of interest exists.

Whatever the objective situation, it is *perceived* or *subjective conflict of interest* that is the immediate determinant of conflict behavior. Thus, the subjective representations of conflict of interest become especially important in understanding or predicting the behavior of the parties. As Figure 5.1 illustrates, subjective or perceived conflict of interest is affected not only by the objective situation but also by psychological characteristics of the two parties and of their organizations. Our emphasis on subjective conflict of interest as the proximal determinant of conflict behavior does not imply

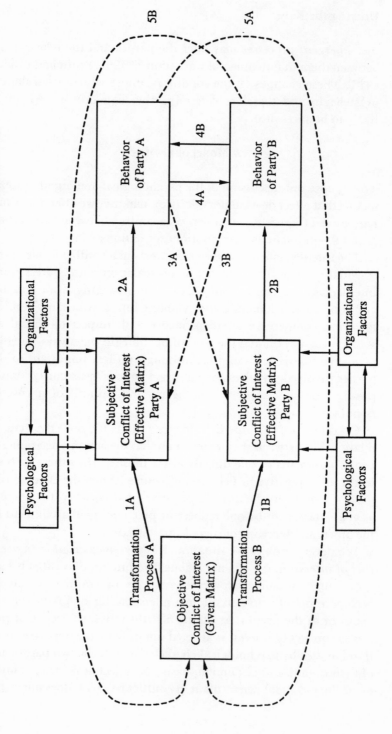

Figure 5.1. Transformational Processes and Action-Reaction Cycles in Conflict Situations.

that objective conflict of interest is unimportant. Both are essential elements in a theory of de-escalation, and objective conflict of interest is in most cases a major predictor of the level of perceived conflict of interest.

However, the objective bases of interdependence and conflict of interest may be either accurately or inaccurately perceived by the parties involved (Jervis, 1976). Either party may be mistaken about the degree of interdependence or even whether it is positive or negative. In the early stages of World War II, both England and the Soviet Union clearly recognized their interdependence with Germany with respect to their own security and sovereignty. However, both Chamberlain and Stalin were mistaken in believing that Hitler viewed this interdependence in positive or mutualistic terms rather than in negative or oppositional terms.

The relationship between objective states of conflict and the parties' subjective representations of those conditions can be understood as "transformations" of payoff matrices (Kelley, 1979, 1983). Following Kelley (1979), our model posits that decision makers do not respond directly to the objective properties of a situation, which he calls the "given matrix." Instead, they respond selectively to certain properties, resulting in an "effective matrix" or "transformed" representation of the situation. It is the effective matrix that is most closely linked to behavior.

In discussing the importance of transformations in social interaction, Kelley (1979, p. 12) offers a functionalistic argument. "Better given outcomes," he suggests "can be assured and/or inefficient conflict processes can be avoided if, through reconceptualization, the persons transform the pattern of their interdependence." Thus, transformations can be considered functional in conflict situations to the extent that they facilitate or promote de-escalation, and dysfunctional to the extent that they inhibit or undermine the process of de-escalation.

Because Kelley is concerned primarily with interpersonal relationships, he gives special attention to the role of psychological factors in the transformation process. These factors, which he terms *dispositions,* include an individual's social values, motives, goals, attitudes, and beliefs. Kelley proposes that these dispositions can be conceptualized as "rules" governing transformations. For example, a superpower leader with a relatively competitive disposition might act in terms of interpersonal rules such as "Always make your opponent blink first," "Always hit twice as hard as you are hit," or "Offer the carrot but be ready with the stick."

At the individual level, these transformational rules may be conscious or unconscious. At the organizational level, they are likely to be codified, integrated, and elaborated as organizational routines, institutional lessons derived from prior conflicts, and espoused political ideologies. These rules in turn are enacted or expressed in behavior toward the other party. The interaction of these behaviors produces escalation or de-escalation.

When two parties are engaged in active conflict, the transformation process becomes complex, and in Figure 5.1 we have attempted to represent something of that complexity. The conflict process can be thought of as beginning with an objective or given payoff matrix, although the point of origin in a conflict is almost always arbitrary. The transformation process, however, is not likely to be the same for both parties, since it is determined not only by the given matrix but also by the enduring properties of the perceiving party. Thus, in a two-party conflict there is one given matrix but two effective matrices, and the effective matrix for each party is the proximal determinant of its behavior. These processes are illustrated in Figure 5.1 by arrows 1A and 1B and 2A and 2B.

The further complexities of conflict interaction illustrated in Figure 5.1 involve the three main effects of conflict behavior. The behavior of each party, as it is perceived, alters the effective matrix of the other (arrows 3A and 3B). The conflict behavior of each also generates direct interactive responses for the other (arrows 4A and 4B). These sequences can be thought of as action-reaction cycles (see Davis and Powell, Chapter Four of this volume). Finally, the conflict behavior of each party can affect the objective conflict of interest between them (arrows 5A and 5B).

Having described the basic elements of the conflict model, it remains for us to elaborate what the model tells us about the de-escalation process. We assume that in the majority of cases objective conflicts of interest, no matter how severe, offer some potential for resolution. Most conflicts have mixed motives, which means that there exist both competitive or distributive solutions that further one party's interest at the expense of the other and cooperative or integrative solutions that promote the joint interests of both parties.

For a variety of reasons, however, opportunities for de-escalation and cooperative resolution may not be perceived by the parties at conflict. In terms of our model, the potential for de-escalation inherent in an objective conflict of interest is then lost in the dysfunctional transformations by which the parties move from objective to subjective conflict of interest. Our interest in de-escalation directs our attention to such missed opportunities and to the factors that account for them. Such factors act as barriers to de-escalation.

Barriers to De-Escalation

The model we have described implies that many failures to initiate and sustain a de-escalatory process can be traced to underlying properties of organizations and psychological characteristics of decision makers and that these factors operate by affecting the transformation process that links objective conflict of interest to subjective or perceived conflict of interest.

Psychological Factors

Many psychological factors can affect decision makers' perceptions of conflict. Previous research (Jervis, 1976; Jervis, Lebow, and Stein, 1986; Tetlock and McGuire, 1986) has identified numerous perceptual, cognitive, motivational, and social-psychological variables that influence how decision makers interpret and respond to international conflict. We will focus on a few factors of particular relevance to understanding why decision makers might fail to initiate or sustain a de-escalatory process. We will categorize these processes as (1) inadequate cognitive representations of the situation, (2) motivational deterrents to de-escalation, and (3) affective factors in de-escalation.

Inadequate Cognitive Representations. To de-escalate a conflict, decision makers must be able to envision a future conflict-free state and the transitions or steps needed to reach that state. Thus, their cognitive representations of the conflict are important. Unfortunately, the sources of inadequacy in those representations are nu-

merous and serious. In this section we consider four of them: biased
construals, inappropriate analogies, zero-sum biases, and reliance
on conflict imagery.

Biased construals. From the standpoint of normative or rational
models of decision making, it might be expected that decision makers would use new information in order to update or revise their
preexisting beliefs about an antagonist. Hints of more conciliatory
behavior or cooperative intentions on the part of an antagonist
would then be taken as evidence of at least the potential for de-
escalation in a given conflict or improvement in the overall relationship between the parties. However, the tendency by decision
makers to assimilate new information in a biased manner in order
to fit preexisting theories or expectations has been well documented, both by international relations theorists (Jervis, 1976) and
by experimental social psychologists (Kramer, 1989; Lord, Ross,
and Lepper, 1979). These studies demonstrate that decision makers
tend to fit incoming information, especially when it is ambiguous
or inconclusive, into their preexisting stereotypes and categories.

Such perceptual differences between parties at conflict and the
importance of those differences in determining their behavior are
also conspicuous in their biased punctuation of an action-reaction
sequence (Swann, Pelham, and Roberts, 1987; Watzlawick, Beavin,
and Jackson, 1967). Party A is likely to see a series of continuing
or escalating conflict behaviors as a sequence of B-A, B-A, B-A, in
which the initial aggressive move is made by the other party, B, and
the moves by A are always defensive responses to those moves. The
perceptions of party B describe the sequence as A-B, A-B, A-B, in
which the roles of aggressor and defender are reversed.

The observable behaviors, of course, are likely to be unpunctu-
ated, forming a sequence in which punctuation is therefore arbitrary, in the eye of the beholder. This is a phenomenon familiar to
every parent, as the ancient and mutual accusation "He/she started
it!" is shouted by both small warriors. And it is no less familiar in
the long sad history of international conflict. Arabs and Israelis, for
example, choose different historical moments of origin in order to
justify their own claims to land and thus to cast the other in the role
of invader.

Use of inappropriate analogies. When trying to decide what course of action to take during a conflict, decision makers may search for or invoke past conflicts for guidance (Neustadt and May, 1986). While invoking analogies is a useful heuristic, it may lead to inappropriate comparisons or conclusions. The lessons supposedly learned from past conflicts or crises may be uncritically applied. For example, when President Kennedy was trying to decide how to deal with the Soviets over Berlin, he compared the situation to conditions preceding World War II, conditions that became highly salient to him while he was researching his book *Why England Slept*. Such analogies may lead to errors of judgment in either direction; for purposes of de-escalation, the problem is that they may cause decision makers to overestimate the hostility or aggressive intent of the other party. Moreover, the lessons themselves may be wrong, as evidenced by the recent critical reexamination of the Cuban missile crisis (Blight and Welch, 1989; Garthoff, 1987).

Worst-case planning, used indiscriminately, can be regarded as a special kind of inappropriate analogy. Kramer, Meyerson, and Davis (forthcoming) show that, as a habitual mode of planning, worst-case planning can lead decision makers to overestimate the level of threat in a situation, overattribute hostile or competitive motives to other parties, and underestimate their responsiveness to cooperative or de-escalatory initiatives.

Zero-sum bias. The zero-sum bias is a tendency to view the world as a war of all against all, in which the quantity of desirable things is fixed and a greater share for one means a lesser share for another. Such a belief plays a central role in what are called operational codes, ways of imposing order on an ambiguous and complex environment. People who hold the zero-sum bias are thus likely to perceive specific conflict situations in terms that make de-escalation costly and undesirable.

There is evidence that the zero-sum bias is common in our culture. Early research with randomly assigned groups of executives showed that the groups developed highly competitive relationships, even though there was no objective scarcity in the desired outcome of personal learning and instructor approval (Blake, Shepard, and Mouton, 1964). More recently, Thompson and Hastie (1988) found evidence that negotiators often assume that their interests are incompatible, even when there is integrative potential in the situation. The construal of the problem as "zero sum" reduces the likelihood that parties will discover integrative or cooperative solutions.

Conflict imagery. In addition to the use of explicit analogies as discussed above, images and metaphors are prominent in the decision-making process and in subsequent explication. Dean Rusk's famous quip to President Kennedy at the height of the Cuban missile crisis that "we were toe to toe and the other guy just blinked" strongly suggests a schoolyard confrontation from which an unambiguous winner and loser must emerge. Metaphors of this kind, which may be invoked consciously or used unconsciously, are more significant for their connotative than for their denotative value. They are a kind of shorthand that carries more meaning than a literal interpretation would imply. They dramatize the issue under discussion. More important, by implying the resemblance of a complex and unfamiliar event to something known and familiar, metaphors suggest known and familiar solutions and thus seem to illuminate the issue at hand. The problem, of course, is that the light thus shed may be false. The tendency of male political leaders to view international conflicts and negotiations in terms of win-lose metaphors derived from their early experience with sports and organizational competitions is disastrously inappropriate when applied to a confrontation between nuclear powers (Frank, 1987; Greenhalgh, 1987; see also Kelley and Schmidt, 1989).

Motivational Deterrents to De-Escalation. Thus far we have been concerned with the effects of cognitive factors on the processing of information under conditions of conflict. We have said nothing about motivational factors that might impede the de-escalation process. All cognitive processes involve some motivational component, but the use of inappropriate analogies, the imposition of a zero-sum framework on interactions irrespective of objective conditions, and addiction to negative images of conflict are tendencies in which the dominant element is cognitive.

By contrast, certain distortions of information about oneself and others show a powerful motivational component; they serve to maintain positive views of the self, either directly or by depreciating others, and they defend in other ways against unacceptable beliefs, perceptions, or feelings (Jervis, 1985; Kramer and Newton, 1989;

Tetlock and McGuire, 1986). These biases reflect subconscious as well as conscious needs to see the world in certain ways, and they assume strong motivational forces of which the person may be only partially aware.

Positive illusions of self. Many studies show that decision makers maintain a variety of positive illusions about themselves and their behavior (Taylor and Brown, 1988). Three categories of such illusions seems especially likely to affect de-escalatory processes: overly positive self-evaluations, unrealistic optimism, and exaggerated perceptions of control or mastery.

Overly positive self-evaluations are not limited to negotiators and decision makers. People generally perceive positive traits or descriptions to be more true of themselves than of others (Brown, 1986). Of special importance for the dynamics of conflict is the tendency for people to perceive themselves as fairer than others (Messick and Sentis, 1979). Kramer and Newton (1989) measured this tendency before and after a simulated conflict. Before the conflict, individuals believed that they were more cooperative, fairer, and more likely to reciprocate concessions than other people. Moreover, after interacting with a person randomly assigned to them, they rated themselves as having acted more fairly and more cooperatively and as having been more reciprocative during the experimental conflict.

Unrealistic optimism includes the tendency of decision makers to believe that their negotiated outcomes will be more favorable than those of others, on average, and that they are less likely than others to experience negative life events. The unreality of such expectations is inferred not from the individual case but from the fact that the expectation to be above average is general. Perceptions of control and mastery show a similar pattern, reflecting a tendency for people to believe that, compared to others, they have greater influence over events than is objectively warranted.

To include such cognitive illusions of the self among the motivational factors that affect de-escalation implies that they serve important psychological functions for the individual, such as protecting self-esteem or making it possible to undertake and persist at difficult and challenging tasks (Taylor, 1989; Taylor and Brown, 1988). Whatever their positive intrapsychic functions, however, the effect of these attributes on de-escalation is likely to be negative. For example, the tendency to maintain overly positive self-evaluations may lead each party in a conflict to construe its own behavior in favorable terms, while evaluating comparable actions by the other in less favorable terms. Both may then regard the efforts they make to de-escalate a conflict as fair and balanced, whereas similar concessions offered by others are viewed as less so. Whether for this or other reasons, decision makers tend to value their own actions or initiatives more highly than those made by an adversary (Stillinger, Epelbaum, Keltner, and Ross, 1989). Stillinger and others, for example, demonstrated in several experiments that individuals overvalue their own concessions, while discounting the importance or value of concessions made by an adversary. In some cases, the mere fact that an adversary is willing to concede something may be taken as evidence that the concession must be of little value. Thus, one nation's willingness to reduce or eliminate some component of its strategic forces may be construed by the other as evidence that the component is obsolete.

Similarly, to the extent that people are generally overoptimistic in their expectations about their own future outcomes, their aspirations for negotiation may be unrealistically high. When both parties have unrealistically high aspirations, it becomes difficult for them to find mutually satisfying or acceptable compromise positions.

Negative perceptions of the other party. To the extent that positive illusions about oneself and one's group, organization, or nation are expressed in relative terms, they imply unrealistically negative attributions to others. The tendency toward such attributions has been a subject of social-psychological investigation for many years and under many conceptual labels, among them prejudice, stereotyping, nationalism, and ethnocentrism. The term *ethnocentrism* was first proposed early in the century (Sumner, 1906), and it has continued in use as a collective concept for a large set of attitudes and perceptions that serve to elevate the in-group in relation to outsiders. (See Brewer and Kramer, 1985, for one review.) To the ethnocentric person, in-group attitudes appear to be universal, in-group beliefs intrinsically true, in-group values centrally human, and in-group actions inherently moral (Seeman, 1983; Janis, 1983).

Such attitudes and perceptions are demonstrably handicapping for negotiation and the integrative resolution of conflicts. For example, stereotyping means that the out-group is seen as monolithic, and responses to representatives of that group therefore tend not to be appropriately differentiated, either individually or situationally. Such stereotyping is not only an initial handicap to negotiation and de-escalation; it tends to be resistant to new information generated in the negotiating process. Indeed, prejudice, of which stereotyping is a manifestation, has been defined as prejudgment that is not reversible when exposed to new knowledge. One effect is reduced likelihood of responding to conciliatory acts (Rothbart and Hallmark, 1988).

Negatively distorted perceptions of one's adversaries, like positively distorted perceptions of oneself and one's groups, have their uses. They may, for example, motivate persistent and even heroic behavior. Nevertheless, unrealistically negative views of one's adversaries, and the psychological processes that sustain such illusions, are among the significant barriers to de-escalation.

Loss aversion. De-escalation almost always requires the acceptance of loss in some sense. The loss may be perceived rather than real; it may be a loss only in relation to previous unrealistic expectations. It may be merely a forgone gain, but the sense of loss is real and it is a barrier to de-escalation. Many of the psychological factors already discussed contribute to this syndrome of loss aversion. For example, people high in self-esteem are likely to feel that they deserve to experience gains rather than losses, and people with ethnocentric views are likely to believe that their negatively valued adversaries are undeserving and overbenefitted.

There is, however, an additional and powerful aspect of loss that is an inevitable part of de-escalation. In order to initiate and sustain a de-escalatory process, decision makers must modify their own behavior. The very term *de-escalation* implies change, and change means the modification or abandonment of a previous course of action. Resistance to change among individuals and groups has been studied for many years (Coch and French, 1948), and more recent research has documented its power in organizational settings. For example, studies on the escalation of commitment (Ross and Staw, 1986; Staw, 1981; Staw and Ross, 1987) and psychological entrapment (Brockner and Rubin, 1985) have demonstrated that decision makers tend to remain committed to a course of action even in the face of mounting evidence that the course of action is costly or flawed. Rather than change their decision, individuals are likely under some circumstances to throw good resources after bad.

Staw (1981) proposes several motivational factors that foster irrational perseverance on the part of decision makers. First, pressures to justify previous decisions may cause them to bolster evidence in their favor and minimize or ignore evidence to the contrary. Such psychological processes Staw characterizes ironically as retrospective rationality. The tendency to rationalize prior actions can reflect both psychological pressures toward self-justification and pressures to appear rational to external audiences to whom decision makers feel accountable (Sutton and Kramer, Chapter Seven of this volume).

In addition to such retrospective rationality, decision makers may succumb to a form of prospective pseudorationality, whereby they evaluate the future probability or value of anticipated positive outcomes to be greater because of the "sunk costs." Having invested substantial resources to achieve a goal, decision makers may perceive the goal to be closer than it actually is and exaggerate the significance of events that suggest its imminence. Among some of the principal U.S. decision makers involved in the management of the Vietnam War, for example, there were frequent unrealistic allusions to being able to see "light at the end of the tunnel." General Westmoreland and President Johnson attached particular significance to the so-called crossover point, the point at which the enemy was allegedly being "attrited" faster than it could replenish its forces (Berman, 1989). Such reference points may represent highly salient, if illusory, indicators of success.

Erroneous perceptions of goal proximity and consequent resistance to change may be especially likely when an organization has a history of success (Starbuck and Milliken, 1988). The Bay of Pigs invasion attempt has been criticized as an example of a poorly conceived decision with a disastrous outcome, but it is important to note that it followed a series of military or quasi-military successes in other countries for which the decision-making process may have been no different.

Studies of commitment and entrapment have focused primarily

on decision makers' concerns about the perceived rationality or consistency of their decisions. In the case of political leaders, concern about other facets of their self-concept may also cause them to remain committed to a course of action long after objective evidence urges change or abandonment. For example, the desire to see oneself as strong, potent, and heroic may impel leaders to persist rather than back down. It may lead also to the adoption of confrontational tactics. Getting the other guy to blink first may be perceived to be as important as peacefully resolving a conflict. The motivation to avoid losing or accepting defeat may also be very strong (Greenhalgh, 1987). Lyndon Johnson, for example, did not want to go down in history as the first president to lose a war. Such motivations may be especially potent among elites who have reached their positions precisely by being tough and perseverant (Frank, 1987).

It is likely that the culture of many organizations encourages the development of such tendencies, first by promoting to positions of leadership people who persist in the face of adversity, and then by rewarding leaders who continue to show such traits. Nor is this entirely irrational; commitment to a course of action, courage in carrying it out, and resistance to discouragement are not trivial virtues, and under most circumstances they may be presumed to contribute to organizational survival. Like other virtues, however, they can be practiced to excess, and it is excess of perseverance that prevents change from escalation or stalemate to de-escalation.

The interaction between psychological and organizational processes is further illustrated by the organizational manifestations of commitment. When decision-making elites in an organization commit themselves to a major policy or course of action, their commitment is likely to have pervasive effects on organization structure. Subunits, specialized positions, or job descriptions are created to carry out the elite decision. Ross and Staw (1986) have used the term *institutional embeddedness* to refer to this process. The single-purpose nature of these subunits and positions may contribute to their efficiency in carrying out one course of action, but it may also make policy change more difficult to enact. Their specialization builds in a kind of organizational inertia that resists change. The disruption of Eisenhower's summit conference with Khrushchev by the shooting down of Francis Powers's secret U-2 reconnaissance plane can be interpreted as an example of this phenomenon. Eisenhower hoped the conference might begin a process of de-escalation, but the U-2 program of military reconnaissance and the planes assigned to it were single-purpose organizational devices not easily diverted from their previously assigned function or usable for other purposes.

Affective Factors in De-Escalation. Although high levels of arousal and affect are obvious concomitants of conflict, they are also much neglected topics for research. In fact, they are not afforded systematic attention in any of the major models of conflict. It is not even easy to find a taxonomy of those affective or emotional states that are relevant to conflict situations, although such a taxonomy would presumably include such feelings as anger, frustration, hopelessness, helplessness, fear, relief, depression, elation, hatred, and affection.

Earlier research on personality factors, which can be considered as tendencies toward different patterns of emotionality, showed rather spotty results in relation to conflict behavior. For example, certain personality characteristics of managers and union stewards, especially their needs for power and dominance, were associated with higher levels of labor-management conflict at the plant level; managers and stewards high in need for affiliation, on the other hand, were more likely to behave accommodatively (Stagner, 1962; Bass and Dunteman, 1963).

Early findings of this kind were not followed up, however. There has been some speculation about personality traits that might lead to constructive approaches to conflict, but they have been little researched in real-life situations. The effects of personality have been investigated in conflict games, but without consistent results (Terhune, 1970; Deutsch, 1971). Perhaps the most general findings thus far are that situational factors attenuate the impact of personality effects (Rapoport and Chammah, 1965; Terhune and Firestone, 1967; Katz and Kahn, 1978) or interact with them (McClintock and Liebrand, 1988).

We have proposed a causal sequence that begins with such situational factors and leads from them to individual transformations, that is, from the objective to the subjective payoff matrix. These transformations we would expect to be moderated or intensified by personality characteristics and emotional states and would in turn affect judgment, choice, and behavior. That causal sequence remains to be fully demonstrated, but it is consistent with earlier research and with the decision model proposed by Janis (Chapter Eight of this volume). Of the four main pathways to defective decision making in that model, one is defined primarily by emotive factors. When such factors are evoked, the decision maker is less likely to undertake the tasks of vigilant problem solving and more likely to rely on simple responses such as "retaliate" or "avoid thinking about it."

Organizational Factors

What does an organizational perspective require us to add to our analysis of barriers to de-escalation? One answer is that we must take account of the organization embeddedness of the interacting parties.

Role Constraints. By including organizational embeddedness as a factor in conflict and negotiation between organizations and nations, we recognize that the decision makers responsible for de-escalating a conflict are not free agents but people behaving in accord with their organizational roles. These roles are enacted in the context of a complex network of organizational relations.

The importance of such roles is apparent when we compare statements of public figures before and after their retirement from public life or even when they move from one organizational role to another. In 1960, President Eisenhower issued a remarkable warning to the American people about the dangers of the military-industrial complex and a hopeful prophesy that some day the yearning of the people for peace would compel their governments to provide it for them. These statements were part of his farewell address to the nation. Similarly, Robert McNamara proposed that the United States might initiate the process of nuclear de-escalation by unilateral cuts in the number of warheads to 50 percent of existing levels, but this proposal was made only after he had left the position of secretary of defense and was speaking as head of the World Bank. Similarly, Caspar Weinberger as head of the Budget Office in President Reagan's cabinet had earned the nickname of "Cap the Knife" for his insistence on severe reductions in the federal budget. In contrast, his performance as secretary of defense set an all-time record for unrestrained demands for increased military expenditures. These examples suggest that pronouncements made easily during exit from office or change from one position to another may be personally or politically impossible from within.

Such differences between statements by the same person before and after a major change in role do not necessarily imply hypocrisy or even a sense of sustained conflict between personal convictions and demands of the organizational role. No doubt some people speak hypocritically and some are tortured by what has been termed person-role conflict. But role expectations affect attitudes and perceptions as well as behavior; indeed, such attitudinal and perceptual changes are probably the main proximal determinants of behavioral change (Lieberman, 1956; Katz and Kahn, 1978).

It is an irony of hierarchical organization that people whose distance from the center of policy-making or proximity to the organizational boundary enables them to take a more critical stance are unlikely to communicate their criticisms. Their hesitancy stems in part from lack of easy access to the decision makers, in part from an understandable tendency toward risk aversion in their careers (Janis, Chapter Eight of this volume), and in part from the effects of socialization in subordinate roles. For example, although Chester Bowles, a junior officer in the Department of State in the early 1960s, felt that the Bay of Pigs invasion plan was seriously flawed, he hesitated to inform the president, feeling it was "not his place" to do so (Janis, 1983; Kennedy, 1988).

Complexities of Role Conflict. The conflict experienced by people in such situations, while personally painful and organizationally significant, is easily understood; it is a clash between personal knowledge and moral values, on the one hand, and considerations of role constraints and career security on the other. Conflicts of this type, which have been called person-role (Kahn and others, 1964), have been much studied, as have the effects of conflicting demands on individuals within a given role (Miles, 1976; Adams, 1976). The research, however, has investigated the effects of role conflict as a source of stress on the individual and has neglected its effects on organizational performance.

The effects of role conflict are greatly complicated when we take into account more than one level of organization. Actions that deliberately escalate conflict at one level may be taken for the purpose of de-escalating it at another level and may be successful in doing so. When President Kennedy discovered that the Soviets had secretly installed missiles in Cuba, he recognized the political necessity for assertive action. If he did nothing, he noted in the midst of the crisis, he would be impeached (Kennedy, 1969, 1988). Similarly, demonstrations and protests against the continued involvement of the United States in the Vietnam War certainly increased conflict within the United States, but at the same time they may have contributed to the ultimate de-escalation of that war.

In a similar way, actions taken to reduce conflict between nations may increase the level of conflict within them, at least in the short run. The assassination of Anwar Sadat after his peacemaking mission to Israel is a case in point. Fear of being labeled disloyal or traitorous may also prevent leaders from taking such initiatives. Sutton and Kramer (Chapter Seven of this book) provide additional examples of how steps taken to de-escalate a conflict at an interorganizational or international level may increase it at a lesser (intranational or intraorganizational) level, thus undermining or interfering with the de-escalation process.

In short, the organizational effects of role expectations are complicated by the fact that there are multiple constituencies whose claims may be incompatible. Special-interest groups, each with its own agenda, may expect national leaders to pursue courses of action that cannot be reconciled. Wise leadership then consists of assessing the costs in advance and choosing the course of action that is most consistent with long-term organizational (or national) survival.

Dysfunctional Tendencies in Information Flow. The exercise of such wisdom is made more difficult by several organizational tendencies that are both common and dysfunctional, all of them affecting the quality and completeness of upward information flow. One of these, the deliberate withholding of information for hierarchical reasons, has already been noted; it is a dysfunctional side effect of hierarchical power.

Another is the inherent tendency to see new things in old ways—that is, to assimilate new information to existing frames of reference rather than to consider altering the frame. At the individual level this is a familiar and to some extent an unavoidable process. Decision makers tend to fit incoming information into preexisting categories and schemes (Fiske and Taylor, 1984; Jervis, 1976). It is exaggerated in organizations by the accumulation of organizational routines, standard operating procedures that have the force of widely shared role requirements. Such routines are an essential element in organizational functioning and efficiency. They constitute an organization's repertoire of readily available responses, and they stipulate, explicitly or implicitly, the external stimuli to which those responses are appropriate. To the extent that the organizational environment is stable, the routines are likely to be adequate. Significant external changes, however, may create demands or opportunities that go beyond the existing organizational repertoire. It is the distortion or disregard of such changes that puts the organization at risk, and it is environmental changes of that significance that are most vulnerable to misinterpretation. (See, for example, Snyder's [1984] discussion of the "ideology of the offensive" and escalation of conflict in the First World War.)

The reasons go beyond considerations of organizational routines. Routines and procedures are embellished and reinforced by organizational ideologies, which make major demands for change matters of principle and value rather than mere pragmatism. Each organization has a distinctive vocabulary of motives—acceptable and unacceptable reasons for doing things, and organizational scholars more generally acknowledge the importance of the concept of culture at the organizational level. Ideology and culture are even more powerfully present at the national level, where they also tend to limit the pace and possibility for change.

The interpretation of external events is not uniform, however, throughout either organizations or nations. Organizations are composed of subsystems that perform different functions—production, maintenance, boundary relations, adaptation, and management (Katz and Kahn, 1978). These different subsystems stand in different relationships to the environment of the organization, and to some extent they have distinctive subcultures. They are likely to differ therefore in their interpretation of external events and in judgment about appropriate organizational responses.

To the extent that such subsystem differences are understood and tolerated by organizational leaders and their expression is accepted or even rewarded, the upward flow of information in the organization is more likely to represent the complexity and diversity of the external world and the changes in it. To the extent that leaders do not recognize and utilize such internal differences, they will be deprived of important information, especially of the kind that calls for significant organizational change (George, 1980). At the national level, leaders have the advantage of the political process, by which subsystem differences of some kinds are made visible and vocal. Nevertheless, we believe that nations, like organizations, suffer from dysfunctional tendencies in the flow of information to top levels of decision making.

Implications for De-Escalation

The psychological and organizational barriers to de-escalation that we have just reviewed are imposing but not insurmountable. Their effect on the transformation process (Figure 5.1) is to exaggerate objective conflicts of interest so that the conflict of interest as perceived by each party is more intense than the objective facts would warrant. Perceptions of common interests are reduced or prevented, as is the recognition of positive changes in the objective situation (Plous, 1985).

The second main effect of these barriers is thus the perpetuation of the status quo, and not only in a static sense. Their effect is inertial, so that organizational processes already in motion are continued. They do this in large part by preventing decision makers from detecting and interpreting appropriately changes in their environments, especially changes in the behavior of their antagonists and/or opportunities for more cooperative relationships.

Even the attempts of decision makers to de-escalate conflicts can be impeded or frustrated by these barriers. On the one hand, the decision makers may initiate policies that have unintended and undesired consequences and, on the other, they may fail to take actions that might be effective in breaking a stalemate or stopping an escalation.

Mere awareness of these barriers may enable parties at conflict to reduce or remove them in some cases. For example, Janis (Chapter Eight) describes the ways in which procedures of vigilant problem solving can overcome the tendency to rely on organizational routines that emphasize continuity rather than change. Reduction of these barriers in turn increases the congruence between objective and subjective (organizationally perceived) conflicts and commonalities of interest. Such congruence does not in itself lead to de-escalation, but it makes de-escalation more likely to the extent that the objective situation makes it desirable.

Approaches to De-Escalation

Our discussion thus far has considered two sets of conditions necessary for the de-escalation of conflict. The first is a state of perceived interdependence between the parties, an interdependence that is either unavoidable, potentially rewarding, or both. Without such interdependence, as we have said, there is no motivation for decision makers either to bear the costs of conflict or to make the effort to de-escalate it. The second set of conditions for de-escalating an existing conflict involves the reduction of barriers—cognitive, motivational, and organizational.

These conditions, however necessary for de-escalation, are not sufficient to initiate the process. For the process of de-escalation to begin, at least one party to the conflict—and preferably both, of course—must perceive the costs and risks of continued conflict as unacceptably high. On this much, researchers on problems of conflict tend to agree. They differ, however, in their emphasis on self-initiated versus third-party-initiated approaches to de-escalation, and they differ also in the kinds of initiating moves that are most likely to be successful.

Unilateral Initiatives

Approaches based on unilateral initiatives (that is, steps that the primary parties themselves can take) focus on two issues. First, how do the parties get the de-escalatory process going? And, second, how do they sustain it?

Perhaps the simplest and most direct way to initiate a de-escalatory change is for one of the antagonists to make one or more de-escalatory moves and thus interrupt an existing stalemate or escalating sequence. Such an initiative is direct in that it immediately alters the interaction pattern, and it is simple in that it requires no prior introduction of third parties or structural changes. One can imagine a move of this kind being made either as the first of an unconditional and unlimited sequence or in more limited contingent fashion. A considerable research literature has developed on the relative effectiveness of such initiatives. (See Lindskold, 1986, for an overview.) With respect to unconditional pacifism, the experimental evidence is discouraging. At least in the laboratory, unvarying cooperative behavior leads to exploitation. Opponents are pleased by unconditional benevolence, puzzled by it, and take advantage of it (Solomon, 1960; Shure, Meeker, and Hansford, 1965; Axelrod, 1984; Deutsch, 1986).

Initiatives that involve *conditional* or contingent cooperation, on the other hand, appear to be effective in eliciting reciprocal cooperation from opponents. Early experimental research along these lines involved games in which a confederate made an initial cooperative move and requested a reciprocal act of cooperation, and the results were consistently positive (Deutsch, 1973; Swingle, 1970). More recently, the computer tournaments developed by Axelrod (1984) generated similar results. Rapaport's tit-for-tat strategy began each game sequence with a single cooperative move but made its second and succeeding moves identical to whatever the opponent's response had been. The strategy was thus retaliative, but it was also forgiving; each new game sequence was again begun with a cooperative move, regardless of what the opponent's behavior had been in the preceding sequence. In two "international tournaments" this strategy proved superior to all others submitted by game theorists, both in eliciting cooperation and in maximizing joint return.

Deutsch's (1986) nonpunitive strategy is similar but more forgiving than tit-for-tat. It involves three successive cooperative moves by a confederate, regardless of whether or not they are reciprocated; thereafter, the confederate (with a few prescribed exceptions) matches whatever the experimental subject did on the preceding trial. The logic of this strategy is that the norm of reciprocity builds in strength over the series of three cooperative moves and that the defensive response thereafter avoids the exploitation to which unconditional continuing cooperation is subjected. Deutsch's results show superior payoffs for this strategy over both punitive and pacific (turn-the-other-cheek) strategies, with the margin of difference increasing as the experimental games continue.

Osgood's (1962) strategy of graduated reciprocation in tension reduction (GRIT) is similar in conception, but the limits on the number of unreciprocated cooperative moves are more flexible. This strategy was first proposed without any accompanying data but, perhaps in lieu of that, Osgood's small book contained in addition to the proposal itself a fictional account of an American president's attempt to utilize the GRIT strategy in dealing with the USSR. From the viewpoint of organizational theory, the story was authentic in capturing the simultaneous, oppositional, and internally divisive developments that these peaceful initiatives stimulated in the two countries. In the Soviet Union the internal struggle was between those forces urging cooperative reciprocal responses and those demanding either no de-escalatory move or the exploitation of a seeming opportunity or weakness. In the United States, the internal struggle was between those supporting the cooperative effort and those who called it ill-advised, impeachable, or treasonable. More recent experimental work (Lindskold, 1986) tends to confirm the effectiveness of Osgood's approach.

Life does not replicate experiments, but Etzioni (1967) made a persuasive interpretation of John F. Kennedy's last months in office as approximating the GRIT strategy, and with considerable success: "For each move that was made, the Soviets reciprocated. Kennedy's 'Strategy for Peace' speech was matched by a conciliatory speech by Khrushchev; Kennedy's unilateral declaration of a cessation of tests was followed by a cessation of production of strategic bombers; spies were traded for spies; and so forth. The Russians showed no difficulties in understanding the gestures and in responding to psychological initiatives; and they participated in a 'you move–I move' sequence rather than waiting for simultaneous, negotiated, agreed-upon moves. Further, they shifted to multilateral-simultaneous arrangements once the appropriate mood was generated, as reflected in the test-ban treaty and other space resolution [sic]."

We cannot know whether, had Kennedy lived, this sequence might have continued. We do know that it was not. As this is written, we seem to be witnessing a major cooperative initiative, this time from the USSR under Gorbachev's leadership. Signs of reciprocation are already apparent. Its duration, the degree of reciprocity it induces, and its ultimate accomplishments remain to be determined.

Both tit-for-tat and GRIT are incremental and conditional strategies that enable each party to adapt to changes in the other's behavior. Both invite cooperation and are receptive to it, and both limit the risks of exploitation. Both are didactic, attempting to teach an opponent that cooperation is wanted but exploitation will be resisted. Osgood's GRIT approach and Axelrod's tit-for-tat strategy differ, however, in their assumptions about how this dual message can best be communicated and cooperation evoked. GRIT relies on the cumulative effects of a series of unilateral concessions to induce reciprocity and begin the de-escalatory process. Tit-for-tat argues for a single conciliatory initiative, followed by another if it is immediately reciprocated, but followed by a retaliatory or uncooperative response if it is not. In a new round of negotiation, however, tit-for-tat again risks a single conciliatory move. Tit-for-tat is thus forgiving, as we have said, but it is also more "myopic" and provocable than GRIT.

Both strategies have characteristic weaknesses and risks. Tit-for-tat may be too provocable (Bendor, 1987); the single cooperative move may not be enough to convince an opponent that the de-escalatory change is real, intended, or sincere. On the other hand, the series of unilateral de-escalatory moves specified by the GRIT strategy may be misunderstood as weakness. And both strategies, when they are brought into the real world, involve the difficulty of inventing or discovering one or more unilateral cooperative moves significant enough to impress an opponent and not so significant that they put the initiating organization or nation at serious risk. Keeping the initial series of unreciprocated moves within the bounds of security is a further limitation of the GRIT strategy that Osgood recognized, as he did the implied race between evoking a cooperative response from the external opponent and yielding to internal demands for less conciliatory behavior.

Both GRIT and tit-for-tat aim to establish a series of reciprocated de-escalatory moves, and both therefore must overcome the tendency of parties at conflict to overvalue their own concessions while devaluing concessions made by their opponents (Stillinger, Epelbaum, Keltner, and Ross, 1989). One way of dealing with this problem is to make the initial cooperative move so large or dramatic that it cannot be easily discounted. It may be that the unavoidable risks involved in making such moves are tolerable when both parties have sufficient retaliatory capacity to assure themselves against extreme exploitation. Research on this issue—the effect of varying magnitude of an initial cooperative move—remains to be done, but several such relationship-transforming initiatives have taken place at the international level in recent years. The visit of President Sadat to Israel is an obvious example, and the first visit of President Nixon to China is another. The initial approach of President Gorbachev to President Reagan might be cited as a third example, although in this case it is difficult to separate the effect of the initial move from that of the several unilateral concessions that followed it.

We can conclude that in spite of yet unanswered questions about the relative effectiveness of different unilateral initiatives, the possibility of de-escalation by actions of the protagonists themselves has been demonstrated both in the laboratory and in the world at large.

Third-Party Approaches

Much of the research on conflict resolution involves some form of intervention by third parties, explicit or implicit. The explicit interventions typically occur in organizational settings, with the third party in the role of mediator, arbitrator, or expert consultant. The implicit third-party interventions, seldom so acknowledged, occur mainly in experimental research. The designers of experiments, by altering payoff matrices, setting rules for communication between opponents, or providing advance instruction about the nature of the game, act as powerful third parties might in real-world settings. The analogy between organizations and nations is perhaps less robust for de-escalation via third-party interventions than for de-escalation by the opponents themselves, since nations seldom invite mediation and almost never accept arbitration, in which opponents agree in advance to be bound by the decision of the arbitrator. The potentialities for third-party interventions at the international level are sufficient, however, to justify some attention to organizational and experimental research on the subject.

The experimental evidence for interventions, perhaps more properly regarded as manipulations, that de-escalate conflict is persuasive with respect to at least four factors: reducing objective conflict of interest or increasing objective commonality of interest, altering the transformation process so that subjective conflict of interest is reduced or commonality is increased, facilitating communication before a move is made, and making it clear that the parties will be required to interact in the future.

In most laboratory games, objective conflict and commonality of interest constitute a single variable; changing the payoff matrix increases one and decreases the other. Experiments show that the proportion of cooperative as compared to uncooperative or defecting choices is highly correlated (.86 in two-person games) with the objective structure of the payoff matrix (Rapoport and Chammah, 1965; Solomon, 1960; Deutsch, 1971). Similar effects, though not quite so strong, have been obtained in the laboratory by varying the orienting instructions to experimental subjects and thus presumably the transformation process. For example, Deutsch (1973) and his colleagues presented the same game to different subjects in three different ways—as an exercise in cooperation and concern with the welfare of one's partner/opponent (cooperative orientation), in maximizing one's own winnings (individualistic orientation), or in maximizing one's winnings at the expense of one's partner/opponent (competitive orientation).

Two peculiarities of most conflict games, especially the widely used Prisoner's Dilemma, are the restriction on communication between the players and the improbability of future interaction with the same partners or opponents. Experimental subjects are not usually allowed to communicate their intentions before acting or to discuss their actions after making a move; they merely act, and their opponents must infer the reasons for past behaviors and predictions for the future solely on the basis of the actions themselves. When the constraint against communication is lifted, as it has been in at least a few experiments, cooperative behavior is significantly increased—except when subjects have been given competitive instructions before the game (Deutsch, 1973; Katz and Kahn, 1978). Finally, the probability of cooperative behavior in a conflict game is increased when the participants know that they will continue to interact with the same people (Marlow, Gergen, and Doob, 1966).

When we consider these findings in terms of the interventions that a third party might make in a real-life situation, their relevance seems somewhat uneven. A third party entering an organizational conflict as mediator or consultant can probably do little to alter the objective conflict of interest (payoff matrix). He or she might be able to do a great deal, however, to alter the transformation, that is, the ways in which opponents perceive and interpret the existing conflicts and commonalities of interest. A third-party consultant should also be able to influence the state of communication between opponents, not so much by lifting a ban on communication as by establishing a norm of communicating in advance the intended move and the reasons for it. The expectation of future interaction is already present in most organizational conflicts, but it is possible for a third party to remind opponents of the long-term value of the relationship at times when the heat of the exchange makes it neglected or forgotten.

Research on third-party interventions in real-life organizations is generally consistent with the experimental findings, although the limited power of the consultant as compared to the experimenter is apparent throughout these studies. For example, Walton (1969) was able to help a "country director" in the U.S. Department of State reduce conflict with a dozen other relevant agencies by creating a new lateral structure, a voluntary monthly meeting of agency representatives who had in common a concern for the country in question. In the language of conflict games, Walton increased commonality of interest by introducing a new game, which would be played by a special subset of the parties at conflict. His assumption was that agreements reached by these agency representatives would then be accepted by their constituents, and this appears to have been the case. We interpret the dynamics of this intervention as a two-stage process, with an increase in objective commonality of interest achieved by creation of the new voluntary group and a subsequent reduction in subjective conflict of interest among the group's agency constituents.

Most third-party interventions in organizational conflicts concentrate on the transformation process and attempt to alter perceptions of conflicts and commonalities of interest in ways that de-escalate conflict behavior. Success along these lines has been reported in many studies, although the evidence is often less quantitative than we wish. Methods of altering the transformation process have emphasized training in integrative problem solving rather than competition or bargaining (Blake, Shepard, and Mouton, 1964; Walton and Dutton, 1969; Blake and Mouton, 1970; Lewis and Pruitt, 1971; Levi and Benjamin, 1977). Other interventions have successfully altered the transformation process by helping one or both parties to reconceptualize the conflict, either by fragmenting along the lines first proposed by Fisher (1964) or by emphasizing the larger context of common interests within which the conflict occurs (Druckman and Zechmeister, 1973; Thierry, 1977). The remaining third-party approaches to de-escalation that are suggested by our review of experimental research, requiring verbal communication between antagonists in advance of actions and stipulating that they will be interacting in the future, are to some extent built into most organizations. Both factors have been reported as conducive to prevention or de-escalation of organizational conflict (Lewis and Pruitt, 1971; Vliert, 1984).

As we have said, the extrapolation from the laboratory and organization to the international level is extremely tentative with respect to third-party interventions, for the most obvious of reasons: in disputes between nations a qualified, effective, and mutually acceptable third party simply may not exist. Especially in the case of the superpowers, no other countries can act as arbitrators and insist on cooperation. Even in disputes between nations of lesser power, a pragmatic wariness about the motives of third parties and an almost fanatic attachment to the principle of national sovereignty often combine to prevent effective intervention from outside.

Third-party interventions in disputes between nations will therefore require the adaptation or invention of forms appropriate to that level rather than the direct application of methods developed in other settings. For example, nations in conflict might agree to create bodies that would then function like third parties. It could be argued that the Standing Consultative Commission, despite its very limited powers, served some such function. A different example, in which a multistate body attempted to intervene between national antagonists, is provided by the Contadora Proposal. Heads of state of six Central American nations convened to develop a proposal for de-escalating the conflict between Nicaragua and the United States. The proposal did not lead directly to a de-escalation of that conflict, although it may have contributed to other efforts to do so. It does, however, suggest ways in which nations might obtain some of the advantages of third-party intervention at its best—saving face, putting psychological distance between key antagonists, providing equal representation, and perhaps making it possible to change actors who have too much invested in the conflict to consider anything but beating their opponents. This is another area where collaboration between organizational researchers and international relations theorists may prove particularly fruitful. There has been a great deal of interest among international relations theorists in recent years in how international alliances, especially security alliances, form. (See, for example, Walt, 1987.) Research by organizational theorists such as Borys and Jemison (1989) on "hybrid organizations," organizations created by two or more sovereign organizations in order to pursue common interests, may shed light on the process by which such internation structures evolve.

Conclusion

In this chapter we have attempted to provide a general framework for conceptualizing the process of conflict de-escalation, whether initiated by agencies external to the conflict or by the protagonists themselves. In doing so, we have suggested the broad outlines of a theory of de-escalation and indicated some of the many remaining tasks.

Our aim throughout the chapter has been to address problems of de-escalation in terms that are relevant to international conflicts and to show how recent research in organizations is at least suggestive for both understanding and resolving international conflicts.

We are sensitive to the limitations of the nation-organization analogy, however, and we have tried to present its limitations as well as its potentialities.

One way of overcoming those limitations is to search for better analogs than that of corporations and nations. Schelling (1960, p. 12), for example, proposed that gang warfare has much in common with war between nations: "Nations and outlaws both lack enforceable legal systems to help them govern their affairs. Both engage in the ultimate in violence. Both have an interest in avoiding violence, but the threat of violence is continually on call. It is interesting that racketeers, as well as gangs of delinquents, engage in limited war, disarmament and disengagement, surprise attack, retaliation and threat of retaliation; they worry about 'appeasement' and loss of face; they make alliances and agreements with the same disability that nations are subject to—the inability to appeal to higher authority in the interest of contract enforcement."

It is likely that gang warfare also presents some of the obstacles to research that we have noted in the case of international relations—especially secrecy and inaccessibility. Nevertheless, the argument holds: the use of smaller social units as models for nation-states has much to teach us, and we should not restrict ourselves to the corporate example.

In the search for such models and their use there is a convergence of interest and opportunity for scholars who study conflict in organizational settings and those concerned with international relations. The traditional compartmentalization of disciplines and specialties has kept them apart. We hope that this chapter may contribute to mutual awareness of their research and to opportunities for collaboration on problems of shared interest. None ranks higher in importance or potential than the de-escalation of conflict.

References

Adams, J. S. "The Structure and Dynamics of Behavior in Organizational Boundary Roles." In M. D. Dunnette (ed.), *Handbook of Industrial and Organizational Psychology*. Chicago: Rand McNally, 1976.

Allison, G. T. *Essence of Decision: Explaining the Cuban Missile Crisis.* Boston: Little, Brown, 1971.

Argyris, C. *Increasing Leadership Effectiveness.* New York: Wiley, 1976.

Axelrod, R. *The Evolution of Cooperation.* New York: Basic Books, 1984.

Bass, B. M., and Dunteman, G. "Behavior in Groups as a Function of Self, Interaction, and Task Orientation." *Journal of Abnormal and Social Psychology,* 1963, *66,* 419-428.

Bendor, J. "Cooperation in an Uncertain World." *American Journal of Political Science,* 1987, *28,* 531-558.

Berman, L. *Lyndon Johnson's War: The Road to Stalemate in Viet Nam.* New York: Norton, 1989.

Betts, R. K. *Nuclear Blackmail and Nuclear Balance.* Washington, D.C.: Brookings Institution, 1987.

Blake, R. R., and Mouton, J. S. "The Fifth Achievement." *Journal of Applied Behavioral Science,* 1970, *6,* 413-426.

Blake, R. R., Shepard, H. A., and Mouton, J. S. *Managing Intergroup Conflict in Industry.* Houston, Tex.: Gulf, 1964.

Blight, J. G., and Welch, D. A. *On the Brink: Americans and Soviets Reexamine the Cuban Missile Crisis.* New York: Hill & Wang, 1989.

Borys, B., and Jemison, D. B. "Hybrid Arrangements as Strategic Alliances: Theoretical Issues in Organizational Combinations." *Academy of Management Review,* 1989, *14,* 234-249.

Boulding, K. B. *Conflict and Defense.* New York: Harper & Row, 1966.

Brewer, M. B., and Kramer, R. M. "The Psychology of Intergroup Attitudes and Behavior." *Annual Review of Psychology,* 1985, *36,* 219-243.

Brockner, J., and Rubin, J. Z. *Entrapment in Escalating Conflicts.* New York: Springer-Verlag, 1985.

Brown, J. D. "Evaluations of Self and Others: Self-Enhancement Biases in Social Judgments." *Social Cognition,* 1986, *4,* 353-376.

Coch, L., and French, J.R.P., Jr. "Overcoming Resistance to Change." *Human Relations,* 1948, *1,* 512-533.

Deutsch, M. "Toward an Understanding of Conflict." *International Journal of Group Tensions,* 1971, *1,* 42-54.

Deutsch, M. *The Resolution of Conflict: Constructive and Destructive Processes.* New Haven, Conn.: Yale University Press, 1973.

Deutsch, M. "Strategies of Inducing Cooperation." In R. K. White (ed.), *Psychology and the Prevention of Nuclear War.* New York: New York University Press, 1986.

Druckman, D., and Zechmeister, K. "Conflict of Interest and Value Dissensus: Propositions in the Sociology of Conflict." *Human Relations,* 1973, *26,* 449–466.

Etzioni, A. "The Kennedy Experiment: Unilateral Initiatives." *Western Political Quarterly,* 1967, *20,* 12–23.

Fisher, R. "Fractioning Conflict." In R. Fisher (ed.), *International Conflict and Behavioral Science: The Craigville Papers.* New York: Basic Books, 1964.

Fiske, S. T., and Taylor, S. E. *Social Cognition.* New York: Random House, 1984.

Frank. J. D. "The Drive for Power and the Nuclear Arms Race." *American Psychologist,* 1987, *42,* 337–344.

Garthoff, R. *Explaining the Cuban Missile Crisis.* Washington, D.C.: Brookings Institution, 1987.

George, A. L. *Presidential Decisionmaking in Foreign Policy: The Effective Use of Information and Advice.* Boulder, Colo.: Westview, 1980.

George, A. L. *Managing U.S.-Soviet Rivalry: Problems of Crisis Prevention.* Boulder, Colo.: Westview, 1983.

Greenhalgh, L. "Interpersonal Conflicts in Organizations." In C. L. Cooper and I. T. Robertson (eds.), *International Review of Industrial and Organizational Psychology.* New York: Wiley, 1987.

Janis, I. L. *Groupthink.* (2nd ed.) Boston: Houghton Mifflin, 1983.

Jervis, R. *Perception and Misperception in International Politics.* Princeton, N.J.: Princeton University Press, 1976.

Jervis, R. "Perceiving and Coping with Threat." In R. Jervis, R. Lebow, and J. Stein (eds.), *Psychology and Deterrence.* Baltimore, Md.: Johns Hopkins University Press, 1985.

Jervis, R., Lebow, R. N., and Stein, J. *Psychology and Deterrence.* Baltimore, Md.: Johns Hopkins University Press, 1985.

Kahn, R. L., Wolfe, D. M., Quinn, R. P., Snoek, J. D., and Rosenthal, R. A. *Organizational Stress: Studies in Role Conflict and Ambiguity.* New York: Wiley, 1964.

Katz, D., and Kahn, R. L. *The Social Psychology of Organizations.* (2nd ed.) New York: Wiley, 1978.

Kelley, H. H. *Personal Relationships: Their Structures and Processes.* Hillsdale, N.J.: Erlbaum, 1979.

Kelley, H. H. "The Situational Origins of Human Tendencies." *Personality and Social Psychology Bulletin,* 1983, *9,* 8-30.

Kelley, H. H., and Schmidt, G. "The 'Aggressive Male' Syndrome: Its Possible Relevance for International Conflict." In P. C. Stern, R. Axelrod, R. Jervis, and R. Radner (eds.), *Perspectives on Deterrence.* New York: Oxford University Press, 1989.

Kennedy, R. F. *Thirteen Days: A Memoir of the Cuban Crisis.* New York: Norton, 1969.

Kennedy, R. F. *Robert Kennedy in His Own Words: The Unpublished Recollections of the White House Years.* New York: Bantam Books, 1988.

Kissinger, H. *The White House Years.* Boston: Little, Brown, 1979.

Kramer, R. M. "Windows of Vulnerability or Cognitive Illusions? Cognitive Processes and the Nuclear Arms Race." *Journal of Experimental Social Psychology,* 1989, *25,* 79-100.

Kramer, R. M., Meyerson, D., and Davis, G. "Deterrence and the Management of International Conflict: Components of Deterrent Decisions." In A. Rahim (ed.), *Conflict Management.* New York: Praeger, forthcoming.

Kramer, R. M., and Newton, E. "Positive Illusions in Negotiations." Unpublished manuscript, 1989.

Lebow, R. N. *Between Peace and War.* Baltimore, Md.: Johns Hopkins University Press, 1981.

Lebow, R. N. *Nuclear Crisis Management: A Dangerous Illusion.* Ithaca, N.Y.: Cornell University Press, 1987.

Levi, A. M., and Benjamin, A. "Focus and Flexibility in a Model of Conflict Resolution." *Journal of Conflict Resolution,* 1977, *21,* 405-425.

Lewis, S. A., and Pruitt, D. G. "Organizational, Aspiration Level, and Communication Freedom in Integrative Bargaining." *Proceedings of the American Psychological Association,* 1971, *6,* 221-222.

Lieberman, S. "The Effects of Changes in Roles on the Attitudes of Role Occupants." *Human Relations,* 1956, *9,* 385–402.

Lindskold, S. "GRIT: Reducing Distrust Through Carefully Introduced Conciliation." In S. Worchel and W. G. Austin (eds.), *Psychology of Intergroup Relations.* (2nd ed.) Chicago: Nelson-Hall, 1986.

Lord, C. G., Ross, L., and Lepper, M. R. "Biased Assimilation and Attitude Polarization: The Effects of Prior Theories on Subsequently Considered Evidence." *Journal of Personality and Social Psychology,* 1979, *37,* 2098–2109.

McClintock, C. G., and Liebrand, W. "Role of Interdependence Structure, Individual Value Orientation, and Another's Strategy in Social Decision Making: A Transformational Analysis." *Journal of Personality and Social Psychology,* 1988, *55,* 396–409.

Marlow, D., Gergen, K. J., and Doob, A. N. "Opponents' Personality, Expectation of Social Interaction, and Interpersonal Bargaining." *Journal of Personality and Social Psychology,* 1966, *3,* 206–213.

Messick, D. M., and Sentis, K. "Fairness and Preference." *Journal of Experimental Social Psychology,* 1979, *15,* 418–434.

Miles, R. H. "Role Requirements as Sources of Organizational Stress." *Journal of Applied Psychology,* 1976, *61* (2), 172–179.

Morley, I. E., Webb, J., and Stephenson, G. M. "Bargaining and Arbitration in the Resolution of Conflict." In W. Stroebe, A. Kruglanski, D. Bar-Tal, and M. Hewstone (eds.), *The Social Psychology of Intergroup Conflict.* New York: Springer-Verlag, 1988.

Neustadt, R. E., and May, E. R. *Thinking in Time: The Uses of History for Decision Makers.* New York: Free Press, 1986.

Osgood, C. E. *An Alternative to War or Surrender.* Champaign: University of Illinois Press, 1962.

Plous, S. "Perceptual Illusions and Military Realities: The Nuclear Arms Race." *Journal of Conflict Resolution,* 1985, *29,* 363–389.

Pondy, L. "Organizational Conflict: Concepts and Models." *Administrative Science Quarterly,* 1967, *12,* 296–320.

Pruitt, D. G., and Rubin, J. Z. *Social Conflict: Escalation, Stalemate, and Conflict.* New York: Random House, 1986.

Rapoport, A., and Chammah, A. M. *Prisoner's Dilemma: A Study in Conflict and Cooperation.* Ann Arbor: University of Michigan Press, 1965.

Ross, J., and Staw, B. M. "Expo 86: An Escalation Prototype." *Administrative Science Quarterly,* 1986, *31,* 274-296.

Rothbart, M., and Hallmark, W. "Ingroup-Outgroup Differences in the Perceived Efficacy of Coercion and Conciliation in Resolving Social Conflict." *Journal of Personality and Social Psychology,* 1988, *55,* 248-257.

Schelling, T. C. *The Strategy of Conflict.* Cambridge, Mass.: Harvard University Press, 1960.

Seeman, M. "Alienation Motifs in Contemporary Theorizing: The Hidden Continuity of the Classic Themes." *Social Psychology Quarterly,* 1983, *46,* 171-184.

Sherif, M. "Superordinate Goals in the Reduction of Intergroup Conflict." *American Journal of Sociology,* 1958, *63,* 349-356.

Shure, G. H., Meeker, R. J., and Hansford, E. A. "The Effectiveness of Pacifist Strategies in Bargaining Games." *Journal of Conflict Resolution,* 1965, *9,* 106-117.

Smoke, R. "The Nature and Control of Escalation." In R. White (ed.), *Psychology and the Prevention of Nuclear War.* New York: New York University Press, 1986.

Snyder, G. H., and Diesing, P. *Conflict Among Nations.* Princeton, N.J.: Princeton University Press, 1977.

Snyder, J. *The Ideology of the Offensive: Military Decision Making and the Disasters of 1914.* Ithaca, N.Y.: Cornell University Press, 1984.

Solomon, L. "The Influence of Some Types of Power Relationships and Game Strategies upon the Development of Interpersonal Trust." *Journal of Abnormal and Social Psychology,* 1960, *61,* 223-230.

Stagner, R. "Personality Variables in Union-Management Relations." *Journal of Applied Psychology,* 1962, *46,* 350-357.

Starbuck, W. H., and Milliken, F. J. "Challenger: Fine-Tuning the Odds Until Something Breaks." *Journal of Management Studies,* 1988, *25,* 319-340.

Staw, B. M. "The Escalation of Commitment: A Review and Analysis." *Academy of Management,* 1981, *6,* 577-587.

Staw, B. M., and Ross, J. "Behavior in Escalation Situations: Antecedents, Prototypes, and Solutions." In B. M. Staw and L. L. Cummings (eds.), *Research in Organizational Behavior.* Vol. 9. Greenwich, Conn.: JAI Press, 1987.

Stein, J. "Calculation, Miscalculation, and Deterrence." In R. Jervis, R. Lebow, and N. Stein (eds.), *Psychology and Deterrence.* Baltimore, Md.: Johns Hopkins University Press, 1986.

Stein, J. "Building Politics into Psychology." *Political Psychology,* 1988, *9,* 245-271.

Stillinger, C. A., Epelbaum, M., Keltner, D., and Ross, L. "The 'Reactive Devaluation' Barrier to Conflict Resolution." Unpublished manuscript, 1989.

Sumner, W. G. *Folkways.* New York: Ginn, 1906.

Swann, W. B., Pelham, B. W., and Roberts, D. C. "Causal Chunking: Memory and Inference in Ongoing Interaction." *Journal of Personality and Social Psychology,* 1987, *53,* 858-865.

Swingle, P. (ed.). *The Structure of Conflict.* Orlando, Fla.: Academic Press, 1970.

Taylor, S. E. *Positive Illusions.* New York: Basic Books, 1989.

Taylor, S. E., and Brown, J. "Illusion and Well-Being: A Social Psychological Perspective on Mental Health." *Psychological Bulletin,* 1988, *103,* 193-210.

Terhune, K. W. "The Effects of Personality in Cooperation and Conflict." In P. Swingle (ed.), *The Structure of Conflict.* Orlando, Fla.: Academic Press, 1970.

Terhune, K. W., and Firestone, J. M. "Psychological Studies in Social Interaction and Motives (STAM), Phase 2: Group Motives in an International Relations Game." CAL Report No. VX2018-G-2. Ithaca, N.Y.: Cornell Aeronautical Laboratory, 1967.

Tetlock, P. E., and McGuire, C. B. "Cognitive Perspectives on Foreign Policy." In R. K. White (ed.), *Psychology and the Prevention of Nuclear War.* New York: New York University Press, 1986.

Thierry, Hk. *Organisatie van Tegenstellingen* [The Organization of Antithesis]. Assen: Van Gorcum, 1977.

Thomas, K. "Conflict and Conflict Management." In M. D. Dunnette (ed.), *Handbook of Organizational Psychology.* Chicago: Rand McNally, 1976.

Thompson, L., and Hastie, R. "Judgment Tasks and Biases in Negotiation." In B. H. Sheppard, M. H. Bazerman, and R. J. Lewicki (eds.), *Research in Negotiation in Organizations.* Vol. 2. Greenwich, Conn.: JAI Press, 1988.

Vliert, E. van de. "Conflict—Prevention and Escalation." In P.J.D. Drenth, Hk. Thierry, P. J. Willems, and C. J. De Wolff (eds.), *Handbook of Work and Organizational Psychology.* Vol. 1. New York: Wiley, 1984.

Walt, S. M. *The Origins of Alliances.* Ithaca, N.Y.: Cornell University Press, 1987.

Walton, R. E. *Interpersonal Peacemaking: Confrontations and Third-Party Consultation.* Reading, Mass.: Addison-Wesley, 1969.

Walton, R. E., and Dutton, J. D. "The Management of Interdepartmental Conflict: A Model and Review." *Administrative Science Quarterly,* 1969, *14,* 73–84.

Watzlawick, P., Beavin, J., and Jackson, D. *Pragmatics of Human Communication.* New York: Norton, 1967.

Chapter 6

Strategic Choice in Conflicts

The Importance of Relationships

Leonard Greenhalgh
Roderick M. Kramer

"Nations," notes Oye (1986, p. 1), "dwell in perpetual anarchy, for no central authority imposes limits on the pursuit of sovereign interests." Oye's characterization of the international environment is representative of a major paradigm in international relations theory. According to this paradigm, nations can be construed as rational actors trying to maximize their own interests in a world composed of similarly motivated strategic actors. Conflicts between nations arise when their interests are perceived to be incompatible. In analyzing how nations respond to such conflicts, game theory and the rational theory of choice have exerted a powerful influence on theoretical conceptions of strategic behavior (Brams, 1985; De Mesquita, 1981; Schelling, 1960).

While both the game-theoretical perspective and the rational choice perspective offer useful insights, there has been an interest in exploring—and a recognition of the need for—new conceptions of international relations. Saunders (1989), for example, has argued that there is a need for a conceptual framework that goes beyond the definition of international relations purely in terms of rational calculation of self-interests. In particular, he suggests that the conventional view that states amass "military and economic power to

181

pursue objectively defined interests at the expense of other states"
(pp. 1-2) needs to be reexamined critically. In its place, he proposes
a framework should be developed that explicitly takes into account
the multiplicity of complex forms of relationship that exist among
nations and that transcend their short-term military and economic
concerns.

In this chapter, we suggest that much can be learned from what
we know about our collectivities that experience conflict, particularly organizations. Nations and organizations have much in common. Both international and interorganizational relations are
shaped by many forms of interdependence. At the international
level, this interdependence manifests itself in many ways. Nations
are interdependent with each other with respect to tangible resources such as oil, strategic minerals, and other raw materials.
Their interdependence extends to less tangible resources as well,
including the desire for status, votes of confidence during international crises, and even security (Jervis, 1976). In a similar way, organizations are interdependent with other organizations for many
crucial resources (Pfeffer and Salancik, 1978). As a result, problems
concerning the regulation of competition for such resources and the
establishment of cooperative relationships are of central concern in
both spheres. Nations and organizations also have in common the
fact that they are structures in which decisions are made by powerful
elites who are accountable to multiple constituencies; and these
constituencies are sources of tension and strain on decision makers.

The study of organizations, however, has proceeded in different
directions from the study of international relations. As a result, it
may contain insights that can illuminate our understanding of international relations. This chapter examines one of these developments—the emerging interest in the importance of *relationships* in
conflict—and provides some examples of how it can be applied to
an understanding of international conflicts. Specifically, we propose a typology of relationships. We then suggest how the perceived
relationship between two parties affects their conception of a conflict situation. Finally, we identify some of the psychological and
institutional factors that influence strategic choice and conflict
outcomes.

Typology of Relationships

Relationships involve the parties' global and enduring perceptions of each other and the stances they adopt as a result. Relationships have been largely overlooked by scholars studying conflicts (Greenhalgh, 1987b). When relationships have been considered, they have been conceptualized in a rather unidimensional way. For example, social psychologists interested in relationships have often focused on the implications of specific forms of interdependence on decision makers (for example, Kelley, 1979) but have ignored other dimensions of relationships. In the formal, game-theoretic sense, interdependence exists when the achievement of one party's goals are dependent on the actions of another. The ease with which interdependence can be operationally defined encourages its use as a proxy for complex relationships, and it has been used widely in experimental studies of interdependence relations.

As important as the notion of interdependence is, however, a richer conceptualization is desirable for capturing the essence of conflicts involving larger collectivities such as organizations and nations. An innovative paper by Saunders (1989) moves us in the right direction by identifying four characteristic properties of relationships between nations that need to be understood: (1) compatible values, interests, or needs; (2) patterns of interaction; (3) limits prescribing the range of actions that are acceptable to each party; and (4) a shared sense of common identity, interests, and destiny.

A broad typology of relationships seems useful at this stage of early paradigm development, and Table 6.1 is offered for its heuristic value in taking us in that direction. The table is not intended as an exhaustive typology but rather is intended to illustrate the range of possible relationships between the parties to a conflict. Development of a more complete typology awaits systematic investigation of the various dimensions along which relationships differ (see Greenhalgh and Chapman, 1990). The contribution of Table 6.1 to our understanding of relationships is that it shows two things. First, it shows that relationships differ qualitatively along several dimensions; second, it shows that international examples have much in common with organizational examples.

The eight types of relationships that are listed in the first column

Table 6.1. Range of Relationships Between Two Parties in Conflict.

Type of Relationship	Predisposition of Participant		Examples	
	Role	Identifying Characteristics	Organizational	International
Symbiosis	True partner	Experiences strong mutual commitment	Joint proprietorship	U.S. and U.K. during WW II
Alliance	Friend	Experiences altruistic motivation	Mentoring	U.S. and Canada
Conditional cooperation	Contractual partner	Cooperates but is wary of exploitation: caveat emptor	Transfer pricing arrangement	U.S. and Mexico
Instrumental interdependence	Meeter of needs	Cooperates only within sphere of common interests	Customer and supplier	EEC
Peaceful coexistence	Loner	Is indifferent to other party	Conglomerate divisions	Switzerland and Austria
Benign competition	Fellow contestant	Seeks own gain, hopefully not at other's expense	Realtors in multiple-listing contract	U.S. and Japan in world markets in 1980s
Rivalry	Unmerciful competitor	Seeks own gain at other's expense	Monopolistic competition	France and Germany
Enmity	Enemy	Engages in spiteful behavior to harm opponent	Feud between companies: lawsuits and countersuits	IRA and the government of Northern Ireland

of Table 6.1 are ordered from most antagonistic to most collaborative. In the second and third columns, sample predispositions of participants in each type of relationship are suggested. Roles are defined here as patterns of response that are perceived by decision makers to be appropriate to the experienced relationship; identifying characteristics are behaviors and cognitions that are detectable to observers, even though they may remain more or less "invisible" to the parties themselves. The listed organizational and international examples are chosen for their familiarity to readers, not because they are perfect exemplars of the type of relationship being illustrated.

The relationship between two parties, as we have defined it here, cannot be described simply in terms of objective facts and the tangible bases of interdependence that exist between them; rather, it exists in the minds of the parties and is therefore an intersubjective phenomenon. Thus, the perceptions of the parties are an essential dimension of the relationship between them. Gorbachev's courting of the various NATO members in the late 1980s can be interpreted as an effort to reshape favorably the relationship between the Soviets and the NATO members, as can his subsequent bold initiatives to redefine Soviet-American relationships as well.

Of course, there may be asymmetries between how the parties perceive or construe their relationship and even considerable variation within a party. For example, different constituencies within one party are likely to maintain discrepant views of the nature of their relationship with another (see Sutton and Kramer, Chapter Seven of this volume).

Introduction to the Model

Figure 6.1 summarizes how the perceived relationship influences the way the different parties construe the conflict between them and its situational context, how these perceptions combine to influence strategic choices, and how these choices in turn affect outcomes. Both choices and outcomes are shown to redefine the relationship because of two feedback loops; thus, past actions determine future responses because they shape fundamental predispositions to predict and interpret the other party's response to problems that arise. The subsections that follow briefly explain the components of the model and how they are related to each other.

Strategic Choice. A key aspect of the relationships between nations, we have argued, is the interdependence between countries with respect to both concrete and intangible resources. Indeed, the exchange of such crucial resources is one of the most common transactions to occur between nations. Organizational relationships entail similar forms of interdependence and must engage in com-

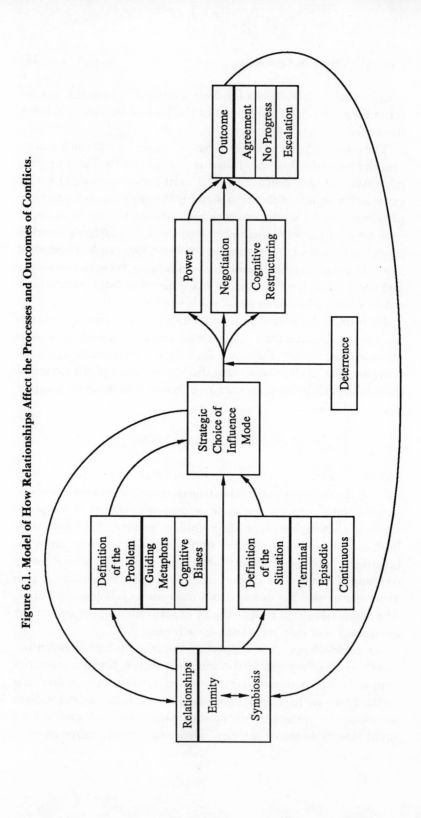

Figure 6.1. Model of How Relationships Affect the Processes and Outcomes of Conflicts.

parable exchanges in order to survive. As Pfeffer and Salancik (1978) have argued, a major goal of most organizations is to guarantee access to those resources that are essential to the accomplishment of their tasks.

The problem of deciding how to respond to the various forms of interdependence that permeate international and interorganizational relations has been a central theme in both the international relations literature and the literature on organizations. As Kahn (1989, p. 185) has cogently noted, "The persisting question for every organization and every nation is how best to manage unavoidable interdependencies." Both literatures have emphasized the central role that decisions or choices made by national and organizational decision-making elites play in the management of such interdependence.

The dilemmas associated with managing interdependence can be conceptualized as posing problems of *strategic choice* for organizational and national elites. Each party must decide which strategies, out of all of those that are available, should be selected in trying to influence the other party. For example, in deciding how best to resolve a conflict with another nation, decision makers may have to choose between using economic sanctions as threats or other more collaborative approaches. Similarly, in trying to manage its relationship with another organization over a shared market, an organization may have to choose between unrestrained competition with the aim of driving the other out of existence or trying to achieve a level of peaceful coexistence by going after different segments of the market. The model depicted in Figure 6.1 identifies some of the factors that influence such choices.

Game-theoretic formulations of the problem of strategic choice, especially in the international arena, have generally addressed issues pertaining to how decision makers can maximize their own outcomes given the presence of other parties trying to do the same. Brams's (1985) analysis of superpower relations is representative of this approach. Such analyses generally assume that the parties involved in a conflict are individualistically motivated (that is, concerned about their own gain alone) and that they have no relationship other than that implied by the payoff matrix. Thus, the boundaries of the relationship are determined exclusively by the structural dimensions of interdependence; psychological dimensions (for example, concern about the other party, feelings of loyalty or attraction), if they are considered at all, are afforded only minimal and perfunctory attention.

Even in the simplest of interdependence games, the problem of strategic choice acquires a surprising complexity. This complexity is aptly illustrated in the ecological versions of Axelrod's (1984) computer tournaments. As soon as we broaden the objectives of a given strategic choice to encompass concerns about its impact on the relationship between the parties, the problem becomes even more complex. Strategic choices made in the "shadow" of relationships, to borrow from Axelrod's elegant terminology, must take account of the effects of the mode of influence selected on the long-term relationship between the parties. These effects include such changes as how the parties perceive each other, the extent to which they are willing to trust each other in future interactions, their willingness to adhere to the agreements they have made, and their readiness to give the other party the benefit of the doubt in an ambiguous situation. Thus, strategic choice is both a product of relationships and a determinant of future relationships, hence the feedback loop depicted in Figure 6.1.

Definition of the Problem. Strategic choices are first of all shaped by the basic cognitive categories that decision makers use to perceive, interpret, and respond to situations. In this chapter, we are particularly interested in two cognitive factors: the imagery used to visualize an abstract problem and how the problem is framed by decision makers in preparing responsive action.

Images and metaphors are the result of basic thought processes that determine how decision makers construe a conflict. Images, along with their more elaborated thought patterns, metaphors, are important because people come to understand complex, abstract phenomena such as conflict in terms of concepts that are simpler and more familiar. When decision makers encounter a new situation, they often interpret it in terms of the degree to which it is similar to or different from already known phenomena. For example, electricity is baffling to most people, but it becomes comprehensible when they think about it as if it were a fluid traveling through a pipe. Thus we speak of electrical "current" and "resistance." In this way, hydraulics functions as a guiding metaphor that allows us to understand electricity. Greer (1969) notes the dependence of scientists on guiding metaphors.

In a more recent paper, Greenhalgh (1987a) explores the importance of metaphors in conflict situations. Consider a member of an elite trying to make sense of what it means to be in conflict with another party. The conflict literature shows that even scholars have trouble defining exactly what a conflict is and what should be incorporated within the domain of the construct. Decision makers who are immersed in a conflict are even worse off; they are faced with the complexity of the total situation, its implications for their constituency and their relationships with the other party, and their emotional problems. During the Cuban missile crisis, for example, President Kennedy expressed concerns about avoiding nuclear war, but also about the effects of different choices he might make on his political future, the possibility that he might be impeached if he failed to demonstrate resolve, the future of America's relationships with its allies, and the impact of his actions on Soviet-American relations. To think about this morass of abstract detail in practical terms, decision makers often tend to simplify the bewildering booming, buzzing confusion of events by using a familiar metaphor to capture the essence of what is going on.

In this respect, guiding metaphors function much like historical analogies. In their recent analysis of how decision makers use history, Neustadt and May (1986) have argued that policymakers, when trying to make sense of current events, often try to find analogies with past events with which they are familiar. For example, one of the strategic options the members of President Kennedy's EX-COMM considered during the Cuban missile crisis was a surprise attack on Cuba aimed at destroying Soviet missile emplacements. In trying to anticipate how the international community might react to such a surprise attack, Robert Kennedy invoked a comparison to the Japanese attack on Pearl Harbor.

In a similar way, using a particular metaphor such as chess to interpret an ongoing conflict selectively draws attention to certain features of the relationship but at the expense of other germane attributes. As a consequence, certain features of the situation may be given too much weight during decision making while others are ignored or underweighted. The choice of metaphor, in other words, greatly influences what gets noticed in a given situation. As another example, a prevalent class of metaphors among Westerners for characterizing conflicts are sports metaphors. Seen from the perspective of these metaphors, conflicts are episodic contests in which each contestant's mission is to beat the other party. The rules of the game may be stretched to the limits of explicit game rules; they may even be violated if it is possible to do so without getting caught. The relationship this metaphor engenders is short term, zero sum, lacking in trust, and inescapably adversarial (Greenhalgh, 1987a). Conflict is seen as a competitive contest from which one winner and one loser will emerge.

These examples highlight some of the strengths and liabilities of guiding metaphors. On the positive side, metaphors function to direct attention toward salient features of the conflict that merit further evaluation or consideration. Similarly, they may help decision makers discover more creative solutions to the conflict. On the negative side, metaphors may constrain thinking so that only certain elements of the relationship are attended to or processed.

In addition to the influence of guiding metaphors, a variety of cognitive processes can also affect strategic choice. These include various judgmental heuristics, such as representativeness and availability, and the simulation heuristic (for example, Jervis, 1976; Jervis, Lebow, and Stein, 1985; Kramer, 1989; Kramer, Meyerson, and Davis, 1990; Stein, 1988).

Definition of the Situation. Strategic choices are also influenced by how decision makers define a conflict situation. Although there are many important dimensions to such definitions, the temporal horizon decision makers adopt during decision making is of particular relevance to the present analysis. In his classic work on coalitions, Caplow (1968) notes the different choices that are predicted when actors have different beliefs about the continuity of their interaction. Similarly, Axelrod (1984) has emphasized the importance of the "shadow of the future" in shaping relationships between strategic actors. In Table 6.2, we offer three definitions of the situation that imply different temporal orientations. A *terminal* situation occurs when one or both of the parties construe their relationship as bounded by the immediate conflict. In the extreme, it occurs when one of the parties views the conflict as a life-and-death struggle, believing that it could cease to exist as an outcome of the conflict. An *episodic* situation, in contrast, occurs when the relationship is dominated by a single transaction in which the history and future of the relationship between the parties are not considered but merely taken for granted. Finally, a *continuous* orientation is one in which the problem giving rise to the conflict is seen as only the current state of an ongoing relationship. In a marital dispute, for example, the two parties may view their immediate conflict as embedded in an ongoing pattern of interaction extending over months or years. In Table 6.2, we present organizational and international examples of these alternative definitions of the situation that form the temporal context in which collectivities interact.

Three points can be made about the definition of the situation that decision makers generate. First, it is necessarily subjective. The objective situation—that which would be observed by a disinterested or omniscient observer—is largely irrelevant. Choices are made on the basis of the reality that the decision makers experience. Second, the particular definition of a situation that a decision maker arrives at is subject to cognitive biases that have important consequences for the severity of the conflict (Greenhalgh, 1986). Associated with these cognitive processes are various affective reactions. Because of these affective reactions, the temporal horizon associated with the relationship may be altered. The emotions generated in a dispute—such as anger, resentment, fear, and hatred—may intensify a decision mak-

Table 6.2. Organizational and International Illustrations of Varying Definition of the Situation.

Definition of the Situation	Organizational Example	International Example
Terminal	Corporate takeover fight	Palestinian charter denying Israel's right to exist
Episodic	Competitors for a U.S. defense contract	U.S. invasion of Grenada
Continuous	Japanese joint ventures	U.S.-Panamanian relations in 1988

er's focus on the immediate situation. As a dispute intensifies, the ongoing, long-term aspects of the relationship may fade in importance in comparison to the immediate confrontation. Consequently, a given conflict may be viewed as terminal or episodic by the parties themselves even though outside observers can see that the current dispute is simply one event in an ongoing sequence of interactions.

Mode of Influence. The primary purpose of this section is to analyze strategic choices in relationships by treating them as decisions regarding the mode of influence that should be used to influence the actions of another party. Specifically, we describe some of the common modes of strategic influence used by nations and organizations. We will focus on three modes of strategic influence available to decision makers. We characterize these three modes of influence as *power-based, negotiated,* and *cognitive* approaches to conflict resolution (Greenhalgh, 1986). We then examine how the nature of the relationship between the parties affects the particular mode of influence they select. Finally, we discuss the role deterrents play in attempts to influence the other party.

Power-based approaches. Power-based approaches to conflict resolution are generally aimed at inducing the other party to accede to one's will. They function primarily by exploiting existing asymmetries in the balance of power. Power-based approaches can assume many forms, including the use of coercive tactics and contingent sanctions. For example, Betts (1987) has described how U.S. presidents have on occasion resorted to the use of "nuclear blackmail" in attempting to force other nations to comply with their policy aims.

The common aim of these approaches is to exert influence on the behavior of the other party by exploiting its fears, needs, or vulnerabilities. Thus, coercive actions are usually directed toward achieving a specific behavioral objective (for example, compliance), with little concern given to building or furthering the relationship between the parties (other than to keep the weaker party dependent or powerless). In this respect, power-based approaches that are coercive erode rather than enhance the relationship between the parties.

It is important to note, however, that power imbalances can be used to achieve more cooperative aims. A more powerful party can use its power in an attempt to actually further the welfare of the other. It may engage in conciliatory actions, such as offering military or economic aid in order to promote a more positive relationship between the parties. Although such actions may be tied to specific short-term strategic objectives (such as persuading a nation to permit an important military base on its territory), they may be simultaneously aimed at improving the longer-term relationship between the parties. They may be stimulated by a desire to foster a sense of reciprocity or strengthen the commitment between the parties.

Unfortunately, the use of power to achieve positive goals can also have negative consequences. It can lead to resentment because such aid reinforces a sense of weakness, indebtedness, and dependency on the part of the recipient. Similarly, if the weaker party is perceived as unappreciative or proves unwilling to reciprocate such benefit, the more powerful party may come to perceive it as ungrateful or hostile.

Decision makers may also use "mixed" strategies (that is, combinations of coercive and conciliatory forms of influence) when trying to influence another party. For example, they may provide technical assistance to promote better agricultural practices, while simultaneously using economic sanctions to discourage unfair trade practices. Unfortunately, there has been little systematic research on the impact of these "carrot-and-stick" influence approaches on relationships. As a result, we know very little about what the optimal mix of such strategies might be or the consequences for relationships of different sequences of positive and negative influence attempts. The lack of research on this topic is regrettable because international and interorganizational relationships typically entail long histories of interactions involving just such mixtures of positive and negative influence attempts.

Up to this point, we have discussed these power-based modes of influence primarily from the standpoint of the more powerful party. Paradoxically, there are situations where a less powerful party can exploit its lack of power to strategic advantages. Schelling (1960) describes a variety of situations involving the use of compellant strategies where, precisely because of their impotence to do otherwise, less powerful parties can induce more powerful parties to pursue, albeit reluctantly, a given course of action. If two parties are separated and lost in a forest, for example, and they both know that only one of them knows how to find the other, the ignorant one can sit back in comfort and relax while the more informed party has to endure the long trek to his or her camp.

Negotiated conflict resolution. Negotiation is a bilateral influence process whereby both parties are engaged in the process of seeking a settlement or agreement regarding their differences. As a process, negotiation consists of a series of offers, concessions, and trades that are initiated by the parties in order to resolve conflict over some given set of issues (for example, access to a shared waterway between two nations, or delivery and payment schedules between two organizations).

Much of the research on negotiations has focused on negotiation outcomes, such as the Pareto-optimality of the agreements that are ultimately reached by the parties (see, for example, Roth, 1989) and individual cognitions (Bazerman, 1983; Bazerman and Neal, 1983). Increasingly, however, attention is being given to the social nature of the negotiation process (Kramer, 1990a; Morley, Webb, and Stephenson, 1988). As a process of social interaction, negotiation is viewed as helping the parties develop a shared perception of the bases of their relationship and the approaches they are willing to use in order to manage that relationship. From this perspective, "what is crucial is not that the negotiators reach agreement but that the agreements can be justified as rules, *defining the terms on which the parties will do business"* (Morley, Webb, and Stephenson, 1988, p. 122; emphasis added).

This view suggests further that the particular form that a negotiation takes depends not only on the issues at stake but on the nature of the prior relationship or history of interaction between the parties. This is particularly evident with respect to the basic decision negotiators face as to whether to engage in integrative versus distributive bargaining when trying to resolve their differences (Lax and Sebenius, 1986; Lewicki and Litterer, 1985; Walton and McKersie, 1965). The aim of integrative bargaining is to increase the joint gains of the two parties. Integrative approaches to negotiation include tactics such as disclosing one's own true interests, needs, and goals to the other party. By engaging in such open exchanges of information, the parties increase the likelihood that they will discover opportunities to simultaneously satisfy or advance each of their goals.

In the case of distributive bargaining, the parties assume from the outset that their interests are incompatible. The negotiation process is conceived of by the parties as a contest over a fixed pie of resources that must be divided between them. Thus, one party's gain is necessarily the other's loss. Because of this zero-sum orientation, they are less likely to consider an open and honest exchange of information as useful. Instead, they may resort to tactics such as deception or disinformation in order to mislead the other party as to the negotiator's true goals, interests, or needs. Since they perceive little opportunity for joint gain, they are also likely to use coercive measures such as threats to force concessions from the other party and maximize their own share of the pie.

The importance of the prior relationship between the parties in shaping the negotiation process is suggested by considering the requirements for decision makers to engage in integrative versus distributive bargaining. For example, in order for a party to engage in integrative bargaining, it may require some level of assurance that its attempts to initiate an honest exchange of information will not be exploited or viewed as indicative of weakness or lack of resolve. Because of such fears, decision makers may decide to use distributive bargaining behavior for purely defensive reasons.

In turn, the form of negotiation that is selected by the parties is likely to impact the subsequent relationship as well. In addition to the immediate positive effects of integrative bargaining on the outcome of a negotiation, there may be substantial long-term collateral effects on the relationship between the parties. Thus, there may be an enhanced awareness of the other party's needs and goals, leading to the development of greater empathy. The use of integrative behaviors can lead to greater interpersonal attraction between the parties and more positive expectations regarding their future interactions. As a result, the parties may begin to view their relationships as deeper and more robust. Conversely, the use of distributive bargaining tactics may undermine the trust of the parties in each other, lead to decreased attraction, and result in the formation of negative expectations regarding their future interaction.

The importance of the nature of the relationship—and in particular how it is construed by the parties—is further illustrated by considering how different the process of negotiation can be across various cultures. In many Western cultures, negotiation is construed by the parties as a relatively formal set of procedures for dispute resolution. The dominant metaphor for the relationship is legalistic. In many cases, in fact, the product of the negotiation is a written contract that explicitly describes the parties' rights and obligations. The boundaries of permissive action are carefully articulated so that each party knows precisely what it can and cannot do. In terms of the impact of the negotiation on the subsequent relationship, attention becomes focused on compliance with the letter of the law rather than the spirit that may have motivated the involvement of the parties in the relationship in the first place.

It is ironic that while the ostensible aim of such explicit negotiations is to provide some assurance against cheating and reduce the perceived risk of exploitation, this excessive focus on legalistic demarcation of the relationship may actually invite the parties to search for loopholes. Drawing decision makers' attention to such boundaries may increase the salience of opportunities to skirt the limits of the contractual relationship. When negotiation is enacted with this metaphor in mind, the relationship tends to be defined narrowly in terms of the contractual rights and obligations and also episodically in terms of the duration of the relationship as specified in the contract.

This conceptualization of the negotiation process can be sharply contrasted with that characteristic of certain other countries such as Japan, where both the process and outcome of negotiations are different (see Tung, 1984, and Zimmerman, 1985, for detailed discussions). The goal of negotiation and the nature of the contract that is being sought, for example, are very different from those of Western culture. The negotiation process is predicated on the assumption that, by negotiating, the parties mutually recognize that a long-term relationship is being entered into. It is the relationship that is central, not the negotiation outcome. Thus, the specific terms of the contract are in many respects less important than the fact that the relationship itself now exists. Moreover, the expectations of the parties and the impact of the negotiation process on their relationship are also quite distinctive from those characteristic of Western culture. The negotiation process is viewed as an opportunity for the parties to develop a long-term relationship through mutual understanding and cooperation. It is acceptable and indeed expected that as conditions change, the parties may have to adjust the terms of the agreement to meet these changed circumstances. Negotiation, like the relationship itself, is a continuous, adaptive social process rather than an episodic interaction defined by a legal contract. In this respect, the contract between the parties is more social and psychological rather than explicit and legalistic.

Cognitive conflict resolution. Cognitive approaches to conflict resolution consist of modes of influence that are aimed at reducing the level of *perceived* conflict between the parties. They entail a process of cognitive readjustment whereby the conflict is no longer perceived as salient to the parties (Greenhalgh, 1986). The primary goal of a cognitive mode of influence, then, is to change the underlying perceptions, attitudes, beliefs, and values of the other party.

One important class of cognitive approaches to conflict resolution consists of the use of persuasive messages. The most extreme examples are brainwashing and propaganda. A variety of more subtle techniques based on impression management and social accounting also exist (Bies, 1987).

Moreover, there are less direct approaches to changing perceptions. For example, one party can attempt to change the other's perceptions by using voluntary restraint in an attempt to elicit cooperation from the other. By exercising such restraint, the party achieves two interrelated goals. First, it communicates its own cooperative intentions to the other. Second, it implicitly signals its trusting the other party not to exploit the relationship in return. A variety of behavioral strategies that are based on the use of incremental conciliatory initiatives are designed to work in this way. Perhaps the best known is the GRIT strategy, which is aimed at building perceptions of trustworthiness and reliability between the parties (see Lindskold, 1978).

Other strategies are designed to change attitudes by inducing a party to engage in a behavior or action consistent with the desired attitude. For example, the "foot-in-the-door" technique is a strategy for increasing behavioral compliance with a request; it consists of a small and inconsequential initial request, followed by a larger, more consequential request. Research has shown that the level of compliance with the larger request is significantly higher when it is preceded by the smaller request than when it is made alone (see Cialdini, 1985; Zimbardo, Ebbesen, and Maslach, 1977). The success of the foot-in-the-door technique is tied to the changes in self-perception that presumably follow compliance with the initial small request.

Although the use of a cognitive strategy may be motivated primarily by a desire to achieve some limited goal (for example, a change in attitude toward a specific arms control proposal), it is important to note that accompanying the changes in perception of the issue might be more general changes in the perception of the relationship between the parties. The process of reaching consensus on a specific issue may generalize to the parties' perceptions of their relationship. For example, the discovery of a mutually acceptable solution to a previously unresolvable conflict may cause the parties to redefine their relationship as one in which such agreements are both possible and can be expected to be forthcoming.

To summarize, we have described three different modes of influence that decision makers can use when trying to manage a conflict arising within an international or interorganizational relationship. One way of thinking about the differences between these approaches is in terms of the depth or level of change in the relationship they imply. In the case of power-based approaches, the change in the relationship may be superficial because compliance is forced and not voluntary. Consequently, there may be little internalization of the change. In the case of negotiation, the relationship may be changed in a more profound sense, because whatever changes are enacted are agreed upon by the parties. Finally, in the case of cognitive approaches, the changes in attitudes and perceptions may reflect the most enduring and profound change in the relationship because they reflect the way the parties have come to actually view the relationship.

The Functions of Deterrents in Relationships. Deterrents are used to dissuade another party from engaging in actions that are perceived to be antithetical to one's interests. A deterrent is a threat to impose penalties or costs so great that they outweigh any conceivable gain the other party might hope to achieve through such actions. In the realm of international relations, deterrence has been most often conceptualized in terms of either conventional or nuclear deterrence, both of which are predicated on the threat to use military power to induce compliance. The theory of deterrence has dominated much of the scholarly literature on influence processes in international relations (see, for example, George, 1974; Jervis, Lebow, and Stein, 1985; Snyder, 1961). The doctrine of mutual assured destruction (or MAD) posits that two countries can maintain a "balance of terror" if each can credibly threaten to impose massive destruction on the other's civilian population and homeland if it is attacked. Because each country is able to reduce the other to a scorched, radioactive wasteland, they maintain a stable, albeit fragile, relationship based on mutual fear and vulnerability.

Organizational theorists have been interested in how deterrents shape interorganizational relations as well (see Wilson, 1989). Perhaps the organizational analog that comes closest to the scorched-earth version of a nuclear deterrent is the "poison pill" in takeover fights for U.S. corporations. Weaker companies have devoted considerable ingenuity to devising poison-pill strategies to deter takeover attempts by other companies. These strategies, which are triggered by the aggression of a stronger company, have the effect of reducing the attractiveness of the target company.

In much of the literature, deterrence has been treated as a power-based mode of influence whose use and effects are considered in isolation from other dimensions of the relationship and other forms of influence that might be used. Less obvious is the use of a deterrent in conjunction with other modes of influence. We regard the imposition of a deterrent as having different effects depending on whether it is used in the context of power-based, negotiated, or cognitive approaches to conflict resolution.

When used in the context of power-based modes of influence, deterrence functions to neutralize the other party's power. During the 1950s, the Eisenhower administration, facing both economic constraints and the presence of a Soviet conventional military superiority in Eastern Europe, decided to use nuclear deterrents to offset this advantage of the Warsaw Pact forces over NATO forces. By threatening to escalate a local, conventional military conflict in

Western Europe to the level of a nuclear confrontation between the superpowers, the United States was able to neutralize what otherwise would have been an overwhelming military advantage for the Soviets.

One of the disadvantages of using deterrents in power-based relationships, of course, is that they stimulate the other party to develop deterrents of its own to balance or counter those already in place. This may lead to escalating action-reaction cycles as each party seeks a decisive deterrent advantage.

The use of deterrents in the context of negotiations is somewhat different. In the case of negotiations, deterrents function to change the other party's incentives to negotiate or settle. Most game-theoretic formulations of distributive bargaining predict settlements on the basis of their improvement over the parties' reservations prices; that is, negotiators are assumed to evaluate the attractiveness of a settlement on the basis of the alternatives associated with no agreement (see, for example, Walton and McKersie, 1965). The reservation price is the value of the settlement at which the negotiators would just as soon walk away from the negotiation and deal with another party. Greenhalgh (1989) uses a game-theoretic analysis to show that deterrents to nonagreement can be used as a coercive contingency that lowers the effective reservation price for the party on whom it is imposed. He shows that a rational negotiator would prefer a settlement—even one with negative absolute utility—rather than suffer imposition of the deterrent. The more odious or aversive the deterrent, the greater the likelihood that the other party will be compliant.

The short-term effects of the use of deterrents are perhaps all too obvious. In negotiation the use of deterrents tends to undermine the potential for integrative bargaining because it implies a lack of trust between the parties. The effects may be even more pervasive in the long term, creating a relationship that is adversarial in essence and that predisposes the parties to a future of distributive bargaining.

In the case of cognitive forms of conflict resolution, the effects of deterrents are more complicated. In general, one expects that imposing a deterrent will inhibit cognitive restructuring. The threat to impose a penalty on the other party if it does not see things the way one would like is unlikely to increase the effectiveness of a persuasive appeal or attraction toward the party; in fact, it is more likely to have the opposite effect. To the extent that most individuals value their autonomy, attempts to coerce them into adopting a particular point of view are likely to solidify rather than reduce their resistance to accommodation. In this regard, the use of deterrents during attempts at persuasion may produce both reactance and resistance in the other party.

The disagreement between Great Britain and Argentina over the Falkland Islands (or the Malvinas, depending on one's point of view) became entrenched when the parties added deterrents. Initially, the parties were involved in a long-standing disagreement over sovereignty that Argentina could possibly have solved in its favor by framing the issue in terms of outdated British colonialism. A graduated series of persuasive appeals might eventually have led to independence of the islands, especially if international pressure were brought to bear on the British. This might have been followed by progressive hegemony as the islands increased their dependence on Argentina, while British ties and influence in the area would have decreased The potential efficacy of a persuasive process was destroyed, however, by Argentina's threat to use force to end Britain's continuing claims on sovereignty. The dispute then escalated into a war, and a power-based solution was ultimately imposed by the British. The recent war between Iran and Iraq and the skirmishes between the United States and Libya concerning the Gulf of Sidra during the Reagan administration display many of these same dynamics.

The destructive effects of deterrents are evident in organizational settings as well. A dispute over management's right to control the work force may be potentially solvable through persuasion in the early phases of a dispute, particularly given that workers and managers have a common interest in the long-run survival and prosperity of the company. However, if the workers threaten to strike if their demands over work rules are not met, management may feel compelled to devise a "counterdeterrent," such as threatening to replace the work force with a more cooperative set of new workers. Quickly, the conflict escalates to the point where cognitive means of conflict resolution are no longer possible. A similar escalation of conflict is sometimes observed at the interorganizational level (for example, marketing wars).

There are, to be sure, circumstances under which the use of deterrents during cognitive conflict resolution produces effects favorable to the party imposing those deterrents. For example, if the other party does yield to the deterrent, attitude change may occur in a direction that benefits the party imposing the deterrent. Research on the forced compliance paradigm and social influence processes such as the foot-in-the-door procedure suggests that initial compliance may lead to subsequent attitude change, through processes of self-perception and dissonance reduction (Zimbardo, Ebbesen, and Maslach, 1977).

Outcome of the Conflict. The particular mode of influence that is selected, of course, determines to a large extent whether a conflict is resolved, remains unchanged, or is exacerbated. We usually characterize these alternatives as agreement, no progress, or escalation. (See Figure 6.1.) We will discuss each outcome briefly, further noting how the mode of influence selected and also the antecedent decision variables affect each outcome. Then we will examine the feedback loop that links the nature of the agreement with the future relationship.

Agreement is a general term applied to a solution that to some degree ends a dispute. But agreement is not a unitary phenomenon. Figure 6.2 shows a range of possible outcomes, all of which might be considered agreements of sorts. They are arrayed in order of decreasing consensus among the parties.

From the standpoint of preserving a symbiotic relationship, full resolution of a conflict can only be achieved through the cognitive changes that characterize true conflict resolution. This outcome is obviously rare in real life, if it exists at all, and it is offered as an anchoring point for the consensus continuum. Even the slightest hint of a deterrent may preclude this solution because decision makers will attribute their reconciled views to imposition of the coercive contingency rather than to true agreement. Unanimous acceptance of a solution does not imply full consensus but encompasses many elements, including the perceived fairness of the process and outcome, the reduction in expectations that is central to reconciling

Figure 6.2. Range of Agreements Showing Various Degrees of Consensus.

Degree of Consensus	Nature of Agreement
High consensus	Full resolution
↑	Unanimous acceptance
	Acceptance with reservations
↓	Grudging acceptance
Low consensus	Suppressed hostility
	Open enmity

diverse interests, and a sense of commitment among the parties to the agreed-upon course of action.

The next two degrees of acceptance, having reservations about what was agreed to and accepting the agreement only grudgingly, seem to result from process problems in negotiation. Acceptance with reservations may mean that there were some shortcomings in the negotiation process or that the incompatibility of interests was severe enough to force considerable sacrifices in order to achieve a negotiated agreement. Process problems involve domination, lack of true participation, misperceptions, and so on. Dissatisfaction can arise from process rules such as majority vote rather than consensus or from a lack of procedures that assure all negotiators a chance to express themselves fully, so that the most vociferous participants overwhelm those who are less assertive.

The last two forms of agreement are perhaps more accurately described as settlements rather than agreements because the outcome is obviously being imposed against one party's wishes. These are settlements in the sense that the parties have given up actively contesting the issues, but it should be obvious from the descriptors that even though overt conflict has ceased, the emotions underlying the conflict remain strong. These types of settlement tend to result from power processes or from the imposition of deterrents on negotiation processes. They are unstable solutions because one party does not really accept them; they last only so long as power is exerted, and they may be undermined at the first opportunity.

The "no progress" outcome shown in Figure 6.1 is often referred to as stalemate or impasse, but we prefer not to use these terms. Stalemate portrays a situation in which neither party, despite its best efforts, can annihilate the other. Likewise, impasse suggests a negotiation attempt that has foundered. No progress on the other hand can also be the result of equal power, conflict avoidance, postponement of interaction, or low priority given to the dispute.

The escalation outcome shown in Figure 6.1 is dealt with in detail in Chapter Five by Kahn and Kramer and so will receive no detailed treatment here. The point to highlight from this analysis is that escalation always results from the *process,* never from the substance of the issues in dispute.

Positive Feedback Loops. As indicated in Figure 6.1 the effects of strategic choice on a relationship can be pervasive. High-consensus processes can improve the dynamics that affect choices and lead to further cooperation; low-consensus (high-domination) processes, in contrast, can produce more adversarial dynamics. Let us trace the effects of a low-consensus process through the model to illustrate the pathways of the positive feedback loops.

A low-consensus process is a stimulus to further conflict. In collective bargaining, for example, a contract that management coercively imposes spawns myriad grievances; similarly, in international conflicts, unfair articles of surrender sow the seeds of the next war. They produce the sensation of having "lost," which motivates the dominated party to "even the score," or "recover lost ground." The low-consensus agreement induces no obligation to comply with the terms of the settlement in the absence of influence.

In addition to producing an agreement that is difficult to implement, a coercive process gives rise to a relationship that is characterized by domination and subjugation. Because of the way the relationship is construed, the losing party does not think about the conflict situation as a problematic event in a long-term relationship. Thus, that party is not motivated to make concessions or otherwise behave in a way that generates goodwill. Instead, the exploited party expects to win the next episode, having resolved to struggle harder and be more cunning or intransigent in order to secure short-term gains. Furthermore, the loser becomes a power seeker, having lost faith in the more consensus-building influence modes of negotiation and conflict resolution. Finally, creative energies are devoted to finding a deterrent that will discourage exploitation rather than to integrative bargaining. All of these factors make escalation more likely than reconciliation. They energize further enmity and divisiveness, and this system tends to accelerate until external pressure is applied or one party destroys the other.

Relationships as Cognitive Structures

We emphasized above that relationship is a subjectively defined phenomenon and as such is deeply rooted in the phenomenology of the parties to a conflict (their attitudes, beliefs, values, cognitions, perceptions, and so on). It might be worthwhile, accordingly, to elaborate in somewhat more detail on the psychological status of the concept of relationship. To do so, we draw on recent social-psychological theory and research on social cognition (Brewer, 1988; Fiske and Taylor, 1984) and attempts to extend social cognition research to organizational and international relations (for example, Kramer, 1989; Lord and Foti, 1986; Weick and Bougon, 1986).

Social cognition research suggests several ways of conceptualizing relationships as cognitive structures. One intriguing possibility is that relationships may be represented in decision makers' memories in the form of prototypes. A *prototype* is a cognitive structure that contains information about the typical or characteristic attributes of an object (Klatzky, 1980). Empirical research suggests that prototypes exist for many of the social and nonsocial objects that we commonly encounter in our lives. On the basis of research, we propose that individuals have a set of more or less well-developed prototypes for relationships. These prototypes represent the major kinds of relationships they have experienced. Thus, for example, national leaders may have prototypes of Communist heads of state, actor-presidents, and rulers of South American countries. Such prototypes may be based on direct experience (such as contact with representatives of a particular category) or learned through cultural forms of transmission (education, propaganda, and so on).

Because there has been little empirical research on this topic, we know relatively little about the number, degree of differentiation, and complexity of relationship prototypes that are characteristic of real-world decision makers. However, prior research on other kinds of prototypes suggests that relationship prototypes may differ considerably across decision makers. For example, the degree of differentiation and complexity of these prototypes may vary as a function of the individuals' prior experiences, the particular generalizations or "lessons" they have extracted from those experiences, and their cognitive complexity. Table 6.1 identifies a variety of possible candidates for relationship prototypes, but there are undoubtedly more.

Although decision makers' prototypic representations of objects may be highly individualistic, research suggests that there are *basic level* categories (that is, those that are higher in typicality or representativeness) and that the features of prototypes at the basic category level may be relatively similar across individuals, at least within a given culture (see, for example, Rosch, 1978). For example, the prototypes that U.S. citizens have of an Iranian terrorist may have in common such attributes as "speaks in an agitated manner," "wears long robes," and "denounces Western discos."

In addition, the cultural, social, and organizational environment within which decision makers operate may shape the development of prototypes. Some institutional environments may facilitate the development and maintenance of more complex cognitive representations of relationships, while others foster more simplistic or primitive thoughts and images. In this respect, organizations provide settings for the creation of collective or consensually validated prototypes (compare Weick and Bougon's 1986 discussion of the role of collective cognitive maps in organizations).

What are the implications of conceptualizing relationship in terms of a cognitive structure such as a prototype? The major implications pertain to the effects that such prototypes can have on information processing and decision making during a conflict. (See also Fiske and Taylor, 1984, and Lord and Foti, 1986, for informative discussions of the functions that schemata serve in social perception and behavioral interaction.) Relationship prototypes have a variety of consequences in this regard, some of which are functional and adaptive and some of which may be quite dysfunctional.

First, the particular prototypes that are available to a decision maker define the range of relationships that the decision maker regards as possible and therefore anticipates in interacting with other parties. Second, and relatedly, prototypes act as filters that are used to interpret incoming information, especially when that information is ambiguous or incomplete. They may, in this regard, direct the decision maker's attention selectively to certain expected or highly salient features of the conflict situation, causing other less prototypic features to be overlooked. Third, prototypes may be used to make inferences about the situation and guide strategic choice. Elements consistent with the prototype may be overweighted during this inferential process, while those that are inconsistent will be regarded as irrelevant cues or noise. To the extent that decision making is driven by the available prototypes, individuals' interpretations and responses to situations that present novel or unexpected features may be problematic. Thus, while prototype-driven information processing may be adaptive in that it allows for the rapid processing of large amounts of incoming information and efficient decision making, it may also lead to biased information processing and low-quality decisions.

Determinants of Strategic Choice

We have not said much thus far about factors that might affect the strategic choices that decision makers are likely to make when trying to influence another party. The identification of such factors is an important next step in developing a model of conflict based on the concept of relationships. It would be useful to know, for example, under what circumstances decision makers are likely to resort to coercive forms of influence rather than to use less provocative tactics such as persuasion or negotiation. The model depicted in Figure 6.1 clearly implies that strategic choices should be influenced, at least in part, by the relationship between the interacting parties, but it does not specify in any detail the nature of this influence. In this section, accordingly, we address that issue.

Because of space constraints, we will not attempt to present an exhaustive or complete analysis of the determinants of strategic choice; rather, we will focus on providing a broad sketch of some of the major psychological and institutional processes that shape strategic choice. One assumption that we make in the following analysis is that different types of relationship imply different degrees of perceived commonality of interests and correspondence of outcomes. For example, relationships such as enmity and rivalry imply disjunctive interests and low correspondence between own and other's outcomes, while alliance and symbiosis imply more conjunctive interests and high correspondence of outcomes.

Psychological Constraints in Strategic Choice. Our analysis of relationships implies three basic factors that might influence strategic choice: (1) decision makers' *goals* or *motives* during decision making, (2) their *expectations* about the other party's likely choice of behavior, and (3) their *perception* of the efficacy of a given mode of influence.

Decision makers' goals and motives. Many game-theoretic and economic models of strategic choice have treated as axiomatic the proposition that individuals will act primarily to maximize their own outcomes (Roth, 1989). Although this assumption has proven to be analytically useful, its power in predicting actual choice behavior in strategic games has often proven rather low. For example, individuals in experimental studies of strategic interaction have frequently been observed to differ considerably in the relative importance or "weight" that they appear to assign to their own outcomes and others' outcomes. (See, for example, Messick and McClintock, 1968; McClintock and Keil, 1983; Kramer, McClintock, and Messick, 1986.) As Ochs and Roth (1989, p. 379) have noted, "At least some agents incorporate distributional considerations in their utility functions." These differences in individuals' preferences for various self-other outcome distributions have been presumed to reflect differences in the goals or motives underlying strategic choice (McClintock and Liebrand, 1988). Three motivational orientations that have been widely observed in these studies that have special importance for understanding strategic choice in the context of relationships are *individualism, competition,* and *cooperation.*

The choice behavior of individualistically oriented decision makers suggests that they are primarily concerned about furthering their own outcomes, regardless of how their choices affect the other party's outcomes. The behavior of these decision makers comes closest to the sort of egocentric, own-outcome maximizing behavior assumed by many game-theoretic models. In contrast, competitively oriented decision makers tend to choose strategies that maximize their *relative* gain over others (hence, they are also sometimes referred to in this literature as "difference maximizers"). Finally, decision makers with a cooperative orientation tend to act in ways that increase their *joint* gains; that is, they try to maximize the combined outcomes of self and the other party.

Decision makers' motivational orientations can influence the specific strategic choice they make when interacting with others. In particular, competitors may use more coercive and distributive strategies, because these strategies are most likely to maximize their relative gain over others. In contrast, individualists may be responsive to the demands of a particular situation, so that their strategic behavior is more contingent. Since these individuals are concerned only with their own gain, they are likely to select whichever strategy (integrative, distributive, cognitive, and so on) they perceive as having the greatest likelihood of maximizing their own gain. Thus, they will adapt their own behavior to that of the party with whom they are interacting. The behavior of cooperators may be similarly adaptive to the other party's strategic behavior. When negotiating against another cooperator, for example, they may reciprocate integrative behavior in order to maximize their joint outcomes. When interacting with a more competitive decision maker, on the other hand, they may resort to distributive tactics in order to avoid exploitation.

We propose here that the motive or goal of decision makers is likely to depend on how they define or construe their relationship with the other party. In other words, the weight given to individual versus joint outcomes during strategic interaction depends on the prior relationship between the parties. Thus, in the case of cooperative or symbiotic relationships, each party may positively weight both its own and the other party's outcomes during decision making. This results in a preference for using modes of influence that further joint rather than individual interests alone. In the case of more neutral relationships (for example, conditional cooperation and instrumental interdependence), the parties may be concerned primarily with maximizing their own interests and relatively indifferent to the outcomes accruing to the other. In these cases, they may view the situation as more episodic and the scope of the relationship as limited to the issues at stake (see Greenhalgh and Chapman, 1990). Finally, in the case of relationships involving enmity or rivalry, the parties may be concerned primarily with maximizing their relative gain over the other. Their orientation will be largely competitive, and they may view the situation as terminal. As a result, they may use coercive power-based strategies and more distributive forms of bargaining.

Decision makers' expectations. Even when decision makers are willing to use positive forms of influence, such as problem solving or persuasion, they may still decide against doing so if they believe that the other party will be unresponsive or might exploit their efforts at cooperation. As Pruitt and Kimmel (1967) note, cooperation depends not only on decision makers having the goal of cooperating but also on the expectation that the other party will cooperate in return. Thus, trust is an important factor mediating strategic choice. In support of this, several recent experimental studies of strategic choice in interdependence situations have found that when expectations of reciprocity are low, decision makers are less likely to risk cooperating with others (Brann and Foddy, 1988; Kramer, Goldman, and Davis, 1990; Messick and others, 1983).

Although the effects of perceived relationship on expectations of reciprocity have not been examined empirically, it is reasonable to argue that trust levels will vary across relationships. For example, in the case of relationships such as enmity and rivalry, decision makers may tend to overestimate the differences between themselves and the other party. Consequently, they may underestimate the potential for reciprocity. These low expectations can affect strategic choice in several ways. First, when expectations of reciprocity are low, individuals may be less likely to communicate openly or initiate other forms of integrative bargaining. For example, one technique that helps parties achieve integrative outcomes is logrolling. In logrolling, the parties agree to "trade off" on two issues, each of which is more important to one party than the other (Lax and Sebenius, 1986; Lewicki and Litterer, 1985). If their expectations of reciprocity are low, the parties may perceive little incentive to proposing such trade-offs or trusting the other person to live up to his or her side of a bargain. Low expectations of reciprocity can also cause negotiators to adopt relatively short-term and instrumental perspectives on their relationships. Specifically, they may be less willing to engage in cooperative strategies such as GRIT (Lindskold, 1973) that are intended to build trust and cooperation but are predicated on longer-term interactions.

In the case of more cooperative relationships, such as alliances and symbiotic relationships, in contrast, the parties' expectations of reciprocity may be much greater. Thus, they may be willing to take greater risks in trusting the other party. Moreover, they may be less reactive to ambiguous information that the other party may be failing to live up to an agreement.

Decision makers' perceptions of the efficacy of strategic choices. We might also expect, again on intuitive grounds, that the selection of influence strategies should be contingent on decision makers' perceptions of the efficacy of those strategies. All else being equal, individuals should select those strategies that they believe will be particularly effective in changing another party's behavior. Perceptions of the efficacy of different strategies may depend, however, on the perceived relationship between the parties. This is suggested by recent work by Rothbart and Hallmark (1988). They found that, when evaluating the efficacy of various influence strategies, individuals judged conciliatory strategies to be less likely to be efficacious when dealing with "out-group" members than when dealing with members of one's own group.

If we construe the perceived closeness of a relationship as a proxy for in-group–out-group status, the implications of these findings are clear. First, they suggest that individuals may select strategies that are excessively coercive or provocative when trying to influence other "out-group" parties. Second, since individuals tend to view themselves as being more responsive to cooperative and conciliatory modes of influence, they may perceive the behavior of another party as excessively hostile or provocative in return. To the extent, of course, that the other party does the same, the result may be a series of reciprocally hostile exchanges that further escalate the conflict between them. In other words, because both parties underestimate the impact of their behavior on the other and simultaneously overreact to the influence attempts of the other, it may be very difficult

for them to reach a state of equilibrium or achieve a sense of closure
to the conflict.

Institutional Constraints on Strategic Choice. In drawing attention to some of the psychological determinants of strategic choice,
we do not intend to overlook or minimize the role of institutional
constraints on such choices. Because decision-making elites in nations operate within complex organizational settings, their strategic
choices will undoubtedly be affected by the properties of those settings. The range of options that decision makers consider and their
behavioral predispositions toward action, for example, may be
heavily influenced by the norms, attitudes, and values within an
organization. Similarly, an organization's culture and its routines
and SOPs are likely to influence which events are seen as important
and meriting further attention or action (March and Weissinger-
Baylon, 1986; Posen, 1984; Snyder, 1984).

Another characteristic feature of complex organizations is the
presence of multiple constituencies that exert pressures on decision
makers to pursue policies and courses of action that are perceived
to be compatible with their own interests. For this reason, analyses
of relationship that focus only on relationships between the
decision-making elite will necessarily be inadequate. For example,
trying to understand the relationship between President Reagan
and Chairman Gorbachev at the interpersonal level would fail to
take into account the impact of the constituencies to whom they feel
accountable. As Sutton and Kramer argue in Chapter Seven, such
pressures create severe strategic predicaments for decision makers.
In response to these predicaments, they are likely to modify their
strategic behavior in order to strike compromises between the competing internal and external pressures. Along these lines, Carnevale,
Pruitt, and Britton (1979) found that individuals are likely to adopt
competitive or contentious tactics when negotiating under constituent surveillance.

Not only may the short-term strategic choices of decision makers
be constrained, but also their ability to propose new definitions of
relationship. In the early 1960s, President Kennedy encountered numerous obstacles in trying to steer Soviet-American relations in a
more cooperative direction; members of the Reagan administration
experienced significant negative reactions from critics when they

expressed optimism regarding the arms control negotiations between Reagan and Gorbachev; and Gorbachev more recently has encountered significant internal opposition to his efforts to change the nature of the relationships between the Soviet Union and some of its allies.

Conclusion and Implications

As we noted at the beginning of this chapter, the study of international relations and that of interorganizational relations have proceeded largely independently of each other. This has been particularly true of the literatures concerning organizational and international conflict. As an inspection of the citations found in any of the major reviews in either of these literatures will attest, there has been surprisingly little cross-fertilization of ideas. This independence is not altogether surprising. The boundaries of empirical inquiry and theory development that characterize a field are often set along clearly drawn disciplinary lines. Theory and research on international relations have largely fallen within the perimeters of political science. While insights from organizational theory have on occasion informed such theory and research (see, for example, Allison, 1971; Posen, 1984; Snyder, 1984), these insights have been imported by political scientists; organizational scholars have remained, at best, only accidental tourists in this field. Of course, there are obvious conceptual problems associated with crossing levels of analysis. These create barriers for any scholar who hopes to span disciplinary boundaries. Among the most obvious of such problems is the simple fact that nations are complex multiorganizational structures. Thus, they may have emergent properties that do not exist at the level of the individual organization.

However, lines of inquiry can be too independent. This occurs when promising new concepts in one field are overlooked in another. We believe that *relationship* is such a concept. The study of conflict in organizations is making headway by exploring the impact of relationships on how conflicts are experienced and addressed, and the reciprocal effects of conflicts on relationships. This chapter has explored the usefulness of this line of inquiry and provided some initial ideas for how this point of view might enrich the study of international relations.

The model we have presented here suggests several promising directions for future research in this area. First, although we have sketched the broad outlines of a model of strategic choice based on the notion of relationships, there is much about this model that remains to be elaborated. In particular, we need a more systematic treatment of the organizational and psychological determinants of strategic choice. We need a model of strategic choice that weaves together these separate literatures. We have utilized the concept of a prototype as a way of conceptualizing individual differences in perceived relationship but have noted that more research is needed to validate this idea.

Second, there is a need for further exploration of organizational analogs that might be useful in understanding international relationships. Borys and Jemison (1989), for example, have recently presented a systematic framework for thinking about what they term "hybrid" organizational arrangements—new combinations of organizations that further the joint interests of the collaborating parties. The study of such forms at the organizational level may inform the development of theory about how international relationships such as regimes (Keohane, 1979; Mares and Powell, Chapter Three of this volume) and alliances (Walt, 1987) evolve, as well as help identify other innovative alternative structures.

We opened this chapter with the uncontroversial observation that interorganizational and international relations are characterized by many forms of interdependence. Not surprisingly, therefore, scholars in these fields have focused much of their discussion of conflict on the importance of interdependence in shaping strategic choice. The broader perspective on relationships that we propose in this chapter implies that although understanding the bases of interdependence between nations or organizations may be a necessary ingredient in any theory of conflict, it may not be a sufficient ingredient. Strategic choice, we would argue, is shaped just as much by the intangible and to a large degree tacit dimensions of relationship between parties. We hope that scholars in both international relations theory and organizational theory will be intrigued by the possibilities that the concept of relationship introduces to the study of both organizational and international phenomena. In particular, we believe that this concept can broaden our view about the nature of strategic choice and conflict in organizations and between nations.

References

Allison, G. T. *Essence of Decision: Explaining the Cuban Missile Crisis.* Boston: Little, Brown, 1971.

Axelrod, R. *The Evolution of Cooperation.* New York: Basic Books, 1984.

Bazerman, M. H. "Negotiator Judgment." *American Behavioral Scientist,* 1983, *27,* 211–228.

Bazerman, M. H., and Neal, M. A. "Heuristics in Negotiation: Limitations to Dispute Resolution Effectiveness." In M. H. Bazerman and R. J. Lewicki (eds.), *Negotiating in Organizations.* Newbury Park, Calif.: Sage, 1983.

Betts, R. K. *Nuclear Blackmail and Nuclear Balance.* Washington, D.C.: Brookings Institution, 1987.

Bies, R. J. "The Predicament of Injustice: The Management of Moral Outrage." In L. L. Cummings and B. Staw (eds.), *Research in Organizational Behavior,* Vol. 9. Greenwich, Conn.: JAI Press, 1987.

Borys, B., and Jemison, D. B. "Hybrid Arrangements as Strategic Alliances: Theoretical Issues in Organizational Combinations." *Academy of Management Review,* 1989, *14,* 234–249.

Brams, S. J. *Superpower Games: Applying Game Theory to Superpower Conflict.* New Haven, Conn.: Yale University Press, 1985.

Brann, P., and Foddy, M. "Trust and the Consumption of a Deteriorating Common Resource." *Journal of Conflict Resolution,* 1988, *31,* 615–630.

Brewer, M. B. "A Dual Process Model of Impression Formation." In T. K. Scrull and R. S. Wyer (eds.), *Advances in Social Cognition.* Vol. 1. Hillsdale, N.J.: Erlbaum, 1988.

Caplow, T. M. *Two Against One: Coalitions in Triads.* Englewood Cliffs, N.J.: Prentice-Hall, 1968.

Carnevale, P. J., Pruitt, D. G., and Britton, S. D. "Looking Tough:

The Negotiator Under Constituent Surveillance." *Personality and Social Psychology Bulletin,* 1979, *5,* 118–121.

Cialdini, R. B. *Influence: Science and Practice.* Glenview, Ill.: Scott, Foresman, 1985.

De Mesquita, B. B. *The War Trap.* New Haven, Conn.: Yale University Press, 1981.

Fiske, S. T., and Taylor, S. E. *Social Cognition.* New York: Random House, 1984.

George, A. L., Farley, P. J., and Dallin, A. (eds). *U.S.-Soviet Security Cooperation: Achievements, Failures, and Lessons.* New York: Oxford University Press, 1988.

George, A. L., and Smoke, R. *Deterrence in American Foreign Policy: Theory and Practice.* New York: Columbia University Press, 1974.

Greenhalgh, L. "Managing Conflict." *Sloan Management Review,* 1986, *27* (4), 45–51.

Greenhalgh, L. "The Case Against Winning in Negotiations." *Negotiation Journal,* 1987a, *3,* 167–173.

Greenhalgh, L. "Relationships in Negotiations." *Negotiation Journal,* 1987b, *3,* 235–243.

Greenhalgh, L. "Cooperation, Competition, and Coercion: Impact of Strategic Choices on Ongoing Relationships." Working paper, Amos Tuck School of Business Administration, Dartmouth College, 1989.

Greenhalgh, L., and Chapman, D. I. "Relationships and Conflict: A Model and Typology." Working paper, Amos Tuck School of Business Administration, Dartmouth College, 1990.

Greer, S. *The Logic of Social Inquiry.* Chicago: Aldine, 1969.

Janis, I. L. *Groupthink: Psychological Studies of Policy Decisions and Fiascoes.* Boston: Houghton Mifflin, 1982.

Janis, I. L. *Crucial Decisions: Leadership in Policymaking and Crisis Management.* New York: Free Press, 1989.

Jervis, R. *Perception and Misperception in International Politics.* Princeton, N.J.: Princeton University Press, 1976.

Jervis, R. *The Meaning of the Nuclear Revolution.* Ithaca, N.Y.: Cornell University Press, 1989.

Jervis, R., Lebow, R. N., and Stein, J. *Psychology and Deterrence.* Baltimore, Md.: Johns Hopkins University Press, 1985.

Kahn, R. L. "Nations as Organizations: Organizational Theory and International Relations." *Journal of Social Issues*, 1989, *45*, 181–194.

Kelley, H. *Personal Relationships: Their Structures and Processes.* Hillsdale, N.J.: Erlbaum, 1979.

Keohane, R. O. *After Hegemony: Cooperation and Discord in the World Political Economy.* Princeton, N.J.: Princeton University Press, 1984.

Klar, Y., Bar-Tal, D., and Kruglanski, A. W. "Conflict as a Cognitive Schema: Toward a Social Cognitive Analysis of Conflict and Conflict Termination." In W. Stroebe, A. W. Kruglanski, D. Bar-Tal, and M. Hewstone (eds.), *The Social Psychology of Intergroup Conflict: Theory, Research, and Applications.* New York: Springer-Verlag, 1988.

Klatzky, R. L. *Human Memory: Structures and Processes.* (2nd ed.) New York: W. H. Freeman, 1980.

Kramer, R. M. "Windows of Vulnerability or Cognitive Illusions? Cognitive Processes and the Nuclear Arms Race." *Journal of Experimental Social Psychology*, 1989, *25*, 79–100.

Kramer, R. M. "Intergroup Conflict in Organizations: The Role of Categorization Processes." In L. L. Cummings and B. M. Staw (eds.), *Research in Organizational Behavior.* Greenwich, Conn.: JAI Press, 1990a.

Kramer, R. M. "The More the Merrier? Social Psychological Aspects of Multi-Party Negotiations in Organizations." In M. H. Bazerman, R. J. Lewicki, and B. L. Sheppard (eds.), *Research on Negotiation in Organizations.* Vol. 3. Greenwich, Conn.: JAI Press, 1990b.

Kramer, R. M., Goldman, L., and Davis, G. "Social Identity, Expectations of Reciprocity, and Cooperation in Social Dilemmas." Unpublished manuscript, Stanford University, 1990.

Kramer, R. M., McClintock, C. M., and Messick, D. M. "Social Values and Cooperative Response to a Simulated Resource Conservation Crisis." *Journal of Personality*, 1986, *54*, 576–592.

Kramer, R. M., Meyerson, D., and Davis, G. "How Much Is Enough? Psychological Components of Guns Versus Butter Decisions." *Journal of Personality and Social Psychology*, 1990, *58*.

Kuhlman, D. M., Camac, C. R., and Cunha, D. A. "Individual

Differences in Social Orientation." In H. Wilke, C. Rutte, and D. M. Messick (eds.), *Experimental Studies of Social Dilemmas.* Frankfurt: Peter Lang, 1986.

Kull, S. *Minds at War: Nuclear Reality and the Inner Conflicts of Defense Policymakers.* New York: Basic Books, 1988.

Lax, D. A., and Sebenius, J. K. *The Manager as Negotiator: Bargaining for Cooperation and Competitive Gain.* New York: Free Press, 1986.

Lewicki, R. J., and Litterer, J. A. *Negotiation.* Homewood, Ill.: Irwin, 1985.

Lindskold, S. "Trust Development, the GRIT Proposal, and the Effects of Conciliatory Acts on Conflict and Cooperation." *Psychological Bulletin,* 1978, *85,* 772-793.

Lord, R. G., and Foti, R. J. "Schema Theories, Information Processing, and Organizational Behavior." In H. P. Sims and D. A. Gioia (eds.), *The Thinking Organization: Dynamics of Organizational Social Cognition.* San Francisco: Jossey-Bass, 1986.

McClintock, C. G., and Keil, L. "Social Values: Their Definition, Development, and Impact upon Human Decision Making in Settings of Outcome Interdependence." In M. H. Blumberg, A. Hare, V. Kent, and M. Davies (eds.), *Small Groups and Social Interaction.* Vol. 2. New York: Wiley, 1983.

McClintock, C. G., and Liebrand, W.B.G. "Role of Interdependence Structure, Individual Value Orientation, and Another's Strategy in Social Decision Making: A Transformational Analysis." *Journal of Personality and Social Pscyhology,* 1988, *55,* 396-409.

Maki, J., and McClintock, C. G. "The Accuracy of Social Value Prediction: Actor and Observer Differences." *Journal of Personality and Social Psychology,* 1983, *45,* 829-838.

March, J. G., and Weissinger-Baylon, R. (eds.). *Ambiguity and Command: Organizational Perspectives on Military Decision Making.* Marshfield, Mass.: Pitman, 1986.

Messick, D. M., and McClintock, C. G. "Motivational Basis of Choice in Experimental Games." *Journal of Experimental Social Psychology,* 1968, *4,* 1-25.

Messick, D. M., Wilke, H., Brewer, M. B., Kramer, R. M., Zemke, P., and Lui, L. "Individual Adaptations and Structural Change as Solutions to Social Dilemmas." *Journal of Personality and Social Psychology*, 1983, *44*, 294–309.

Morley, I. E., Webb, J., and Stephenson, G. M. "Bargaining and Arbitration in the Resolution of Conflict." In W. Stroebe, A. W. Kruglanski, D. Bar-Tal, and M. Hewstone (eds.), *The Social Psychology of Intergroup Conflict*. New York: Springer-Verlag, 1988.

Neustadt, R. E., and May, E. R. *Thinking in Time: The Uses of History for Decision Makers*. New York: Free Press, 1986.

Ochs, J., and Roth, A. E. "An Experimental Study of Sequential Bargaining." *American Economic Review*, 1989, *79* (3), 355–384.

Oye, K. A. "Explaining Cooperation Under Anarchy: Hypotheses and Strategies." In K. A. Oye (ed.), *Cooperation Under Anarchy*. Princeton, N.J.: Princeton University Press, 1986.

Pfeffer, J. *Power in Organizations*. Marshfield, Mass.: Pitman, 1981.

Pfeffer, J., and Salancik, G. *The External Control of Organizations: A Resource Dependence Perspective*. New York: Harper & Row, 1978.

Posen, B. R. *The Sources of Military Doctrine: France, Britain, and Germany Between the World Wars*. Ithaca, N.Y.: Cornell University Press, 1984.

Pruitt, D. G., and Kimmel, M. J. "Twenty Years of Experimental Gaming: Critique, Synthesis, and Suggestions for the Future." *Annual Review of Psychology*, 1967, *28*, 363–392.

Pruitt, D. G., and Rubin, J. Z. *Social Conflict: Escalation, Stalemate, and Conflict*. New York: Random House, 1986.

Rosch, E. "Principles of Categorization." In E. Rosch and B. B. Lloyd (eds.), *Cognition and Categorization*. Hillsdale, N.J.: Erlbaum, 1978.

Roth, A. E. "An Economic Approach to the Study of Bargaining." In M. H. Bazerman, R. J. Lewicki, and B. L. Sheppard (eds.), *Research on Negotiation in Organizations*. Vol. 3. Greenwich, Conn.: JAI Press, 1989.

Rothbart, M., and Hallmark, W. "In-Group–Out Group Differences in the Perceived Efficacy of Coercion and Conciliation in Resolving Social Conflict." *Journal of Personality and Social Psychology*, 1988, *55*, 248–257.

Saunders, H. H. "An Historic Challenge to Rethink How Nations Relate." Working paper, 1989.

Schelling, T. C. *The Strategy of Conflict*. Cambridge, Mass.: Harvard University Press, 1960.

Snyder, J. *The Ideology of the Offensive: Military Decision Making and the Disasters of 1914*. Ithaca, N.Y.: Cornell University Press, 1984.

Staw, B. M., and Ross, J. "Behavior in Escalation Situations: Antecedents, Prototypes, and Solutions." In B. M. Staw and L. L. Cummings (eds.), *Research in Organizational Behavior*. Vol. 9. Greenwich, Conn.: JAI Press, 1987.

Stein, J. "Building Politics in Psychology." *Political Psychology*, 1988, *9*, 245-271.

Tetlock, P. E. "Policy-Makers' Images of International Conflict." *Journal of Social Issues*, 1983, *39*, 67-86.

Tetlock, P. E. "Monitoring the Integrative Complexity of American and Soviet Policy Rhetoric: What Can Be Learned?" *Journal of Social Issues*, 1988, *44*, 101-131.

Tung, R. L. "How to Negotiate with the Japanese." *California Management Review*, 1984, *26*, 62-77.

Walt, S. M. *The Origins of Alliances*. Ithaca, N.Y.: Cornell University Press, 1987.

Walton, R. E., and McKersie, R. B. *A Behavioral Theory of Labor Negotiations*. New York: McGraw-Hill, 1965.

Weick, K. E., and Bougon, M. G. "Organizations as Cognitive Maps: Charting Ways to Success and Failure." In H. P. Sims and D. A. Gioia (eds.), *The Thinking Organization: Dynamics of Organizational Social Cognition*. San Francisco: Jossey-Bass, 1986.

Wilson, R. "Deterrence in Oligopolistic Competition." In P. Stern, R. Axelrod, R. Jervis, and R. Radner (eds.), *Perspectives on Deterrence*. New York: Oxford University Press, 1989.

Zimbardo, P., Ebbesen, E. B., and Maslach, C. *Influencing Attitudes and Changing Behavior*. Reading, Mass.: Addison-Wesley, 1977.

Zimmerman, M. *How to Do Business with the Japanese*. New York: Random House, 1985.

Chapter 7

Transforming Failure into Success

Spin Control in the Iceland Arms Control Talks

Robert I. Sutton
Roderick M. Kramer

"Some of us are like a shovel brigade that follow a parade down Main Street cleaning up," Mr. Regan said with a laugh. "We took Reykjavik and turned what was a sour situation into something that turned out pretty well."

Donald Regan, White House chief of staff, *New York Times*, Nov. 16, 1986

One of the most dramatic ways in which nations interact with each other is through meetings involving their heads of state. Economic summits, arms control negotiations, and other formal, face-to-face encounters have played an increasingly important role in managing international relations during recent years. Nonetheless, the ability of heads of state to reach agreements during and after such meetings is often hindered, and is always shaped, by the constituencies to whom they feel accountable. The nuances of this process have not, however, received much attention, either from international relations theorists or from organizational scholars. The impressions that heads of state create—either intentionally or unintentionally—among key constituencies is one such nuance.

This chapter uses the example of the 1986 Iceland arms control talks between President Reagan and Chairman Gorbachev to develop grounded theory about the use of impression management by organizational actors. Although the specific events associated with these talks have faded from the headlines, the events at Reykjavik still stand as a striking case study of how presidential administrations use symbolic actions to maintain and enhance their image among important constituencies.

In developing our argument, we first explain how our perspective is an extension of current work by organizational theorists on the symbolic role of management. We then consider how our perspective follows from and contributes to existing social-psychological theory on impression management. This conceptual background sets the stage for our treatment of the Iceland arms control talks. We propose that three causally linked phases of impression management were associated with these talks. On the American side, the first phase consisted of attempts by the Reagan administration to set expectations or provide a "frame" for the forthcoming meeting between Reagan and Gorbachev. The second phase entailed acknowledging that the talks had failed, creating a predicament for Reagan and his advisers. The third phase consisted of attempts by key members of the administration to transform the failure into a success by "imparting positive spin." These three phases are useful, we argue, for understanding how impression management by members of a presidential administration affected the social construction of reality held by key audiences. By skillfully using several impression management strategies, these impression managers were able to convince key audiences that although the outcome of the Iceland talks appeared to be a failure, it was actually a success.

The Symbolic Role of Management

Recent perspectives on organizations portray elites such as chief executive officers and top management teams as "managers of meaning" who interpret organizational events in order to enhance and protect the intertwined images of their organizations and themselves (Pfeffer, 1981). Indeed, Weick and Daft (1983, pp. 90–91) have argued that "the job of management is to interpret, not to get the work of the organization done."

Managerial interpretations of organizational events are essential because they legitimize organizational actions to both internal and external constituencies (Meindl, Ehrlich, and Dukerich, 1985; Pfeffer, 1981; Salancik and Meindl, 1984); the effectiveness of any organization depends on the continuing participation and support of such exchange partners. In other words, shaping the perceptions of the "organizational audience" is an essential component of the leadership role.

This view of organizational elites is useful for understanding the behavior of presidents and their administrations. Presidents and their aides who make decisions regarding foreign policy and national security are not only concerned with the impact of their decisions on so-called objective issues such as the balance of power between nations and trade relations. They are also concerned about how such decisions will be perceived by important constituencies to whom they feel responsible or accountable. Thus, a central component of both organizational and political leadership is symbolic acts that are calculated to shape the perceptions of key "audiences" for whom they must perform.

Leaders as Impression Managers

This chapter builds on the view that the job of management is to interpret key events for organizational audiences. We contend that leaders of both organizations and presidential administrations are similar to other individuals in other contexts where there is pressure to maintain positive images, reputations, and identities. To do so, they are motivated to engage in impression management. Indeed, political decisions and actions by presidential administrations appear to reflect an increasing concern with the images they project to others, their popularity among important constituencies, and the preservation and protection of their reputations. As the quotation by Donald Regan at the beginning of this chapter suggests, appearance may be regarded as more important than reality.

Impression management has been the subject of literally hundreds of laboratory studies. (See Chatman, Bell, and Staw, 1986; Schlenker, 1980; Tedeschi, 1981, for overview.) Many of these studies focus on techniques that actors use to attenuate the negative effects of identity-threatening situations or "predicaments" (for example, apologizing, blaming others, reinterpreting the event) or on techniques for accentuating the positive effects of identity-enhancing situations (for example, claiming responsibility, using self-deprecation).

Despite the number of such studies, however, there are still many gaps in our knowledge about the impression management process. This chapter addresses at least three such gaps: (1) how individuals who engage in impression management in laboratory experiments differ from organizational actors who engage in impression management in field settings; (2) how *ambiguity* about whether an event is identity threatening or enhancing affects the impression management process; and (3) how impression management can be viewed as a dynamic rather than static process. Each gap is considered below.

Impression Managers in the Laboratory Versus the Field. Most prior research on impression management has been conducted in laboratory settings; only a few researchers have studied impression management in natural settings such as organizations (Gardner and Martinko, 1988; Staw, McKechnie, and Puffer, 1983; Sutton and Callahan, 1987) and university classrooms (Cialdini and others, 1976). In the present chapter, we consider a real group of impression managers (members of the Reagan administration) and their transactions with a real audience (the press). Moreover, while impression management can be used to enhance or protect the image of both individuals and social systems, most existing research and theory focus on the individual level of analysis (Chatman, Bell, and Staw, 1986). This chapter considers efforts by a group of impression managers to enhance the image of their organization, the Reagan administration. This last point is crucial because, as we will argue in more detail, the process of impression management that involves multiple actors and audiences is shaped by forces not evident at the dyadic level of analysis.

A comparison of Figures 7.1 and 7.2 illustrates how impression

**Figure 7.1. Basic Elements of Laboratory Studies
of Impression Management.**

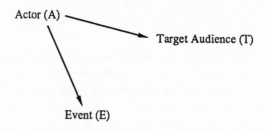

Figure 7.2. Elements of Impression Management in Organizations.

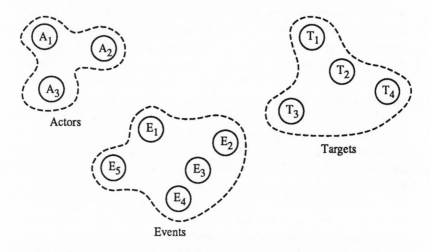

management by individuals in the laboratory differs from impression management by organizational leaders in field settings. By extension, the figures illustrate some ways in which the conceptual perspective developed here differs from most prior work. Figure 7.1 summarizes how impression management is usually modeled in laboratory studies. An actor (typically a confederate) tries to maintain or enhance his or her image in the eyes of some target audience (usually the subject of the experiment). The impression management predicament arises because the actor has experienced an identity-threatening event (for example, spilling a cup of coffee) or an identity-enhancing event (for example, winning an award). The efficacy of the impression management strategy (for example, taking responsibility, denying responsibility, joking, self-deprecation) is usually assessed by the experimental subject, who constitutes the entire "target audience."

This laboratory approach is useful because it is parsimonious and allows the researcher carefully to control for or carefully to screen out extraneous sources of variation and social complexity. Unfortunately, however, as Figure 7.2 indicates, this approach greatly oversimplifies impression management problems that are typically faced by corporate and presidential elites who are trying to protect or enhance the images of their organizations.

Organizational elites—be they top management teams or the president's cabinet—are composed of multiple actors. As a result, the process of impression management becomes decidedly more complex. The complexities include some of the following. First, there may be a problem of coordinating the various accounts provided by different actors. This does not arise in laboratory studies of individuals. Multiple actors who are trying to enhance the identity of the same organization may say and do things that contradict each other. Second, some members of the elite group may be perceived as having greater credibility than others. Third, the perceived credibility of members of the elite group may vary, depending on the issue.

Fourth, an individual actor may engage in behavior that protects his or her own image but damages the image of the organization as a whole. Fifth, the aggregate images of individual actors may be only loosely related to the image of the social system as a whole. For example, audience members for a particular organization may perceive that it is a good company with poor management or a poor company with good management.

Sixth, some impression management strategies available to groups cannot be used by individuals. For example, when an identity-threatening event occurs (for example, poor financial performance in a firm or a political scandal), organizations can identify a scapegoat, place blame on that person, banish him or her from the collectivity, and claim that the once soiled entity has been transformed into a purified and untarnished entity (Bonazzi, 1983).

Moreover, impression management by organizational actors, when it occurs in natural settings, differs from the typical laboratory model because organizational actors face the more complex problem of presenting a favorable image to multiple targets. Conveyed images that create a good impression among some members of the audience may create a poor impression among other members. For example, the top management of a firm that is experiencing mild financial difficulties may use bold strategies calculated to impress stockholders, such as pay cuts and employee layoffs. These same strategies, however, can create a poor impression among lower-level employees, soil the firm's reputation in the community, and make it difficult to recruit new employees.

Finally, organizational elites in natural settings face the problem of maintaining a favorable image in the context of multiple concurrent events, some of which are identity threatening and some of which are identity enhancing. This creates additional sources of complexity because the target audiences' *overall* image of the elites is not shaped by a single event. Rather, audiences evaluate each new event in the context of a large number of identity-threatening and identity-enhancing events. This fact of organizational life creates the opportunity for organizational actors to use impression management strategies that are not usually available to laboratory subjects. When an identity-threatening event occurs, they can answer questions from members of the organizational audience by calling attention to the other "wonderful" things that they have done or are doing, thereby deflecting attention from events with less flattering implications.

Ambiguity of Events: Identity Threatening or Identity Enhancing? The second contribution of this chapter is to consider the process of impression management when the meaning of an event is ambiguous. Previous research on impression management has focused almost exclusively on events that are unambiguously identity threatening or enhancing. Thus, organizational researchers have focused on unambiguous indicators of financial performance such as annual reports (Salancik and Meindl, 1984; Staw, McKechnie, and Puffer, 1983) and bankruptcy (Sutton and Callahan, 1987). In laboratory experiments, examples of clearly threatening predicaments include inducing subjects to lie or to spill index cards (Tedeschi and Riordan, 1981). Because the emphasis of experimental studies has been on controlling the independent variables, great pains have been taken to assure that the experimental manipulations are unambiguous. In contrast, the event examined here, the Iceland arms control talks, is an example of a predicament that was ambiguous because it was unclear initially whether the outcome of the talks was identity threatening or identity enhancing to the Reagan administration.

Studying events that are clearly identity threatening or enhancing has advantages for both theory building and testing. For example, this distinction enabled Tedeschi and Reiss (1981) to propose that actors would respond to identity-threatening situations with excuses (efforts to deny or minimize responsibility) or justifications (efforts to reduce construed negativeness) and to identity-enhancing situations with entitlings (efforts to gain responsibility) or enhancements (efforts to increase the construed positiveness of the event).

Yet many events that occur in life—both within and outside organizations—are ambiguous, particularly with respect to whether they enhance the identity of the actor or threaten it. For example, approximately eighteen months after Lee Iacocca became chief executive officer of the Chrysler Corporation, it experienced a quarter in which it lost about a quarter-million dollars. Prior research on impression management by organizational elites (for example, Staw, McKechnie, and Puffer, 1983) used such financial losses as evidence of an identity-threatening event. Iacocca, however, argued that this was Chrysler's *best* quarter in years and described the small loss as a sign that the firm would soon be profitable. Some observers of the automotive industry accepted Iacocca's version of the story, while others contended that the firm was still in deep trouble.

Thus, when an event of such ambiguity occurs, some members of the organizational audience may perceive it to be identity threatening, while other members may perceive the same event to be identity enhancing. Even the impression managers may be unsure of the meaning of the event. When such ambiguous events occur, the impression manager faces a dilemma that is implied, but not made explicit, by the Tedeschi and Reiss model. Should excuses and justifications be used? Or should entitlings and enhancements be used? In addition, impression managers may feel pressure to use excuses and justifications with audiences that disapprove of the event, and entitlings and enhancements with audiences that approve. These pressures can cause impression managers to engage in hypocrisy.

Impression Management as a Dynamic Process. The third gap in the literature addressed by this chapter is that impression management is viewed here as a dynamic process. While Figure 7.2 offers an enriched view of impression management, it is consistent with most prior research because it portrays impression management as a static rather than a dynamic process. In our analysis we wish to emphasize the give-and-take that occurs between impression managers and target audiences. Moreover, the success or failure of impression management attempts are treated as independent events in most prior work. The perspective presented here emphasizes that the efficacy of a given impression management attempt depends heavily on the prior history of impression management attempts by the group of actors and on the anticipated future relationship between impression managers and the audience.

Specifically, analysis of the Iceland case, along with our reading of existing literature on impression management (for example, Schlenker, 1980; Tedeschi, 1981) and Weick's (1979) writings on cycles of interlocked behaviors, has led us to propose the "impression management cycle" as a basic building block for research. Figure 7.3 portrays this cycle. We propose that an impression management cycle begins when some stimulus (an identity-threatening or identity-enhancing event or new data about such an event) arises that requires organizational actors to explain their role in the event, to explain specific features of the event, or both. This initial account may be accepted or rejected by the target audience. Audiences may use a variety of criteria to evaluate whether the initial account is satisfactory, including the following: (1) Is it plausible? (2) Are the actors credible? (3) Is the account politically acceptable?

The cycle ends if the audience does not question the actor's initial explanation. Indeed, if the audience is satisfied with the account, then neither the audience nor the actor is motivated to pursue the story since the salience of the stimulus is low. There is, after all, agreement about the meaning of the stimulus and thus ambiguity is low. We argue that in the case of many organizational predicaments, it is more often the case that audience members are

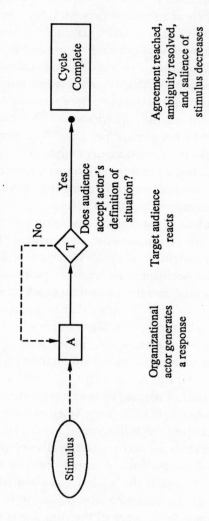

Figure 7.3. Impression Management Cycle.

Stimulus

Organizational
actor generates
a response

Target audience
reacts

Does audience
accept actor's
definition of
situation?

No

Yes

Cycle
Complete

Agreement reached,
ambiguity resolved,
and salience of
stimulus decreases

unconvinced by at least some parts of the impression manager's initial account. First, some constituencies may challenge the truthfulness or completeness of the account offered. Second, as we noted above, the various members of the top management team have the problem of coordinating their accounts. Thus, the consistency of the overall story may be called into question by the audience if conflicting accounts have been offered by different members of the impression management team. Third, as the story unfolds, new evidence may be introduced that requires additional explanation by the impression managers. Fourth, accounts that satisfy one audience may dissatisfy others. Thus, audiences that were satisfied with earlier accounts but are dissatisfied with the latest accounts may raise challenges that evoke new cycles of interaction between actors and audiences.

We propose that the impression manager is under pressure to continue responding to such audience reactions until both parties reach a negotiated settlement or shared interpretation of the event. In Weick's (1979) terminology, the cycles of interlocked behavior continue until the organizational actors and the target audiences have reduced, or eliminated, perceived equivocality regarding the event. As Figure 7.3 indicates, we propose that three outcomes indicate the end of an impression management cycle: (1) agreement is reached, (2) ambiguity is resolved, and (3) the salience of the stimulus decreases.

Phases of Impression Management in the Iceland Talks

The conceptual groundwork described above sets the stage for our analysis of the Iceland arms control talks. Before presenting the details of the analysis, it may be useful to describe briefly the data we used in our study. We gathered evidence about the Iceland talks from a variety of sources, including transcripts of press conferences and television interviews with key actors in the Reagan administration. For example, we viewed all of the ABC "Nightline" segments pertaining to the Iceland talks. We also collected reports about the talks from *Time, Newsweek, U.S. News and World Report,* the *Washington Post,* and the *New York Times.* The following chronology outlines the key events associated with these talks.

September 19, 1986: Soviet Foreign Minister Eduard Shevard-nadze delivers a letter to President Reagan from Soviet Premier Gorbachev proposing that the two of them meet prior to their official summit meeting for a less formal presummit discussion.

September 20, 1986: Reagan agrees that such a meeting might be worthwhile. Over the next few days, President Reagan, Secretary of State Shultz, and Secretary of Defense Weinberger reaffirm the value of such a meeting and begin laying the ground work for such a meeting. They indicate, however, that the Daniloff case remains an obstacle.

September 30, 1986: Daniloff is released and plans for the summit move forward.

October 11 and 12, 1986: The Iceland talks are held.

October 13, 1986: Newspaper accounts present a grim and almost universally negative postmortem. Administration efforts to engage in impression management, or "impart positive spin," are evident. These efforts continue into November, when attention begins to be deflected away from the Iceland talks and toward questions concerning illegal aid to the contras and weapon sales to Iran in exchange for American hostages.

This qualitative evidence about the Iceland arms control talks led us to identify three distinct phases of impression management involving members of the Reagan administration (the impression managers) and members of the press (the target audience). These phases are (1) setting expectations or "framing" the forthcoming event, (2) acknowledging the predicament, and (3) transforming the failure into a success, a process popularly characterized as "imparting positive spin." We propose that there were causal relationships among the three phases; specifically, we argue that the content of each prior phase shaped and constrained the content of subsequent phases.

The context in which these phases unfolded reflected a series of impression management predicaments that are analogous to the more complex case outlined in Figure 7.2 rather than the relatively simple case presented in Figure 7.1. In the Iceland talks, there were multiple organizational actors (Reagan and his aides) who acted as impression managers for a single social system (the Reagan administration). There were also multiple target audiences for such impression management. The diverse questions and comments raised in the press represented a wide range of interests, including American conservative, moderate, and liberal factions; European allies; and the Soviets, as well as the press's own interests. There were also multiple events. The Iceland talks themselves were composed of multiple events and occurred in the context of other events that required impression management by the Reagan administration, such as the Daniloff spy case and the emerging Iran "Arms for Hostages" affair.

The three phases were necessary before a negotiated settlement could be reached between the organizational actors (the Reagan administration) and their target audiences (represented by the press) about the real meaning of the Iceland talks. Numerous cycles of negotiation between organizational actors and audience were needed because new events occurred or were revealed as the situation unfolded, and the meaning of each new piece of information had to be negotiated. Moreover, much of the information associated with the Iceland talks was ambiguous; indeed, it was often unclear whether unfolding events threatened or enhanced the image of the Reagan administration. According to our model, when ambiguity is high, more cycles of negotiation are required. In Weick's (1979) terminology, the cycle of interlocked behavior had to continue longer because perceived equivocality about events was high.

This phase model and the evidence that gave rise to it are elaborated below.

Phase 1. Setting Expectations (Framing the Forthcoming Event)

> Reagan announced prior to the Iceland talks: "Success is
> not guaranteed. But, if Mr. Gorbachev comes to Iceland in
> a truly cooperative spirit, I think we can make some
> progress."
>
> *New York Times,* Oct. 9, 1986

The first phase entailed negotiations between the Reagan team and the press regarding expectations about the forthcoming talks. During this period, members of the Reagan administration and the audience (represented by members of the press) engaged in a series of both tacit and explicit negotiations regarding expectations about the possible success of the talks and how broad the agenda for the talks should be. Of particular importance seemed to be reaching a shared perception regarding how optimistic one should be about the potential for the talks to produce substantial progress in the area of arms control.

This period can be viewed more generally as a phase that arises when a predicament can be *anticipated* by organizational actors. This phase may be especially important to organizational elites when they anticipate that there is considerable risk that the upcoming event will be identity threatening (for example, the event is perceived to have a high probability of failure). Thus, prophylactic or "defensive" impression management may be used to prepare the audience for the anticipated predicament.

In the case of the Iceland talks, we observed considerable evidence that vigorous negotiations occurred regarding the appropriate definition of the situation. The impression management cycles observed during this phase consisted primarily of members of the Reagan administration proposing various definitions of the situation in order to set expectations about outcome from the upcoming talks. ("Organizational actor generates a response" in the terminology of Figure 7.3.) These proposed definitions were met with a series of "interrogations" from members of the target audience. ("Target audience reacts" and "does not accept the actor's definition of situation" in the terminology of Figure 7.3.) The forms these interrogations took included demands for clarification, qualification, and quantification.

The members of the Reagan administration reacted initially as if scheduling the talks was an unqualified identity-enhancing event. Indeed, Gorbachev's proposal to hold the talks initially received a very favorable reaction from the world press. The *New York Times* published an article on October 2, 1986, entitled "Keeping Score," in which it suggested that Gorbachev deserved the credit for arranging the superpower meeting that would salvage the East-West dialogue. Since this predicament was construed as identity enhancing by members of the Reagan administration, Tedeschi and Reiss's (1981) perspective predicts that members of the administration would try to use "entitlings" to encourage audience members to perceive that the administration shared responsibility (and credit) for the event. Sure enough, Reagan stated on October 2 that although the idea for the talks was Gorbachev's, the United States had proposed the *dates* for the meeting!

Moreover, initial statements to the press by Shultz and Reagan about the talks were largely positive and generally optimistic regarding the potential for progress at the upcoming talks. Reagan, for example, stated on October 1 that the "chances [for arms control] are better than they have been in many years." But this upbeat definition of the situation was challenged by both the press and other critics of the administration. First, the talks were viewed as having been made possible by the trade of a jailed American reporter (Daniloff) who had been accused of spying in the Soviet Union in exchange for a jailed Soviet official accused of spying in the United States. Critics argued that this act violated American negotiating principles and that the Reagan administration had paid too much in order to secure Soviet participation in the upcoming talks. Second, the Reagan administration was accused of being too eager and willing to negotiate. Specifically, conservative critics complained that the administration had adopted too conciliatory a stance for the upcoming talks.

The Reagan administration responded to these criticisms on October 2 and October 3. The press reported that the administration was trying to "dampen expectations," that the president was now voicing only "cautious optimism," and that other officials wished to avoid "heightened expectations."

In the period between October 2 and October 9, this initial cycle continued. Critics repeated the charge that the administration was too conciliatory, and the administration answered that, in fact, it had only modest expectations. At this juncture, another constituency, previously silent, entered the arena. Human rights advocates began to put pressure on the Reagan administration to link the arms control talks to progress on human rights issues. In response to these diverse criticisms that his administration was not being tough enough on the Soviets, Reagan replied that he was not going to be "snowed into believing that the leopard is changing its spots." Thus, the press and public were being reassured that they should not worry.

As this sequence of events illustrates, the Reagan administration first tried to introduce a definition of the situation. However, this definition was not accepted by a variety of key audiences. As a result, several rounds of explicit and implicit negotiation were required before a definition of the situation that was acceptable to both the administration and these key audiences was developed. In our model, this negotiated view of the situation is seen as a provisional rather than a final settlement, since new facts and new ambiguities were introduced as the talks and associated events unfolded. In addition, these cycles of negotiation led the impression managers— who had first interpreted the situation as unambiguously good—to reinterpret the situation as one that could either turn out well or turn out badly.

Phase 2. Acknowledging the Predicament

> The dejection in the President's carriage as he walked
> out of Hofdi house, the disappointment etched into every
> line of Secretary of State George Shultz's face as he briefed
> the press, had flashed an unmistakable message to TV
> watchers around the world: the summit meeting with
> Mikhail Gorbachev had ended in failure. Worse, headlines
> were spreading the impression that Reagan had thrown
> away the promise of a nuclear-free world by clinging to his
> vision of a space-based defense—even if there might be no
> missiles to defend against.
>
> Newsweek, Oct. 27, 1986

The second phase evident during the Iceland talks entailed acknowledging that an identity-threatening predicament had in fact occurred. The Reagan administration acknowledged during this phase that some failure had in fact occurred, but proposed a definition of the situation that was designed to protect its image. Phase 2 can be viewed more generally as the organizational analog of the identity-threatening situations described by Tedeschi and Reiss (1981). According to their framework, when an event is construed by impression managers as negative, they feel compelled to respond with excuses (efforts to deny or minimize responsibility) or justifications (efforts to reduce negativeness). Adding the dynamic perspective advocated in our model, the cycles of negotiation between the organizational actors (the Reagan administration) and the audience (represented by the press) focused on the issue of just *who* was to blame for the failure to reach an arms control agreement.

When the talks ended on the night of October 12, the press reported that "historic gains" had been near but that the talks had failed. Each side accused the other of responsibility for this failure. The Soviets asserted that the failure was a direct result of the Reagan administration's commitment to the Star Wars "fantasy." In return, President Reagan claimed that he had no illusions about the Soviets or their ultimate intentions. He stated, "We prefer no agreement than to bring home a bad agreement to the United States" (*New York Times*, Oct. 13, 1986).

Thus, the event was acknowledged to be a failure and a disappointment both by Reagan administration officials and by Gorbachev and his aides, but each side disagreed about which side was ultimately responsible for the failure. All parties agreed that the talks were a clear failure and thus were unambiguously threatening to the images of the negotiation partners.

At this point, conflicting accounts regarding the "correct" interpretation of this outcome began to appear in the American press. Senator Sam Nunn, for example, suggested that Reagan was not prepared to negotiate seriously and had missed a historic opportunity. Reagan was further criticized in the American press for clinging rigidly to Star Wars. Some scientists were quoted as arguing that it was a poor concept for a weapon but a good bargaining chip that should have been used in the negotiations. In contrast, the White House communications director claimed that it was "Reagan's finest hour." In sum, although there was a general feeling that an opportunity had been present to make real gains and had somehow been missed, there was also some ambiguity about the true nature of the outcome.

Phase 3. Transforming the Failure into a Success— "Imparting Positive Spin"

> Look at the polls. The American people are behind us.
> The point was we wanted to tell people what happened
> inside, so the outsiders will understand the enormity of the
> accomplishments that the President made. It wasn't a
> defeat at all, but it might have been characterized that way
> if we had sat still. . . . Why not tell what happened? Why
> not let it all hang out? Why not? We have nothing to be
> ashamed of.
>
> Donald Regan, as quoted in the
> *New York Times,* Oct. 16, 1986

The third phase of our model entails efforts by impression managers to offer new interpretations of the past events (Weick and Daft, 1983). These interpretations are aimed at transforming an event that audiences initially perceive as a failure into an event that they come to perceive as a success. According to our model, these iterative efforts to impart positive "spin" end when consensus between the organizational actors and their audiences is reached. These agreements typically concern such issues as the significance of the event, who deserves responsibility for it, and the extent to which it is identity threatening or identity enhancing.

As we illustrate below, the members of the Reagan administration were apparently able to reinterpret the events at Iceland as a success, and this "new and improved" social construction of reality was accepted by members of the American public. This case thus provides a striking illustration of how organizational leaders can manage meaning in order to enhance and protect the intertwined images of their social systems and themselves.

The transformation of a widely construed failure into a widely construed success appears not to have been considered in the impression management literature. In Tedeschi and Reiss's (1981) model, for example, and in a widely cited book by Schlenker (1980), the negative effects of identity-threatening events are presumed to be attenuated or neutralized through the use of excuses, justifications, and apologies. But these authors do not consider situations in which an initially negative event is transformed into an identity-enhancing event to which actors eventually respond with entitlings (efforts to gain responsibility). Nor do they offer a framework for understanding this transformation process. The ambiguous features of real events and the iterative dynamics of impression management in the real world—not to mention the remarkable impression management skills of real politicians—that we propose can be used to explain how such profound interpretation shifts can occur.

As noted above, perceptions that the Iceland talks had failed and the Reagan administration had let a historic opportunity slip away were widespread on Monday, October 13, the day after the talks ended. The Reagan administration immediately launched what White House Communications Director Patrick Buchanan described as "the most extensive and intensive communications plan I've ever been associated with in the White House" (*New York Times,* Oct. 15, 1986). Officials of the Reagan administration indicated that the goal of this media campaign was to *reverse* newspaper and television accounts that characterized Reagan's adherence to the Star Wars program as the primary reason that an agreement had not been reached at Iceland. The approach of the Reagan administration was to challenge this attribution directly. Buchanan stated, "Basically our story is this. The president made the most sweeping, far-reaching arms control proposal in history. Gorbachev said, 'No.'" Buchanan further characterized initial press analyses that the Reagan administration had failed as simply "mistaken."

The three top aides in the White House held forty-four briefings and interviews "on the record" during the week following the talks, as well as dozens of other such conversations "off the record." This level of access was unprecedented in the Reagan administration. *Newsweek* (Oct. 19, 1986) commented that the "summit had begun with a news blackout but ended up producing a whiteout of pronouncements, amplifications, and amended remarks."

Interestingly, aides within the administration even acknowledged that this impression management was occurring. As one aide noted to a *New York Times* reporter, Shultz (who had looked so dejected the night talks ended) and other senior officials were actively trying to "reshape perceptions" of the Reykjavik meeting. As another unidentified White House aide put it, "We were focusing on the one yard we didn't gain. Well, what about the ninety-nine yards we did? We kept saying, 'Let's focus on that.'" Even Shultz had changed his tune and was now characterizing the talks as a "watershed" event because "for the first time the two sides agree to dramatic reductions in nuclear and strategic arms."

Opinion polls suggested, moreover, that the efforts of these impression managers may have successfully protected and enhanced the intertwined identities of the president and his administration. Consider the trends that the *New York Times*/CBS News poll revealed about past and present public opinion of Reagan's Soviet policies (*New York Times,* Oct. 19, 1986). The October 1986 poll was taken during the height of the Reagan administration's effort to "impart positive spin" on events at Iceland:

Who do you think is more to blame for the failure to reach an agreement?

	Reagan	Gorbachev	Both equally
October 1986	14%	45%	25%

Which leader do you feel is more committed to reaching an arms control agreement?

	Reagan	Gorbachev	Both equally
October 1986	63%	9%	15%

How much confidence do you have in President Reagan to negotiate an arms control agreement with the Soviet Union?

	A lot	A little	None at all
July 1985	28%	52%	17%
October 1986	53	35	8

The opinion polls were not the only evidence that President Reagan and his fellow impression managers were successful in providing interpretations that transformed what had been a perceived failure into a perceived success. This view that the social construction of reality had changed was acknowledged widely. Donald Regan was not the only one to argue that the Reykjavik talks "turned out pretty well" for the president and his administration. On October 22, 1986, the *New York Times* reported that NATO's Nuclear Planning Group backed Reagan's stance at Iceland. Similarly, Chancellor Helmut Kohl of Germany stated that rather than being upset at Reagan's failure to reach an arms control agreement, he felt that "Reykjavik was broken off at the right time. It's time for stock taking." Even Senator Kennedy (an avid administration critic) admitted that while the Reagan administration didn't really deserve credit for the positive outcome, nonetheless, the image of the administration had benefited from the Iceland talks. "The man in the street would have applauded Reagan whether he came back from Iceland in triumph or failure. His popularity would have gone up whether he had signed or just talked tough to the Russians."

Taken together, we believe this evidence supports our view that the Reagan administration and its audiences were moving toward what we have termed a negotiated settlement or consensus regarding the "proper" interpretation of the events at Reykjavik. The cycle of give-and-take about the meaning of the Iceland talks was approaching completion. Members of diverse organizational audiences were coming to agree that the talks had been a success, an identity-*enhancing* outcome for the Reagan administration and not a failure, as initially thought. Further, despite Senator Kennedy's arguments, we contend that the massive impression management campaign undertaken by members of Reagan's staff did, in fact, play a significant role in helping their "audience" develop this social construction of the talks.

Nonetheless, it is also important to consider an additional explanation at this juncture. Efforts by both the Reagan administration and the press to understand and interpret events at Iceland decreased after late October. This pattern suggests that the salience of the situation had dropped because equivocality had been reduced through the negotiation cycle. But the story disappeared almost completely once the Irangate scandal began to unfold. This pattern is also consistent with our perspective on impression management by organizational actors. Organizational impression management for a "target" event almost always occurs in the context of many other events. Thus, other events (Irangate in this case) may reduce the salience of a "target" event. Indeed, the impression management cycle for the target event may halt even though equivocality still remains as organizational actors and audiences—who have bounded rationality (March and Simon, 1958)—turn their attention to more salient and vivid events. Thus, the salience of a given impression management predicament must be judged relative to other predicaments faced by the impression managers and their audiences.

Conclusions

The case of the Iceland arms control talks suggests that, at least for some research questions, there may be a symbiotic relationship between organizational theory and international relations. This case illustrates how organizational theory can be used to enhance our understanding of relations between nations. Prior theory building and research on the symbolic role of leaders of organizations served as a conceptual point of departure that led us to view leaders of nations as managers of meaning who interpret international events in order to enhance and protect the intertwined images of their administrations and themselves.

Conversely, the case of the Iceland talks provides an example of how evidence about relationships between nations can be used to develop theory about organizations. This case provided empirical grounding for our perspective on impression management by organizational elites. The Iceland talks demonstrate the problem of pleasing multiple constituencies with opposing preferences, which is not evident in prior research on impression management by laboratory subjects, who are unencumbered by organizational roles. This case also illustrates the dynamic processes through which impression managers and their audiences come to agree on the meaning of events, and it exemplifies the possibility that an event may be so ambiguous that both impression managers and their target audiences are unsure whether it is identity enhancing or identity threatening. These insights about impression management by the leaders of social systems have been given scant attention in the literature on symbolic management by organizational leaders.

The perspective presented here on impression management by leaders of organizations and nations is, however, by no means complete. We hope that in addition to attending to the conceptual arguments emphasized in the body of this chapter, scholars who use the perspective presented here as a starting point will grapple with—and perhaps resolve—two persistent difficulties that have troubled us throughout the development of the chapter.

The first difficulty is that researchers may be unable to untangle the efficacy of impression management by leaders from the romance of leadership. Our assumption in interpreting the events following the Iceland talks is that despite the presence of a potentially identity-threatening event, skilled use of impression management by the Reagan administration transformed an apparent failure into an apparent success. An alternative explanation is that even a failure can increase a leader's popularity if it also increases his or her visibility. Meindl and Ehrlich's (1987) experimental research indicates that—independently of leaders' objective performance—people are so enamored of their leaders that they tend to view a person's performance more favorably just because he or she occupies a leadership role.

Regardless of success or failure, widely publicized events such as peace talks or wars may make leaders especially visible to their constituents, thus amplifying the romance of leadership. President Kennedy seemed aware of this alternative explanation when, following the botched secret invasion of Cuba at the Bay of Pigs, he was told of a Gallup poll showing that an unprecedented 82 percent of Americans were behind his administration. Schlesinger (1965, p. 273) reports that Kennedy responded by joking, "It's like Eisenhower; the worse I do, the more popular I get."

The second difficulty stems from the argument that the job of management is to interpret, not to get the work of the organization done. This perspective, if taken to its logical conclusion, suggests that as long as managers can convince key constituencies that the organization is efficient, that it is doing high-quality work, and that its members are behaving ethically, it does not matter how inefficient the organization is, how poor the quality of work is, or how unethically the members behave.

From a conceptual perspective, this view is somewhat troubling because it suggests that—despite the domination of logical positivism in the social sciences—the features of organizations can never be understood objectively. But organizational theory can be changed if it can be demonstrated that viewing organizations as objectively knowable entities is logically and empirically untenable. The practical implications of this view are far more troubling. It suggests that to the extent that leaders are blessed—or trained—in the art of imparting positive spin, they need not worry about the efficiency, performance, or ethics of their organizations. The most successful leader would be the one who is most skilled at blaming others when things go wrong, at taking credit when things go well, and—as the story of the Iceland talks implies—at convincing others that even events that appear to be undesirable or evil are actually desirable or noble. We are troubled by this implication because we would rather live in a world populated by organizations that are effective and ethical than a world populated by organizations led by people who can convince us—no matter what the facts—that their organizations are effective and ethical.

References

Bonazzi, G. "Scapegoating in Complex Organizations: The Results of a Comparative Study of Blame-Giving in Italian and French Public Administration." *Organization Studies,* 1983, *4,* 1-18.

Chatman, C. A., Bell, N. E., and Staw, B. M. "The Managed Thought: The Role of Self-Justification and Impression Management in Organizational Settings." In H. P. Sims, D. A. Gioia, and Associates (eds.), *The Thinking Organization: Dynamics of Organizational Social Cognition.* San Francisco: Jossey-Bass, 1986.

Cialdini, R. B., and others. "Basking in Reflected Glory: Three (Football) Field Studies." *Journal of Personality and Social Psychology,* 1976, *34,* 366-375.

Gardner, W. L., and Martinko, M. J. "Impression Management: An Observational Study Linking Audience Characteristics with Verbal Self-Presentations." *Academy of Management Journal,* 1988, *31,* 42-65.

March, J. G., and Simon, H. *Organizations.* New York: Wiley, 1958.

Meindl, J. R., and Ehrlich, S. B. "The Romance of Leadership." *Administrative Science Quarterly,* 1987, *30,* 78-102.

Meindl, J. R., Ehrlich, S. B., and Dukerich, J. M. "The Romance of Leadership and the Evaluation of Organizational Performance." *Academy of Management Journal,* 1985, *30,* 91-109.

Mintzberg, H. "An Emerging Strategy of 'Direct' Research." *Administrative Science Quarterly,* 1979, *24,* 580-589.

Nisbett, R., and Ross, L. *Human Inference: Strategies and Short-*

comings of Social Judgment. Englewood Cliffs, N.J.: Prentice-Hall, 1980.

Pfeffer, J. "Management as Symbolic Action." In L. L. Cummings and B. M. Staw (eds.), *Research in Organizational Behavior.* Greenwich, Conn.: JAI Press, 1981.

Richardson, K. D., and Cialdini, R. B. "Basking and Blasting: Tactics of Indirect Self-Presentation." In J. T. Tedeschi (ed.), *Impression Management Theory and Social Psychological Research.* Orlando, Fla.: Academic Press, 1981.

Salancik, G. R., and Meindl, J. R. "Corporate Attributes as Strategic Illusions of Management Control." *Administrative Science Quarterly,* 1984, *29,* 238–254.

Schlenker, B. R. *Impression Management.* Pacific Grove, Calif.: Brooks/Cole, 1980.

Schlesinger, A. M., Jr. *A Thousand Days: John F. Kennedy in the White House.* Boston: Houghton Mifflin, 1965.

Staw, B. M., McKechnie, P. I., and Puffer, S. M. "The Justification of Organizational Performance." *Administrative Science Quarterly,* 1983, *28,* 582–600.

Sutton, R. I., and Callahan, A. L. "The Stigma of Bankruptcy: Spoiled Organizational Image and Its Management." *Academy of Management Journal,* 1987, *30* (3), 405–436.

Tedeschi, J. T. *Impression Management Theory and Social Psychological Research.* Orlando, Fla.: Academic Press, 1981.

Tedeschi, J. T., and Reiss, M. "Identities, the Phenomenal Self, and Laboratory Research." In J. T. Tedeschi (ed.), *Impression Management Theory and Social Psychological Research.* Orlando, Fla.: Academic Press, 1981.

Tedeschi, J. T., and Riordan, C. A. "Impression Management and Prosocial Behavior Following Transgression." In J. T. Tedeschi (ed.), *Impression Management Theory and Social Psychological Research.* Orlando, Fla.: Academic Press, 1981.

Weick, K. E. *The Social Psychology of Organizing.* Reading, Mass.: Addison-Wesley, 1979.

Weick, K. E., and Daft, R. L. "The Effectiveness of Interpretation Systems." In K. S. Cameron and D. A. Whetten (eds.), *Organizational Effectiveness: A Comparison of Multiple Models.* Orlando, Fla.: Academic Press, 1983.

PART 3

Decision and Control

Chapter 8

Reducing Avoidable Errors

A New Framework for Policy-Making and Crisis Management

Irving L. Janis

Top-level leaders in government and in organizational life, however else they may differ from one another, have this in common: they function as crisis managers. That is, when situations arise in which the well-being and integrity of the system (or organization) as a whole are at stake, top executives are called upon to respond. Their response in such cases involves decisions that define policy, initiate a chain of implementing decisions and actions, and thus shape the future of the system, nation, or organization.

International crises involving superpowers are the most important exemplars of such situations. All too often the policy decisions made shortly before and during major international crises fail to meet the objectives of the top-level leaders who function as crisis managers. A large body of research indicates that top-level U.S.

This chapter is based on Janis (1989), which presents a fuller elaboration of the theoretical model, including much more detailed discussion of (a) the evidence bearing on the key assumptions, (b) the potential values and limitations of the model, and (c) the hypotheses derived from the model that have direct implications for improving the quality of crisis management.

249

crisis managers have frequently displayed gross symptoms of defective decision making throughout the nuclear age. (See, for example, George, 1980; Janis, 1986; Lebow, 1987; Neustadt and May, 1986.) Intensive studies of the way international crises have been managed by United States presidents and their main advisers since the end of World War II indicate an absence of gross symptoms in only a small percentage of the crises (Herek, Janis, and Huth, 1987; Janis, 1989). And, as will be described later in this chapter, recent research findings show that symptoms of defective decision making are related to two types of unsuccessful outcomes: failure to protect U.S. national interests and failure to promote international stability by lowering the level of superpower conflict.

Obviously, during superpower crises there are grave risks of gross misunderstandings and miscalculations that can have catastrophic consequences. In a future confrontation, the same kinds of misunderstandings and miscalculations could lead inadvertently to all-out nuclear war, even though the leaders on both sides want to avoid it.

In this chapter I shall describe a new theoretical framework for analyzing policy-making processes, a framework that has a number of direct implications concerning what can be done to reduce the likelihood of avoidable errors in crisis management. The prescriptive implications could prove to be especially useful for two major policy problems posed by international crises:

- What can be done to keep clashing interests of the nuclear superpowers from mounting, so as to prevent confrontations that create dangerous crises?
- Whenever a crisis does occur, how can it be managed from the outset to prevent it from spinning out of control and escalating to nuclear war?

The prescriptive implications are also pertinent to dealing effectively with other types of crises facing the leaders of all nations as a result of mounting threats of worldwide ecocatastrophes. These include the dangers posed by the depletion of the ozone layer and the resulting overexposure of people all over the world to ultraviolet rays (which produce dangerous skin cancers along with other disastrous biological effects), by deforestation (especially of the tropical rain forests that are being transformed into grazing lands or urbanized), and by the "greenhouse effect" (from excessive heat in the atmosphere generated by industrial production all over the earth, which can produce drastic changes in climate resulting in melting of the polar ice caps and ultimately the destruction of the entire life-sustaining global environment).

Sources of Errors

Unsuccessful outcomes of crucial policy decisions have many different causes, some of them beyond the control of leaders and others controllable, even if not actually controlled. Genuinely unforeseeable events may block the implementation of a wise decision, for example, and unforeseeable countermoves by adversaries or competitors may prevent policy decisions from attaining their intended effects. Leaders may bring to crucial decisions a baggage of oversimplified beliefs and ideological stereotypes that include faulty assumptions about the requirements for good solutions or about the consequences of choice. Even when policymakers are open-minded, the available evidence may be too ambiguous to correct their erroneous assumptions. Or policymakers may be given erroneous information that appears accurate because it comes from seemingly authoritative reports or expert testimony with no signs of disagreement. And to all this must be added the unknown or chance factors commonly called bad luck.

Nevertheless, among the major causes of unsuccessful outcomes in policy decisions, one is very much under the control of the leaders themselves: *the quality of the decision-making procedures used either to arrive at a new policy or to reaffirm an existing one.* Good decision-making procedures do not guarantee good outcomes, of course. Nor do defective procedures (inadequate information search, biased appraisal of consequences, and lack of contingency planning) guarantee that a policy decision will be a fiasco. Uncontrollable, unknown, and chance factors can occasionally result in "good luck" as well as bad. But the likelihood of failure is substantially less if sound procedures of information search, appraisal, and planning are used. (For evidence bearing on this important point see pp. 270–276.)

Prospects for Developing Pertinent Theory

If we had a valid theory describing linkages between policy-making procedures and good versus poor outcomes, we could extract valuable prescriptions for improving the quality of policy-making in government, business, and public welfare organizations. Do we have anything approaching such a theory at present? Unfortunately not. What we do have are numerous unintegrated hypotheses supported to varying degrees by empirical evidence, much of which is subject to debate and disagreement among social scientists. (See Abelson and Levi, 1985.) Nevertheless, there are scattered pieces of research that can be used to evaluate and consolidate hypotheses from the work of psychologists, political scientists, sociologists, economists, historians, management scientists, and scholars in other social science disciplines. So far as the development of theory is concerned, this area is still in a very early stage. There are many contending theorists, some of whom clash head on while others simply ignore or bypass their rivals without bothering to analyze points of divergence or convergence, all of which creates an atmosphere of theoretical chaos.

Despite all the fragmentation and lack of agreement to be found in the research literature, it seems to me that many bits of theorizing and pieces of sound empirical evidence can be fitted together to form a fairly coherent view of decision-making processes. In my opinion, the time to start integrating the seemingly divergent theoretical perspectives is already at hand. Perhaps the pessimists are right when they tell us that we shall never have a comprehensive theory that encompasses fully all the complicated psychological, sociological, political, and economic factors that influence the making of consequential policy decisions. But I see no reason for being inhibited about taking steps in the direction of bringing more order out of the chaos of clashing concepts by sketching in rough outline an integrative theoretical framework that describes the social and psychological sources of error in policy-making. In any case, that is what I have attempted to do, as will become apparent in the next sections of this chapter.

Considerable skepticism about the prospects for any such attempts is to be anticipated, especially among the many social scientists who believe it is utterly unrealistic to expect in the foreseeable future a valid comprehensive theory in this domain. Kinder and Weiss (1978), for example, take the pessimistic position that the best we can hope for at present is a "few notions" that are not well-integrated to account for "some of the processes for some of the people some of the time." But if the theoretical framework I am attempting to construct is as promising as I think it is, I expect social science theory to attain a much more ambitious objective within the near future—a theoretical model that can account for most decision-making processes for most policymakers most of the time.

Key Postulates

My theoretical model is based on four main assumptions or postulates. *The first postulate is that the quality of the procedures used to arrive at a fundamental policy decision is a major determinant of a successful outcome.* Until recently there has been practically no dependable evidence bearing directly on this assumption.

A second postulate is that most top-level leaders, including crisis managers in government and other large organizations, are capable of carrying out the essential steps of vigilant problem solving. Those steps are represented in Figure 8.1, which summarizes the main components described by social scientists who have studied policy-making and crisis management. (See, for example, Katz and Kahn, 1966, and 1978.) The figure is not intended as an ideal model for the making of policy decisions but as a realistic *descriptive* model of what most executives demonstrate by their actions that they are *capable* of doing when they try to do the best job of decision making they can under the circumstances. The model describes what executives can do within the confines of incomplete knowledge, unresolvable uncertainties, limited capacity to process information, bureaucratic power struggles, and all the other usual con straints that can hamper sound thinking about the generally

Figure 8.1. Main Steps in the Vigilant Problem-Solving Approach to Decision Making.

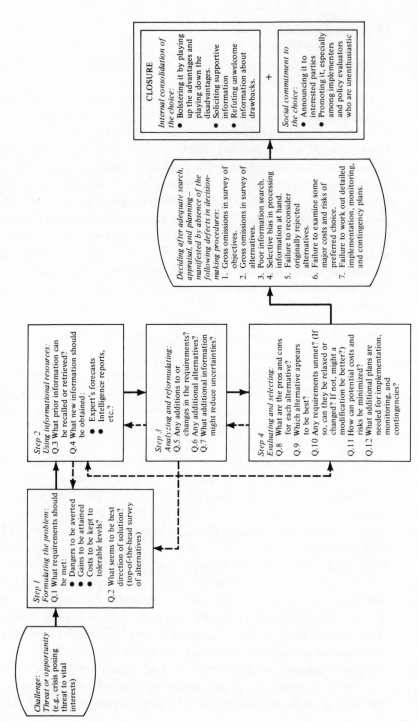

Source: Adapted from *Crucial Decisions: Leadership in Policymaking and Crisis Management*, by I. L. Janis, 1989, p. 91. New York: Free Press. Copyright © 1989 by The Free Press, a division of Macmillan, Inc. Reprinted by permission of the publisher.

ill-defined policy problems that require crucial decisions. The hall-mark of high-quality decision making is that by the time the pol-icymakers arrive at their final choice and move toward closure, they have carried out the essential steps of vigilant problem solving (by answering all the key questions listed in Figure 8.1) sufficiently well that they do not display any of the symptoms of defective decision making (listed on the fourth column of the figure).

A third postulate, which is quite familiar to social scientists and widely accepted, is that policymakers generally make little or no effort to use the high-quality procedures of vigilant problem solv-ing for arriving at a policy decision if they regard the issue as rel-atively unimportant. Nor should they. The *costs* of vigilant problem solving are substantial, and misplaced vigilance would be wasteful. For newly emerging problems that are not perceived as threatening any vital national interests, governmental policymakers typically resort to what is sometimes called "quick-and-easy" deci-sion making, also commonly referred to as a "seat-of-the-pants" approach. Especially during the early stages of a crisis, however, such perceptions are likely to be incorrect. Thomas Schelling (1962) has commented on the *"poverty of expectations"* that prevented U.S. civilian leaders and military commanders in 1941 from realiz-ing that the warning signals they were getting from the intercepted Japanese government communications, which U.S. cryptographers had discovered how to decode, might point to an oncoming Japa-nese attack against Pearl Harbor and other United States military bases. "Unlike movies," Schelling points out, "real life provides no musical background to tip us off to the climax."

Numerous obstacles prevent policymakers from using a vigilant problem-solving approach, including psychological constraints that result in failures to tone down the deafening, scary music that swells up when crisis managers are overreacting to ambiguous warning signals. Overreactions or underreactions to warnings can occur when crisis managers are in a state of high emotional stress, as is indicated in the third column of Table 8.1. This table summa-rizes all the major constraints, both external and internal, that can obstruct vigilant problem solving.

The fourth postulate, which pertains to all the various con-straints listed in the upper half of Table 8.1, is much less obvious

**Table 8.1. Major Constraints That Can Obstruct Vigilant
Problem Solving and Typical Decision Rules to Cope with Them.**

Cognitive Constraints	Affiliative Constraints	Egocentric (Self-Serving and Emotive) Constraints
Limited time	Need to maintain: power status compensation social support	Strong personal motive: e.g., greed, desire for fame
Perceived limitations of available resources for information search and appraisal		Arousal of an emotional need: e.g., anger, elation
Multiple tasks	Need for acceptability of new policy within the organization	Emotional stress of decisional conflict
Perplexing complexity of issue		
Perceived lack of dependable knowledge		
Ideological commitments		

Cognitive Decision Rules	Affiliative Decision Rules	Egocentric (Self-Serving and Emotive) Decision Rules
Availability	Avoid punishment	Personal aggrandizement: "What's in it for me?"
Satisficing	"Rig" acceptance	
Analogizing	Exercise one-upmanship in the power struggle	Angry retaliation
Nutshell briefing		Audacity: "Can do!"
Operational code	Groupthink: preserve group harmony	Elated choice: "Wow! Grab it!"
		Defensive avoidance: procrastinate, pass the buck, or bolster
		Hypervigilant escape: "Get the hell out fast."

Source: Adapted from *Crucial Decisions: Leadership in Policymaking
and Crisis Management,* by I. L. Janis, 1989, p. 149. New York: Free Press.
Copyright © 1989 by The Free Press, a division of Macmillan, Inc. Reprinted by permission of the publisher.

and more debatable than the other three postulates, so it cannot be expected to be generally accepted by social scientists until it is extensively investigated in studies of many different kinds of policy decisions in a variety of organizations. *The fourth postulate states that even when policymakers believe that a threat or opportunity poses an extremely important problem, they will not adopt a vigilant problem-solving approach unless they perceive or intuitively presume all salient constraints to be sufficiently manageable that none has to be given very high priority.*

According to this postulate, whenever policymakers consciously or preconsciously evaluate one or another of the problem-solving, affiliative, or egocentric constraints as so potent and difficult to manage that dealing with it is more important than finding a high-quality solution to the problem, they will adopt a simplistic strategy. When a policymaker uses that type of procedural strategy, he or she relies primarily upon a few simple decision rules to cope with the dominating constraint instead of carrying out the essential steps of vigilant problem solving. The most commonly used decision rules are listed in the bottom half of Table 8.1. They have been described in detail on the basis of my review of the social science literature and my own current comparative case study research on American presidential policy-making during international crises (Janis, 1989, chaps. 2, 3, 4, and 8). The fourth postulate asserts that even when policymakers realize that vital interests of the nation are at stake, they will rely upon simple decision rules to deal with a crisis if any one of the constraints against vigilant problem solving is dominant. In such instances, which seem to occur fairly frequently, what the crisis managers do is tantamount to giving the constraint top priority; they do not engage in adequate information search or appraisal of alternatives and fail to carry out other essential steps of vigilant problem solving. As a result they fail to correct the common types of misperceptions and miscalculations that even the most brilliant and knowledgeable policymakers are likely to make when confronted with a crisis, including the conceptual errors arising from the relatively stable cognitive schemas that policymakers regularly employ to make sense out of what seems to be happening.

The harmful effects of applying oversimplified and misleading ideological assumptions, stereotypes, and judgmental heuristics can sometimes be mitigated if decision makers engage in vigilant information search and appraisal, even when they feel right at the outset that they know enough about the problem to conclude that there is only one course of action that is clearly the best way to handle it. Although vigilant problem solving cannot be expected to detect and rectify all the misconceptions, it increases the likelihood that the worst ones—those most discrepant from available facts— will be corrected before a final decision is made. (See Fiske and Taylor, 1984; Nisbett and Ross, 1980.)

Of course, in every crisis there are imminent deadlines and other forms of time pressure that interfere with carrying out the tasks required by the four essential steps of vigilant problem solving represented in Figure 8.1. Nevertheless, even in an extraordinary crisis when only a day or two is available for search and appraisal, the government or a major corporation can mobilize the resources to carry out a fairly substantial information search rapidly by obtaining comprehensive briefings from several independent experts who have already assimilated much of the pertinent background information. Also, multiple briefings can quickly be obtained from leading proponents of diverse policy positions, who can be counted on to highlight the defects of the alternatives they oppose. In just a few hours, it may be possible to go through various steps of vigilant problem solving sufficiently to avoid overlooking fatal flaws, thereby preventing gross errors that could readily arise if such steps were not taken.

In every major crisis, there are likely to be powerful constraints in addition to time limitations that are obstacles to vigilant problem solving. Fatigue takes its toll when crisis managers are rushing full steam ahead to take protective action before it is too late. National leaders also suffer from information overload as intelligence reports and bits of advice from experts flow in. Usually there are impressive and sometimes alarming raw data on the adversary's state of military readiness from sophisticated monitoring devices, with little opportunity to analyze most of it. As a crisis mounts, national leaders find it extremely difficult to peer through the dense fog of confusing intelligence information bearing on what the leaders of adversary nations are doing and why they might be doing it.

At the same time, crisis managers are likely to be exposed to strong political, organizational, and informal social pressures from various departments and agencies, from the Congress, from their political party, from the press, and from representatives of powerful interest groups who favor certain policy options and strongly oppose others. Such managers know that if they do not conform at least partially, their failure to do so could adversely affect their relationships with other powerful people within the government and perhaps also with important constituencies outside the government, with which they are affiliated.

Then, too, the crisis managers need to cope with internal constraints imposed by their own emotional needs, most notably the need to ward off distressing feelings of anxiety. In many instances policymakers do not realize that they are doing so. In my case studies of major crises faced by U.S. leaders the end of World War II, I find frequent indications that emotional stress is a source of personal motivation that affects top-level crisis managers at times when they are grappling with dangerous confrontations of the superpowers. Individuals who have played a prominent role in U.S. crisis management acknowledge the powerful effects of stress. This is apparent in pertinent comments by key members of the White House Executive Committee that dealt with the Cuban missile crisis in 1962. (See Kennedy, 1969; McNamara, 1986; Rusk, 1983.)

It must be emphasized, however, that being keenly aware of powerful constraints like the ones just described does not always prevent crisis managers from carrying out the steps of vigilant problem solving. From the standpoint of effective problem solving, there certainly is nothing wrong with paying close attention to the constraints. On the contrary, the essential first step involves specifying all the various requirements to be met in order to arrive at a good solution to the problem. These requirements include taking account of time pressures, organizational resources, social pressures from dominant power holders and constituencies, and all sorts of other constraints that could affect the way the decision is arrived at, the substance of the policy decision, or both. Thus, when a constraint is salient but does not interfere, it nevertheless influences the policy-making process right from the outset, because the requirements essential for dealing with each of the salient constraints are added to other requirements posed by the crisis.

Crisis managers who adopt a vigilant problem-solving approach concentrate on the primary objective of working out a good solution to satisfy—as well as can be done under the circumstances—the major requirements posed by the threats that are creating the crisis, with due regard for potential risks that could result in disastrously high costs to the nation. They strive to arrive at a policy solution without too much expenditure of time and without overusing organizational resources. They also take account of other types of constraints; for example, they seek a course of action that will contain the threats to vital national interests but one that also will not adversely affect their relationships with other top-level people in the government and will not be disregarded or undermined by those expected to implement the policy decision. In addition to trying to make sure that the chosen course of action will be accepted by other power holders and implementers within the government, policymakers may also strive to satisfy their own emotional needs, such as those evoked by the psychological stress of making a crucial decision. They aim for a solution to the crisis that will not continue to create emotional tension and cause them to lose sleep at night.

Every vital policy decision during a crisis has so many ramifications that no one can expect to meet fully all of the objectives. Compromises and trade-offs, which are always necessary, will be made most judiciously, with minimal risk of overlooking a fatal drawback, if crisis managers use a vigilant problem-solving strategy. When they adopt that strategy, they strive to find a high-quality solution that will take into consideration the entire set of requirements, including those added because they are taking account of various constraints that cannot be ignored. But according to the fourth postulate, the vigilant problem-solving strategy will be used by crisis managers only if they expect the constraints to be manageable. If they regard any one of the constraints as so crucial that it must be allowed to play a dominant role in arriving at a choice, they will rely almost entirely upon a simple decision rule to take care of the constraint instead of using the decision rules as supplementary aids to problem solving in a way that does not interfere with careful search, critical thinking, and planning.[1]

The Constraints Model

Figure 8.2 presents a preliminary descriptive model that embodies the four key postulates. It shows the main social and psychological components that are determinants of vigilant problem solving. The model also highlights the determinants of three other procedural strategies, involving reliance on three different types of decision rules. Relying on any of those simple rules is likely to lead to errors as a result of failing to carry out the essential steps of vigilant problem solving when dealing with serious challenges that affect vital interests.

As in most flow charts, this one starts at the upper left and terminates (in one or another of the four "END" boxes) at the lower right, with mediating processes represented in between. If you look at the box at the upper left, you can see that the psychological processes that enter into the making of a policy decision begin when power holders become aware of a challenge in the form of a threat or opportunity that poses a problem because the power holders' organization or nation will suffer losses (or opportunity costs) if it continues business as usual without making any changes. The challenge may occur precipitously as a result of a single dramatic event or communication (such as an ultimatum threatening war from a rival nation), or it may build up gradually from a series of relatively unobtrusive events or communications (such as gradual blocking by a rival nation of access to foreign markets).

Illustrative types of informational inputs that are among the main antecedent conditions are shown in the first column of Figure 8.2. (Additional types of antecedent conditions not shown in the first column—organizational rules and traditions, personality predispositions of policymakers, and leadership practices—are discussed in Janis, 1989, chaps. 8, 9, and 10.)

The core of the model consists of the mediating psychological processes represented in the second and third columns of Figure 8.2. The second column shows the key questions evoked by the challenge; the third column shows the type of procedural strategies that policymakers will adopt as a result of the answers they give to the key questions.

The fourth column shows the expected consequences of each of

Figure 8.2. Descriptive Model Representing Psychological Effects of Dominant Constraints on Policy Making.

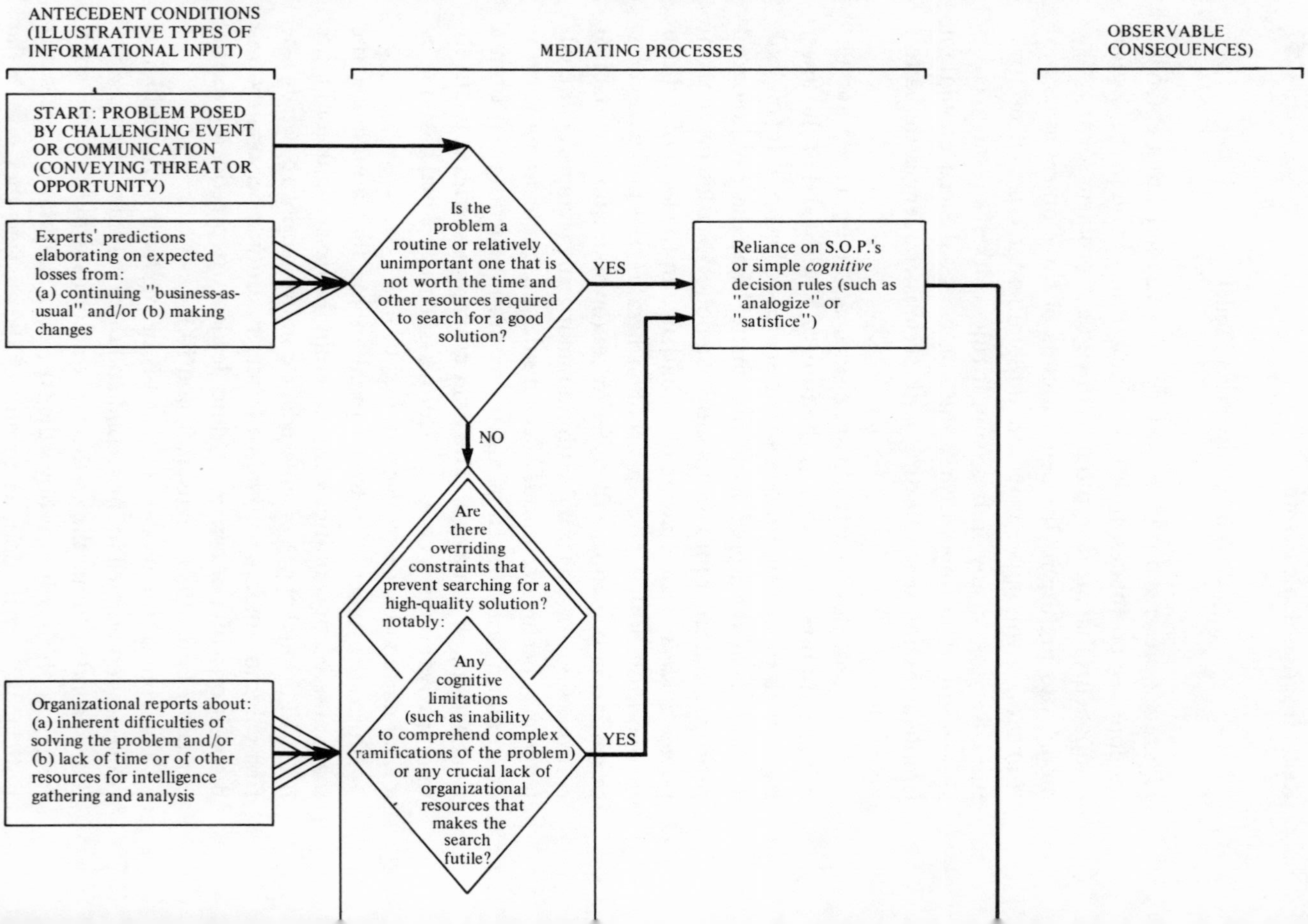

ANTECEDENT CONDITIONS
(ILLUSTRATIVE TYPES OF
INFORMATIONAL INPUT)

MEDIATING PROCESSES

OBSERVABLE
CONSEQUENCES)

START: PROBLEM POSED
BY CHALLENGING EVENT
OR COMMUNICATION
(CONVEYING THREAT OR
OPPORTUNITY)

Experts' predictions
elaborating on expected
losses from:
(a) continuing "business-as-
usual" and/or (b) making
changes

Organizational reports about:
(a) inherent difficulties of
solving the problem and/or
(b) lack of time or of other
resources for intelligence
gathering and analysis

Is the
problem a
routine or relatively
unimportant one that is
not worth the time and
other resources required
to search for a good
solution?

YES

NO

Are
there
overriding
constraints that
prevent searching for a
high-quality solution?
notably:

Any
cognitive
limitations
(such as inability
to comprehend complex
ramifications of the problem
or any crucial lack of
organizational
resources that
makes the
search
futile?

YES

Reliance on S.O.P.'s
or simple *cognitive*
decision rules (such as
"analogize" or
"satisfice")

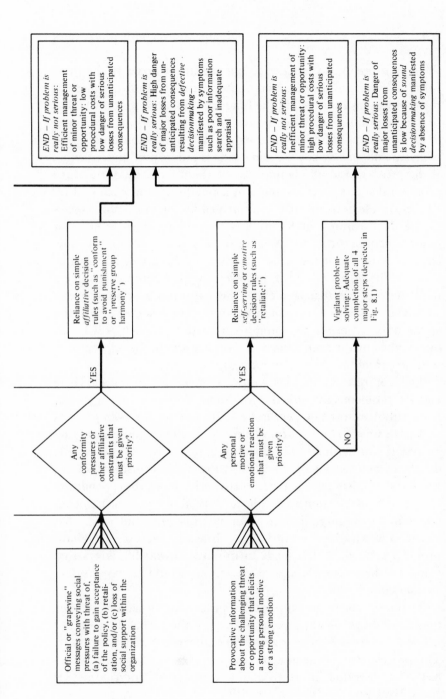

Source: Adapted from *Crucial Decisions: Leadership in Policymaking and Crisis Management,* by I. L. Janis, 1989, pp. 154–155. New York: Free Press. Copyright © 1989 by The Free Press, a division of Macmillan, Inc. **Reprinted by permission of the publisher.**

the four procedural strategies designated in the boxes in the third column. The overall evaluation of the adequacy of management of the problem, as indicated in the final column, depends on whether or not the problem actually turns out to be really serious (according to the consensus of honest judgments of knowledgeable observers—which are not necessarily the same as their public pronouncements). If the problem actually is *not* serious, the use of any of the three procedural strategies involving a quick-and-easy approach that relies on simple decision rules (represented by the upper three boxes in the third column of Figure 8.2) would be judged as efficient management of the minor threat or opportunity. There will be low costs for arriving at the decision, with low danger of any serious losses to the organization. If, however, the problem proves to be a really serious one, management of the major threat or opportunity would be evaluated as extremely deficient. The low cost of arriving at the policy decision by using a simplistic approach will be far outweighed by the high danger of serious losses to the organization resulting from the poor procedural strategy used.

The opposite evaluations would be made for instances where vigilant problem solving is the dominant procedural strategy used. If the problem turns out *not* to be really serious, the policymakers will have wasted a great deal of time and other organizational resources to deal with a minor threat or opportunity that poses little danger of any serious organizational losses from miscalculations. But if the problem proves to be a really serious one, the expenditure of time and other resources will be more than offset by the tremendous gain for the organization from averting potential losses that might otherwise have ensued. In such a case the use of vigilant problem solving, which tends to minimize avoidable errors that could be disastrous for the organization, would be regarded as sound management.

As policymakers go through the process of answering the key questions shown in the second column of the model, they do not necessarily verbalize to themselves either the question or the answer. The process may occur at a preconscious level, which can be detected by observing indirect verbal and nonverbal indicators. (See Janis, 1989, pp. 189-200 and 316-319.)

Crisis managers' answers to the key questions about the importance of the challenge and to the key questions about constraints may frequently be quite unrealistic as a result of gross misunderstandings of warnings, misconceptions, and faulty inferences based on misleading ideological assumptions. Also, they may be misled by incorrect information and deliberate manipulations by interested parties who have a vested interest in steering the choice toward their own preference. Many studies in the social sciences can be drawn upon to formulate plausible propositions about the conditions under which policymakers are likely to give unrealistic answers to the key questions.

Pathways to Success and Failure. A number of different pathways are shown in the model, only one of which is likely to end up bringing glory and attributions of greatness to national leaders who are responsible for managing crises. That one requires them to give negative answers to all the key questions when confronted by each major threat. First, such leaders must believe that an important problem is posed by the challenge, which cannot be delegated or solved immediately off the top of their heads. Second, they must judge, consciously or preconsciously, that all the various constraints can be managed without allowing any of them to be dominating considerations that override all of the other requirements for a good solution. If, and only if, these two conditions are met, the pathway leads to the box at the bottom of the third column, which includes the entire set of four essential steps of vigilant problem solving, requiring the policymaker to answer conscientiously a set of twelve additional questions, as depicted in Figure 8.1.

In answering the twelve questions, vigilant policymakers use various guiding principles. For example, the tit-for-tat reciprocity principle may be taken into account to help specify the requirements for an effective course of action in response to an adversary's aggressive moves (Axelrod, 1984); the elimination-by-aspects principle may be used to help narrow down the alternatives to the most promising ones (Tversky, 1972). The answers suggested by such principles are regarded by the policymakers as tentative first approximations, which they reevaluate during later stages of vigilant problem solving in light of whatever new information has been gathered. Along with the guiding principles, the policymakers also use simple decision rules as *suggestive leads* that can facilitate the search for a good solution without replacing or interfering with intensive information search and critical thinking. This limited usage contrasts sharply with the high degree of reliance on such rules that characterizes the seat-of-the-pants strategies represented in the other three boxes in the third column of Figure 8.2.

Four of the pathways depicted in Figure 8.2 are mediated by a simplistic approach. All four end up with many symptoms of defective decision making as a result of the crisis managers' reliance on simple decision rules. The seven main symptoms of defective decision making were introduced earlier in this chapter (in the second-to-last column of Figure 8.1, p. 254). Those symptoms correspond to failures to meet the seven criteria for high-quality decision making extracted by Janis and Mann (1977, pp. 10–14) from the extensive research literature on effective procedures used by individual executives and by groups of policymakers in government, business corporations, and public welfare organizations.

The four defective pathways can be seen somewhat more easily in Figure 8.3, which summarizes the essential features of the model represented in Figure 8.2. (It also includes a number of major determinants of the defective pathways, which will be discussed in the final section of this chapter.)

The first pathway is mediated by the policymaker's judgment that the problem is too trivial to bother with. Sometimes this judgment is erroneous, usually because warnings about potential losses are ambiguous and presented in such an unimpressive way that they constitute too weak a challenge to reach the threshold for gaining the attention of busy executives or for competing successfully with many other troubles that appear to be more worthy of time and energy. If the policymakers' answer to the first key question is yes, they typically dispose of the problem quickly by adopting simple *cognitive* decision rules, such as those embodied in adages like "let sleeping dogs lie."

The second pathway also leads to a quick-and-easy approach involving reliance on simple *cognitive* decision rules, but it is mediated by the policymakers' judgment that there are overriding problem-solving constraints that prevent them from seeking a high-quality solution. Among the most common of such constraints are the policymakers' realization that the complex ramifications of the problem exceed their cognitive capabilities and that the organization lacks available resources for intensive information search, appraisal, and planning.

A third pathway that leads to a seat-of-the-pants approach is mediated by overriding concern about affiliative constraints, which makes for reliance on simple *affiliative* decision rules. This type of constraint arises when an executive becomes aware of demands for conformity to the wishes of other power holders in the organization who are in a position to threaten anyone who fails to conform with extreme retributions, such as being removed from office or being excluded from top-level meetings. Much more often, however, the anticipated social punishments for failing to conform involve more subtle threats of social disapproval. An entirely different but equally powerful affiliative constraint becomes dominant when policymakers who are working together in a cohesive group display the "groupthink" syndrome, which involves reliance on the simple decision rule to "preserve group harmony by going along uncritically with whatever consensus seems to be emerging" (see Janis, 1982).

The fourth pathway that leads to many symptoms of defective decision making is mediated by the policymakers' self-serving motives or emotional state. Despite their best conscious efforts, policymakers sometimes cannot avoid being influenced by emotive constraints created by intense arousal of anxiety, guilt, anger, elation, or other strong emotions. They are also subject to the same kind of internal constraints when they have a strong emotional bias in favor of one particular solution to the problem or against various alternatives that might be viable candidates for a good solution.

The model represented in Figures 8.2 and 8.3 is intended to be applicable to a chief executive or to anyone else in a leadership role who is charged with responsibility as a policymaker. It can also be applied to middle- and low-level personnel, including staff who submit policy recommendations to the top level and departmental administrators who modify new organizational policies by putting their own personal stamp on the way the policies formulated by top-level management are implemented.

The model can be used to analyze sources of error in the decision-making process, whether an executive is making a policy decision entirely on his or her own or is participating in a group decision

Figure 8.3. Four Pathways to Policy Decisions of Poor Quality in Response to Major Challenges Contrasted with the Pathway to Vigilant Problem Solving.

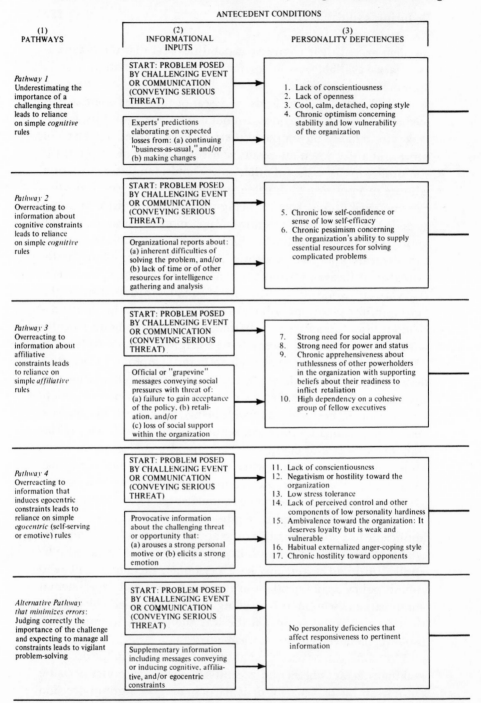

Source: Adapted from *Crucial Decisions: Leadership in Policymaking and Crisis Management,* by I. L. Janis, 1989, pp. 212–213. New York: Free Press. Copyright © 1989 by The Free Press, a division of Macmillan, Inc. Reprinted by permission of the publisher.

Figure 8.3. Four Pathways to Policy Decisions of Poor Quality in Response to Major Challenges Contrasted with the Pathway to Vigilant Problem Solving, Cont'd.

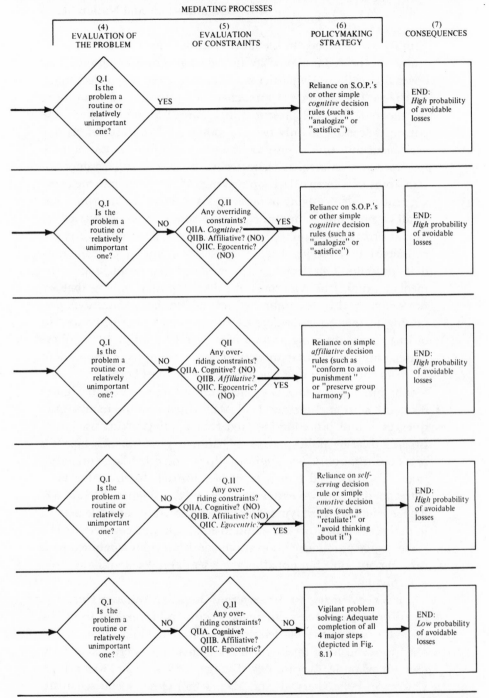

Note: This figure reproduces the key components of the constraints model represented in Figure 7-1 in *Crucial Decisions: Leadership in Policymaking and Crisis Management*, with another set of antecedent conditions added: personality deficiencies.

with fellow members. In the latter case, the investigator would examine the procedures used by the advisory group, committee, or board that collectively participates in making the policy decision.

Mixed, Intermediate Approaches. For purposes of exposition, the theoretical model presented in Figures 8.2 and 8.3 shows the pathways leading to only two end points of a continuum. At one extreme of the "quality-of-procedures" continuum are the simplistic procedural strategies, characterized by a very large number of symptoms of defective decision making. At the other extreme is the vigilant problem-solving approach, characterized by no symptoms at all or only one symptom (from the common garden variety of human error to be expected whenever someone attempts to carry out conscientiously a series of complicated tasks). But there are intermediate procedural strategies to be considered that result in an intermediate number of symptoms of defective policy-making that are not represented in the figures. A few additional assumptions pertaining to these intermediate categories need to be introduced in order to make the basic features of the model applicable to policy-making approaches that are neither entirely simplistic nor vigilant problem solving but that combine components of both.

The missing intermediate categories not represented in Figures 8.2 and 8.3 are included in Table 8.2, which lists the main consequences of four procedural approaches to policymaking used from time to time by policymakers in national governments, business corporations, public welfare institutions, and other large organizations. The first and fourth types of approach listed in the table correspond to the two extremes represented in Figures 8.2 and 8.3. The second and third types of approach shown in the table pertain to policy-making processes of intermediate quality, characterized by some degree of reliance upon simple decision rules combined with carrying out some but not all of the essential tasks of vigilant problem solving.

Evidence Bearing on Assumptions About Process and Outcome. Does it really make any difference whether policymakers show few or many symptoms of defective decision making? Some social scientists who have investigated policy-making assert that it does. (See, for example, Etzioni, 1968; George, 1980; Katz and Kahn, 1978; Lawrence, 1985; Neustadt and May, 1986.) Other social scientists,

Table 8.2. Consequences of the Vigilant Problem-Solving
Approach to Policy-Making Compared with Those of Three Other Approaches.

Type of Approach in Policymaker's Repertoire	Amount of Time and Effort Required	Quality of Decision Making: No. of Defective Symptoms	Probability of Avoidable Errors
1. Vigilant problem solving	Very large	0-1	Low
2. Quasi-vigilant	Moderate to large	2-3	Moderate
3. Quasi-simplistic	Small to moderate	4-6	Fairly high
4. Simplistic	Very small	7	Very high

Source: Adapted from *Crucial Decisions: Leadership in Policymaking and Crisis Management*, by I. L. Janis, 1989, p. 163. New York: Free Press. Copyright © 1989 by The Free Press, a division of Macmillan, Inc. Reprinted by permission of the publisher.

however, think that it does not. It seems quite fashionable these days, especially among some leading theorists in management studies and political science, to take a very jaundiced view of the prospects for improving crisis management and policy-making. (See, for example, Lindblom, 1980; Nelson, 1977; Starbuck, 1983, 1985.) A major consideration frequently mentioned by the pessimists is that even the most sophisticated and skilled policy analysts who use the best available procedures are likely to be seriously mistaken about some of the crucial facts and about some of the main inferences they draw from the apparent facts on the basis of their ideological preconceptions and stereotypes. These conceptual errors result in faulty framing of the problem from the very outset and gross miscalculations concerning the expected consequences of alternatives.

I certainly agree that conceptual errors occur frequently at the outset of policy-making and fairly often remain uncorrected. But like other social scientists who do not agree with the pessimists, I believe that these errors can be and sometimes are corrected in response to the new information policymakers obtain when they conscientiously go through the successive steps of vigilant problem solving (as described in Figure 8.1, p. 254). In my research on international crises, I have encountered examples of such corrections in foreign policy decision making by national leaders in the Truman, Nixon, and Johnson administrations. (See Janis, 1989, chap. 5.) It remains an empirical question as to whether or not residual errors are so pervasive even when policymakers carefully go through the procedures necessary to carry out vigilant problem solving that by and large it makes no essential difference in the outcome whether they use those procedures or not.

The first of my key postulates contradicts the views of the pessimists. It asserts, in effect, that *for consequential decisions that implicate vital interests of a nation or organization, use of a vigilant problem-solving approach, with judicious information search and analysis (within the constraints usually imposed by limited organizational resources), will generally result in fewer miscalculations and therefore better outcomes than any other approach.* To put it yet another way, in terms of the components shown in Figure 8.1, *the fewer the steps of vigilant problem solving that are carried out adequately—as manifested by symptoms of defective policymaking—the higher the probability of undesirable outcomes from the standpoint of the nation's goals and values.*[2]

Direct evidence bearing on the first two postulates is provided by a systematic study by Herek, Janis, and Huth (1987). The main purpose of our study was to determine the extent to which favorable outcomes in international crises affecting the United States are related to the quality of policy-making by the nation's leaders. In order to investigate the relationship between quality of decision-making processes and outcome of policy decisions, we assessed the U.S. government's management of each of nineteen international crises by making detailed ratings of the presence or absence of each of the seven symptoms of defective policy-making listed in the fourth column of Figure 8.1. We imported into this research on international relations some of the methodological refinements that have been developed in systematic research in the field of social psychology—including special procedures designed to prevent contaminated judgments and to control for other artifacts that can give rise to spurious results.

The study involved four major steps. First, on the basis of independent ratings by three outside experts on international conflicts, a sample of nineteen major crises since World War II was selected.

Second, bibliographic sources describing the decision-making process in each crisis were collected and their adequacy was rated by the experts. Third, the source materials judged to be most dependable were used to score the decision-making procedures during each crisis in terms of the seven symptoms of defective policy-making. Fourth, independent ratings of the crisis outcomes were obtained from two outside experts who remained "blind" to the decision-making process scores and to the hypotheses under investigation.[3] The two outside experts, both of whom have conducted extensive research on international crises, provided independent ratings on two outcome variables for the effectiveness of crisis management by U.S. policymakers for each crisis. First, they rated the crisis outcome's effect on U.S. vital interests: whether they were advanced, hindered, or unaffected during the days and weeks following the crisis. Second, they rated the level of international conflict during the days and weeks following the end of the crisis: whether there was an increase, decrease, or no change in tension, stability, hostility, or the likelihood of war between the United States and the Soviet Union or China. The two experts' ratings were combined to yield a score of –1 if both agreed that the crisis outcome was negative, +1 if both agreed that it was not negative, and 0 if they disagreed. When we compared the ratings on outcomes obtained from the two experts, we found a fairly high degree of agreement, indicating a satisfactory degree of interanalyst reliability.

The results in Figure 8.4 show a strong relationship between quality of decision making as manifested by number of symptoms of defective decision making (rated by the investigators) and unfavorable outcomes (based on the average ratings of the two outside experts). Quantitative correlational data show that higher symptom scores are significantly related to more unfavorable outcomes for U.S. vital interests ($r = .64$, $p = .002$) and to more unfavorable outcomes for international conflict ($r = .62$, $p = .002$). These results clearly indicate that crisis outcomes tended to have more unfavorable effects for U.S. interests and were less likely to decrease international conflict when the policy-making process was characterized by a relatively large number of symptoms of defective decision making.[4] The findings are consistent with the expectations that policymakers sometimes use vigilant problem-solving procedures and that

**Figure 8.4. Relationship Between Decision-Making Quality
and Crisis Outcomes.**

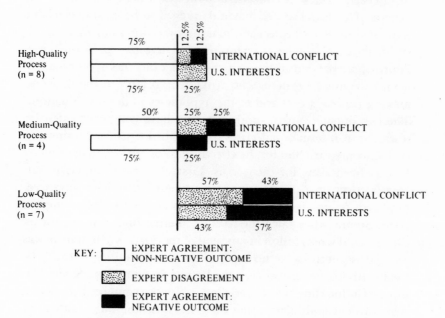

Source: Adapted from "Decisionmaking During International Crises: Is
Quality of Process Related to Outcome?" by G. Herek, I. L. Janis, and P.
Huth, 1987, *Journal of Conflict Resolution, 30*, p. 517. © 1987 by Journal
of Conflict Resolution. Used by permission of SAGE Publications, Inc.

Note: This figure reproduces Figure 1 in Herek, Janis, and Huth (1987)
with one slight change to correct the minor error listed under *Erratum* in
the December 1987 issue of the *Journal of Conflict Resolution* (vol. 31,
p. 672).

when they do so their decisions are more likely to meet their goals
than when they do not. Contrary to the generalization asserted by
the pessimists, the quality of the decision-making process *is* related
to the policy decision's outcome.

While the correlations between process and outcome support the
hypothesis that low-quality decision making leads to unfavorable
outcomes, they do not prove this causal relationship. One type of
alternative explanation is that the significant correlations result

from the influence of a third (unobserved) variable. It is possible, for example, that more serious crises are usually associated with more defective decision making and with less favorable outcomes because more serious crises are more stressful and involve more difficult decisions with higher stakes than do less serious crises. In order to check on this possible type of third-factor explanation, we obtained ratings from two additional experts on seriousness of the crises and difficulty of the decision making. To test the extent to which the correlations between process and outcome were affected by these variables, we constructed stepwise regression equations for each of the two outcome variables (U.S. vital interests and international conflict). This method can be used to control statistically for the effects of any third factor for which ratings are available. The results of this statistical analysis indicated that the substantial correlations we obtained between process and outcome could not be accounted for by a third factor of the type we examined—seriousness or difficulty of the crisis.

Of course, there is always the possibility that other hidden factors we did not look into could be responsible for the observed correlations. Because our data are correlational, we cannot conclude that the quality of decision-making processes, as indicated by the number of symptoms of defective decision making, plays a causal role in producing the policy decision outcomes. It is a plausible interpretation, however, not contradicted or disconfirmed by any of the results. The findings of the present study thus bear out the surmises of quite a large number of social scientists who have concluded that poor-quality procedures used in arriving at a policy decision give rise to avoidable errors that increase the likelihood of obtaining an unsatisfactory outcome. Stein and Tanter (1980), for example, assert an equivalent proposition in terms of favorable outcomes in their analysis of policy decisions made by Israeli government leaders during international crises. "Other things being equal," they state, " 'good' procedures are more likely to produce 'good' outcomes" (p. 8). Their account of "good" procedures includes the key components of vigilant problem solving.

In order to test the generality of the positive relationship between process and outcome, further research is needed with other samples of crisis decision making. Such research could help to define the limiting conditions under which the relationship can be expected to be observable.

Earlier I mentioned that a popular trend in present-day discussions of management science and political science is to take a very dim view of the prospects for achieving better outcomes from improving policy-making processes in government or in other large organizations. This view leads to the expectation that little or no improvement in crisis prevention or crisis management can be expected from introducing systematic methods of problem solving and other aids to effective decision making. The significant relationships between process and outcome in international crises observed in the Herek, Janis, and Huth (1987) study favor a different view of the policy-making process. The findings support the expectation that international conflict management could be improved by introducing appropriate systematic problem-solving procedures into the policy-making process. Such procedures could make for more successful outcomes, reducing the severity of international conflict while furthering the policymakers' national security objectives and other vital interests.

Implications for Research on Crisis Management

The constraints model presented in Figures 8.2 and 8.3 and Table 8.2 provides the rudiments of a theoretical framework for describing alternative procedural strategies used by crisis managers and other policymakers to arrive at policy decisions. It is intended to serve the main functions of scientific explanation. Two of the most important of those functions are to help us understand connections among diverse phenomena and to make relevant predictions about future events.[5]

The model might prove to be especially valuable in investigations that seek to determine the probable causes of any policy fiasco for the purpose of trying to understand what has gone wrong, with an eye to making recommendations about how to prevent recurrences of such errors in the future. It offers a set of alternative explanations to be investigated, explanations that differ markedly from popular models currently being used implicitly, if not explicitly, by many investigative committees in governments and other large organizations throughout the world. The most popular model is based on the notion that the main cause of gross policy errors usually is chronic negligence or incompetence on the part of one or more persons in positions of responsibility within the organization. Those who rely on this model expect their investigation will end up putting the finger on negligent culprits or incompetent bunglers. Their main presumption is that chronic defects in crisis management can be eliminated if the leaders who botched up the crisis under investigation are replaced by new ones with better qualifications for their leadership roles. In contrast, the constraints model does not direct investigators to look primarily for individuals who are chronically negligent or incompetent when seeking to explain one or more instances of defective policy-making. Instead, the constraints model offers a number of alternative causal sequences as probable causes of error in policy-making. It incorporates a variety of theoretical concepts, ranging from bureaucratic politics to misleading judgmental heuristics, that have emerged piecemeal from research bearing on policy-making processes in the social sciences. The constraints model, of course, is much broader in scope than any of the component theoretical concepts that it attempts to integrate into a more comprehensive framework.

Whether carrying out applied research for the practical purpose of preventing the recurrence of policy errors in one particular organization or basic research for the scientific purpose of understanding how and why policy errors occur in different kinds of organizational settings, investigators using the constraints model would be prompted to start their inquiry by looking into the five alternative causal sequences represented in Figure 8.2 (pp. 262–263) and summarized in Figure 8.3 (pp. 268–269). All five of those pathways are closely linked with existing bodies of theory in one or another of the social science disciplines.

In Figure 8.3, the two columns designated as antecedent conditions—infomational inputs and personality deficiencies—are useful for formulating hypotheses about the conditions under which crisis managers will display one or another of the defective pathways (1–4) rather than the nondefective pathway that minimizes errors and requires carrying out the essential steps of vigilant problem solving (shown in Figure 8.1, p. 254). A number of hypotheses can be derived from the model for three different areas of inquiry:

1. Research on *personality variables* and other dispositional characteristics of top-level policymakers (such as the variables listed in the third column of Figure 8.3) that might be pertinent to finding out who will be good crisis managers and who will not
2. Research on *effective leadership practices* that promote vigilant problem solving among members of a crisis management group, including practices that counteract the detrimental effects of various types of informational inputs (such as certain of the ones listed in the second column of Figure 8.3), which foster reliance on simple decision rules
3. Research on *organizational variables*—norms, structures, and cultural characteristics that foster a vigilant problem-solving approach by top-level crisis managers whenever vital interests of the nation are at stake, including organizational features that affect the flow and processing of pertinent informational inputs (like the ones listed in the second column of Figure 8.3)

I shall present an illustrative set of hypotheses for each of the three areas, in order to illustrate the potential value of the constraints model for generating new hypotheses that appear to be worth pursuing. All the various hypotheses formulated with the aid of the constraints model will require careful investigation. They are intended to be added to the research agendas of psychologists, political scientists, sociologists, management experts, and other scholars in the social sciences who are interested in discovering the conditions for effective policy-making, which could be pertinent for improving the quality of policy-making in our society. Such improvements are urgently needed in the coming decades, as I pointed out at the beginning of this chapter, to prevent worldwide disasters from ecocatastrophes and nuclear holocaust. At a less cataclysmic level, the suggested improvements might help government agencies or subunits deal effectively with threats to their survival.

Personality Variables. One of my main working assumptions is that leaders who differ in dispositional attributes, such as chronic level of conscientiousness, have characteristically different ways of responding to the various types of informational inputs listed in the second column of Figure 8.3, which affect one or another of the answers they typically give to the key questions represented in the fourth and fifth columns of the figure. If we examine the constraints model from the standpoint of differences in *threshold* of responsiveness to warnings and other informational inputs in light of the research literature on personality differences, it is possible to generate a number of plausible hypotheses concerning the role of personality deficiencies. Using this approach, I have arrived at seventeen hypotheses that seem sufficiently plausible to warrant systematic investigations. These hypotheses specify *who* is most likely to display symptoms of defective decision making as a result of being generally inclined to ignore, misinterpret, or overreact to certain types of information, symptoms that increase the probability of avoidable errors. Specialists in personality research undoubtedly will think of additional personality variables pertinent to responsiveness to informational inputs, which will enable them to formulate additional hypotheses that are equally or perhaps more plausible.

The first row in Figure 8.3 embodies four hypotheses about personality deficiencies. The entries in that row state, in effect, that under conditions where a problem is posed by a challenging event or communication conveying a serious threat to vital national interests, crisis managers who have any of four personality characteristics (listed in the third column of the first row) will tend to ignore the threat and to deal with the problem as a routine or relatively unimportant one. They will rely upon standard operating procedures or other simple decision rules, which makes for a high probability of avoidable losses if the threat materializes.

Each of the next three rows in Figure 8.3 can be read in a comparable way as embodying additional hypotheses about personality deficiencies that make for failure to respond adequately to informational inputs pertaining to any emerging or ongoing crisis. The entire set of seventeen hypotheses represented in Figure 8.3, which emphasizes the *interaction* between informational inputs and personality dispositions, may provide a fresh perspective for research on the role of personality in effective crisis management.

The hypotheses about personality variables have their counter-

parts as prescriptive hypotheses that specify what can be done
within an organization to improve the quality of policy-making.
Each of them, if verified in subsequent research, would have something to say about the types of people who should be recruited and
promoted as promising candidates for high-level positions as policymakers. (Further elaborations of the seventeen hypotheses and
their implications for selection of crisis managers are presented in
Janis, 1989, chap. 9.)

Leadership Hypotheses. I have developed twenty hypotheses
about effective leadership, derived from the constraints model (Janis, 1989, chap. 10). Some of the hypotheses are fairly well known,
having already been suggested by management experts. For these
hypotheses, the constraints model provides a more comprehensive
theoretical rationale than the piecemeal ad hoc rationales to be
found in much of the management literature. A few hypotheses
derived from the constraints model specify leadership practices that
are not likely to be familiar to practitioners or to research specialists
in the field of management. They provide additional examples of
the potential value of the constraints model for generating original
hypotheses that appear to be plausible and that warrant systematic
investigation.

Each of the hypotheses about leadership practices, if verified, will
have direct practical implications for improving the quality of crisis
management policy-making in government and other large organizations. Executives who want to improve their effectiveness in ful-
filling leadership functions in the sphere of policy-making might
be able to change in the recommended direction once they realize
that certain of *their own actions* are imposing detrimental constraints that could be eliminated. Some of the hypotheses may make
top-level crisis managers more aware of the constraints imposed by
external circumstances and point to the steps that can be taken to
prevent those constraints from interfering with the quality of their
group's decision-making processes.[6]

The hypotheses provide tentative answers to a central question
for behavioral science research on leadership: what can an individual leader do to eliminate common types of error made by an executive committee or advisory group whose members participate in
crucial decisions, such as those made during major crises? Accord-

ing to the constraints model, any leadership practice that increases the likelihood that executives who function as crisis managers or policy planners will give negative answers to the four key questions (shown in the triangles in Figure 8.2) increases the likelihood that those participants will use a vigilant problem-solving approach.

For purposes of explicating the implications of the constraints model, it is helpful to return once again to the diagram of pathways to defective policy-making shown in Figure 8.3. One of the main implications is that when a major crisis arises a leader needs to *counteract* the influence of various types of informational inputs (listed in the second column of Figure 8.3) that induce members of a policy-making group to give positive answers to the key questions about constraints. By inducing those participants to change so as to answer no to all the key questions, according to the model, a leader will prevent them from resorting to a simplistic approach, which results in gross symptoms of defective decision making.

Although the hypotheses about leadership practices apply most directly to the chief executive or whoever is designated as the chairperson of the policy-making group, they also apply to any influential member who takes the lead in directing the group's activity. That is to say, the leadership practices pertain not only to the actions of the *formal* leader but also to the actions of any member who functions temporarily as an *informal* leader by attempting to insert a new business item on the agenda or to change the group's procedures in conducting its deliberations. All the hypotheses about effective leadership practices for crisis management appear to be plausible and worth pursuing in subsequent research in light of well-established concepts and findings in social psychology and management sciences. For illustrative purposes, five of the hypotheses are given below.

The likelihood of successful outcomes of major crises will be increased if a leader takes steps to prevent gross miscalculations and other common types of errors by engaging in the following leadership practices, each of which contributes to enhancing the quality of crisis management.

1. *Whenever most members of a policy-making group regard a threat as sufficiently important to require prompt action but judge the problem it poses as not very serious because they believe that an*

"obvious" solution is readily available, take steps to create constructive doubts in their minds by raising critical questions about any seemingly obvious solution: If a leader does this, he or she will tend to prevent a poor-quality decision by fostering vigilant problem solving.

2. *Whenever an impending threat poses a problem that members of the group believe is a very difficult one requiring an excessive drain on themselves or their organizational resources to carry out a full-scale information search and appraisal, take steps to counteract the members' judgments that there are insurmountable obstacles to finding a high-quality solution:* If a leader does this (for example, by calling attention to available expertise and other organizational resources of which the members are unaware), the likelihood that the group will make a poor-quality decision on the basis of using simple decision rules will be reduced.

3. *Whenever members of a policy-making group are failing to make progress despite persistent problem-solving efforts to deal with a very difficult set of issues posed by a major crisis and are beginning to show signs of discouragement, fractionate the complex set of problems into smaller subproblems:* If a leader does this, the likelihood that the group will abandon a vigilant approach and resort to a simplistic approach will be reduced. This fractionating tactic, which breaks down a complicated set of problems into separate ones that are seen as more manageable, was well publicized when Henry Kissinger, as a peace negotiator in the Middle East following the Arab-Israeli War in 1973, used it successfully. If a group is able to work out one or more satisfactory partial solutions, each "small win" encourages the members to keep working on the remaining subproblems. As a result of positive changes in their expectations about the manageability of the constraints, the group members will subsequently be more likely to work out an integrated solution that satisfactorily combines the partial solutions of the various subproblems into a fairly high-quality policy decision.

4. *During a crisis, whenever some or all members of the group are temporarily displaying intense emotional stress, anger, grief, guilt, elation, or any other strong emotion, intervene to counteract the adverse influence of the members' strong emotional needs that go along with their temporary state of high arousal* (for example,

by temporarily postponing any definitive decision and shifting the group's attention to a different problem on the agenda, which could restore a vigilant problem-solving set among the members or at least stem the tide of emotion that would otherwise continue to build up): If a leader does this, he or she will tend to prevent the quality of decision making from deteriorating from the members' tendency to rely upon a simple decision rule that gives priority to satisfying the strong emotional need.

5. *Whenever a policy-making group appears to be reaching the end of its deliberations, after settling upon a consensus as to the best available course of action, make a rapid, rough-and-ready diagnosis of residual symptoms of defective decision making and then take steps to eliminate them:* If a formal or informal leader does so, he or she will tend to improve the overall quality of the policy decision. Even without knowing which particular constraint may be responsible for a persisting symptom, such as biased assimilation of new information, a few measures such as the following could be sufficient to eliminate it: call each symptom of defective decision making to the attention of the group and ask the members to discuss the appropriate key questions that enter into the vigilant problem-solving strategy (shown in Figure 8.1, p. 254); when the persisting symptom is failure to work out implementation, monitoring, and contingency plans, elicit and discuss critical feedback from key implementers by inviting representatives of the main organizational units responsible for implementing the policy decision to give the group their frank appraisals of the options under consideration along with information concerning implementation obstacles or setbacks to be expected.

Obviously one must be skeptical about any prescriptive inferences drawn from any of the hypotheses about what a leader should do to improve the policy-making process in his or her organization until those inferences have been tried out sufficiently in field settings to ascertain whether they actually work well enough to be worth the cost and effort they may require and also to be sure that they are free from unacceptable side effects. But they appear to be promising leads, well worth the trouble and expense of being tried out in an open-minded way not only by research investigators but also by qualified members of advisory groups who participate at least peripherally in the policy-making process and who want to improve the process. The prescriptive implications that prove to be ineffective could then be eliminated from further consideration, and those in need of modification could be revised.[7]

Organizational Structure and Process. Each of the hypotheses about leadership practices has direct implications for *organizational norms,* including leadership role prescriptions. That is to say, any of the specified leadership practices that stand up well when investigated could be incorporated into prescriptive hypotheses about standard procedures and changes in the operational code of an organization's top-level policymakers. If they prove to be feasible and effective in the judgment of well-qualified observers, including the top-level policymakers themselves, those leadership practices could be consolidated by formulating new institutionalized norms and accountability requirements rather than leaving such choices entirely up to each individual leader. The new norms and requirements would pertain directly to the organization's policy-making procedures by specifying who is expected to do what in order to arrive at sound policy decisions.

Aside from norms about leadership practices, it is possible directly to change organizational structure, procedure, and staffing patterns to facilitate crisis diagnosis and management. Here I suggest changes in advocacy structures, staff specialization and development, implementation processes, and accountability procedures.

Multiple Advocacy. Vigilant problem solving would be facilitated if an organization were to adopt the system of "multiple advocacy" recommended by Alexander George (1972, 1980). He proposes that organizations adopt a three-tier structure when making important decisions. First, the chief executive or top-level leader presides over the system, taking the role of a magistrate and evaluating the relative merits of the competing positions. Second, there is a custodian of the decision-making process. This is usually a vice president or special assistant, whose job as honest broker is to maintain and supervise the adversarial and collegial nature of policymaking within the organization. Finally, there are the advocates who are chosen by the custodian to argue competing positions in policy-planning meetings by the chief executive.

George (1980) points out that multiple advocacy does not guarantee a good decision-making process in every instance. The system can malfunction if the advocates do not cover the full range of options, if no advocate can be found for an unpopular option, if advocates for a minority position do not have full access to secret intelligence reports and other essential organizational resources, or if the advocates thrash out their disagreements privately, bringing a unanimous recommendation to the chief executive. That is the reason for the "custodian," the person who is responsible for protecting the organization against incomplete or sham multiple advocacy.

Staff Development and Specialization. If there is no system of multiple advocacy, the quality of crisis decision making would probably be enhanced by adding a decision-process expert to the staff and by adding a "threat screening" staff. For purposes of diagnosing defects in the policy-making process and taking steps to correct the defects, the top-level crisis managers might benefit if a skilled decision process expert were available to serve as a consultant or as a member of their policy-making group. For example, when appropriate to do so, the decision process expert could help the crisis management group to generate best case, worst case, and most likely scenarios. These can be elicited if the chairperson or decision-process expert simply asks the group to discuss three questions about each course of action under consideration:

1. If we choose this option, what is the best outcome that could be expected, on the assumption that everything goes pretty much the way we intend?
2. If we choose this option, what is the worst that could be expected, on the assumption that things do not work out the way we intend?
3. If we choose this option, what is the most likely outcome?

Obtaining the group's answers to these questions could be advantageous not only for exploring nonobvious consequences of the alternatives that might otherwise be overlooked but also for developing detailed contingency plans for whichever course of action is selected. Generating the various scenarios also might be helpful occasionally in counteracting initial biases among members, both those who are overly optimistic about what appears to be the best available course of action (by assuming the best case and not thinking about possible costs and risks) and those who are overly pessimistic about it (by assuming and thinking only about the worst case).

The potentially positive and negative consequences that emerge from the group's discussion of the anticipated scenarios could form the basis for much more detailed analysis of the problems posed by a crisis, which might make the group members more open to pertinent information that they had been ignoring and less preoccupied with side issues or tangential arguments. With the help of a decision-process expert who has technical skills in the decision analysis, a set of decision trees might be constructed. These diagrams could show the crisis managers in schematic form the decision alternatives and their probable consequences, with some indications of probability estimates for each of the possible outcomes. As Behn and Vaupel (1982) point out in their book on how to construct and use decision trees (*Quick Analysis for Busy Decision Makers*), "decision 'saplings' (simple decision trees with only a few branches) . . . can help even when lead time [for making a decision] is very short. Intuition still plays an important role, as it does in any decision, but it can be aided and focused by using a simple decision sapling to concentrate one's analytical and intuitive energies on the essence of the dilemma" (p. 6).

In order to know when and how to raise questions in a productive way, particularly when vital policy decisions have to be made under great time pressure, it is essential for the leader to do a considerable amount of homework prior to the meetings of a policy-making group—and to encourage the members to do the same. The participants need to become sufficiently knowledgeable about the facts and the best available estimates to be able to spot inconsistencies and gaps in any new information that seems to require drastic reappraisal of a contemplated course of action. But there is little time for homework assignments in the schedules of overworked executives. All the more reason for an organization to maintain a competent staff to screen potential threats and opportunities and to institute effective procedures for evaluating new challenges that might require high-level policy decisions. An adequate screening system can reduce the number of problems the policymakers have to deal with, enabling them to concentrate their time and energy on those of paramount importance. It may also reduce the number of avoidable crises that arise from failing to appraise warning signs correctly before the threats materialize. Thus, if an organization has developed efficient operations for screening potential challenges, it would be possible for the top-level policymakers to have time to do the necessary homework on the major problems they are trying to solve.

Implementation Processes. Social scientists who study organizations have become increasingly aware of inadequacies of the so-called "classical" hierarchical model of the exercise of power in policy-making. According to that model, policy formulators at the top choose and instruct policy implementers who, as subordinates, proceed to carry out the directives obediently in a "nonpolitical" way. In a detailed critique of the "classical" model, Nakamura and Smallwood (1980) cite a large number of research investigations indicating that the process of implementation often does not unfold in a sequential "unidirectional" fashion such that policy formulation precedes policy implementation (for example, Bardach, 1977; Lipsky, 1978; McLaughlin, 1976; Pressman and Wildavsky, 1973; Rein and Rabinovitz, 1978; Radin, 1977; Van Meter and Van Horn, 1975).

All the studies they cite emphasize limitations of the policymakers at the top who supposedly run things. For example:

> McLaughlin emphasized a reciprocal process of "mutual adaptation" between policy makers and implementers; Bardach classified and analyzed a wide variety of "games" that implementers can play to impede, frustrate, and to subvert policy; and Radin's case study depicted the political intrigue that can surround attempts to implement specific policies. . . . After reviewing this shift in emphasis away from policy makers and toward policy implementers, one might even suspect that the "classical" model had been turned upside-down, which is precisely what M.I.T. political scientist Michael Lipsky suggests. . . . According to Lipsky, "There are many contexts in which . . . policy is effectively 'made' by the people who implement

it." Each of these recent studies has produced a more circular view of the policy process. This process appears to be characterized by a fluid and reciprocal series of interrelationships between different groups of actors rather than a straight-line "classical" hierarchy that points directly from the top to the bottom [Nakamura and Smallwood, 1980, pp. 18–19].

The circular rather than linear view of the sequence, as these authors describe it, calls attention to feedback loops between policy formation and implementation. Feedback comes not only from implementers but also from other evaluators, some of whom are likely to be interested parties who are self-appointed monitors. As Lindblom (1980, p. 4) says, "one group's solution becomes another group's problem." He points out, as an example, that if the federal government comes out with a new economic policy that raises prices of agricultural products, it solves the farmers' problem but evokes protests from consumer groups.

Social scientists who pursue the full implications of the feedback concept find themselves rediscovering the virtues of representative democracy. Of particular interest here are the implications for effective leadership and organizational norms that can be discerned when we consider the change from a linear to a circular conception of policy formation in conjunction with the constraints model.

One obvious implication is that innovative leadership with regard to introducing policy changes is not limited to top-level management. It can sometimes come from the bottom of the organization, from people who have not been assigned any authority at all to formulate policy. The constraints model, as indicated earlier, is applicable to lower-level administrators provided that their decision-making behavior can be observed sufficiently to enable their procedural strategy to be diagnosed.

For any new policy directive that comes down from the top, implementers at all levels of the organization have the choice as to whether to carry it out as they think it is intended, to ignore it, or to modify it in one way or another. The constraints model is directly applicable to instances where middle-level or lower-level personnel function as innovative leaders either by implementing an official policy in a way that changes it or by introducing new practices to fill in policy gaps and cope with recurrent problems that had been ignored by the official leaders at the top. The constraints model also indicates the conditions under which people at any level in the hierarchy who engage in innovative decision making will use a vigilant problem-solving strategy or one of the seat-of-the-pants strategies, and the consequences of these alternative approaches.

The feedback model of organizational power, when combined with the constraints model, also has major implications for the leadership role of the top-level power holders. Consider, for example, the large number of requirements that top-level policy planners need to take into account in order to promote satisfactory implementation. Rein and Rabinovitz (1978) point out that in addition to making sure that a policy will meet legal requirements and will be properly understood and intellectually defensible (in terms of institutional maintenance, protection, and growth), effective policy planners must make sure that it is administratively feasible, that it does not violate organizational norms, and that it will "attract agreement among contending influential parties who have a stake in the outcome" (p. 315). These implementation requirements always need to be met in addition to whatever other requirements pertain to the problems that the policy planners are trying to solve. The likelihood that all the various requirements will be taken into account sufficiently to yield a high-quality decision, according to the constraints model, depends partly upon whether or not the policy planners adopt a vigilant problem-solving approach.

Effective leadership requires policymakers, including those functioning as crisis managers, to be especially responsive to feedback from implementers and others affected by any of their policy decisions. Because no organization is ever a perfect representative democracy, policy-making groups are always unrepresentative in various ways. Most often there is inadequate representation of the lower-level personnel in the organization who are expected to implement the new policy. A chief executive can at least partially overcome this deficiency if there is a standard organizational rule to have knowledgeable representatives of the various groups of implementers in the crisis management group, and if careful attention is paid to the information they supply about the pitfalls to be expected from attempts to implement various policy alternatives. If representation is still not complete, vigilant information search needs to be carried out by consulting with spokespersons from the various groups that will be called upon to implement the new policy.

After announcing a policy decision designed to prevent a crisis from developing, a chief executive and other policymakers need to be vigilantly alert to signs that implementers are not acting in accordance with the policy or signs that the policy is not succeeding when implemented as intended. The modification stage of policymaking in response to feedback is probably facilitated when new policies are introduced on a *small scale* and on a *trial basis*—if time permits—so as to provide ample opportunity to "debug" them before applying them full scale across the board. Deliberately introducing a planned trial-and-error strategy of this kind would be expected to improve the quality of an organization's policy decisions and thereby increase the incidence of relatively successful outcomes. But the policymakers would have to sustain a vigilant problem-solving approach to deal with whatever setbacks and complications arise throughout the period when attempts are being made to implement each new policy.

When crisis managers are making a decision about what to do to deal with a threat that appears to be very serious, they are less likely to display symptoms of defective decision making if there is an organizational requirement for the group to construct a decisional balance sheet (as an accountability requirement). It would oblige them to list briefly the known pros and cons for each alternative that has been considered. The decisional balance sheet procedure (described in Janis and Mann, 1977, and in Wheeler and Janis, 1980) can be introduced by a leader or by a decision-process expert simply by asking one of the members of the group to prepare a first draft of a grid with a separate row for each alternative and with separate columns for expected positive consequences and expected negative consequences (costs and risks). These columns can be subdivided into high, moderate, and low probability consequences.

The first draft of the grid can be presented to the group on a large chalkboard or screen, with plenty of blank spaces left to be filled in. The leader can then ask the group to examine each alternative in detail and to fill in additional entries of pros and cons. The entries in the initial balance sheet grid and the new ones to be added by the group could include positive and negative consequences for whatever vital organizational or national interests are at stake and also for broad political, economic, social, moral, and humanitarian objectives. If the leader or any member of the group believes that there are viable alternatives that have not yet been considered, they can be added to the balance sheet. Their pros and cons can then be spelled out and examined in comparison with the entries for the original set of alternatives.

There are several benefits to be expected from spending the time and effort necessary for constructing a balance sheet, which make it something more than a simple bookkeeping operation for recording what the members of the policy-making group already know. First of all, it often leads decision makers to become aware of gaps in their knowledge, especially about drawbacks of the most attractive alternative and the positive features of the others, which makes them realize that they need to obtain more information to fill in the gaps. It also helps decision makers to carry out a comprehensive evaluation of the alternatives. By looking over the entries in the balance sheet grid, decision makers often start using a more complex set of criteria for making the final choice rather than focusing attention on only one or two criteria. When decision makers compare the entries for one alternative with another, it may also help them to notice possible trade-offs that could make one alternative clearly superior to the others. Then, too, the negative entries for whichever alternative is chosen increase the decision makers' awareness of the need to work out detailed contingency plans so as to be prepared for meeting anticipated drawbacks.

A supplementary organizational norm might specify that after a group has completed constructing a balance sheet, the leader should help realize its benefits by raising appropriate questions, such as the following:

1. What information do we need that is still missing?
2. Does your tentative choice based on comparing the balance sheet entries agree with your intuitive or gut feelings? If not, what considerations might we have left out?
3. Is the alternative that looks best *good enough?* Does it meet all

of our main objectives? If not, can we modify it in some way—
maybe by partially combining it with one of the other
alternatives—to satisfy the most essential requirements?

4.   If we feel ready to commit ourselves to the best alternative, what
contingency plans would we need to make—taking account of
the entries listed in the minus column for that alternative—
before starting to implement our decision?

Although I have presented the above hypotheses about organizational structure and process as separate from the hypotheses about
personality and leadership, they are obviously intertwined. Changes
in structure have implications for leadership practice; personality
style affects leadership performance. However, presenting these
hypotheses separately calls attention to the broad range of interventions available to increase crisis management effectiveness.

Making the Model More Complete

There is a major deficiency in the constraints model that needs to
be discussed in order to call attention to a new set of problems for
research that could lead to filling in some gaps to make the model
more complete. The deficiency has to do with the incomplete formulations of the antecedent conditions that induce or contribute to
each of three types of constraints that are key components of the
model represented in Figures 8.2 and 8.3. If the model in its present
form is on the right track, it poses a number of new questions,
particularly about antecedent conditions. These questions require
basic social science inquiries directed toward increasing our understanding of when, how, and why a simplistic approach rather than
vigilant problem solving is used in making policy decisions: What
are the conditions that incline policymakers to give positive answers
to the key questions about being able to manage the cognitive constraints? The major affiliative constraints? The major egocentric
constraints? Which decision rule (or set of rules) do policymakers
rely upon when each of the major constraints becomes dominant in
the policy-making process? Without answers to these questions, the
constraints model of policy-making does not enable us to make

predictions as to which decision rule (or set of rules) is more likely to be used when a policymaker does not adopt a vigilant problem-solving approach.

To make the model more complete it will be necessary to add further assumptions about the conditions under which policymakers rely upon each of the decision rules that short-circuits the essential steps of vigilant problem solving and leads to avoidable errors. Ultimately, studies directed toward answering the new set of research questions posed by the model should enable us to specify for each of the most commonly used cognitive, affiliative, and egocentric decision rules the prime antecedent conditions that play a causal role in its being used by policymakers and the particular types of avoidable errors that are most likely to result from relying upon it.

In order to illustrate the kinds of hypotheses that are starting to emerge from this new line of inquiry oriented toward making the model more complete, Table 8.3 shows an error-sequence outline for an emotive rule that I have noted in a number of my case studies of international crises (Janis, 1989). An error-sequence outline specifies (a) the antecedent conditions that lead to reliance on a particular decision rule to deal with a particular type of constraint, (b) the telltale signs of the first step of the mediating *modus operandi,* indicating that the constraint is exerting a powerful influence on the policymakers during the period they are working on the decision, (c) the telltale signs of the second step of the mediating *modus operandi,* indicating that the particular decision rule is dominating the decision-making process, and (d) the consequences in terms of observable symptoms of defective decision making.

Table 8.3 describes the elated choice ("Wow! Grab it!") rule. This simple decision rule is likely to be invoked if a policymaker, after having been frustrated by difficulties in finding a good solution, suddenly becomes elated when he or she discovers a choice alternative that beautifully satisfies a few of the most essential requirements without having any apparently insurmountable defects. The policymaker's strong positive emotional state of exuberance operates as a constraint that interferes with vigilant problem solving. It is expressed by such phrases as "Wow! This is a better solution than you could hope for, so grab it; don't take any chance of losing the wonderful opportunity by wasting time looking into it any further."

Table 8.3. Error-Sequence Outline for Reliance on the Elated Choice ("Wow! Grab It!") Rule to Cope with Elation as an Emotive Constraint.

Antecedent Conditions	Telltale Signs of Positive Excitement as an Emotive Constraint	Telltale Signs of Relying on the Elated Choice Rule	Consequences for Quality of Decisionmaking
A. *Essential conditions* 1. Vital problem: Perceived need for a good solution. 2. *Initially depressed or frustrated* because no satisfactory alternative can be found that meets all major requirements during intensive search. 3. Unexpected discovery of a promising new alternative: Satisfies some hitherto unmet major requirements. B. *Facilitating conditions* 4. Tradition of relaxing some requirements for a target of opportunity. 5. Deadline pressures: Augments sense of "grab it or lose it." 6. Apparent competition: Someone might "grab it away from you."	1. Manifestations of strong feelings of *elation.* 2. Verbal expressions of relief about dilemma, with marked increase in optimism about solving it. 3. Resistance to delaying the choice—concern about losing a unique opportunity.	1. Enthusiasm expressed about the "Wow" choice: global praise with strong emphasis on requirements that are met. 2. Strong desire for closure: Sense of "This is it! No need to search or deliberate any longer." 3. Minimizing of requirements that are not met with optimism about overcoming known obstacles (the high costs and risks). 4. Impatient with skeptics who question the "Wow" choice.	1. Initial canvassing of objectives may be thorough but some objectives are overlooked when the "Wow!" choice is made. 2. Search for good alternatives is curtailed after discovery of the "Wow" choice. 3. Information search is curtailed after discovery of the "Wow!" choice. 4. Processing of new information is biased in favor of the "Wow!" choice. 5. Originally rejected alternatives are not reconsidered even when unsolicited new information favors them. 6. Potential costs and risks of the "Wow!" choice are ignored or minimized. 7. Little implementation and contingency planning.

Source: Adapted from *Crucial Decisions: Leadership in Policymaking and Crisis Management*, by I. L. Janis, 1989, p. 197. New York: Free Press. Copyright © 1989 by The Free Press, a division of Macmillan, Inc. Used by permission of the publisher.

When elation and the "Wow!" rule dominate their feelings and thoughts, policymakers are inclined to move rapidly toward closure even though their information search and deliberations are grossly incomplete. This tendency appears to have been a major contributing factor in the momentous decision made by President Harry Truman and his advisers to approve the use of America's first A-bombs to destroy Japanese cities in 1945.[8]

Even if policymakers start off being vigilant in their efforts to find a good solution, they stop being so once they become elated about a new alternative and start using the "Wow!" rule. They no longer try to ferret out faulty assumptions about benefits to be expected, hidden costs, and as yet undetected ways in which essential requirements might fail to be met, which could lead them to continue searching for a better alternative. Instead, they discount and minimize any signs suggesting that there might be high costs or potential risks. If they encounter unwelcome information indicating that the political or moral costs of carrying out the attractive course of action will be so excessively high as to exceed what they had regarded from the outset as the upper limit, they are willing to waive the original requirement. They feel that it is entirely justifiable to do so in order to take advantage of the extraordinary "target of opportunity." In an elated state about having found a wonderful solution, policymakers maintain high optimism about overcoming all obstacles, even though information may be available to them indicating that such expectations are not warranted.

The main point of an error-sequence outline like the one in Table 8.3 is that it specifies the main antecedent conditions that increase the chances of a given constraint's being perceived consciously or preconsciously by a policymaker as so overwhelmingly important that he or she will answer yes to the corresponding constraint question in Figure 8.2. The specifications of the antecedent conditions can be regarded, in effect, as additional hypotheses about the circumstances that tend to make the constraint dominant. The outline also designates the consequences of giving it top priority by using the simple decision rule at the expense of ignoring other major requirements for a good solution to the policy problem at hand. Each such outline also lists the telltale signs or symptoms that can be used to determine whether or not the policy-making process is dominated by the constraint, as well as the potentially detrimental effects on the quality of decision-making processes. [9]

Currently I am working on the task of formulating (and illustrating with detailed case study material) the error-sequence outlines for all the simple decision rules listed in Table 8.1. These outlines can be regarded as supplements to the constraints model, filling in gaps in the category of antecedent conditions that make for a positive answer to one or another of the key questions about constraints. Further amplifications of the antecedent conditions can be expected from comparative case study investigations, which will provide an empirical basis for constructing error-sequence outlines that will take account of suggestive findings from psychological experiments and other types of inquiry. Research projects are obviously needed to explicate and verify each error-sequence outline (like the one in Table 8.3) for each of the most commonly used decision rules. The findings could flesh out the bare bones of the theoretical analysis of the role of constraints represented in Figures 8.2 and 8.3 by providing the missing specifications essential for improving predictions about when an individual executive or a group engaging in policy-making will rely primarily on simple cognitive, affiliative, or egocentric decision rules. And, of course, the new findings are needed to enable one to predict *which particular rule* policymakers will use in various circumstances.

As the theoretical framework becomes more fully elaborated on the basis of empirical findings, it should become increasingly helpful to social science investigators and to organization troubleshooters, enabling them to extract more valid "lessons of history" than can be inferred on the basis of the impressionistic analyses now being used. Ultimately, those lessons could lead to improvements in the way crucial policy decisions are made. Once again, it must be emphasized that improvements are urgently needed to prevent incipient crises from developing and to prevent the ones that do develop from spinning catastrophically out of control.

Notes

1.   A dominating constraint that is given priority, as I have already indicated, need not necessarily be one that the policymaker is consciously aware of. Emotional stress, for example, typically

operates as a constraint at the preconscious level. Crisis managers might fail to adopt a vigilant problem-solving strategy because of this emotive constraint, despite being very confident that they can manage all the other external and internal constraints that they are aware of. When confronted with the worrisome problems posed by an international crisis that could result in outbreak of war, their own intense emotional reactions to the distressing dilemmas could play such a dominant role that they resort to a simplistic strategy, using either the "hypervigilance" decision rule ("get the hell out of the dilemma fast") or the "defensive avoidance" rule ("don't think about it: procrastinate, pass the buck, or bolster whichever alternative seems least objectionable at the moment").

2. For a review of *indirect* evidence bearing on the first two postulates, see Janis, 1989, chap. 6. Much of the indirect evidence comes from studies designed to test predictions from an "expected utility" model of decision making. Some correlational evidence indicates a relationship between quality of information search and outcome. But the findings from both types of studies are equivocal, especially because the investigators did not make any observations of the decision-making process itself and the findings could be accounted for in other ways.

3. Taking account of the possibility that outcome ratings might be influenced by personal political ideology, we deliberately chose experts from opposite ends of the conservative-liberal continuum in their personal views about the cold war.

4. The findings in Figure 8.4 show that a substantial percentage of the crisis management decisions (eight out of the nineteen cases) were of fairly high quality, as manifested by no symptoms or only one symptom of defective decision making. This finding is consistent with the second key assumption, which asserts that many, if not all, national policymakers are capable of using a vigilant problem-solving approach, even though for the majority of policy decisions they may use it only partially or not at all.

    In this study we also observed considerable variability in the number of symptoms displayed by the same crisis managers during different crises, which is consistent with the assumption that policymakers are likely to use a vigilant problem-solving strategy in making crisis decisions under some circumstances but not under other circumstances. For example, the top-level policymakers in the Nixon administration displayed all seven symptoms of defective decision making in the Indo-Pakistani war crisis, while they displayed few symptoms in two other crises. Policymakers in the Eisenhower and Kennedy administrations displayed the fewest symptoms. But it is well known from studies of presidential decisions that they did not always engage in vigilant problem solving. For example, their handling of two moderately important crises not included in our sample—the U-2 incident (Eisenhower) and the Bay of Pigs invasion (Kennedy)—have been characterized as extremely defective (see Donovan, 1984; Janis, 1982). Thus, it appears that while there are variations arising from individual differences in decision-making capabilities of different groups of policymakers (such as those occurring in different presidential administrations), the same president and his group of policymakers, as expected from the third and fourth postulates (stated on pages 255–257), show considerable variation in the quality of their decision making from one policy decision to another.

5. In order to fulfill the main functions of a descriptive theory of policy-making processes, the model requires further elaboration to indicate when and how it can be applied. I have attempted to formulate the requisite elaborations in Chapter 8 of my book *Crucial Decisions* (1989).

6. The leadership practices specified in the hypotheses, unfortunately, are not low-cost means for bringing about improvements. On the contrary, most of them are probably quite costly, especially because they require additional time and effort from leaders, from crisis management groups, and in some instances from their support staffs. Furthermore, certain of the leadership practices might turn out to have unintentional side effects that create less tangible costs, such as creating animosity and low morale among members of an advisory group, which could result from facilitating open debates about alternative options. In order to ascertain whether any one of the hypotheses is valid, research evidence will be needed to see if the benefits definitely outweigh the obvious costs and the losses that might result from undesir-

able side effects. It is my expectation that ultimately many of the hypotheses will prove to be sufficiently valid to warrant recommending the designated leadership practice as prescriptions for leaders who want to improve the quality of their organization's policy-making procedures. If so, those hypotheses could also form the basis for recommending ways to improve the curriculum of schools of management and in-service training courses designed to groom executives for top-level positions.

7. The hypotheses about leadership practices are formulated in terms that pertain directly to the way a leader conducts formal meetings and informal contacts with members of an executive committee or policy planning group. Most of the hypotheses, however, are intended to be equally applicable when a leader makes a policy decision largely on his or her own, after consulting briefly with only one or two advisers, provided that the information, evaluations, or advice they give could in any way influence the overall quality of the policy-making process.

Although the hypotheses derived from the constraints model appear to be plausible, none of them has been sufficiently investigated to warrant being regarded as empirically well supported. They are tentative propositions about potentially effective leadership practices to be added to the unfinished agenda for research on policy-making.

Of the twenty hypotheses about effective leadership practices that have been derived from the constraints model (Janis, 1989, chap. 10), only five are presented on pp. 281–283. The other fifteen hypotheses are as follows:

1. *Whenever the discussion of a problem by a management group reveals lack of consensus about its importance, encourage all the members to adopt a vigilant problem-solving approach:* If a leader does this at times when one small subgroup regards the issue as important enough to warrant vigilant attention, even though others take the opposite position, he or she will tend to prevent the group from arriving at ill-considered cursory decisions that fail to deal effectively with emerging crises.

2. *Whenever the policy-making group has arrived at a consensus to the effect that an emerging threat is of such low im-*

portance at present that it can be delegated, tabled, or completely ignored, advise all those who participate in the decision to have relatively low confidence in their judgment and to maintain a vigilant set: If a leader does this, he or she will reduce the chances of failing to deal effectively with emerging crises before they mount to dangerously high levels. The purpose of fostering a vigilant set in such circumstances is to induce the members of the group to be ready to reopen the issue if new evidence indicates that more is at stake than was thought at the time the decision was made.

3. *Whenever members of a policy-making group assert that it will be very difficult or impossible to gain acceptance within the organization for certain options that they regard as strong potential candidates for dealing effectively with the problem, take steps to counteract their tendency to overemphasize this organization constraint* (for example, by asking the participants to consider the potentialities of their group for persuading others in the organization to accept the best available option on its merits and by calling attention to comparable instances in the past when opposition melted following adoption of a high-quality solution): If a leader does this, the likelihood that the group will abandon a vigilant problem-solving approach essential for working out a high-quality solution will be reduced.

4. *Whenever the members of a policy-making group show signs of relying upon a simple decision rule to conform in order to avoid recrimination, take steps to counteract the strong social pressures* (for example, by making an effort to persuade powerful people to desist if they are subjecting members of the group to demands for conformity): If a leader does this, the likelihood that the group will abandon the search for a high-quality solution will be reduced.

5. *Take steps to counteract the tendency of subordinates to withhold or distort bad news out of concern for possible recrimination from the top-level managers:* If a leader does this, information supplied to the policy-making group by key personnel throughout the organization who function as sources of intelli-

gence and advice will be of higher quality, which will increase the quality of the entire decision-making process.

6. *Whenever there are indications that some members of the policy-making group are opposed to a course of action the leader favors, avoid yielding to the temptation to "rig" the meeting in ways that would squelch the opposition:* If a leader does this, the group's decision-making process generally will be of higher quality.

7. *Whenever a policy-making or crisis management group is functioning as a compatible team with a fair or high degree of esprit de corps, take steps to counteract the tendency to adopt the simple decision rule that makes for "groupthink"—to conform with the majority opinion in order to preserve group harmony:* If the formal leader does this (for example, by putting into practice various antigroupthink measures specified in Janis, 1982, pp. 262–271), the decision-making process will tend to be of higher quality.

8. *Whenever incentives are present at the outset that might tempt some or all members of a policy-making group to favor a policy option that will satisfy self-serving motives, openly mention the temptation at the initial meeting and call attention to the laws, ethical norms, and role obligations designed to be safeguards against conflicts of interest:* If the designated leader (or one of the members who emerges as a temporary informal leader) does this, he or she will reduce the likelihood that self-serving motives will interfere with the search for high-quality solutions.

9. *Whenever there are indications during a series of meetings of a policy-making group that some members are starting to be unduly influenced by self-serving motives, take steps to counteract any such tendency* (for example, by conveying a genuine attitude of moral disapproval during group meetings in response to any comments suggesting that it might be justifiable to allow a self-serving motive to influence evaluations of policy options and by conducting private discussions with the group members who appear to be giving priority to a self-serving motive but are not openly admitting it): If a formal or informal leader does this, the likelihood that self-serving mo-

tives will continue to interfere with efforts to arrive at a high-quality policy decision will be reduced.

10. *Whenever the members of a policy-making group are moving toward a consensus on a policy option that will give priority to a self-serving motive or an emotional need, defer a final decision and introduce counteracting incentives by making salient their accountability to other power holders who will object:* If a formal or informal leader does this, he or she will tend to prevent an ill-conceived policy decision.

11. *Arrange for all members of the policy-making or crisis management group (including the leader) and for all key members of their staffs to be given stress inoculation training via a series of crisis simulation exercises before any anticipated crisis of great magnitude occurs:* If a leader does this, there will be substantially less likelihood that the groups's performance will be impaired as a result of the internal (egocentric) constraints imposed by emotional stress when the time comes for them to function as crisis managers.

12. *During a severe crisis, when the members of the policy-making or crisis management group are undergoing considerable stress, present communications that are likely to alleviate acute feelings of apprehensiveness so as to reduce the tendency to give priority to the internal constraint imposed by the need to cope with anxiety or other strong emotions:* If the formal leader (or else one of the members with sufficient stress tolerance who is capable of functioning as an informal leader) does this, he or she will reduce the chances that the members will adopt a defective coping pattern of defensive avoidance or hypervigilance.

13. *Whenever the danger of severe losses appears to be so imminent that some or all members of the policy-making or crisis management group believe the deadline is too short to allow time to work out a good solution to deal with the harrowing crisis, take steps to counteract the adverse effects of extreme time pressure, which augments the tendency to give priority to the need to alleviate emotional stress:* If a formal or informal leader does this, he or she will reduce the chances that the quality of decision making will deteriorate as a result of hypervigilant reactions among members of the group.

14. *During any long, drawn out crisis, whenever members of a crisis management group are undergoing prolonged emotional stress, present communications that are likely to build up a realistic basis for hope:* If a formal or informal leader does this, particularly at times when an attempted course of action has failed to resolve the crisis and some members are starting to express pessimism about finding a satisfactory solution, he or she will tend to prevent the disruptive effects of the internal constraint that is imposed when demoralization occurs under conditions of high emotional stress, which makes for reactions of defensive avoidance and thereby greatly impairs the quality of decision making.

15. *Whenever the leader surmises that the group of policymakers is not functioning at its highest potential level despite his or her repeated, corrective efforts (including measures of the type to which Hypothesis 5, p. 283, refers), make a careful diagnosis of the constraints that are probable sources of the interference and then take steps to counteract their adverse influence:* If a leader does this, the likelihood of the process continuing to be of poor quality right up to the point of final closure will be reduced.

For each of the hypotheses, additional specifications have been formulated to indicate more precisely what kinds of actions a leader would have to carry out if he or she were to adopt each of the leadership practices that is expected to counteract reliance on simplistic decision rules in order to promote a vigilant problem-solving approach (Janis, 1989, chap. 10). For example, the following specifications have been added to the last hypothesis. Among the steps that could be taken to counteract the adverse influence of whichever constraints are diagnosed are the following:

a. Call the group's attentions to signs that the constraint is exerting undue influence.
b. Attempt to eliminate the constraint by changing the objective conditions that are producing it—for example, if there are indications that members of the group are being excessively constrained by time pressures, attempt to "buy"

more time by negotiating with adversaries to have a temporary "cease fire" agreement or the equivalent until new proposals can be worked out.

c. Attempt to persuade the members not to give any persisting constraint undue weight. Advise them to treat it as one of the many requirements to be taken into account when seeking a satisfactory solution, not as the single most important requirement that cannot be traded off in a compromise, if necessary, to attain other more essential objectives.

8. President Truman and several of his close advisers saw the A-bombs as providing a unique opportunity to end the war without the huge losses of American lives required by prior military plans for invading the Japanese home islands. Secretary of State James Byrnes enthusiastically informed the president that "the bomb might well put us in a position to dictate our own terms at the end of the war" (Truman, 1955, p. 87). Henry L. Stimson, secretary of war in Truman's cabinet, when briefing the president referred glowingly to the new weapon as "a master card in our hand" (Feis, 1960). There are numerous indications that when making plans to use the atomic bomb against Japanese cities, Truman and his advisers regarded it as a master card for the purpose of bringing a rapid end to the war in Japan. They were so enthusiastic about the attractive technological solution for saving American lives that they failed to make detailed queries of the government's intelligence sources as to the likelihood that Japanese leaders might already be on the verge of surrendering and that diplomatic maneuvers might succeed without using the A-bombs to kill tens of thousands of Japanese civilians.

9. The entire pattern shown in the error-sequence outline must be observed, with independent evidence bearing on each of the four sets of variables, in order to be at all confident about drawing a conclusion that a given constraint was exerting a strong influence and that heavy reliance on the simple decision rule to deal with that constraint was one of the probable causes of a poor-quality decision. When there is evidence that a simple decision rule was being used by a policymaker but no inde-

pendent evidence indicating that the plausible constraint was present and exerting a strong influence during the time when the policy decision was being made, it would be unwarranted to make a circular inference that the policymaker must have given a positive answer to the key question concerning the hypothesized constraint. There are always alternative causal sequences that could account for the use of a particular decision rule, some of which might have as much face plausibility as the one that implicates the hypothesized constraint. In general, when the constraints model is used as an aid to investigations of the probable causes of a defective policy decision, evidence of indicators bearing on the policymakers' judgment of the importance of the problem and responsiveness to the various types of constraints is always required in order to make reliable and valid inferences about how the policymakers answered the key questions listed in the second column of Figure 8.2, pp. 262–263.

Investigations of the probable causes of badly managed crises, even when carried out for the practical purpose of preventing the organization from repeating the same mistakes, can contribute suggestive leads concerning hitherto neglected antecedent conditions that foster reliance on simple decision rules to deal with powerful constraints. Such investigations might also lead to the discovery of error sequences that have not yet been described in the social science literature.

In order to validate the hypotheses embodied in a tentative error-sequence outline (such as the one in Table 8.3) and also to investigate each of the various hypotheses derived from the constraints model in the three areas of personality, leadership practices, and organizational structure, the full range of behavioral research methods could be used. These include comparative case studies, correlational analyses, experiments in social-psychological laboratories, and field experiments in natural settings.

References

Abelson, R. P., and Levi, A. "Decision Making and Decision Theory." In G. Lindzey and E. Aronson (eds.), *The Handbook of Social Psychology.* (3rd ed.) New York: Random House, 1985.

Axelrod, R. *The Evolution of Cooperation.* New York: Basic Books, 1984.

Bardach, E. *The Implementation Game: What Happens After a Bill Becomes a Law.* Cambridge, Mass.: MIT Press, 1977.

Behn, R. D., and Vaupel, J. W. *Quick Analysis for Busy Decision Makers.* New York: Basic Books, 1982.

Donovan, R. J. "Ike: How Great a President?" *New York Times Book Review,* Sept. 9, 1984, p. 1, pp. 46–47.

Etzioni, A. *The Active Society.* New York: Free Press, 1968.

Feis, H. *Between War and Peace: The Potsdam Conference.* Princeton, N.J.: Princeton University Press, 1960.

Fiske, S. T., and Taylor, S. E. *Social Cognition.* New York: Random House, 1984.

George, A. L. "The Case for Multiple Advocacy in Making Foreign Policy." *American Political Science Review,* 1973, *66* (3), 751–785.

George, A. L. *Presidential Decisionmaking in Foreign Policy: The Effective Use of Information and Advice.* Boulder, Colo.: Westview, 1980.

Herek, G., Janis, I. L., and Huth, P. "Decisionmaking During International Crises: Is Quality of Process Related to Outcome?" *Journal of Conflict Resolution,* 1987, *31,* 203–226.

Janis, I. L. *Groupthink: Psychological Studies of Policy Decisions and Fiascoes.* Boston: Houghton Mifflin, 1982. (Revised and enlarged edition of *Victims of Groupthink,* 1972.)

Janis, I. L. "Problems of International Crisis Management in the Nuclear Age." *Journal of Social Issues,* 1986, *42,* 201–220.

Janis, I. L. *Crucial Decisions: Leadership in Policymaking and Crisis Management.* New York: Free Press, 1989.

Janis, I. L., and Mann, L. *Decisionmaking: A Psychological Analysis of Conflict, Choice, and Commitment.* New York: Free Press, 1977.

Katz, D., and Kahn, R. L. *The Social Psychology of Organizations.* New York: Wiley, 1966.

Katz, D., and Kahn, R. L. *The Social Psychology of Organizations.* (2nd ed.) New York: Wiley, 1978.

Kennedy, R. F. *Thirteen Days: A Memoir of the Cuban Crisis.* New York: Norton, 1969.

Kinder, D. R., and Weiss, J. A. "In Lieu of Rationality: Psychological Perspectives on Foreign Policy Decision Making." *Journal of Conflict Resolution,* 1978, *22,* 707–735.

Lawrence, P. R. "In Defense of Planning as a Rational Approach to Change." In J. M. Pennings and Associates (eds.), *Organizational Strategy and Change.* San Francisco: Jossey-Bass, 1985.

Lebow, R. N. *Nuclear Crisis Management: A Dangerous Illusion.* Ithaca, N.Y.: Cornell University Press, 1987.

Lindblom, C. E. *The Policy-Making Process.* (2nd ed.) Englewood Cliffs, N.J.: Prentice-Hall, 1980.

Lipsky, M. M. "Implementation on Its Head." In W. D. Burnham and M. W. Weinberg (eds.), *American Politics and Public Policy.* Cambridge, Mass.: MIT Press, 1978.

McLaughlin, M. "Implementation as Mutual Adaptation." In W. Williams and R. Elmore (eds.), *Social Program Implementation.* Orlando, Fla.: Academic Press, 1976.

McNamara, R. S. *Blundering into Disaster: Surviving the First Century of the Nuclear Age.* New York: Pantheon, 1986.

Nakamura, R. T., and Smallwood, R. *The Politics of Policy Implementation.* New York: St. Martin's Press, 1980.

Nelson, R. R. *The Moon and the Ghetto.* New York: Norton, 1977.

Neustadt, R. E., and May, E. R. *Thinking in Time: The Uses of History for Decision Makers.* New York: Free Press, 1986.

Nisbett, R., and Ross, L. *Human Inference: Strategies and Shortcomings of Social Judgement.* Englewood Cliffs, N.J.: Prentice-Hall, 1980.

Pressman, J. L., and Wildavsky, A. *Implementation.* Berkeley: University of California Press, 1973.

Radin, B. A. *Implementation, Change, and the Federal Bureaucracy.* New York: Teachers College Press, 1977.

Rein, M., and Rabinovitz, F. F. "Implementation: A Theoretical Perspective." In W. D. Burham and M. W. Weinberg (eds.), *American Politics and Public Policy.* Cambridge, Mass.: MIT Press, 1978.

Rusk, D. *Maximum Peril.* Videotape produced by A. Singer. New York: Alfred P. Sloan Foundation, 1983.

Schelling, T. "Foreword." In R. Wohlstetter, *Pearl Harbor.* Stanford, Calif.: Stanford University Press, 1962.

Starbuck, W. H. "Organizations as Action Generators." *American Sociological Review*, 1983, *48*, 91–102.

Starbuck, W. H. "Acting First and Thinking Later: Theory Versus Reality in Strategic Change." In J. M. Pennings and Associates (eds.), *Organizational Strategy and Change*. San Francisco: Jossey-Bass, 1985.

Stein, J. G., and Tanter, R. *Rational Decision Making: Israel's Security Choices*. Columbus: Ohio State University Press, 1980.

Truman, H. S. *Memoirs*. Vol. 1. *Year of Decisions*. Garden City, N.Y.: Doubleday, 1955.

Tversky, A. "Elimination by Aspects: A Theory of Choice." *Psychological Review*, 1972, *79*, 281–299.

Van Meter, D. S., and Van Horn, C. E. "The Policy Implementation Process: A Conceptual Framework." *Administration and Society*, 1975, *6*, 447.

Wheeler, D., and Janis, I. L. *A Practical Guide for Making Decisions*. New York: Free Press, 1980.

Chapter 9

Decision Rules, Decision Styles, and Policy Choices

Fritz W. Scharpf

Prefatory Notes by Fritz W. Scharpf

Organization theory, as I see it from the outside, is being pulled in different directions. One of them is still defined by the Weberian model of bureaucratic organization or the neoclassical theory of the firm, both of which view organizations as instruments for the achievement of exogenous purposes defined by their owners or sponsors. Analytically, they equate organizational action with the rational choices of a unitary actor who possesses an internally consistent preference function. In order to approximate this decision-theoretical model, organizations are assumed to be hierarchically integrated. Goals and courses of action are then specified by a well-informed top management that also has the power to define organizational rules, to issue directives, and to provide incentives (positive and negative) to subordinates. Subordinates in turn are willing to follow rules and obey directives as long as their own diverging interests are effectively neutralized by a positive "inducements-contributions balance" (Simon, 1957b). Organization research within this classical perspective is more often prescriptive than descriptive or explanatory, and it tends to focus attention narrowly on factors that affect the efficiency with which the postulated goals of an organization are in fact pursued by its members. The use of this

model for an understanding of international security issues seems
to be quite limited.

The opposite direction or organizational perspective not only
challenges the rational-choice assumptions of the classical model
but discards them altogether. In this view, organizational decisions
are anything but goal oriented, well informed, or hierarchically
integrated. In one variant, they are simply seen as the outcome of
chaotic processes that resemble "garbage cans" in which the divergent interests and concerns of multiple (and often confused) actors
are associated haphazardly by mere temporary coincidence (Cohen,
March, and Olsen, 1972; March and Olsen, 1976; March and
Weissinger-Baylon, 1986). Alternatively, organizations are viewed as
being trapped in their own rigid routines; empirical observations
that seem to suggest successful goal orientedness therefore should
not be ascribed to organizational rationality or learning but to processes of evolutionary selection in hazardous environments (Kaufman, 1971; Hannan and Freeman, 1977, 1984, 1988). Whatever may
be the descriptive realism or intellectual fascination of these and
similarly antirational approaches, however, it is clear that they do
not offer much promise for the practical solution of international
problems.

Compared to these equally extreme, hyperrational or nonra-
tional approaches, a third strand of theory seems more promising
when one is interested in lessons that organization research could
provide for international security. It is also a view that seems particularly persuasive to the political scientist, since it treats organizational decisions as outcomes of bargaining processes within
coalitions of active participants (Cyert and March, 1963) or, more
directly, as political processes within the organization considered as
a "polity" (Zald, 1970; Pettigrew, 1973). What makes this approach
attractive is that it dispenses with the unrealistic notion of the unitary organizational actor without eliminating the possibility of purposeful organizational action. It acknowledges the diversity of
interests and worldviews among the members of an organization,
and it is able to do justice to the importance of power differentials
and of formal authority relations and decision rules. But it also
admits the possibility that actors may know what they are doing and
that they may be able to anticipate the outcomes of their interactive

choices and select their own strategies accordingly. In short, in coalition bargaining and in political action, not everybody, and perhaps nobody, will be able to achieve his or her most preferred outcomes—but that does not preclude the possibility that the outcomes actually achieved were anticipated and intentionally brought about by purposeful actors.

This chapter is framed within that political perspective. It uses game theory as a relatively precise language for describing and analyzing constellations of interdependent purposeful choices. But it is also critical of the simplifying assumptions that are usually introduced when the analytical models of mathematical game theory are used for descriptive, explanatory, or prescriptive purposes in real-world situations. Indeed, the point that is emphasized here seems particularly pertinent for international security issues. It is often not possible to predict the choices of actors from an analysis of their "objective" interests or of the "official" payoffs of an interaction alone. What matters just as much as the "given matrix" of real outcomes is the underlying interpretation of the relationship between the parties. (Kahn and Kramer, in Chapter Five of this volume, examine the transformation of given matrices to subjective matrices, and the implications of such transformations for de-escalation of conflict.) Game theoretic applications, on the other hand, assume often without further inquiry that the parties must be exclusively self-interested or "individualistic" in their orientation. In reality, however, they may have defined their interactions as being "cooperative," "competitive," or even as a relationship among mortal enemies.

The point is that those "interaction orientations" may be much more volatile than the underlying "objective" situations, and if changed, the game that is being played among the parties may change its character beyond recognition. Sadat's visit to Jerusalem comes to mind, as does Ronald Reagan's and Mikhail Gorbachev's redefinition of U.S.-Soviet relations. The game-theoretical literature has pointed to many other cases in the international and other fields that illustrate the importance of perceptions (and misperceptions) of the game that is in fact being played (Stein, 1982; Jönsson, 1983; Plous, 1985). Thus one of the most useful lessons for international security might be to pay extremely close attention to the correct identification, and constructive management, of the players' changing definitions of the nature of their interaction.

(The remainder of this chapter is reprinted from Fritz W. Scharpf, "Decision Rules, Decision Styles, and Policy Choices," *Journal of Theoretical Politics*, 1989, *1* [2], 149–176. © 1989 Sage Publications Ltd., London. Used with permission.)

Introduction

Much of comparative political science research may be characterized as an attempt to explain and predict the influence of political institutions on the choice of public policy.[1] Yet there is, so far, no cumulative progress toward a body of coherent, empirically supported general theory, or even toward agreement on a common set of independent and dependent variables and testable hypotheses (Feick and Jann, 1988). By now, that state of affairs can, surely, no longer be attributed to a scarcity of comparative policy studies, as one might still have surmised twenty-five years ago (Lowi, 1964). Instead, the difficulties seem to arise from the highly contingent nature of the postulated relationship itself, and they are likely to persist unless research is able to deal effectively with this problem.

But what are the sources of contingency in the relationship between political institutions and policy choices? When we consider the formation of public policy (as distinguished from its implementation), we may assume that institutions—a shorthand term for organizational capabilities and the rules governing their employment—will constrain, but not completely determine, policy choices. Nevertheless, certain policy options will be empirically infeasible, or at least severely disadvantaged by the absence of requisite capabilities, and others will be normatively prohibited by given sets of effective rules. In short, certain policy options are unlikely to be chosen under certain institutional conditions.[2]

How much such negative predictions would be worth in practical (or information theoretical) terms depends on the relative importance of the choices that are precluded by given institutional constraints, compared to those that are not. Ordinarily, however, the range of feasible and permissible options is so wide that institutional hypotheses alone could at best explain only a small portion of the empirical variance of policy outputs (and still much less of the variance of policy outcomes). The rest must be explained by a considerable variety of "contextual factors," including differing conditions of the policy environment, differing interests and goals of policymakers, and differing belief systems[3] through which policymakers are interpreting cause-and-effect and means-end relationships. Thus, policy choices are simultaneously influenced by at least four sets of factors, institutional, situational, preferential, and perceptional, rather than by institutional constraints alone.

Now it is true that the presence of additional variables need not discourage institutional analyses of policy choices—as long as we could still be sure that they are in fact explaining some part of the empirical variance. But even that assumption is thrown into doubt by the prevailing methodology of comparative policy research, which uses statistical methods for the discovery, as well as for the confirmation, of empirical regularities. If we have theoretical reasons to think that an outcome is influenced by several factors, these are high-risk strategies. Bivariate analyses concentrating upon a single independent variable or multivariate analyses that use only a few variables may produce spurious correlations that would disappear with the introduction of additional factors (Blalock, 1961). Yet the number of variables that are theoretically relevant in an explanation of policy choices is so large that we are likely to run out of cases (even in "pooled time-series analyses") whenever we try to run multivariate analyses for the complete set.[4] As a consequence, quantitative cross-national policy studies are often limited to very small subsets of an unknown universe of potentially relevant explanatory factors. Different studies are likely to focus upon different subsets, and even when they use the same set of variables, their findings are likely to be unstable if uncontrolled background factors should differ from one study to another. In short, there is no reason to expect convergence when cross-national studies are used to discover (rather than to test) theory.

Comparativists who are aware of these difficulties sometimes try to reduce the number of relevant variables by self-consciously applying the "most similar systems design" (Przeworski and Teune, 1970) to their selection of cases. It may be possible, for instance, to

hold constant much of the environmental, preferential, and perceptional variance if we focus on a standardized set of severe and
obvious policy problems—in the hope that these "single exit" conditions (Latsis, 1972; Zintl, 1987) will also have concentrated the
minds of political actors upon convergent goals and hypotheses.
Additionally, analyses may be limited to subsets of policymakers
with common interests and ideological orientations and, presumably, shared goals and perceptions. When these assumptions are
approximately correct, it is indeed more plausible that the remaining differences in policy choices might in fact be due to differences
in institutional constraints.

But we must realize that these are limited solutions. Single-exit
assumptions often founder on the realities of ideological conflict
and historical change, and the search for ideologically homogene-
ous preferences and perceptions will often end up with so few cases
that the remaining situational and institutional differences will
again confound comparative explanations. Thus the conclusion
seems inevitable that neither cross-national quantitative studies nor
the "discovery of grounded theory" (Glaser and Strauss, 1967) in
matched case studies will generally be able to cope with the range
of contingent linkages between political institutions and policy
choices.

That does not mean that we should abandon the hope of developing and validating general theory in the field of comparative
policy research. But the less we are able to trust the generality of our
empirical findings, the more urgently we need to improve the trustworthiness of the theoretical models that we are submitting to empirical tests. To do so, we need to complement the inductive
discovery of grounded theory with a significant investment in the
construction of theoretical models with a higher degree of internal
plausibility, and external compatibility with preexisting empirical
and theoretical knowledge (Willer, 1978; John, 1980; Layder, 1982).
These must necessarily consist of relatively narrow but well-
understood "partial theories" that can be combined, in historically
specific configurations, in more complex explanations of real-
world phenomena. While axiomatic theorizing cannot, by itself,
produce knowledge about the real world, it may sharpen the expectations that guide our search for and help us to make better use of

the evidence that is available. In that spirit, the present chapter will try to develop some abstract and partial propositions about the range of possible linkages between political institutions and policy choices.

Boundary Rules, Decision Rules, and Policy Choices

In more abstract models it is of course no longer possible to use the concrete dependent variables of empirical research, that is, specific policy choices evaluated by the goals of given policymakers. They need to be replaced by more abstract descriptors of the quality of policy choices. At the most general level, these may be defined along three dimensions of a social welfare function: interpersonal, intertemporal, and substantive.

1. In the *interpersonal* (or intergroup) dimension, the criterion is *inclusiveness:* to what extent will different institutional arrangements extend or reduce the range of interests that are taken into account in policy choices? Do they tend to emphasize the defense of narrowly defined particular interests or the pursuit of broadly defined collective interests?

2. In the *intertemporal* dimension, the criterion is *stability:* to what extent are institutional conditions conducive to policy choices that are able to stand the test of time in the sense that they will reflect not momentary impulses or short-term interests but, in the words of one of the great justices of the United States Supreme Court, "the sober second thought" of the community (Stone, 1936, p. 25; Bickel, 1962, pp. 23–28)?

3. In the *substantive* dimension, the criterion is *social optimality:* to what extent will institutions favor policy choices that are able to eliminate Pareto-inferior solutions by avoiding unnecessary welfare losses and by exploiting opportunities for increasing total social welfare?

But how could institutional arrangements affect the interpersonal, intertemporal, and substantive quality of policy choices? Institutions, it will be remembered, are here defined as configurations of organizational capabilities (assemblies of personal, material, and informational resources that can be used for collective action) and of sets of rules or normative constraints structuring the interaction of participants in their deployment. Thus institutions create the power to achieve purposes that would be unreachable in their absence (Thompson, 1970). However, the power to achieve collective purposes is also the power to destroy, to oppress, to exploit, and to command. It is likely to be resisted unless its exercise is supported by norms assuring compliance—and they in turn cannot be effective without rules specifying conditions and limits for the exercise of organized power. Among these rules,[5] two will receive special consideration here as particularly powerful predictors of policy choices: "boundary rules" defining the units of collective action, and "decision rules" governing the transformation of preferences into binding decisions.

Within a policy context, *boundary rules* are important at two levels: they define collective identities, and they also define units within which "governance" replaces "contracting" as a procedure for reaching jointly binding decisions.

At the first level, *identities* define the reference systems by which policy choices are evaluated. Even within the confines of methodological individualism, it must be conceded that individuals are capable of developing "we identities" at various levels of identification (Elias, 1987, pp. 269–274)—the family, the clique, the firm, the local community, the labor union, the nation-state. Any one of these collective identities may, at one time or another, become the effective referent for the comparison of alternative courses of action. Whenever that is true, individual action can only be explained and predicted by reference to the utility of the relevant collective unit whose membership is circumscribed by boundary rules.

At the second level, collective units are characterized by *governance* as an institutionalized capacity for purposeful action that rests ultimately on the power of the group or organization (or of its representatives) to appropriate and commit resources and capabilities of members without their present consent. Who is bound by such decisions is, of course, again determined by boundary rules.[6] Collective units with this capacity for governance may be treated as "corporate actors" in their own right (Coleman, 1974).

The power of governance, however, will not reach very far unless it is based on widely accepted *decision rules* that specify who is entitled to participate in which decisions, and how collective

choices are to be reached in the face of disagreement among legitimate participants. At the most general level, these decision rules
may specify hierarchical, majoritarian, or unanimous procedures
for conflict resolutions. *Hierarchy* implies the unilateral power of
one participant (or of a few participants) to determine the choices
of all others, *majority* invests the numerically larger faction with
the same power, and *unanimity* makes governance dependent upon
the agreement of all.

As a consequence, institutionalized boundary rules unite and
separate. They unite individuals (or rather, role segments of individuals) who share a certain collective identity, and they separate
them from others whose identity is recognized as being different.
More important, they unite individuals among whom coordination
may be imposed through intra-unit governance, and they separate
them from others with whom purposeful coordination[7] is only
achieved through contracting.[8]

Yet as important as the distinction between governance and contracting may be, it is not as clearly dichotomous as it might seem.
One theoretical bridge between the extremes is provided by the
Coase theorem (Coase, 1960), which demonstrates that in the absence of transaction costs all coordinative and regulatory functions
of government could also be achieved by contract—albeit with different distributive consequences. The underlying assumption about
transaction costs has since given rise to an economic theory of organization that, at first, has drawn a sharp dividing line between
"hierarchical" and "market" forms of coordination (Williamson,
1975). In the meantime, lawyers and sociologists have (re)discovered
a variety of more stable and encompassing or socially embedded
"relational" or "hierarchical" contract relations (Macneil, 1978,
1983; Dore, 1983; Stinchcombe, 1985; Powell, 1987) that are far removed from the "spot contracts" among perfect strangers that were
presumed to be characteristic of the "market" end of the dichotomy.
As a consequence, transaction cost economics now also recognizes
intermediate types of coordination that fall between the extreme
forms of pure markets and pure hierarchies (Williamson, 1979,
1985). Thus, the categorical difference between inter-unit "contracting" and intra-unit "governance" tends to become a matter of degree when relational contracts are included on the one side,[9] and

governance by unanimous agreement is allowed on the other side.[10] Recognition of this fact may help us to achieve a more cumulative social science in which economists have much to learn from studying so-called public institutions, and political scientists from studying the interactions among so-called private organizations.

The Importance of Negotiating Systems. But what is the practical importance of this middle ground for the analysis of public policy choices? When we consider only formal decision rules,[11] we might get the impression that hierarchical and majoritarian forms of governance predominante so completely in the *public sector* that governance by unanimous agreement should be considered as an empirically rare and exotic exception that merits theoretical attention only as a limiting case. Yet Gerhard Lehmbruch and Arendt Lijphart have directed our attention to the importance of de facto unanimity among competing political camps in the "consociational democracies" of some small European countries that are, of course, formally governed by majority (Lehmbruch, 1967, 1968, 1979; Lijphart, 1969). Similarly, Philippe Schmitter's (1979, 1981) "neocorporatist" patterns of interest intermediation also imply the consensual settlement of issues that are formally subject to the exercise of hierarchical government authority. In the same vein, Renate Mayntz found negotiated settlements to be characteristic features of the implementation of environmental regulations even though the relationship between government agencies and private firms is clearly hierarchical in a legal sense (Mayntz and others, 1978). In our own studies of federal state relations in Germany, we also observed a practice of unanimous agreement even in policy areas where majority decisions, or even unilateral decisions by the federal government, are formally prescribed (Scharpf, Reissert, and Schnabel, 1978; Garlichs, 1980; Reh, 1986; Posse, 1986). Similarly, Shepsle and Weingast (1981; Weingast, 1979) have found a tendency toward unanimous decisions (rather than the "minimum winning coalitions" predicted by public choice theory) in the committees of the U.S. Congress operating under simple majority rules. The list could easily be extended to other institutional contexts. In short, recent studies of decision making in the public sector seem to emphasize the practical need for consensus and the importance of unanimity even in situations where formal decision rules would permit, or even require, either unilateral/hierarchical or majority decisions.[12]

In the private sector, on the other hand, hierarchy is assumed to be the decision rule within organizations, while contracts based upon unanimous agreement are the only legitimate means of coordination between private-sector organizations. Nevertheless, relational or hierarchical contracts may include explicit arrangements for unforeseen contingencies that approximate governance systems in the sense that certain decisions (for example, by an arbitrator) are accepted despite continuing disagreement. Of even greater practical importance may be the embeddedness of a great variety of formally separate contracts in longer-term and more encompassing relations among the parties. As a consequence, the costs of exit from such relationships may increase to the point where they will in fact approach "the properties of a minisociety" (Williamson, 1979, p. 238) whose requirements are respected even if they are disliked. Among the most prominent examples are the "clans" of cooperating firms in Japanese industry (Ouchi, 1980, 1984) or the stable networks of suppliers and customers that are characteristic of "just-in-time" production or of "flexible specialization" in some European regional economies (Piore and Sabel, 1984; Sabel, 1987). For all we know, many varieties of more common contractual relations may also have similar characteristics.

To summarize, between the extreme types of purposeful coordination, defined by "markets" (spot contracts) and "hierarchies," there exists a broad middle ground of consensual negotiation systems within and between organizations (Figure 9.1). Their practical importance seems to be considerable, and is probably increasing, in the public as well as in the private sector.

Unfortunately, however, the policy implications of such negotiating systems are theoretically much less well understood than those of either pure markets or clear-cut hierarchical or majoritarian decision systems. Leaving pure markets aside, it is nevertheless possible to develop some preliminary hypotheses about the likely consequences of consensual, majoritarian, and hierarchical forms of coordination for the interpersonal inclusiveness, intertemporal stability, and substantive optimality of policy choices.

Policy Implications of Decision Rules. To begin with the criterion of *interpersonal inclusiveness,* all decision systems are likely to

Figure 9.1. Typology of Coordination Mechanisms.

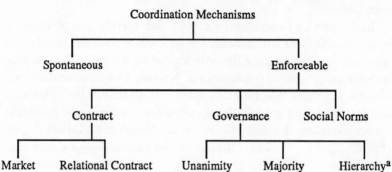

[a]At a next level, one might distinguish among different forms of hierarchies, depending upon whether they are based merely on a preponderance of power, or are supported by "traditional," "democratic," or "contractual" forms of legitimation.

favor the interests of their *members* over those of *outsiders*—which once more emphasizes the importance of boundary rules. Whether decision rules will make much of a difference in that regard is more uncertain—except that systems operating under unanimity may find generosity particularly difficult to achieve since unselfish decisions can be blocked by the veto of a single egotist. The case is clearer when we consider issues of internal *distribution among members*. As is recognized in the Coase theorem itself, the potential for redistribution is reduced as one moves from governance to contract and from hierarchical to unanimous decisions. While hierarchical authorities or hegemonic powers are free to disregard any interests and to choose any distributive rule,[13] and while majoritarian decisions may at least disregard minority interests,[14] unanimity eliminates the possibility of involuntary redistribution. That does not exclude unequal contractual exchanges—but these are derived from a preexisting inequality of bargaining positions (that is, of the relative attractiveness of alternative options when the bargain is not concluded) rather than from the decision process itself (Nash, 1950, 1953; Bacharach and Lawler, 1981). Thus, consensual decision rules permit each party to defend the existing pattern of distribution, while majority and hierarchy create at least the opportunity for involuntary redistribution (which may, of course, increase as well as decrease existing inequality).

With regard to the *intertemporal stability* of policy choices, hierarchical decision systems have perhaps the greatest freedom to consider long-term as well as short-term concerns (but see note 13), and majoritarian parliamentary systems may tend to maximize short-term benefits when elections are frequent and pluralities uncertain. By comparison, the implications of unanimity seem more uncertain: freed from (some of) the pressure of party competition and more secure in their expectations of continuing participation, decision makers are less compelled to maximize short-term advantages. But given the high transaction costs associated with unanimity, effective policy choices will often depend on complexity-reducing and conflict-avoiding redefinitions of the problem at hand (Scharpf, Reissert, and Schnabel, 1978)—and limiting discussion to incremental changes and their short-term consequences is surely one of the most common techniques for reducing complexity (Braybrooke and Lindblom, 1963).

Finally, with regard to *substantive* criteria of allocative efficiency or *optimality*, unanimity is favored in principle (that is, in the absence of transaction costs) by public-choice theorists (Buchanan and Tullock, 1962, pp. 85–96). Precisely because the rule excludes involuntary redistribution, agreement can only be obtained for policy choices through which nobody loses and some are made better off, or through which the winners are able to compensate the losers and still make a gain. When that is so, the trend of decisions will approach the frontier of Pareto optimality. Under the additional assumption that the original distribution is normatively acceptable, unanimity will then be the ideal rule, compared to which majority decisions are likely to produce inferior outcomes—even though transaction costs may make them a practical necessity.

However, as I have tried to show elsewhere (Scharpf, 1988c), the normative attractiveness of unanimity is critically dependent upon what Elinor Ostrom (1986b) has called the "default condition" or "reversion rule" that specifies the consequences of nonagreement. In single-shot negotiations among independent parties, nonagreement leaves everybody free to pursue his or her alternative options individually. Under such conditions, unanimity is indeed likely to maximize individual liberty and to increase allocative efficiency. In on-going decision systems, by contrast, from which exit is impossible or very expensive, nonagreement is more likely to imply the continuation of earlier policy choices.[15] Where that is the case, unanimity protects vested interests in existing regulations and government services regardless of any changes in external circumstances or political preferences that would preclude contemporary agreement on these same measures. Thus, once we move from single-shot decisions to ongoing decision systems, there is no reason to associate either efficiency or libertarian values with unanimity or with contractarian institutions: they will perpetuate "involuntary" governance and socially inefficient "political rents" by protecting the past gains of "distributional coalitions" (Olson, 1982) against policy change. Thus, in ongoing decision systems and under conventional assumptions about the motives of decision makers, unanimity is likely to be associated with a growing body of public policies that are illibertarian and substantively inferior to those that might have been obtained under hierarchical or majority decision rules.

This is about as far as it seems possible to discuss the policy consequences of different decision rules in the abstract and in advance of further empirical work. Yet these are, at best, *ceteris paribus* hypotheses that must necessarily leave a very large amount of variance unexplained. Thus any attempt to "test" them in comparative empirical research is likely to be confounded by the fact that institutions with similar decision rules will work differently in different countries and at different times, and that similar policy patterns may be produced within highly dissimilar institutional arrangements. The difficulty would be most acute if all of the additional determinants of policy choices were highly idiosyncratic, time–space specific contextual factors that could only be accounted for in "historical explanations" of very limited generality. Conversely, the difficulties of theory testing would be reduced if it were possible to develop additional hypotheses of similar generality about other factors interacting with the influence of institutional decision rules. In the remainder of this chapter, I will focus on one such set of factors that seems to modify the decisional tendencies associated with different rules.

Styles of Decision Making

The reference is to a set of cognitive and normative patterns characterizing the way in which interests are defined and issues are framed and resolved under the applicable rules. To characterize such patterns, I have used the term *styles of decision making* in an earlier paper (Scharpf, 1988c). In spite of considerable differences in terminology, I have also found a high degree of substantive convergence on three distinct categories in the literature.[16] Taking my terminological cues from Johan Olsen and colleagues (Olsen, Roness, and Saetren, 1982), I have used *confrontation, bargaining,* and *problem solving* for my own classification of decision styles.

Confrontation refers to competitive interactions in which winning, or the defeat of the other side, has become the paramount goal, and in which the battle can typically be decided only by superior prowess or force. In a *bargaining* relationship, by contrast, individualistic participants are unconcerned about the relative advantage of the other side and exclusively motivated by their own utilitarian self-interest. The typical outcome is a compromise. *Problem solving* implies the pursuit of common goals and the cooperative search for solutions that are optimal for the group as a whole. While the intended meanings of all three categories may be intuitively obvious, it seems useful to provide more rigorous definitions for them through the application of game-theoretical analyses. To do so requires a brief look at the fundamentals.

When discussing factors that may affect the definition of interests and the framing of issues, one must necessarily presuppose a certain degree of loose coupling between objective reality and the perception of interests. This departure from parsimonious rational-choice assumptions would not be useful if real-world interactions were often of the kind presumed by the dichotomy between "symbiotic" and "competitive" relationships. In both cases, misperceptions of the "objective" game situation (pure coordination or pure zero-sum) by rational actors would be too idiosyncratic and infrequent to justify much theoretical or practical interest. In the real world, however, purely competitive or purely symbiotic interest constellations are extremely rare, and probably unstable, compared to "mixed-motive" constellations in which the parties have common as well as competitive interests at the same time.[17] It is their objective ambivalence, pulling participants simultaneously toward cooperation and toward conflict, that also creates room for the redefinition of the interests and issues at stake. Thus, in the game-theoretical literature, much attention is focused on four prototypical mixed-motive games, Assurance, Prisoner's Dilemma, Chicken, and Battle of the Sexes (Figure 9.2).[18]

By and large, however, the discussion is concentrated on "noncooperative" solutions obtainable without the possibility for binding agreements. Within that frame of reference, the application of conventional solution concepts to these four gamess[19] will lead either to equilibria that are suboptimal for both parties or to outcomes that are unstable.[20] Yet the emphasis that these famous "paradoxes of rationality" have received in the literature may be quite misleading for the analysis of public policy formation.

Policy processes take place within the institutional context of an established "state" that provides for the possibility of binding contracts and of binding governmental decisions, and policy choices are usually (though not invariably) binding not only for their target populations but for policymakers as well. That is generally true of negotiated settlements among public entities as well as between public and private organizations and in collective bargaining among private associations. But even under hierarchical or majoritarian decision rules, courts are bound by the rule of *res judicata*, and sovereign parliamentary majorities might face electoral sanctions if they should lightly rescind their own enactments. In short, the impossibility of binding commitments, assumed in analyses of noncooperative games, is typically not to be presupposed in real-world policy processes.

But when the assumption is relaxed, the choice of a negotiated solution becomes a trivial problem in three of the four prototypical mixed-motive games.[21] In Assurance as well as in the Prisoner's Dilemma and in Chicken, it is obvious that voluntary agreement could never be obtained for those outcomes in which the cooperation of one party is exploited by the defection of the other one (D/C or C/D). But once the possibility of exploitation is eliminated, there is no doubt that both parties will prefer the outcome obtained by mutual cooperation (C/C) over that which is expected in the case

Figure 9.2. Payoff Matrices of Four Mixed-Motive Games.

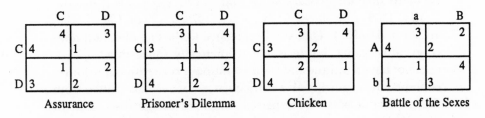

Note: Payoffs ranked from 1 (worst) to 4 (best); C = Cooperate, D = Defect; A = her, B = his preferred choice.

of mutual defection (D/D). In each of these three cases, therefore, cooperative solutions seem entirely unproblematic if binding agreements are possible.[22] The same is not true, however, in Battle of the Sexes. While it is clear that both would prefer one of the coordinated outcomes (A/a or B/b) over the possibility of each going her or his own way (A/B), that is by no means the end of their difficulties, since they must still choose between two solutions whose distributional characteristics are significantly different from each other. If the Prisoner's Dilemma, Chicken, and Assurance are modeling the problem of *whether* the parties are able to cooperate, Battle is about *on whose terms* they should agree.

Before we go further, it is important to note that the characteristics of Battle apply to an extremely wide range of real-life constellations. Not only intimate partners but also business firms engaged in joint ventures; unions and management in collective bargaining; interministerial (Mayntz and Scharpf, 1975), federal-state, and inter-European policy coordination (Scharpf, 1988c) or political parties in a coalition (Tsebelis, 1988), and many similar joint undertakings are all confronted with the same problem: while the benefits of cooperation are more attractive than the outcomes expected in the case of nonagreement, cooperation is seriously threatened by distributive conflict over the choice among cooperative solutions (or over the allocation of the costs and benefits of cooperation). It is probably fair to say that in the great majority of ongoing relationships that is the major obstacle to cooperative solutions.

In spite of its enormous practical significance, however, Battle of the Sexes has received much less attention in the game-theoretical literature than the Prisoner's Dilemma or Chicken games (Luce and Raiffa, 1975, pp. 90–94; Hamburger, 1979, pp. 128–130; Snidal, 1985, pp. 931–932). That surely is related to the fact that, as a non-cooperative game, Battle is not theoretically interesting, since it does not have a unique and stable solution if conventional solution concepts are applied.[23] As a consequence, interest has shifted from the positive analysis of expected outcomes to the discussion of "fair" solutions in the context of pragmatic treatises on the "art and science of negotiation" (Raiffa, 1982). From the vantage point of empirical political science, however, that may not be the most promising line to pursue. Instead, it seems useful to apply to Battle some findings of experimental game research that have challenged another, even more generally held, assumption of game-theoretical analysis. These findings are directly pertinent to our interest in operational definitions of different styles of decision making.

Game theory started as a branch of economics (Neumann and Morgenstern, 1944), and it has always maintained the motivational assumptions of microeconomic theory. Foremost among these is an individualistic "live-and-let-live" definition of the utility that players are supposed to seek: all of them are single-mindedly maximizing their own expected utility with no concern for the payoffs received by other players (except as far as may be necessary to anticipate their moves). But that is, surely, not the full range of potential human motivations. Actors may be engaged in strategic interaction not only as strictly self-interested individuals but also as competitors or even as mortal enemies, as partners in a common enterprise, or even as participants in an altruistic helper-client relationship. None of these can be accommodated by the dominant economic paradigm.[24]

Social scientists and psychologists have, of course, long objected on similar grounds to the motivational simplifications of microeconomics without being able to replace or complement them with similarly powerful analytical tools. Thus we should be interested in a new conceptualization of such objections in a form that seems to facilitate rather than to preclude application of the analytical tools of game-theoretical and, more generally, rational-choice analyses to a wider range of social and political intereactions. The conceptual innovation was achieved by Harold Kelley and John Thibaut (1978, pp. 14-17), who summarized a series of findings in experimental game research by distinguishing between the "given matrix" of objectively defined payoffs and an "effective matrix" that in fact determines the strategy choices of the players.

The distinction rests on the recognition that actors act on the basis of subjective interpretations of reality rather than on the basis of objectively given facts. By itself, of course, that truism would be theoretically unhelpful, substituting an unmanageable variety of cognitive and normative factors for the stark simplifications of microeconomic theory. That trap is avoided by the proposition that the empirical variance of subjective interpretations of reality may be significantly reduced by specifying a limited number of ways in which relationship between the utilities of the parties may be perceived. They are expressed by transformation rules converting the payoffs of each player in the "given matrix" into different sets of subjectively valued[25] payoffs in the "effective matrices."

Three of these transformation rules seem to be included in most studies: the maximization of one's "own gain," the maximization of one's "relative gain" compared to that of the other party, and the maximization of the "joint gains" of all parties (Messick and Thorngate, 1967; McClintock, 1972; Kelley and Thibaut, 1978, pp. 140-150). While other rules are sometimes mentioned in the literature,[26] and while it may be possible to identify empirical or historical examples for all theoretically conceivable cases of a systematically complete catalogue of transformation rules, these three are surely of the greatest practical importance in ordinary policy processes. Since they also happen to correspond directly to our three styles of decision making, they will be the subject of the remaining discussion (Figure 9.3).[27]

Under the first rule, "own gain maximization," the given matrix is reproduced in identical form. The rule thus corresponds to the *individualistic* or utilitarian assumptions of microeconomics and conventional game theory, according to which actors not only have correct and complete information about the consequences of their choices but are guided only by their own utility and are indifferent to the payoffs achieved by the other side. By the same token "own gain maximization" provides a precise operational definition of the

**Figure 9.3. Individualistic, Competitive, and Cooperative
Transformations of Battle of the Sexes.**

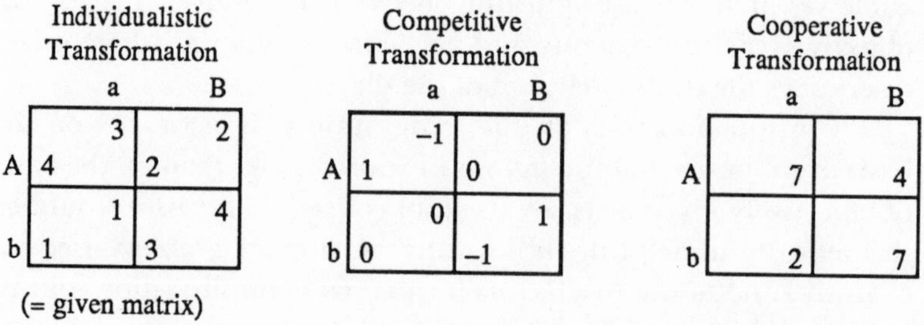

	Individualistic Transformation		Competitive Transformation		Cooperative Transformation	
	a	B	a	B	a	B
A	3 / 4	2 / 2	−1 / 1	0 / 0	7	4
b	1 / 1	4 / 3	0 / 0	1 / −1	2	7

(= given matrix)

attitudes and behavioral tendencies associated above (p. 323) with
the *bargaining* style of decision making. Since actors are assumed
to be self-regarding and nonenvious, bargaining is conducive to the
common search for compromises through which both parties are
able to improve their position compared to the status quo.

This search for compromises is likely to lead to optimal outcomes in the Assurance, Chicken, and Prisoner's Dilemma games.
Even in Battle of the Sexes, the parties may be able to agree on the
obvious compromise of turn taking if the game is played repeatedly
over identical stakes (Kelley and Thibaut, 1978, pp. 101–102); and
if outcomes are continuously variable, they may be able to "split the
difference" (Nash, 1950, 1953). Unfortunately, however, real-world
negotiations must often deal with unique problems and "lumpy"
or qualitatively different solutions. When they correspond to the
constellation of interests described by Battle of the Sexes, bargaining
provides no criterion that would allow the parties to agree on the
choice of one of the coordinated solutions (A/a or b/B).[28]

The second rule, "relative gain maximization," represents a *competitive* transformation of the given matrix. The criterion now is
winning or losing in comparison to the other player rather than
finding mutually agreeable compromises. The rule has excellent
credentials in sociological and psychological theories of reference
groups and of relative deprivation (Stouffer and others, 1949; Merton and Rossi, 1957; Runciman, 1966; Pettigrew, 1967),[29] and it also
agrees with the emphasis on competition in the socialization of
individuals in Western culture (Deutsch, 1985). Examples that come

to mind are competitive sports, electoral competition among political parties, or the arms race. Among our three styles of decision
making, the rule corresponds to the one we have labeled *confrontation*. When it is applied to any one of the mixed-motive
games, the "effective matrix" becomes zero-sum. Under majority
and hierarchy, one side will be able to impose its preferred solution
on the losers, but if the decision rule is unanimity, neither party will
voluntarily agree to the other's domination. In Battle of the Sexes,
the players will then prefer the equality of noncoordination (A/B)
to asymmetrical coordination (Aa or bB), even though that outcome is objectively inferior to the one obtainable by voluntary
submission.

Finally, the third rule implies a *cooperative* or "solidaristic"
transformation of the "given matrix," so that "an actor seeks those
alternatives that afford both herself and the other the highest joint
outcome" (McClintock, 1972, p. 447). If both parties apply the rule,
the difference between their individual payoffs will become irrelevant, and they are both free to engage in a search for "integrative"
solutions (Walton and McKersie, 1965; Pruitt and Lewis, 1975)—
which corresponds to our definition of the *problem-solving* style of
decision making. Examples may be found among happy marriages,
successful sports teams, solidaristic unions, or political parties during the honeymoon period of a new coalition government. Applied
to Battle of the Sexes, the rule suggests that the players should be
happy to accept either one of the coordinated solutions without
regard to the question of distribution.[30]

What is important for our purposes is that both the competitive
and the cooperative rules would transform Battle of the Sexes from
a game without solution into one with predictable solutions. But
these solutions differ significantly in their objective properties as
these are defined by the "given matrix." Thus, if the parties will
overcome their subjective interpretations and revert to an objective
view of the real world (as they are likely to do now and then), they
will discover that the outcomes achieved through problem solving
are superior for either of them (but still different). Hence, if the
transformation rule or interaction logic could be chosen at will,
both players would be better off with a cooperative or problem-
solving view of their relationship. Yet the continuing conflict over

distribution would probably frustrate any purely instrumental adoption of "as-if" valuations.

What is psychologically more likely instead is an oscillation between competition and cooperation, or perhaps the cyclical changes of cooperative, individualistic, and competitive attitudes that have been observed in long iterations of the noncooperative Prisoner's Dilemma (Kelley and Thibaut, 1978, p. 231). In the case of Battle, one might thus expect that one of the parties, finding the search for advantageous solutions obstructed by disagreement in the bargaining style, might turn to problem solving to improve their common welfare. But then her resentment over the unequal distribution of benefits could easily rise to the point where she will switch to confrontation in order to "get even" regardless of her own losses. Once that has happened, the relationship might break altogether, or (if exit is impossible) the experience of common misery might persuade both parties to begin a new round of bargaining over mutually more attractive solutions.

The Interaction of Decision Rules and Decision Styles

Where does that leave us in our search for the parsimonious explanation of policy choices? We have been able to identify three distinct social-psychological mechanisms, corresponding to the decision styles of bargaining, confrontation, and problem solving, that influence the likelihood of socially superior or inferior policy choices quite independently from the applicable rules of decision. Of these, confrontation will systematically lead to socially suboptimal outcomes.[31] On the other hand, the most common and in many ways psychologically most robust bargaining style (which would produce socially acceptable outcomes in Prisoner's Dilemma and Chicken games) is often likely to generate endless disagreement, blockades, and socially suboptimal outcomes when the interest constellation resembles Battle of the Sexes.[32] Finally, problem solving, which would be the socially most desirable decision style, seems always threatened by an erosion of "cooperative" or "solidaristic" attitudes. The obvious next step is to explore more systematically the interaction effects between decision rules and decision styles (Figure 9.4). They are presented here in the form of two-by-three

Figure 9.4. Influence of Decision Rules and Decision Styles on Outcomes in Four Mixed-Motive Games.

Assurance

Decision Style	Decision Rule: Unanimity	Decision Rule: Hierarchy
Problem Solving	(1) 8 ——— 4 / 4	(2) 8 ——— 4 / 4
Bargaining	(3) 4 / 4 ——— 4 / 4	(4) 4 / 4 ——— 4 / 4
Confrontation	(5) 0 / 0 ——— 2 / 2	(6) –2 / 2 ——— 1 / 3

Prisoner's Dilemma

Decision Style	Decision Rule: Unanimity	Decision Rule: Hierarchy
Problem Solving	(1) 6 ——— 3 / 3	(2) 6 ——— 3 / 3
Bargaining	(3) 3 / 3 ——— 3 / 3	(4) 1 / 4 ——— 1 / 4
Confrontation	(5) 0 / 0 ——— 2 / 2	(6) –3 / 3 ——— 1 / 4

Chicken

Decision Style	Decision Rule: Unanimity	Decision Rule: Hierarchy
Problem Solving	(1) 6 ——— 3 / 3	(2) 6 ——— 3 / 3
Bargaining	(3) 3 / 3 ——— 3 / 3	(4) 2 / 4 ——— 2 / 4
Confrontation	(5) 0 / 0 ——— 1 / 1	(6) –1 / 1 ——— 2 / 4

Battle of the Sexes

Decision Style	Decision Rule: Unanimity	Decision Rule: Hierarchy
Problem Solving	(1) 7 ——— 3 / 4	(2) 7 ——— 3 / 4
Bargaining	(3) ? ——— ?	(4) 3 / 4 ——— 3 / 4
Confrontation	(5) 0 / 0 ——— 2 / 2	(6) –1 / 1 ——— 3 / 4

Note: In each cell, the numbers above the line represent the equilibrium outcome in the "effective matrix"; those below the line represent the corresponding payoffs in the objectively "given matrix."

tables whose cells contain the game-theoretical solutions for the possible combinations of rules[33] and styles in each of four archetypical games.

The upper row in each cell in Figure 9.4 represents the outcome that is likely to be chosen in the (subjectively defined) "effective matrix," and the numbers in the lower row represent the corresponding objective outcomes in the "given matrix." While the interpretation of some of the resulting patterns may be intuitively obvious, some are sufficiently interesting to merit further elaboration.

1. In all games, the same socially optimal outcomes are obtained whenever a *problem-solving* style is assumed to govern policy choices (top row of cells). That is a reminder of the power of common orientations. Institutional arrangements make a difference if, and to the extent that, individuals who would otherwise pursue different or conflicting strategies need to be coordinated or constrained. By the same token, however, if solidaristic goals and common cognitive orientations can be generated and maintained among participants, decision rules and institutional arrangements in general have much less of an influence on policy choices. A good example is provided by the mobilization of union solidarity with an embattled Labour government during the "social contract" period in Britain between the autumn of 1975 and 1977. In spite of a highly fragmented and decentralized industrial relations system, British unions were then able to practice a voluntary form of incomes policy that was at least as effective in combatting wage inflation as was the wage restraint achieved by the much more concentrated and centralized Austrian, German, and Swedish union organizations.[34]

Ironically, solidaristic ideology may account for both the presence and the absence of hierarchical power in organizations. The "iron law of oligarchy" (Michels, [1915] 1962) in traditional labor unions and socialist parties, for instance, is surely assisted by the assumption of common goals, delegitimating "individualistic" concerns for the representation of member interests or for the dangers inherent in hierarchical power. The same may be true of fundamentalist religious organizations. Conversely, solidaristic social movements may resist any form of formal organization in the belief that cooperation and coordination are assured by common goals and worldviews alone. Yet hierarchical power corrupts, "individualistic" or "competitive" self-interest is never exorcised permanently, and the world is too ambiguous to assure the continuing convergence of perceptions. Thus solidarity is a fragile condition and is likely to need all the institutional help that it can get. More research on the conditions generating, maintaining, and eroding the collectively beneficent decision style of problem solving is clearly needed.

2. If problem solving maximizes the production of collective welfare irrespective of decision rules, *confrontation* is collectively suboptimal[35] under almost all conditions (bottom row in all diagrams). But here decision rules do make a difference: under *unanimity*, confrontation results in mutual blockage, so that opportunities for increasing total welfare through coordination remain unexploited. When the game resembles Chicken, the parties may even suffer jointly from carrying out their mutual threats. The equality that they in fact achieve is that of equal misery. When that is the case, confrontation is unlikely to persist indefinitely, since both parties have an objective interest in exploring other decision styles.

Under *hierarchy*, by contrast—that is, when one side is able to dictate the solution—outcomes achieved in the confrontational style will be unequal. They are to the advantage of the dominant side in the Prisoner's Dilemma and in Chicken. But when objective interests are more harmonious, as they are in the Assurance game, the confrontational pursuit of distributional advantages may perversely produce inferior outcomes even for the dominant party. On the other hand, if the game constellation resembles Battle of the Sexes, the maximization of distributional inequality by hierarchical domination (or by "bloody-minded" majorities, for that matter) may even lead to outcomes that are objectively superior for the disadvantaged party compared to those that it could achieve under *unanimity*. Under such conditions, the distributional inequality of outcomes may reinforce rather than undermine the prevailing confrontational decision style.

3. The social-psychologically most robust perception of self-interest is generally assumed to be "individualistic." When this *bargaining* style is combined with the rule of *hierarchy*, the outcomes are (subjectively and objectively) optimal for the dominant party. How well the weaker party will do under these circumstances de-

pends entirely upon the character of the game: in Assurance, it will achieve its best possible payoff, in Battle its second-best result, and in the Prisoner's Dilemma its worst-case outcome. But if the decision rule is *unanimity*, the outcomes achieved in a bargaining spirit will be objectively optimal for both parties in all games except for Battle of the Sexes. In the Assurance game, both will achieve all the benefits obtainable through problem solving without the need to generate and maintain solidaristic perspectives. Under conditions of Chicken or the Prisoner's Dilemma, furthermore, bargaining under unanimity will be able to protect the weaker party against extreme exploitation. This surely helps to explain the frequent resort to "consociational" or "Proporz" decision systems in countries with high levels of religious, ethnic, or class conflict (Lehmbruch, 1979).

However, as was pointed out above, consensual negotiations do not work well in Battle of the Sexes. Here individualistic bargaining is likely to be difficult, and outcomes are unpredictable under unanimity, while hierarchy would easily produce favorable outcomes even for the weaker party. The last proposition seems to correspond with the empirical finding that labor-dominated and capital-dominated political economies (while differing in their distributive outcomes) have done better in terms of economic growth, employment, and price stability during the crises of the 1970s and early 1980s than countries where neither capital nor labor enjoyed a hegemonic preponderance (Schmidt, 1986, 1987).

Thus, the intersection of unanimity and bargaining in Battle of the Sexes merits further attention. If, as we have assumed, Battle represents a game constellation of great practical importance, if the domain of unanimity is growing within the public sector as well as in interactions between the public and private spheres, and if bargaining is the most robust or default style of decision making[36]— then we need more systematic knowledge about the potentially pathological policy implications of this particular constellation.[37] Equally important is the search for mechanisms that might overcome the immobilism that is characteristic of policy-making in consensual negotiating systems. One promising field for exploration might be institutional arrangements that help to disentangle the contradictions and mutual interferences created by the simultaneous pursuit of common and conflicting interests. If decisions over the production of collective benefits could be procedurally separated from decisions over the distribution of benefits and costs (as they are in some industrial relations regimes), the parties might collaborate in successful "productivity coalitions" without forcing one side or the other to generally accept an inferior distributive outcome (Scharpf, 1988b). A crucial ingredient in such procedural arrangements might be a basic understanding about rules of distributive justice and their spheres of application (Deutsch, 1985; Walzer, 1983).

Conclusion

Given the complexity of our subject, it is perhaps not surprising that more questions have been raised than answered. Nevertheless, the conceptualizations proposed here could open the way to developing a greater number of "partial theories" of considerable relevance for the explanation of real-world policy choices. The constellations defined by the intersection of three dimensions of variables—type of game, decision rules, and decision styles—are sufficiently specific to allow a considerable reduction of the contingency of choice situations. At the same time, the three dimensions are analytically transparent enough to permit the deductive development of well-understood theoretical models for each of the intersecting constellations. Given their greater complexity and specificity, these models will be able to explicate a larger portion of their contextual conditions (McGuire, 1983; Vayda, 1983; Greenwald, Pratkanis, Leippe, and Baumgardner, 1986) rather than submerge them in one inchoate *ceteris paribus* clause. Thus the empirical exploration, and perhaps even testing, of partial hypotheses should be greatly facilitated.

These hopes, of course, depend entirely upon our ability to operationalize and empirically identify the variables that have been specified theoretically. Presumably, that task is a feasible one for the definition of the decision rules that are in fact applied (Ostrom, 1988). But while a growing number of intuitively plausible studies have used game-theoretical concepts for the interpretation of real-world choice constellations, the methodology that would allow us to determine empirically, in a controlled way, what type of games are in fact being played is still quite unclear. Even less is known about the empirical identification of decision styles whose under-lying concepts have so far only been applied in carefully controlled social-psychological experimentation. So the task is set for a good deal of developmental effort before we can even hope to demonstrate the usefulness of the propositions suggested here for comparative policy research. But given the theoretical impasse of empirical policy research discussed in the introduction, an investment in more basic developmental work may nevertheless be our one best hope.

Notes

1. Even more ambitiously, political scientists often try to link institutional differences directly to policy *outcomes,* such as inflation or unemployment or mortality rates, in quantitative cross-national comparisons. Such associations are likely to be unstable, however, unless explanatory models also include valid (multidisciplinary) specifications for the causal linkages between characteristics of policy environments, policy output, and outcomes.

2. The matter is complicated further by equifinality and institutional learning. If environmental conditions requiring specific solutions persist long enough, countries in comparable situations are likely to come up with functionally equivalent policy responses regardless of institutional differences.

3. "Keynesian" and "monetarist" policymakers, for instance, did draw quite different policy conclusions from the changes in the world economic environment in the 1970s (Scharpf, 1987).

4. If we try to increase the number of cases by going beyond the fifteen or so OECD countries that are generally considered comparable, we also introduce additional dimensions of empirical variation that add to the number of variables that need to be controlled.

5. In a paper defining the agenda for institutional analysis, Elinor Ostrom (1986a, pp. 468–471) distinguishes among seven types of rules, all of which may shape the choice of public policy. Her list includes boundary rules, scope rules, position rules, authority rules, information rules, aggregation rules, and payoff rules. Of these, boundary rules define "the entry,

exit, and domain conditions for individual participants,"
while aggregation rules (for which I have chosen the term
decision rules) are employed for "weighing individual choices
and calculating collective choices at decision nodes."

6. Ideally, the units defined by boundary rules at both these levels would coincide. In practice, that is not necessarily so: the
reference system of decision makers may be narrower or more
inclusive than the collectivity over which governance is exercised, or the two may even be disjoint (as in the case of a
military occupation).

7. That leaves out two other important modes of coordination,
social norms and "spontaneous field control" (Dahl and
Lindblom, 1953, pp. 99-104), or "ecological coordination,"
achieved through unilateral adaptation to an environment
constituted by other actors.

8. As Ian Macneil (1987) has emphasized, the difference is not the
presence or absence of compulsion since contracts are also
based on power—defined by the relative dependence of parties
on the goods or services offered by the other side. What matters
is whether I decide for myself or whether decisions are made
for me (with or without my participation).

9. In the literature, a further distinction is introduced between
"classical contracts," conforming to our description of "spot"
contracts, and "neoclassical contracts," referring to longer-
term relationships with provisions for adjusting to uncertain
future events that are, however, less elaborate than those associated with "relational contracts" (Williamson, 1979). This
further emphasizes the continuity among the various forms of
coordination.

10. Thus the more important distinction might be drawn between
interactions from which low-cost exit is possible, and "ongoing" interaction systems without exit. But again, the distinction becomes a matter of degree when the "embeddedness" of
spot contracts and the potential exit from tightly integrated
organizations are considered.

11. Conventionally, decision rules may be attributed to different
decision arenas in the following way:

Arena	Decision Rules
Within public-sector organizations	Hierarchy, majority
Between public-sector organizations	Hierarchy, unanimity
Between public and private sector	Hierarchy, unanimity
Within private-sector organizations	Hierarchy, majority
Between private-sector organizations	Unanimity

12. This is not to suggest that the distinction between de facto and formal decision rules should be unimportant. Consensual decision systems operating in the shadow of formal hierarchy or majority rules are on the whole less likely to be exploited by recalcitrant dissenters than decision systems operating under formal unanimity. But if de facto rules have achieved legitimacy, the practical difference may not be very great (Scharpf, 1988c).

13. If hierarchy needs to be legitimated, the source of legitimacy (traditional, contractual, or democratic) will significantly affect its freedom of choice. Of particular interest is the case of democratic legitimation through electoral competition among elites. If elections are frequent and competition is intense, hierarchical decisions may be systematically biased toward the most egotistic, myopic, and narrowly defined interests of constituents. Lyndon Johnson put it all in a nutshell with his quip that "You got to be reelected to be a statesman," and it is no wonder that the "statesmen" in the U.S. Congress often come from one-party constituencies.

14. That presumes the existence of stable majority coalitions. If coalitions are unstable, redistribution may be impossible even under the majority rule, as the losers of the last round will always be able to bribe some members of the former majority to switch sides (Mueller, 1979, p. 220).

15. Dennis Mueller (1979, p. 214) comes close to recognizing the problem when he mentions that the unanimous adoption of one proposal on the Pareto frontier will henceforth prevent the adoption of all other proposals from the Pareto-efficient

set. What is added here is the possibility that the earlier choice is moved away from the frontier, not by another collective decision but by changing circumstances or preferences. "Sunset legislation" could not eliminate this problem since it would violate those interests that are better off under the existing statute.

16. A close reading reveals a surprising degree of convergence between seemingly unrelated conceptualizations. Mary Parker Follett (1941), for instance, discussed the resolution of industrial conflict through domination, compromise, or integration, while Russell Hardin (1982) uses conflict, contract, and coordination as descriptors for different forms of collective action. At the organizational level, Amitai Etzioni (1961) seems to refer to similar variables in his distinction between coercive, utilitarian, and normative commitments and controls; and the same seems to be true, at the level of political systems, of Thomas Bonoma's (1976) characterization of unilateral, mixed, and bilateral power systems. Of course, not all pertinent conceptualizations in the literature come in triads. March and Simon (1958, pp. 129–131) suggest four categories: problem solving, persuasion, bargaining, and politics (of which the first two are collapsed here). Walton and McKersie (1965) limit their discussion to distributive and integrative bargaining, while Midgaard (1983) discusses tug-of-war and cooperative bargaining, both corresponding to bargaining and problem solving in the terminology proposed here. The same correspondence exists with the notions of negative and positive coordination between ministerial departments (Scharpf, 1972; Mayntz and Scharpf, 1975, pp. 145–150).

17. The game of pure coordination will turn into the mixed-motive Assurance game if there is any uncertainty about the other party's understanding of the interest constellation; it may be transformed into a Prisoner's Dilemma if there is suspicion of free-riding; or it may assume the character of Battle of the Sexes if the distribution of the costs and benefits of joint action becomes an issue. Conversely, pure competition will be transformed into the mixed-motive game of Chicken if the

common interest in avoiding mutual destruction is realized by
the participants.

18.   While the Prisoner's Dilemma and Chicken games are too
well known to need introduction, the Assurance game is best
described by Jean Jacques Rousseau's tale of a band of savages
on a stag hunt: If they all stay together, they will catch the big
game and all will eat well. But if one of them defects to catch
a rabbit, he alone will eat (though less well), while all others
go hungry. The Battle of the Sexes (alias Hero) game is usually illustrated by the couple who would like to spend an
evening going out together, but she would prefer the opera
and he a ball game. One might also think of a two-career
academic couple having to choose among universities offering
appointments that differ in their attractiveness for her and
him.

19.   In empirical research it is, of course, necessary to reconstruct
the payoff matrices of the games that are in fact played by the
parties. They need not resemble any one of these archetypical
game constellations, and they are unlikely to be symmetrical.
Nevertheless, these four games are suggestive of important
types of real-world relationships.

20.   In the Assurance game (assuming that the parties are unable
to trust each other's rationality) and in the Prisoner's Dilemma game, the suboptimal equilibrium (D/D) is obtained
if both parties apply the minimax rule. In Chicken, the minimax rule would produce a cooperative outcome (C/C), which,
however, is not a game-theoretical equilibrium. In Battle,
minimax strategies would lead to a suboptimal outcome (A/
B), which is also unstable.

21.   The same is, of course, true of all imposed solutions, that is,
when one party is able to determine the outcome under hierarchical or majoritarian decision rules. I will return to that
point in the concluding section.

22.   Andreas Ryll has pointed out to me that this is necessarily true
only in situations that are plausibly represented as a two-
person game. When the number of players increases, the collective optimum may no longer be unique, and the difficulties
of choosing among multiple optima with differing distribu-

tive characteristics may be similar to those encounters in Battle (Sen, 1969, pp. 12–15).

23. Applying the minimax rule, the players would converge upon a suboptimal outcome (A/B), which (by contrast to the Prisoner's Dilemma) is not a game-theoretical equilibrium. Hence both players would like to leave that cell, but if they should do so without coordination, they will end up with their least preferred payoffs (a/b).

24. Rational-choice theorists have spent a good deal of effort trying to derive altruistic or collective or, at minimum, Kantian preferences from individualistic premises (Sen, 1977; Collard, 1978; Harsanyi, 1980; Kennett, 1980a, 1980b; Margolis, 1982; Kolm, 1983). It is probably fair to say that these efforts have led to a negative conclusion. Nonindividualistic preferences are logically autonomous from rather than derivatives of individual egotism.

25. Transformation rules thus do not address the problem of perceptional distortions (Nisbett and Ross, 1980; Kahneman and Tversky, 1984). They continue to assume that the parties correctly perceive the objective payoffs of the given matrix.

26. McClintock as well as Kelley and Thibaut discuss an "altruistic" (maximize other's gain) transformation, but assume that it is of little practical significance. This is questionable when the role of judges or the need for trust in the altruism of professional helpers is considered (Barber, 1983). Kelley and Thibaut (1978, p. 145) also mention the possibility of an "egalitarian" transformation (minimize relative gain) that might be relevant in socialist communities. But that does not seem to exhaust the potential range of human motives: ethnic and religious conflict often seems to imply a "punitive" transformation (minimize other's gain), and some choices even also seem motivated by a desire for self-punishment. A complete typology might thus include the following transformations or "logics of interaction": maximize/minimize own gain, maximize/minimize other's gain, maximize/minimize relative gain, maximize/minimize joint gains.

Of course, not all of these rules are empirically and historically equally likely to prevail (Hirschman, 1977). Nevertheless, I expect that the rational-choice approach will not be fully accepted in the social sciences unless it will transcend its exclusive focus on individualistic motives. Once the full range of human motivations is included, it is also likely that the conditions governing the shift from one logic of interaction to another will become theoretically more interesting than the further explication of specific logics.

27.   In order to simplify the presentation, it is assumed that identical transformation rules will be applied by both parties. In real-world interactions, that is not necessarily the case. The dynamics of asymmetrical transformations are certainly important but cannot be explored here.

28.   The famous Nash solution of normative bargaining theory eliminates the crucial element of Battle, that is, the need to choose between distinct and distributively different solutions—by assuming that outcomes are continuously variable (or can be made so through side payments or package deals). Where that is the case, outcomes will represent the respective bargaining power or threat positions of the players. That solution may be hard to identify in practice, and outcomes may depend much on the strategies and tactics of negotiation (Bacharach and Lawler, 1981; Fisher and Ury, 1983), but there is no reason to expect that the collective optimum will be systematically violated—as it is likely to be when Battle of the Sexes is played over distinct and "lumpy" outcomes.

29.   Theories of relative deprivation could also suggest an "egalitarian" transformation, minimizing rather than maximizing relative gain. Under unanimity, however, that would not alter the choice of outcomes.

30.   It is here that the disregard of the perceptual dimension may seriously impair the predictive value of the theory. Solidaristic communities, or "sects" in the typology developed by Mary Douglas and Aaron Wildavsky (1982), are notorious for their internecine feuds rooted in cognitive difference that are interpreted as defection from the common goal. Thus, as a next step in theory development, propositions regarding rules and styles of decision making need to be connected to propositions

about commonalities and differences of belief systems or "cognitive maps" (Axelrod, 1976; Jönsson, 1983; Sabatier, 1987).

31. This is not in conflict with the attribution of social benefits to market competition. First, economic theory presupposes individualistic rather than competitive motives in the sense used here. Second, "social optimality" is a relative concept that must be defined by reference to a specific collectivity. In the text, it refers to the common interests of participants rather than to the interests of a wider public. To illustrate the point, ideal markets define a Prisoner's Dilemma in which cartels (cooperation) would be "socially optimal" for firms (prisoners) but not for the consumers represented by the cartel office (the sheriff).

32. The constellation may also have important cognitive implications. In games of pure coordination, in the mixed-motive Assurance game and in Prisoner's Dilemma and Chicken, each played as a cooperative game, the parties have a positive interest in improving the correctness of each other's views of the world in order to expedite agreement on a mutually agreeable solution. The same may also be true in zero-sum and mixed-motive constellations with a clear preponderance of power, where the "winner" may have every interest in the prospective "loser's" ability to correctly anticipate the likely outcome of a fight. Not so in a game without solution, like Battle, that is being played in a bargaining spirit under the unanimity rule. Here the parties may have a positive interest in inducing misperceptions that exaggerate their own and underrepresent the other side's alternative options. Hence the concern of negotiations research with the possibilities of tactical information and impression management (Raiffa, 1982; Fisher and Ury, 1983).

33. To simplify, I am only considering unanimity and hierarchy—defined as a situation in which a dominant player is able to determine the outcome for both parties. In this form of presentation, majority would not differ from hierarchy.

34. But the British social contract collapsed in 1978, when union leaders were no longer able to maintain their solidaristic commitment against the pressures of intra- and interorganiza-

Organizations and Nation-States

tional competition. By contrast, countries with a greater degree of institutional concentration in their industrial relations found it much easier to maintain an economically optimal degree of wage restraint (Scharpf, 1987, pp. 97–117, 212–251; 1988a).

35. Again it is necessary to keep in mind the system reference of such characterizations (see note 32). Thus it is entirely possible that confrontation at one level (for example, in collective bargaining) will facilitate solidaristic integration at the level below (for example, within unions and employers associations).

36. The default character of bargaining is reinforced by the predominance of "utilitaristic" organizations, such as business firms, interest associations, or government bureaucracies, in real-world negotiation systems. The role definitions of their agents do not usually permit the solidaristic or confrontational redefinition of the interests at stake (which, however, may be achieved by the personal authority of leaders who are able to transcend their organizational roles).

37. No more than a beginning has been achieved in the analysis of the "joint decision traps" created by de facto unanimity in German federalism and in the European Community (Scharpf, 1988c).

References

Alford, R. R., and Friedland, R. *Powers of Theory, Capitalism, the State and Democracy*. Cambridge: Cambridge University Press, 1985.

Axelrod, R. (ed.). *Structure of Decision: The Cognitive Maps of Political Elites*. Princeton, N.J.: Princeton University Press, 1976.

Bacharach, S. B., and Lawler, E. J. *Bargaining: Power, Tactics, and Outcomes*. San Francisco: Jossey-Bass, 1981.

Barber, B. *The Logic and Limits of Trust*. New Brunswick, N.J.: Rutgers University Press, 1983.

Barnard, C. I. *The Functions of the Executive*. Cambridge, Mass.: Harvard University Press, 1947.

Bickel, A. M. *The Least Dangerous Branch: The Supreme Court at the Bar of Politics.* Indianapolis, Ind.: Bobbs-Merrill, 1962.

Blalock, H. M. *Causal Inferences in Non-Experimental Research.* Chapel Hill: University of North Carolina Press, 1961.

Bonoma, T. V. "Conflict, Cooperation and Trust in Three Power Systems." *Behavioral Science,* 1976, *21,* 499–513.

Braybrooke, D., and Lindblom, C. E. *A Strategy of Decision: Policy Evaluation as a Social Process.* New York: Free Press, 1963.

Buchanan, J. M., and Tullock, G. *The Calculus of Consent: Logical Foundations of Constitutional Democracy.* Ann Arbor: University of Michigan Press, 1962.

Coase, R. "The Problem of Social Cost." *Journal of Law and Economics,* 1960, *3,* 1–44.

Cohen, M. D., March, J. G., and Olsen, J. P. "A Garbage Can Model of Organizational Choice." *Administrative Science Quarterly,* 1972, *17,* 1–25.

Coleman, J. S. *Introduction to Mathematical Sociology.* New York: Free Press, 1964.

Coleman, J. S. *Power and the Structure of Society.* New York: Norton, 1974.

Collard, D. *Altruism and Economy: A Study in Non-Selfish Economics.* New York: Oxford University Press, 1978.

Cyert, R. M., and March, J. G. *A Behavioral Theory of the Firm.* Englewood Cliffs, N.J.: Prentice-Hall, 1963.

Dahl, R. A., and Lindblom, C. E. *Politics, Economics, and Welfare. Planning and Politico-Economic Systems Resolved into Basic Social Processes.* New York: Harper & Row, 1953.

Deutsch, M. *Distributive Justice: A Social Psychological Perspective.* New Haven, Conn.: Yale University Press, 1985.

Dore, R. "Goodwill and the Spirit of Market Capitalism." *British Journal of Sociology,* 1983, *34,* 459–482.

Douglas, M., and Wildavsky, A. *Risk and Culture.* Berkeley: University of California Press, 1982.

Elias, N. "Wandlungen der Wir-Ich Balance." ["Changes in the We-I Balance."] In N. Elias, *Die Gesellschaft der Individuen.* Frankfurt: Suhrkamp, 1987.

Etzioni, A. *A Comparative Analysis of Complex Organizations.* New York: Free Press, 1961.

Feick, J., and Jann, W. " 'Nations Matter'—Vom Eklektizismus zur Integration in der Vergleichenden Policyforschung?" [" 'Nations Matter'—From Eclecticism to Systematic Integration in Comparative Policy Research."] *Politische Vierteljahreschrift,* 1988, *29,* 196–220.

Fisher, R., and Ury, W. *Getting to Yes: Negotiating Agreement Without Giving In.* Harmondsworth: Penguin, 1983.

Follett, M. P. "Constructive Conflict." In H. C. Metcalf and L. Urwick (eds.), *Dynamic Administration: The Collected Papers of Mary Parker Follett.* New York: Harper & Row, 1941.

Garlichs, D. *Grenzen Staatlicher Infrastrukturpolitik: Bund/ Länder-Kooperation in der Fernstrassenplanung.* [*Limits of Governmental Infrastructural Policy: Federal/State Cooperation in Highway Planning.*] Köningstein/Ts: Anton Hain, 1980.

Glaser, B. G., and Strauss, A. L. *The Discovery of Grounded Theory: Strategies for Qualitative Research.* Chicago: Aldine, 1967.

Greenwald, A., Pratkanis, A. A., Leippe, M. R., and Baumgardner, M. H. "Under What Conditions Does Theory Obstruct Research Progress?" *Psychological Review,* 1986, *93,* 216–229.

Hamburger, H. *Games as Models of Social Phenomena.* New York: W. H. Freeman, 1979.

Hannan, M. T., and Freeman, J. H. "The Population Ecology of Organizations." *American Journal of Sociology,* 1977, *82,* 929–964.

Hannan, M. T., and Freeman, J. H. "Structural Inertia and Organizational Change." *American Sociological Review,* 1984, *49,* 149–164.

Hannan, M. T., and Freeman, J. H. "The Ecology of Organizational Mortality: American Labor Unions, 1836–1985." *American Journal of Sociology,* 1988, *94,* 25–52.

Hardin, R. *Collective Action.* Baltimore, Md.: Johns Hopkins University Press, 1982.

Harsanyi, J. C. "Rule Utilitarianism, Rights, Obligations and the Theory of Rational Behavior." *Theory and Decision,* 1980, *12,* 115–133.

Hirschman, A. O. *The Passions and the Interests: Political Arguments for Capitalism Before Its Triumph.* Princeton, N.J.: Princeton University Press, 1977.

John, R. "Theory Construction in Sociology: The Competing Approaches." *Mid-American Review of Sociology,* 1980, *5,* 15-36.

Jönsson, C. "A Cognitive Approach to International Negotiation." *European Journal of Political Research,* 1983, *11,* 139-150.

Kahneman, D., and Tversky, A. "Choices, Values, and Frames." *American Psychologist,* 1984, *39,* 341-350.

Kaufman, F. X., Majone, G., and Ostrom, V. (eds.). *Guidance, Control, and Evaluation in the Public Sector: The Bielefeld Interdisciplinary Project.* Berlin: De Gruyter, 1986.

Kaufman, H. *The Limits of Organizational Change.* Tuscaloosa: University of Alabama Press, 1971.

Kelley, H. H., and Thibaut, J. W. *Interpersonal Relations: A Theory of Interdependence.* New York: Wiley, 1978.

Kennett, D. A. "Altruism and Economic Behavior. I: Developments in the Theory of Public and Private Redistribution." *American Journal of Economics and Sociology,* 1980a, *39,* 183-198.

Kennett, D. A. "Altruism and Economic Behavior. II: Private Charity and Public Policy." *American Journal of Economics and Sociology,* 1980b, *39,* 337-354.

Kolm, S. C. "Altruism and Efficiency." *Ethics,* 1983, *94,* 18-65.

Latsis, S. "Situational Determinism in Economics." *British Journal for the Philosophy of Science,* 1972, *23,* 207-245.

Layder, D. "Grounded Theory: A Constructive Critique." *Journal for the Theory of Social Behavior,* 1982, *12,* 103-123.

Lehmbruch, G. *Proporzdemokratie: Politisches System und Politische Kultur in der Schweiz und Osterreich.* [*Proportional System and Political Culture in Switzerland and Austria.*] Tübingen: Mohr, 1967.

Lehmbruch, G. "Konkordanzdemokratie im politischen System der Schweiz." ["Consocial Democracy in the Swiss Political System."] *Politische Vierteljahresschrift,* 1968, *9,* 443-459.

Lehmbruch, G. *Parteienwettbewerb im Bundesstaat.* [*Party Competition in the Federal State.*] Stuttgart: Kohlhammer, 1976.

Lehmbruch, G. "Consociational Democracy, Class Conflict and the New Corporatism." In P. C. Schmitter and G. Lehmbruch (eds.), *Trends Toward Corporatist Intermediation.* Newbury Park, Calif.: Sage, 1979.

Lijphart, A. "Consociational Democracy." *World Politics*, 1969, *21*, 207–225.

Lowi, T. J. "American Business, Public Policy, Case Studies, and Political Theory." *World Politics*, 1964, *16*, 677–715.

Luce, R. D., and Raiffa, H. *Games and Decisions: Introduction and Critical Survey*. New York: Wiley, 1975.

McClintock, C. G. "Social Motivation—A Set of Propositions." *Behavioral Science*, 1972, *17*, 438–454.

McGuire, W. J. "A Contextualist Theory of Knowledge: Its Implications for Innovation and Reform in Psychological Research." In L. Berkowitz (ed.), *Advances in Experimental Social Psychology*. Vol. 16. Orlando, Fla.: Academic Press, 1983.

Macneil, I. R. "Contracts: Adjustments of Long-Term Economic Relations Under Classical, Neoclassical, and Relational Contract Law." *Northwestern Law Review*, 1978, *72*, 854–905.

Macneil, I. R. "Values in Contract; Internal and External." *Northwestern University Law Review*, 1983, *78*, 340–418.

Macneil, I. R. "Political Exchange as Relational Contract." Unpublished manuscript, European University Institute, Florence, 1987.

March, J. G., and Olsen, J. P. *Ambiguity and Choice in Organizations*. Bergen: Universitetsforlaget, 1976.

March, J. G., and Simon, H. A. *Organizations*. New York: Wiley, 1958.

March, J. G., and Weissinger-Baylon, R. (eds.). *Ambiguity and Command: Organizational Perspectives on Military Decision Making*. Marshfield, Mass.: Pitman, 1986.

Margolis, H. *Selfishness, Altruism, and Rationality. A Theory of Social Choice*. Cambridge: Cambridge University Press, 1982.

Mayntz, R., Derlien, H. U., Bohne, E., Hesse, B., Hucke, J., and Müller, A. *Vollzugsprobleme der Umweltpolitik—Untersuchung der Implementation von Gesetzen im Bereich der Luftreinhaltung und des Gewässershutzes*. [*Implementation Problems in Environmental Policy—The Control of Air and Water Pollution*.] Materialien zur Umweltforschung, Rat von Sachverständigen für Umweltfragen (Ed.), Stuttgart: Kohlhammer, 1978.

Mayntz, R., and Nedelmann, B. "Eigendynamische Soziale Prozesse. Anmerkungen zu einem analytischen Paradigma." ["Self

Dynamic Social Processes. Notes on Analytical Paradigm."] *Kölner Zeitschrift für Soziologie und Sozialpsychologie*, 1987, *39*, 648–668.

Mayntz, R., and Scharpf, F. W. *Policy-Making in the German Federal Bureaucracy*. Amsterdam: Elsevier, 1975.

Merton, R. K., and Rossi, A. S. "Contributions to the Theory of Reference Group Behavior." In R. K. Merton, *Social Theory and Social Structure*. (Rev. ed.) New York: Free Press, 1957.

Messick, D. M., and Thorngate, W. B. "Relative Gain Maximization in Experimental Games." *Journal of Experimental Social Psychology*, 1967, *3*, 85–101.

Michels, R. *Political Parties*. New York: Collier Books, 1962. (Originally published 1915.)

Midgaard, K. "Rules and Strategy in Negotiations: Notes on an Institutionalist and Internationalist Approach." *European Journal for Political Research*, 1983, *11*, 151–166.

Mueller, D. C. *Public Choice*. Cambridge: Cambridge University Press, 1979.

Nash, J. F. "The Bargaining Problem." *Econometrica*, 1950, *18*, 155–162.

Nash, J. F. "Two-Person Cooperative Games." *Econometrica*, 1953, *21*, 128–140.

Neumann, J. von, and Morgenstern, O. *Theory of Games and Economic Behavior*. Princeton, N.J.: Princeton University Press, 1944.

Nisbett, R., and Ross, L. *Human Inference: Strategies and Shortcomings of Social Judgement*. Englewood Cliffs, N.J.: Prentice-Hall, 1980.

Olsen, J., Roness, P., and Saetren, H. "Norway: Still Peaceful Coexistence and Revolution in Slow Motion." In J. Richardson (ed.), *Policy Styles in Western Europe*. London: Allen & Unwin, 1982.

Olson, M. *The Rise and Decline of Nations, Economic Growth, Stagflation, and Social Rigidities*. New Haven, Conn.: Yale University Press, 1982.

Ostrom, E. "A Method of Institutional Analysis." In F. X. Kaufman, G. Majone, and V. Ostrom (eds.), *Guidance, Control, and Evaluation in the Public Sector: The Bielefeld Interdisciplinary Project*. Berlin: De Gruyter, 1986a.

Ostrom, E. "An Agenda for the Study of Institutions." *Public Choice*, 1986b, *48*, 3–25.

Ostrom, E. "The Commons and Collective Action." Unpublished manuscript, Workshop in Political Theory and Policy Analysis, Indiana University, 1988.

Ouchi, W. G. "Markets, Bureaucracies and Clans." *Administrative Science Quarterly*, 1980, *25*, 129–141.

Ouchi, W. G. *The M-Form Society: How American Teamwork Can Recapture the Competitive Edge*. Reading, Mass.: Addison-Wesley, 1984.

Pettigrew, A. M. *The Politics of Organizational Decision-Making*. London: Tavistock, 1973.

Pettigrew, T. E. "Social Evaluation Theory: Convergences and Applications." In D. Levine (ed.), *Nebraska Symposium on Motivation*. Lincoln: University of Nebraska Press, 1967.

Piore, M. J., and Sabel, C. F. *The Second Industrial Divide. Possibilities for Prosperity*. New York: Basic Books, 1984.

Plous, S. "Perceptual Illusions and Military Realities. The Nuclear Arms Race." *Journal of Conflict Resolution*, 1985, *29*, 363–389.

Posse, A. U. *Föderative Politverflechtung in der Umwelpolitik. [Federal-State Joint Decision Making in Environmental Policy.]* Innenpolitik in Theorie und Praxis 16. Munich: Minerva-Publikation, 1986.

Powell, W. W. "Neither Market Nor Hierarchy: The Limits of Organizations." Unpublished manuscript, Center for Advanced Study in the Behavioral Sciences, Stanford University, June 1987.

Pruitt, D. G., and Lewis, S. A. "Development of Integrative Solutions in Bilateral Negotation." *Journal of Personality and Social Psychology*, 1975, *31*, 621–633.

Przeworski, A., and Teune, H. *The Logic of Comparative Social Inquiry*. New York: Wiley, 1970.

Raiffa, H. *The Art and Science of Negotiation*. Cambridge, Mass.: Harvard University Press, 1982.

Reh, W. "Politikverflechtung im Fernstrassenbau der Bundesrepublik Deutschland und im Nationalstrassenbau der Schweiz: Eine vergleichende Untersuchung zur Effizienz und Legitimation des Bürokratischen Föderalismus." Unpublished doctoral dissertation, University of Mannheim, 1986.

Runciman, W. G. *Relative Deprivation and Social Justice: A Study of Attitudes to Social Inequality in Twentieth-Century England.* Berkeley: University of California Press, 1966.

Sabatier, P. A. "Knowledge, Policy-Oriented Learning, and Policy Change." *Knowledge: Creation, Diffusion, Utilization,* 1987, *8,* 649–692.

Sabel, C. F. "The Reemergence of Regional Economics: Changes in the Scale of Production." Unpublished manuscript, Massachusetts Institute of Technology, 1987.

Scharpf, F. W. "Komplexität als Schranke der politischen Planung." ["Complexity as a Limiting Factor in Political Planning."] *Politische Vierteljahresschrift,* 1972, *4,* 168–192.

Scharpf, F. W. *Sozialdemokratiche Krisenpolitik in Europa.* [*The Political Economy of Social Democratic Europe During a Decade of Crisis.*] Frankfurt: Campus, 1987.

Scharpf, F. W. "A Game-Theoretical Interpretation of Inflation and Unemployment in Western Europe." *Journal of Public Policy,* 1988a, *7,* 227–257.

Scharpf, F. W. "Verhandlungssysteme, Verteilungskonflikte und Pathologien der Politischen Steuerung." ["Negotiation Systems, Distribution Conflicts, and Pathologies of Political Control."] In M. G. Schmidt (ed.), *Staatstätigkeit: International Vergleichende Analysen, Politische Vierteljahresschrift,* 1988b, *19,* 16–87.

Scharpf, F. W. "The Joint Decision Trap." *Public Administration,* 1988c, *66,* 239–278.

Scharpf, F. W., Reissert, B., and Schnabel, F. "Policy Effectiveness and Conflict Avoidance in Intergovernmental Policy Formation." In K. Hanf and F. W. Scharpf (eds.), *Interorganizational Policy Making. Limits to Coordination and Central Control.* Newbury Park, Calif.: Sage, 1978.

Schmidt, M. G. "Politische Bedingungen erfolgreicher Wirtschaftspolitik—eine vergleichende Analyse westlicher Industrieländer." ["Political Preconditions of Successful Economic Policy—A Comparative Analysis of Western Industrial Nations."] *Journal für Sozialforschung,* 1986, *26,* 251–273.

Schmidt, M. G. "The Politics of Labor Market Policy: Structural and Political Determinants of Full Employment and Mass Unemployment in Mixed Economies." In F. G. Castles, F. Lehner, and M. G. Schmidt (eds.), *Managing Mixed Economies*. Berlin: De Gruyter, 1987.

Schmitter, P. C. "Still the Century of Corporatism?" In P. C. Schmitter and G. Lehmbruch (eds.), *Trends Toward Corporatist Intermediation*. Newbury Park, Calif.: Sage, 1979.

Schmitter, P. C. "Interest Intermediation and Regime Governability in Contemporary Western Europe and North America." In S. Berger (ed.), *Organizing Interests in Western Europe: Pluralism, Corporatism, and the Transformation of Politics*. Cambridge: Cambridge University Press, 1981.

Sen, A. K. "A Game-Theoretic Analysis of Theories of Collectivism in Allocation." In T. Majumdar (ed.), *Growth and Choice*. New York: Oxford University Press, 1969.

Sen, A. K. "Rational Fools: A Critique of the Behavioral Foundations of Economic Theory." *Philosophy and Public Affairs*, 1977, *6*, 317–344.

Shepsle, K. A., and Weingast, B. R. "Political Preferences for the Pork Barrel: A Generalization." *American Journal of Political Science*, 1981, *25*, 96–111.

Simon, H. A. *Administrative Behavior. A Study of Decision-Making Processes in Administrative Organization*. (2nd ed.) New York: Free Press, 1957a.

Simon, H. A. "A Formal Theory of the Employment Relation." In H. A. Simon (ed.), *Models of Man. Social and Rational*. New York: Wiley, 1957b.

Snidal, D. "Coordination Versus Prisoner's Dilemma: Implications for International Cooperation and Regimes." *American Political Science Review*, 1985, *79*, 923–942.

Stein, A. A. "When Misperception Matters." *World Politics*, 1982, *34*, 487–526.

Stinchcombe, A. L. "Contracts as Hierarchical Documents." In A. L. Stinchcombe and C. A. Heimer, *Organization Theory and Project Management. Administering Uncertainty in Norwegian Offshore Oil*. Oslo: Norwegian University Press, 1985.

Stone, H. F. "The Common Law in the United States." *Harvard Law Review*, 1936, *50*, 4–26.

Stouffer, S. A., and others. *The American Soldier, I: Adjustment*

During the Army Life. Princeton, N.J.: Princeton University Press, 1949.

Thompson, J. D. "Comment: Power as Energy or Power as a Reflection of Things." In M. N. Zald (ed.), *Power in Organizations*. Nashville, Tenn.: Vanderbilt University Press, 1970.

Tsebelis, G. "Nested Games: The Cohesion of French Electoral Coalitions." *British Journal of Political Science*, 1988, *18*, 145–170.

Vayda, A. P. "Progressive Contextualization: Methods for Research in Human Ecology." *Human Ecology*, 1983, *11*, 265–281.

Walton, R. E., and McKersie, R. B. *A Behavioral Theory of Labor Negotiations: An Analysis of a Social Interaction System*. New York: McGraw-Hill, 1965.

Walzer, M. *Spheres of Justice. A Defense of Pluralism and Equality*. New York: Basic Books, 1983.

Weingast, B. R. "A Rational Choice Perspective on Congressional Norms." *American Journal of Political Science*, 1979, *23*, 245–263.

Wiesenthal, H. "Akteurrationalität. Überlegungen zur Steuerungsfähigkeit politischer Akteure in der Beschäftigungskrise." ["Actor Rationality. Reflections on the Control Capacity of Political Actors in the Employment Crisis."] Unpublished manuscript, Faculty of Sociology, University of Bielefeld, 1987.

Willer, D. "What Is Exact Theory?" In R. Smith and B. Anderson (eds.), *Theory Development*. New York: Halstedt Press, 1978.

Williamson, O. E. *Markets and Hierarchies: Analysis and Antitrust Implications*. New York: Free Press, 1975.

Williamson, O. E. "Transaction-Cost Economics: The Governance of Contractual Relations." *Journal of Law and Economics*, 1979, *22*, 233–261.

Williamson, O. E. *The Economic Institutions of Capitalism: Firms, Markets, Relational Contracting*. New York: Free Press, 1985.

Zald, M. N. (ed.). *Power in Organizations*. Nashville, Tenn.: Vanderbilt University Press, 1970.

Zintl, R. "Der Homo Oeconimicus als Generalist oder als Spezialist? Über die Verwendung Rationalistischer Rekonstruktionen der Mikroebene." ["The Homo Oeconimicus as Generalist or as

Specialist? On the Use of Rationalist Microlevel Reconstructions."] Unpublished manuscript, Universität der Bundeswehr, Munich, 1987.

Chapter 10

Loss of Control

Problems of Nuclear Command

Richard N. Lebow
Mayer N. Zald

Prefatory Notes

Our strategy in this volume has been to apply and extend organizational concepts to problems of international relations. One area in which the relevance of organizational processes for issues of national security seems very great is command and control of the nuclear arsenal.

Issues of environmental scanning and information gathering, decision making and discretion, delegation of authority and responsibility, implementation of decisions, and problems of the balance between delegation and control of subordinates are very old in organizational theory yet resonate with modern developments. Oliver Williamson's first major contributions (1964, 1970) to modern organizational theory dealt with the control-loss problem, and modern principal-agent theory deals with the issue of how to design organizations so that agents are tied to principals' objectives. The parallel issues have long been recognized in the conduct of war. The sovereign and his chief advisers have the problems of dealing with other nations, making decisions about war and peace, and executing these decisions by means of diplomatic and military agencies. The problem of the control of subordinates has long standing in international relations, and the possibility of accidental wars and the limits of command have long been known.

These problems are especially acute in managing and controlling nuclear weaponry, since the possibilities of escalation and enormous costs so greatly exceed those in conventional warfare. A very sophisticated literature has developed. It is called CCCI (or C^{3}I), for command, control, communication, and intelligence, and it deals with the central organizational problems of decision making, delegation, and control: what to do if the president is incapacitated; where to locate command centers if an attack occurs; how to build in safeguards against false warnings of attack; how to establish communication links with potential aggressors to minimize mistaken readings of intentions; how to control the delivery of missiles under conditions of limited communication (for example, between central command centers and missile-carrying submarines). Scholars such as Bruce Blair (1985); Ashton Carter, John D. Steinbruner, and Charles A. Zraket (1987); Paul Bracken (1983); and Ned Lebow (1987), who have a sophisticated and detailed knowledge of the workings of government, the military, and nuclear command and control systems, have laid bare the organizational options and dilemmas. Because this literature is already so well developed, we have drawn upon it rather than undertaking our own original investigation.

This chapter, "Loss of Control," is reprinted from Ned Lebow's excellent book *Nuclear Crisis Management* (1987). In it Lebow describes several different ways in which nuclear war might come about. All of his scenarios have organizational analogs in civilian situations. For instance, he describes how information overload and compression of decision time can contribute to escalation. Moreover, he shows how the necessity to delegate launch authority in a time of crisis and requests for release from hierarchical control would work their way up the chain of command. Field commanders would attempt to maximize their discretion. Problems due to overload and the press to delegation under crisis conditions are not unique to the military; they occur in other organizations as well.

Although much of the C^{3}I literature is very sophisticated and very specialized, we believe that even here the scholars of organizational and international relations have much to contribute to each other.

First, there is a growing literature on "normal" organizational accidents (Perrow, 1984) and on the management of high-risk systems (Weick, 1985, 1987) that might be useful to C³I analysts. The organizational literature is especially useful in terms of thinking about how organizational culture, socialization, informal understanding, and local practice contribute to reliability and unreliability. All these features of organization life are subject to purposeful change, and documented efforts to manage such changes may be useful to planners and designers of C³I systems.

Second, however, C³I is an area where the international relations literature may contribute to organizational theory and research. Students of C³I have learned much that may clarify interorganizational relations. For instance, the intelligence and early warning systems developed between the Great Powers may help illuminate problems of oligopolistic communication. Analysis of reliability problems in the control of nuclear weapons may illuminate, or throw into stark relief, problems of managing decentralized global corporations. The benefits of the analogy flow both ways.

Mayer N. Zald

(The remainder of this chapter is reprinted from Richard Ned Lebow, *Nuclear Crisis Management.* Copyright © 1987 by Cornell University. Used by permission of the publisher, Cornell University Press.)

In this chapter I take up our second sequence to war, loss of control, and I describe several different ways in which it could lead to unintended nuclear war between the superpowers. I identify the likely causes of each of these paths of war and show the extent to which they are structural attributes of the superpowers' alert and response systems. A high level of risk is, I shall show, inherent in strategic force generation.

Loss of control is analytically distinct from preemption. In neither sequence is war a desired outcome, but in the case of preemption war nevertheless results from a deliberate decision by leaders on at least one side to wage it. When loss of control leads to war, by contrast, it does so because of the actions of subordinates that leaders are unaware of or unable to prevent.

Loss of control can nevertheless be a contributing cause of preemption. If, in a crisis, leaders become convinced that war is inevitable, because they can no longer maintain control over their forces, they may decide to use them preemptively if they think preemption will confer a significant military advantage. Loss of control is also linked to miscalculated escalation, but here the sequence is reversed. Miscalculated escalation refers to steps up the political-military escalation ladder in a crisis, steps taken to moderate adversarial behavior that instead provoke further escalation by the adversary. It can thus lead to war by loss of control. This chapter illustrates the dynamics of this process in the context of strategic alerts.

Loss of control can have political or institutional causes. In the former case disaffected officials try to sabotage policy or impose a new policy of their own; this was an important cause of war in 1914. Institutional loss of control is a more complex phenomenon. It occurs when individuals, acting on orders, or at least within the accepted confines of their authority, nevertheless behave in ways that interfere with, undercut, or are contrary to the objectives that national leaders are pursuing. Institutional loss of control arises because policy decisions in large bureaucracies often have significant unanticipated consequences.

Military Rigidity

Modern political and military organizations are complex bureaucracies. Their characteristic modes of operation can be quite inappropriate to the needs of political leaders in a crisis. Crisis management requires political finesse in the formulation of policy and a surgical precision in its execution. Generally, large bureaucracies are incapable of either. It is for this reason that political leaders frequently rely on a small coterie of trusted advisers to help them cope with foreign policy. "Kitchen cabinets" of this kind are useful, but they cannot by themselves manage a major international crisis. To the extent that policy calls for extensive diplomatic contacts, military alerts, or actual operations, leaders must of necessity rely on the assistance of the relevant bureaucracies. Political leaders whose demands clash with normal bureaucratic modes of operation are almost certain to encounter resistance.

Even well-run military organizations are likely to be quite rigid. They are avowedly hierarchical, steeped in tradition, and dependent on complex routines. In crisis, moreover, military leaders also tend to emphasize objectives different from those of political leaders. For these reasons, the history of postwar crisis management is filled with instances of civil-military conflict. Here I outline five of the more important organizational sources of such conflict.

First, the military relies on prepackaged routines. Both superpowers have developed weapons and strategies to respond to the kinds of challenges they believe their countries are most likely to face. But these forces, conventional or nuclear, cannot be maintained at full combat readiness, which is too expensive and impractical, and so they are for the most part kept at much lower levels of alert. Procedures have been devised to bring them up to higher levels of readiness at relatively short notice. The ability of the services, individually and collectively, and presumably of their Soviet counterparts to carry out a wide range of options increases as a function of readiness. As a consequence, military organizations will generally insist on moving up to higher alert levels in time of crisis. Even when fully alerted, however, they are likely to resist (or even prove incapable of implementing) options that differ significantly from those they have previously prepared to execute.

Second, the military "factors" problems. Most military operations are composed of distinct routines. These routines are developed by subunits of the services, each of which has a defined area of responsibility within an overall hierarchical structure. Individuals responsible for preparing or implementing military options are likely to consult with subordinate and superior commands, but they may have little or no contact with horizontal commands that are charged with preparing or implementing other aspects of the same operation. Consequently, decisions made by planners almost inevitably reflect a narrow, even parochial view of the problem and may be formulated entirely in ignorance of the political goals that military action is meant to achieve. Those at the apex of the hierarchy, by comparison, are likely to be more sensitive to the political

objectives of the government but less knowledgeable about the details of the operation. The obvious danger for crisis management is
that no one in the system is likely to know the full range of behavior
that any step up the ladder of escalation entails.

Third, options are "staffed" by middle-level officials. Colonels
and their civilian equivalents are generally responsive to a set of
criteria very different from those that motivate political leaders.
When they formulate options, they shape them in terms of standard
operating procedures and tailor them to service capabilities and
preferences. The resulting plans are likely to maximize traditional
military objectives at the expense of precision, flexibility, control,
or other values that political leaders will come to consider critical
in crisis. As political leaders are almost certain to be ignorant of the
details of these options, they will probably remain unaware of the
problems they threaten until they occur. By then, it is often too late
to do anything about it.

Fourth, the military resists political "interference" in the planning and execution of actions. It generally views political intervention in the planning process as a threat to organizational independence. Resistance will be greatest when political directives clash
with service traditions, preferences, and operating procedures. Even
more likely to provoke conflict is political supervision of military
operations, which violates two sacrosanct principles of military organization: the chain of command and the autonomy of the local
commander. The chain of command, a mechanism for preserving
the hierarchical structure of the military, stipulates that orders
should proceed step-by-step down the hierarchy until they reach the
officer responsible for their execution. Traditionally the officer on
the spot carries out those orders as he sees fit. This discretionary
authority is designed to cope with rapidly changing battlefield
conditions.

Finally, the military emphasizes military as opposed to political
objectives. The military approach to conflict is dominated by the
quest for military superiority. Superiority is seen as the essential
condition for deterrence and, should that fail, for winning any war.
Because they stress capabilities over intentions, military officers
tend to be unaware of, or uninterested in, the political constraints
and pressure that affect adversarial leaders. They are correspond-

ingly insensitive to the ways in which their striving for military superiority constitutes an important source of tension with adversaries. In keeping with this outlook, the military is likely to advocate crisis policies that work on the other side's capabilities, not on its intentions. This traditional military outlook is a sure recipe for disaster in the nuclear era, but this is something civilian authorities are more likely to recognize. Attempts they make to restrain military efforts to gain or maintain superiority, or in a crisis to subordinate military advantage or preparedness to broader political goals, are almost certain to meet military opposition.

German mobilization plans on the eve of World War I illustrate the pernicious effects of all of the above-mentioned institutional characteristics of the military. The German Army's almost total autonomy enabled it to plan for war in a political vacuum. When the July crisis came, Germany's political leaders were confronted with a military plan that had been formulated solely with reference to narrow organizational criteria and requirements. They discovered its inadequacy only after it was too late—or so the generals said—to do anything about it. . . .

The Cuban missile crisis provides an interesting contrast to the July crisis. Students of that confrontation have documented the extent to which Kennedy's management of that crisis provoked civilian-military conflict. For the most part, they have taken the military to task for its intransigence (Abel, 1966; Schlesinger, 1965; Allison, 1971; Sagan, 1985). On one level these criticisms are valid; military parochialism interfered with the president's efforts to avoid unduly provoking the Soviet Union, and it could have impeded a diplomatic resolution to the crisis. But the criticisms are also naive. Leopards do not change their spots; it is unrealistic to expect the American military to have been receptive to Kennedy and McNamara's effort to orchestrate and direct the blockade from the White House. "Micromanagement," a novel experience for the Pentagon, was certain to provoke anger and opposition.

The civil-military tensions that arose during the missile crisis resulted from the Kennedy administration's efforts to protect itself against the kinds of institutional mishaps that contributed to war in 1914. Kennedy and McNamara were remarkably prescient about the organizational impediments likely to obstruct their crisis strategy. Kennedy later attributed this in part to his just having read Barbara Tuchman's *The Guns of August,* a book that made a big impression on him (Kennedy, 1969).

In a sense, American civil-military relations during the Cuban crisis warrant being viewed in a positive light. What is remarkable in retrospect is neither the extent of the conflict nor the number of unforeseen and potentially disastrous incidents that took place. Rather, it is the fact that the conflict was not more serious and its effects more destabilizing. Kennedy and the military both deserve credit in this regard; Kennedy for his insight, and military leaders for the degree to which, when pushed, they departed from routine and improvised procedures that responded to presidential directives and needs.

The Dilemma of Contradictory Objectives

Organizational rigidity constitutes an enduring but partially controllable threat to the efforts of national leaders to manage crises in accord with their political objectives. A potentially more serious problem is the contradiction between the measures necessary to prevent an accidental or unauthorized firing of a nuclear weapon, on the one hand, and those required to guarantee the country's ability to retaliate after being attacked, on the other. This dilemma becomes particularly acute at high levels of strategic alert. There it constitutes the single most serious cause of potential instability.

There is an inherent vulnerability of U.S. command and control to nuclear attack and creates uncertainty about the nation's ability to retaliate. According to Bruce Blair, author of the most comprehensive study of this problem, measures introduced in the 1960s to protect against accidental and unauthorized use of nuclear weapons make the prospect of retaliation even more uncertain (Blair, 1985). These safeguards were at least in part a political response to public concerns of the day. They were implemented at a time when policymakers were ignorant of their real strategic consequences. Blair does not call for their repeal; rather, he wants a series of measures designed to reduce the current vulnerability of command and control. In his opinion, this constitutes the nation's strategic Achilles heel.

While Blair and those who share his point of view worry about the prospects for U.S. retaliation, other students of command and control are more concerned about the problem of control. They fear that procedures already instituted to help ensure retaliation significantly raise the risk of war by accident or miscalculation. The most serious danger in a crisis, in their view, is not the mutual temptation to preempt in order to take advantage of the vulnerability of the adversary's command and control. Rather, it is the difficulty that both sides will have in halting escalation once significant military preparations get under way.

The most forceful exponent of this thesis is Paul Bracken. He warns of the possibility of a nuclear Sarajevo, brought about by the interaction of complex institutions that leaders neither understand nor control. "The lesson of World War I," he observes, "was less that war can come about from the actions of obtuse leaders than that a nation's actions in crisis are profoundly influenced by the security institutions built years before the crisis occurs. The process of alerting and mobilizing forces, and of applying those forces, outran the political control apparatus. It even outran the strategies of the states involved" (Bracken, 1983, p. 3).

Bracken is pessimistic about the superpowers' ability to master an acute crisis between them. Contemporary leaders are, he admits, more aware of the dangers of loss of control than were their predecessors in 1914. But they also command more complex and less predictable military organizations: "Even if today's leaders understand the enormously destructive consequences of war, which are far more apparent now than in 1914, the construction of fatalistically complex nuclear command organizations parallels the conflict institutions built in the decade before 1914, but on a far more spectacular and quick-reacting scale" (Bracken, 1983, p. 3).

The command and control systems of the superpowers have matured, as Bracken shows, over the course of the last thirty years. The two most significant developments in this regard have been the vertical and the horizontal integration of these systems. Vertical integration links the warning and intelligence apparatus with the control machinery for nuclear weapons. Horizontal integration consists of tighter central control over nuclear weapons, including the determination of when, if ever, those weapons would be used as well as the targets assigned to them (Bracken, 1983).

Both kinds of integration were prompted by the need to establish greater control over the operational environment. The essential requirement in this regard is timely information about military preparations by adversaries. Such intelligence was made possible by a proliferation of sophisticated electronic and photographic sensors, computerized information processing, complex software algorithms, and control centers.

New procedures also had to be devised to speed up and manage strategic alerts. Thousands of nuclear weapons and their delivery systems, dispersed among numerous scattered commands, necessitated centralized nuclear planning in order to preassign targets and coordinate the delivery of weapons. It required redundant and secure communication channels to keep these forces abreast of adversarial preparations, bring them up to higher states of readiness, or actually authorize them to use their weapons. This requirement made a unified command structure essential.

The result was extraordinarily sensitive and complex systems in which the warning and alerting processes were fused as part of quick-reacting command and control networks. In the United States the institutional heart of this system is the North American Aerospace Defense Command, created in 1957 to serve as the central processor of warning information. NORAD also plays a critical role in an elaborate system of checks and balances designed to prevent accidental or unauthorized use of nuclear weapons. Most important alerting actions or emergency procedures can come into effect only in response to the declaration of the requisite alert level by two separate and independent commands. Institutional checks are built into every level of the system, down to the "two-man rule" that governs the actual launching of a weapon. The strategic bureaucracy deliberately replicates the guiding principle of the federal government, the separation of powers, ensuring that important decisions require the cooperative action of two separate branches.

So far, the combination of institutional checks and physical restraints has prevented an accidental or unauthorized launch. The possibility of such a disaster seems extremely remote under day-to-day operating conditions. It is much more likely to occur in a crisis, however, because of the stresses to which the system would be exposed and the ways in which stress could aggravate structural problems. The system could then behave in unprecedented and dysfunctional ways. We can briefly summarize some of the more troubling and intractable problems of the U.S. alert and response system.

Information Overload. Since the 1960s, photographic, electronic, and signals intelligence has been producing a growing stream of data, a stream beyond the ability of existing centers to process. More and more fusion and operations centers were set up to cope with this influx, but they have never really been able to do so. In a crisis, sensory overload could degrade the timeliness and quality of intelligence, increasing the possibility of faulty assessment. Beyond the confines of the relatively streamlined nuclear alerting systems, moreover, the problem of overload is even more acute. In 1984 the Defense Department reported that its communication networks had transmitted 56.7 million messages, and this total did not include voice transmissions or information in data-processing systems. In time of crisis, standing orders prohibit the transmission of non-essential administrative messages. Even so, operational officers worry, it could take five to ten hours for critical messages to get through (Halloran, 1985).

Institutional Compartmentalization. Fusion and control centers have proliferated, a growth paralleled by an enormous expansion of the strategic forces and their command centers. The result has been a large and highly fragmented strategic bureaucracy. It is now impossible for any single individual to develop intimate knowledge of the entire system and its component parts. The view of the people within the system has accordingly become increasingly compartmentalized and parochial. Coordination becomes more difficult, heightening the prospect that in a novel situation, components of the system would work at cross-purposes or in ways that would produce entirely unanticipated consequences.

Compression of Decision Time. In the 1950s the United States expected to have many hours of advance warning of nuclear attack. Warning today is measured in minutes; missiles fired from offshore submarines would take only five to eight minutes to destroy many of the nation's most important command and control centers, submarine pens, and bomber bases. A variety of systems have been developed to provide more timely warning of attack. Probably the most important of these is a constellation of satellites with infrared sensors capable of detecting Soviet ICBM and SLBM launches. These satellites transmit real-time data to ground stations in Colorado, Germany, and Australia, which in turn send the data not only to NORAD but also to SAC and the National Military Command Center in the Pentagon. Presumably all three centers have the authority to act on the basis of a warning conveyed in this manner. Time pressure has necessitated some circumvention of institutional checks and balances. In the future it may compel even more far-reaching breaches of these organizational safeguards.

Informal Procedures. Any complex system subject to severe time constraints has difficulty in performing its assigned task if it is run strictly by the book. In practice, informal understandings develop among its operators. These take the form of alternative and simplified procedures that facilitate performance by circumventing cumbersome institutional safeguards. The military, Bracken reports, has resorted to such shortcuts; officers have discovered ways of getting around many of the formal requirements of the nuclear command organization in order to carry out their assigned missions. Alternative procedures of this kind, established by oral agreement, are invisible from the outside until they are put into practice. So we do not know how widespread they have become; but we can be sure they have undermined some of the most important safeguards built into the system.

A similar development within the Soviet Union has paralleled the horizontal and vertical integration of the U.S. strategic warning and response system. The two systems have also become tightly coupled. This link was initially a side effect of the capability of each superpower to track the other's military preparations. But now both superpowers also have a growing capability to monitor each other's warning systems. As the two alert and response systems interact with each other on something close to an instantaneous basis, they can be described as components of a single gigantic nuclear system.

On a day-to-day basis the tight coupling of the two alert and response systems is not destabilizing. Each superpower can observe—that is, verify—that the other's forces are operating in the normal manner. Soviet forces are also kept at a lower state of readiness than American forces, something that also minimizes interaction between the two systems. Most important of all, both systems, it is believed, function in a dampening mode; they work on the supposition that something is wrong with information indicating an enemy attack. In the case of the United States, the system about which we know more, a warning triggers actions designed to test and (it is hoped) discredit it before it is accepted as the basis for action. Finally, all the organizational and physical safeguards that both sides have instituted to prevent an accidental or unauthorized launch are fully in effect.

For all of these reasons, the United States has coped successfully with over fifteen hundred false alarms. These have been triggered by causes as diverse as a misleading radar image, the erroneous broadcast of a training tape indicating that a nuclear attack was under way, and the failure of a computer chip, which prompted transmission of the same message. None of these events triggered a war because of what the military, with its love of jargon, calls "dual phenomenology": the reliance on two or more independent sensors to confirm an attack. Nevertheless, many of these incidents triggered some preparatory measures before they were diagnosed as false alerts. In 1980, in response to the computer chip failure, NEACP and B-52s were readied for takeoff, and the airborne command post of the U.S. commander in the Pacific was actually launched (Hart and Goldwater, 1980, p. 4; *New York Times,* 1979a, 1979b, 1980a, 1980b).

Incidents such as these illustrate the propensity of tightly coupled systems to produce overcompensating effects (Perrow, 1984). Bracken reports that additional alerting and preparatory measures would have gone into effect had the computer chip error been discovered a little more belatedly. Almost a hundred B-52s would have been launched and sent north toward their failsafe position, and alert messages would have been sent to ICBM crews as well as to conventional forces in Europe and Korea. The president would have been awakened at approximately 2:30 A.M. and told that he had minutes to evacuate Washington, decide on the country's war plan, and order a response (Bracken, 1983). Even these actions would likely not have led to war. They could have triggered Soviet counterpreparations, however, which would have brought both superpowers to unnecessary and dangerously high levels of nuclear readiness.

The more serious threat is posed by an accident or miscalculation in time of crisis. During a period of high tension more sensors would be activated and assigned to strategic warning. The stream of data entering superpower command and control channels would increase manyfold, and the two warning and response systems would become coupled even more tightly. Military and civilian leaders would also be more disposed to give credence to warnings of attack. If the crisis became sufficiently acute, it might in effect reverse the procedure for responding to warnings: policymakers might authorize a significant level of response *before* ascertaining the validity of a warning. A Soviet response could then provide an American counterresponse. . . . A false alarm could accordingly prompt the superpowers to move up the strategic escalation ladder to dangerously high levels of alert.

Bracken breaks new ground in our understanding of the dangers inherent in superpower crisis. Together with the pioneering work of John Steinbruner, his book ought to alert policymakers and military planners to problems that until recently they have largely ignored (Steinbruner, 1981–82). We can help by specifying the different ways by which system malfunctions could lead to war, which would impart verisimilitude to the somewhat abstract warnings that Steinbruner and Bracken provide. It would also be useful in a practical sense, because different kinds of malfunction almost certainly lead to war in different ways. By identifying these different paths to war, we would take the first step toward making some judgments about their probability and most likely causes.

Such a task is clearly beyond the scope of this chapter. I do intend to make a start in this direction, however, by describing three generic ways in which a system malfunction could provoke a war. These are mistaken retaliation, war by chain reaction, and war precipitated by third parties. I also examine possible scenarios for each of these paths to war. These scenarios should help us think more clearly about the problem and possible means for coping with it.

Mistaken Retaliation

The first possibility to consider arises from the near certainty that in the course of an acute crisis, the president would choose to pre-delegate some degree of launch authority. At least the theoretical possibility would thereby exist that some officer could use or order the use of nuclear weapons in the absence of a command to do so by the National Command Authority (NCA).

To dramatize the implications of predelegation, Bracken (1983) invokes the metaphor of a revolver. A revolver has two control mechanisms: a safety catch and a trigger. As long as the safety catch is locked, the trigger cannot fire the gun. Once the catch is released, control of the weapon passes to the trigger. The strategic arsenal can be likened to a revolver with one safety catch and many triggers. When negative control is in effect, the safety catch is engaged; none of the triggers can fire a nuclear weapon. However, the vulnerability of the NCA to attack requires that arrangements be made to predele-gate launch authority, either in advance of an attack or in response to indications that one has started. Presumably, the more acute the crisis and the perceptions of vulnerability, the further down the chain of command would launch authority be predelegated. If and when the strategic system is shifted to positive control, any one of these triggers could fire the nuclear gun.

Very little is known in practice about delegation of launch au-thority. The subject is highly sensitive, and the few officials, past and present, who have any knowledge of it have been understand-ably reluctant to speak out. Congressional inquiries have estab-lished that the president alone has the authority to order the use of nuclear weapons, but that he may delegate this power without limit (Congressional Research Service, 1975; U.S. Congress, House, 1976). Launch authority is no different constitutionally from any of the other executive powers of the president.

Successive administrations have refused to comment on predele-gation, but some information has nevertheless emerged from the statements of former officials. General Earl E. Partridge, a former commander of NORAD, admitted in a 1957 interview that he had been given the power to use nuclear weapons in specified emergency situations (*U.S. News and World Report,* 1964). General Lauris Norstad, former NATO commander, hinted to journalists that he had been granted similar leeway by President Kennedy (*U.S. News and World Report,* 1964). Daniel Ellsberg insists that presidents Eisenhower, Kennedy, and Johnson delegated launch authority to six or seven 3- and 4-star generals, the officers in charge of each of the unified and specified nuclear commands. He claims to have uncovered presidential letters authorizing these officers to use these weapons on their own authority in the aftermath of a Soviet attack (*New York Times,* 1977). Evidence unearthed by congressional hearings in 1975 and 1976 seems to bear out Ellsberg's claim (U.S., Congress, House, 1976). Looking Glass, usually commanded by a 2-star SAC general, may also be able to initiate a launch order. Former National Security Agency official Raymond Tate has admitted that the airborne command posts and Looking Glass possess the authorization codes. If so, they can not only verify and relay NCA commands but also take action on their own (Tate, 1980).

After reviewing all the available public evidence, Paul Bracken concludes that predelegation of launch authority extends at least as far down the chain of command as the unified and specified commands. In time of crisis, when forces are being brought to a high state of readiness, he believes, predelegation would almost certainly have to extend further down the chain of command. In Europe the extreme vulnerability of command centers to almost instantaneous destruction appears to necessitate more widely distributed launch authority in order to guarantee retaliation (Bracken, 1983).

No delegation of launch authority would be entirely discretionary; presidents are intensely jealous of their prerogatives and do not willingly relinquish authority. All kinds of restrictions would almost certainly hedge in any prior authorization to use nuclear weapons. They would be designed to preserve presidential authority as well as guard against the ill-considered use of such weapons. But whatever the restrictions imposed, the very fact of predelegation increases the risk that missiles might be launched.

In a serious crisis, and even more so in a conventional war, numerous requests for release authority would work their way up the chain of command. Some students of the alerting process contend that these requests would start to come in earlier than is generally expected. Commanders would want to have authorizations in their pocket for fear it would take too long to obtain them when and if they actually needed them (personal communication). The NCA would process requests for release authority and, depending upon the circumstances, could grant some or all of them. It is even conceivable that the president, overburdened by political responsibilities, would allow the secretary of defense to pass on the merits of the requests.

Grants of release authority could lead to hundreds or even thousands of armed weapons in the hands of field-grade officers. Pershing II or nuclear artillery batteries that were under attack and in danger of being overrun could launch their weapons, perhaps in the erroneous belief that a nuclear war had already begun. One weapon fired in this manner might be enough by itself to start a full-scale nuclear war. Alternatively, it could set in motion a chain of reprisals leading quickly to full-scale theater nuclear war.

Such a chain of events could bring nuclear war even in the absence of conventional conflict. The most likely initiator would be a submarine. American sea-launched ballistic missiles lack the physical locks (PALs) that protect other nuclear weapons. To prevent an unauthorized launch, the navy relies instead on institutional safeguards. The launching of a missile requires the concerted action of four officers and eleven seamen at various stations of the boat. All four officers must throw switches or turn keys within moments of one another; the missile cannot be fired if any one of them fails or refuses to participate (Stanford, 1976; Ball, 1985–86).

The navy insists that an SSBN could launch a missile only in response to an Emergency Action Message sent by the NCA. In practice, however, the navy recognizes the difficulty of communicating with submarines on station under wartime conditions and the vulnerability of all existing means for doing so. No doubt this is why naval officials have consistently opposed the introduction of PALs on submarines; such an innovation would necessitate a coded message from the NCA to arm the missiles. The navy's position on the matter encourages speculation that submarine captains must have secret standing orders to execute nuclear operations, in certain well-defined conditions, without an EAM. This supposition is supported by what little evidence exists in the public record (*Los Angeles Times*, 1984; Ball, 1985–86).

The real restraint on an SSBN captain is the crew; the captain would have to convince *them* that a launch was warranted. They might agree if they believed that nuclear war had already begun and that the NCA had been destroyed. A communications failure could erroneously engender such a conclusion, especially at the height of an acute crisis. The implications to the crew would be all the more alarming if the submarine had been attacked or had detected a Soviet effort to track and acquire it as a target. This is no mere speculation; the United States forced Soviet submarines to surface during the Cuban missile crisis and was prepared to use depth charges to do so. Conceivably the Soviets could do the same in some future confrontation if war seemed imminent or even highly likely.

An SSBN being hunted or trailed by the Soviets would confront a dilemma. The ambiguity of the situation would dictate careful efforts to establish what was really going on, but those efforts would require the submarine to come close to the surface, in order to trail or put up an antenna. Either action would make the boat vulnerable, the very last thing its captain would want to do in the circumstances. A safer course of action would be to try to evade Soviet units in the vicinity and only afterward attempt to communicate with other elements of the fleet or the NCA. If for any reason the submarine was unable to break away or communicate with the outside, its captain would find himself in a delicate position. He would be sorely tempted to launch his missiles if he believed his submarine was about to be destroyed. One Ohio-class submarine carries twenty-four missiles, each with four warheads, some of them almost certainly aimed at Soviet cities or targets in or near cities. Devastation of Soviet cities would be more than ample provocation to trigger a major nuclear reprisal against the United States. It is possible that misleading circumstantial evidence could lead a submarine to start a nuclear war when its captain and crew believed that they were retaliating.

There is a second submarine scenario to consider. Unlike the United States, the Soviet Union keeps most of its SSBNs in home waters. The boats may constitute a reserve strategic force; certainly the Soviets have made elaborate efforts to develop the naval and air forces necessary to protect them (Berman and Baker, 1982; Breemer, 1985). The American Navy has bridled at the notion of a Soviet SSBN sanctuary, and since John Lehman became secretary of the navy at the onset of the Reagan administration, it has seemingly become committed to going after the Soviet Navy in its home waters. For American attack submarines, this has long been routine practice (Watkins, 1986). It has been publicly reported that they routinely patrol in areas where Soviet SSBNs would seek to hide. They are also known to have penetrated Soviet territorial waters in the vicinity of major Soviet naval bases and on several occasions to have collided with Soviet vessels (Ball, 1985–86; *New York Times,* 1975a, 1975b, 1976).

Aggressive patrolling of this kind, in the opinion of retired admiral Worth Bagley (1977, p. 12), "risks an incident in time of tension." The Soviets could interpret it as an indication that the United States thought war was likely and was putting itself in a more advantageous position to fight it. If American attack submarines appeared to threaten its SSBNs, the Soviet Navy would be chaffing at the bit to force them to back off. A Soviet move of this kind would, under the tensest of situations, risk a naval encounter. An engagement between the Soviet Navy and American submarines could easily involve nuclear weapons. The U.S. rules of engagement apparently permit submarine captains to protect themselves *in extremis* with nuclear weapons (Ball, 1985–86).

War by Chain Reaction

The second way in which war could arise from system malfunction is as the result of an escalating spiral that leads to war by accident or preemption. The previous scenarios assumed that strategic forces were already at a high level of readiness; this sequence, by contrast, is itself the cause of such an alert.

High levels of strategic alert can result from an action-reaction cycle between Soviets and Americans that drives both superpowers to higher levels of military readiness than either independently would have chosen to implement. As Paul Bracken (1983, pp. 59–60) notes,

A threatening Soviet military action or alert can be detected
almost immediately by American warning and intelligence systems and conveyed to force commanders. The detected action
may not have a clear meaning, but because of its possible consequences protective measures must be taken against it. The
action-reaction process does not necessarily stop after only two
moves, however. It can proceed to many moves and can, and
often does, extend to air- and land-based forces because of the effect of tight coupling. In certain political and military situations,
this action-reaction process can be described as a cat-and-mouse
game of maneuvering for geographic and tactical position. In
more ominous circumstances, it may be seen as a jockeying for
positions before the first salvo of an all-out war.

Such a phenomenon is made more probable by the growing capability of the American and Soviet alerting systems to monitor
each other, not just the military actions that both systems produce.
The effect is to compress the action-reaction cycle. It may also intensify it, because the inherent ambiguity of intelligence of this kind
permits, or even encourages, the most threatening kinds of interpretation. High alert levels, regardless of how they come about, would
seriously interfere with whatever efforts were under way to resolve
the crisis. To quote Bracken (1983, p. 64) again:

> The interdependencies and synergies that were safely ig-
> nored during the peacetime cat-and-mouse game then begin to
> enter the picture. Tight coupling of the forces increases, infor-
> mation begins to inundate headquarters, and human, pre-
> programmed-computers, and organizational responses are
> invoked. Each response, whether it arises from a human op-
> erator or a computer, is intended to meet some narrow precau-
> tionary objective, but the overall effect of both Soviet and
> American actions might be to aggravate the crisis, forcing alert
> levels to ratchet upward worldwide. Although each side might
> well believe it was taking necessary precautionary moves, the
> other side might see a precaution as a threat. This in turn
> clicks the alert level upward another notch.

High levels of readiness threaten to spill over into war in two distinct ways. By definition, they entail some degree of strategic force readiness, dispersal of theater nuclear systems, activation of wartime command posts, and possibly even the spontaneous or organized evacuation of cities. The other side could readily interpret actions of this kind as indications of an impending attack. Such actions could prompt preemption, for any of the reasons analyzed in the previous chapter.

Strategic alerts also risk war by mistaken retaliation. Either side could initiate hostilities in the mistaken belief that it was responding to an enemy attack. We have already described two scenarios of this kind, both of them the result of system failures or misjudgment at the bottom of the nuclear chain of command. The same thing could also occur at the national command level, taking the form of a launch in response to a false warning of attack.

The vertical integration of the intelligence systems responsible for providing warning of attack permits the linking together or "fusing" of data collected from diverse sources into a more comprehensive assessment of threat. The ability to do so increases in a crisis, because warning of attack is given a much higher intelligence priority. Because of well-documented human propensity to impose order on events and to see in them a meaning deeper than reality often warrants, moreover, analysts will tend to view the resulting information flow as pieces of a puzzle (Heider, 1958; Michotte, 1963; Jones and others, 1971; Ross, 1978; Jervis, 1976). An exaggerated threat assessment could result. Events that in ordinary circumstances might be seen as unrelated would more likely be interpreted as part of some coordinated plan by the adversary (Bracken, 1983).

Physical or human failures in the alerting system, in tandem with an exaggerated perception of threat, could prompt extreme overreaction. Suppose, for example, that BMEWS or one of the PAVE PAWS radars is down because of scheduled maintenance or a failure of critical components. Frantic efforts to bring it back on line began at the onset of the crisis, but they have been unsuccessful. As the political situation begins to unravel, a U.S. early warning satellite reports that an SSBN, several hundred miles off the east coast, has just launched seven missiles. (Erroneous reports of this kind have sometimes been received during severe thunderstorms.)

With the relevant PAVE PAWS down and the missiles out of range of the older FSS-7 radars, NORAD would be in a quandary. Most of the other available radars would be useless, because the small MIRV payloads of modern SLBMs are invisible to them. To wait for PARCS in Grand Forks to verify that the United States was really under attack would waste precious minutes in which Soviet warheads could be zeroing in on their targets. To be on the safe side, NORAD and SAC might just arm the Minutemen, send the bombers aloft, and order additional communications aircraft aloft. They would probably also convene a "missile attack conference" with the president.

The Soviets possess the capability to monitor our alert levels and would detect some or all of the U.S. responses to the satellite warning. Not knowing that these were precautionary measures initiated in response to a false alert, Soviet officials might fear they were offensive in intent. The Soviets might move to a higher state of strategic readiness. Some analysts contend that U.S. intelligence is good enough to monitor Soviet strategic communications and to report that the Strategic Rocket Force, and perhaps theater nuclear forces as well, have received some kind of alert order or action message. This information, coming hard on the heels of the still unconfirmed satellite report, would intensify U.S. fears that SLBMs had actually been launched—that they were a precursor to a massive ICBM assault. After all, we would have no way of knowing that the Soviet action was only a response to our alert. An anxious president could order further steps to improve the prospects of retaliation, bringing the country to the very brink of war.

Up to this point our imaginary scenario has involved no human error or unanticipated interaction of components of the warning system. The United States and the Soviet Union have progressed toward full wartime readiness as the result of deliberate decisions taken in response to one faulty sensor. But if, in addition to time constraints and tight coupling, we allow for some kind of system malfunction, compounded perhaps by human error, the chance of catastrophic failure increases enormously.

What, for example, if the training tape that caused the famous 1979 alert had been fed into the computer during a crisis? At that time the monitors at NORAD, the National Military Command

Center in the Pentagon, the Pacific Command, and elsewhere showed that the United States was under attack from both land- and sea-based missiles. Such a tape would have only confirmed a misleading satellite report. In 1979 it took six minutes to determine what was wrong with the system, although only about a minute, the air force alleges, to realize that something had gone awry. At the height of a crisis, however, even that one minute would be more than enough time for a president mistakenly to contemplate retaliation against the Soviet Union.

SAC officers contend that it could not happen, because an exercise would never be conducted during a crisis. Perhaps they are right. But if asked beforehand, they doubtless would have sworn that the computer on which the tape was played could never have fed into the on-line warning system—something that inexplicably *did* happen. My point is not that the event will repeat itself, but rather that there is tremendous uncertainty about how such a complex and tightly coupled system would perform in a crisis. A faulty computer chip, poorly designed software, an operator error, any one of a hundred things or, worse still, a combination of them could result in an accidental war.

Representatives of NORAD dismiss these concerns and the scenarios associated with them as extremely unrealistic. They stress the low probability of component failures and the redundancy built in to all critical operations of the system. In their view a system failure has a minuscule probability of occurring, because it would have to be the multiple of a large number of individual failures. Even if they are right—and there is good reason to doubt it—they can give no assurance that a catastrophic failure could not happen.

Nuclear Alert and Response: A High-Risk System

The history of complex systems is punctuated by disquieting examples of failures that the designers and operators of the system were convinced could never happen. Most of them, including the Great Northeast Blackout of November 1965 and the Three Mile Island incident of 28 March 1979, resulted from the synergistic interaction of physical and human errors. The effects of initial component or subsystem failures were compounded by the failure of system operators to recognize the nature and extent of the problems because the failures were entirely unanticipated. In the case of Three Mile Island and the DC-10 crash of 25 May 1979 at O'Hare airport in Chicago, which was caused by the loss of an engine, human intervention based on faulty diagnosis of the problem greatly aggravated the effects of the failures (President's Commission on the Accident at Three Mile Island, 1979; Perrow, 1984; Stern and Aronson, 1984).

High-risk systems have characteristics that make them especially dangerous. Charles Perrow, author of a highly regarded comparison of high-risk technologies, argues that the danger stems from the way in which failures can interact and magnify their consequences. According to Perrow (1984, p. 4),

> The argument is basically very simple. We start with a plant, airplane, ship, biology laboratory, or other setting with a lot of components (parts, procedures, operators). Then we need two or more failures among components that interact in some unexpected way. No one dreamed that when X failed, Y would also be out of order and the two failures would interact so as to both start a fire and silence the fire alarm. Furthermore, no one can figure out the interaction at the time and thus know what to do. The problem is just something that never occurred to the designers. Next time they will put in an extra alarm system and a fire suppressor, but who knows, that might just allow three more unexpected interactions among inevitable failures. This interacting tendency is a characteristic of a system, not of a part or an operator.

In some systems, complexity of this kind is not necessarily fatal: accidents do not threaten human life, or their effects can somehow be minimized. There is enough available slack, spare time, and other ways of getting things done. But in tightly coupled systems, processes take place very quickly. They cannot easily be halted, and it is correspondingly difficult to isolate their effects.

Better equipment or different procedures can sometimes reduce the tightness of the coupling or minimize its effects. In air traffic control, for example, better organization and equipment have reduced interactive complexity and tight coupling in recent years. In other systems, among them nuclear power plants, neither technical improvements nor organizational innovations have succeeded in making them less accident-prone. The reason, according to Perrow (1984, pp. 4–5), is that such systems are based on organizational structures that have "large internal contradictions." Procedural changes cannot resolve these contradictions. Technological "improvements" only increase interactive complexity and tighten the coupling, making the system even more susceptible to certain kinds of accidents.

Nuclear response systems have several characteristics that make them appear even more accident-prone than many other kinds of high-risk systems. First, we are dealing with *two* systems, not just one. Individually, the strategic alerting networks of the superpowers have been described as the most complex systems ever designed by humans. When those two networks are considered together, they constitute another quantum leap in complexity.

Second, a catastrophic failure, if it occurred, could result not from one or the other national alert and response system, but from the interaction of the two. But we know next to nothing about how these systems would interact. What limited knowledge we do have is based on their performance at the lowest levels of alert, which is not very useful in predicting interactions at times of crisis. In the absence of detailed information about Soviet alert and response procedures, simulation will not help us either. Even if this information were available, simulations would still be of only limited utility in "debugging" the system, because they cannot begin to replicate anything close to the full range of possible interactions. Nor could they reliably factor in Soviet decision-making patterns and perspectives, which, by all accounts, are quite different from ours.

Third, evidence from the purely national level gives us little reason for confidence in the reliability of either side's warning system. The American system, as we have seen, has experienced numerous difficulties, some of them attributable to violations of procedure, others to the failure or malfunction of physical components. Many of these problems, according to General William Hilsman, former head of the Defense Communications Agency, are the kinds of things that "everybody would have told you were technically impossible"

(Roderick and Magnusson, 1983, p. 55). Critics of the system have also pointed to organizational and technical shortcomings; among them the computer software has come in for special criticism (U.S. General Accounting Office, 1981; U.S. Congress, House, 1981; Ford, 1985). Unreliable software is a particularly serious matter, because the nature of any problem might not become apparent until after something had gone seriously wrong (Lin, 1985).

The Soviet early warning system is less redundant and less technically sophisticated than its American counterpart. Up to 1986 the Soviets have never been able to maintain a full constellation of early warning satellites in orbit (Johnson, 1984; Ball, 1985–86). Their over-the-horizon radars are not connected to anything close to state-of-the-art technology for processing information. Nor do they provide coverage of all of the azimuths from which the Soviet Union can be attacked (U.S. Department of Defense, 1984). Their sensors have a propensity for malfunction even greater than that of U.S. sensors. The Soviets also operate under greater time constraints, because a large percentage of their retaliatory forces consists of vulnerable land-based ICBMs.

Complex Soviet systems are, there is reason to suspect, simply less reliable than their American counterparts. Soviet air transport is notoriously unsafe. Soviet airliners lack many of the safety features of American-built craft and generally do not have the same level of redundancy in vital subsystems. Soviet air control systems and procedures are also reported to be much less sophisticated. Soviet nuclear plants were known to be another problem area even before the meltdown at Chernobyl in April 1986. Many incorporate even fewer safety devices than Chernobyl and most American plants. In 1957–58 a major nuclear accident in Kyshtym in the Urals apparently contaminated a wide area with radiation. A Soviet biological and chemical weapons facility in Novosibirsk is reported to have had a major accident in April–May 1978 leading to the death of three hundred people (Medvedev, 1979; Trabalka and others, 1979; Gelb, 1981; Stratton, Stillman, Barr, and Agnew, 1979). Soviet missiles also have a bad safety record (Meyer, 1985).

To their credit, Soviet political leaders appear to take at least as great an interest in the internal control of nuclear weapons as do their American counterparts. Deep distrust of the loyalty of subordinates is one of the hallmarks of the Soviet system, and it has prompted Soviet leaders to maximize their control at every level of the formulation and implementation of policy. American leaders have always felt reasonably confident about their ability to prevent an unauthorized launch; Soviet leaders apparently do not. This lack of confidence may help to explain why the Soviets have continued to rely so heavily on land-based missiles; such assets are more vulnerable than submarines, but they are also easier to control from Moscow. It may also explain why Soviet forces were traditionally kept at a lower state of readiness than American forces (Berman and Baker, 1982; Meyer, 1985).

There is further evidence of Soviet concern with maintaining tight central control over nuclear weapons. Consider, for example, close involvement of the Committee on State Security (KGB) in their development and deployment. The KGB managed the Soviet nuclear weapons program until after Stalin's death; at least one Soviet source maintains that nuclear weapons did not become available to the military until 1954 (Vershinin, 1966, 1967). Even then the KGB controlled and guarded nuclear bombs and warheads at depots that were often well removed from weapons sites. As for missile systems deployed in Eastern Europe, the warheads and bombs that they would carry are retained, it is reported, inside the Soviet Union. Not until the mid-1960s did the Soviets place nuclear warheads on ICBMs on day-to-day alert (Barron, 1974; Penkovskiy, 1965; U.S. Department of Defense, 1978).

Third- and fourth-generation Soviet missiles and their control centers allegedly have electronic safeguards akin to PALs (Berman and Baker, 1982). The KGB nevertheless continues to play an important role in protecting against unauthorized use of nuclear weapons. KGB troops still maintain control over storage depots for these weapons, and they probably have instructions not to hand them over to the military until verifying orders through their own, independent communication channels to Soviet political leaders (Meyer, 1984, 1985). Reports suggest, furthermore, that Soviet ICBM launch centers have four-man crews—two of them KGB officers (Cockburn, 1983; Meyer, 1985; Prokhanov, 1982).

This Soviet emphasis on control makes it likely that Soviet delegation of launch authority, if it takes place at all, will occur at a later stage in a crisis than the equivalent American decision (MccGwire, personal interview, Nov. 5, 1985). It can be considered a plus for crisis stability. When Soviet devolution occurs, however, or once warheads are married up to theater-based delivery systems, control is likely to become precarious very quickly. Stephen Meyer ventures the judgment that because of its concern for control, "the Soviet political leadership would withhold nuclear release authority until prepared to see the military actually use weapons" (Meyer, 1985).

In the United States the transition from negative to positive control is envisaged by defense officials as a smooth if anxiety-provoking transition. Soviet leaders, in contrast, appear to believe that as they move toward war readiness, at some point they will experience a sharp discontinuity in their ability to maintain control over Soviet nuclear forces. This difference in attitude holds implications for crisis stability that cut two ways. Soviet determination to maintain central control as long as possible discourages high alert levels, and to that extent it is beneficial. But it is clearly destabilizing once these levels are reached—and all the more so if American leaders are aware of the problem. It gives both sides a strong incentive to preempt; the Soviets out of fear that it is their last clear chance to mount a coordinated attack, and the Americans out of fear that the Soviets are about to do so.

A fourth factor that makes alert and response systems appear accident-prone is that neither superpower has ever had a full dress rehearsal. We do not know how they would perform in a real crisis. To be sure, parts of the American system, and no doubt the Soviet system as well, have been tested in exercises and simulations. Exercises almost always reveal shortcomings the first time any reasonably complicated procedure goes into effect. Many other kinds of complex systems can be tested repeatedly, however, while obvious political constraints prevent alert and response systems being frequently tested. Even infrequent rehearsals of all or significant parts of the American system would arouse serious political opposition. It could also convey the impression to West European allies and the Soviet Union that the United States was turning into a militarized society seriously contemplating nuclear war. Rehearsals could themselves be destabilizing; they would likely prompt a range of precautionary alerting measures by the other side.

These obstacles put a premium on limited tests and simulations as means of debugging the alert and warning systems. Unfortunately, such methods may not be being exploited to their fullest potential. Some retired officers who have participated have confided that American tests and simulations are seldom based on realistic assumptions. One reason for this, they allege, is concern that failure of any components under operational conditions would expose NORAD to congressional criticism and, as a result, to closer scrutiny.

The fifth and final point to ponder is the implications of the reluctance of the operators to admit to others—and perhaps to themselves—the full extent of the system's vulnerabilities. This is disturbingly reminiscent of pre-World War I Germany, where war games were consistently rigged in order to demonstrate the feasibility of the Schlieffen Plan. The general staff subsequently used the results of these exercises to convince itself of the wisdom of its strategy (Snyder, 1984; Barnett, 1975). Everything went well until the plan had to be executed against an adversary who was not predisposed to conspire with the general staff to bring about the plan's success.

The nuclear navy and SAC are bastions of "technological optimists" (Kendall, personal communication, 1985). Officers in both believe that their weapons and their command and control are reliable and robust. Most of them are reluctant, even unwilling, to consider the possibility of a catastrophic failure, especially one triggered by human error. Their attitude is attributable in the first instance to cognitive bias; these officers work with these systems every day and have developed a high degree of confidence in them. But the bias is also motivated, because the recognition that war could arise from component failure, operator error, or disastrously faulty judgment by the NCA must be unsettling in the highest degree.

Critics, by contrast, are invariably "systems pessimists." They have adopted this perspective as the result of *their* experience, usually personal or historical knowledge of complex systems that have failed. Critics tend to argue by analogy; they draw parallels between the system under discussion and ones that have failed. System operators generally find this kind of argument unconvincing; they are prepared to listen only to scenarios that describe ways their specific system could fail and the reasons for it. The Nuclear Regulatory Commission, for example, refused to take industry critics seriously until they pinpointed the possibility of specific component failures and consequences that could lead to wider system failure. Even then, most of their dire predictions were dismissed as utterly fanciful. The critics began to gain credibility only after Three Mile Island and other less dramatic breakdowns of the kind the industry said could never happen (Perrow, 1984).

In the case of strategic warning, critics can never become as conversant with the system as its operators. So many important details are highly classified, and will remain so, that outsiders inevitably lack credibility in the eyes of the operators. This is alarming. The misplaced faith of the operators of the warning and response system in its inherent robustness could contribute significantly to some future system failure.

War Precipitated by a Third Party

In 1914 third parties were instrumental both in bringing about the crisis and also in preventing its resolution. A similar threat exists today. Tensions between the superpowers could be aggravated dramatically by either the independent military actions of a client state or a nuclear alert by a third power. The 1973 Middle East war testifies to the dangers of the former case. The Israelis succeeded in cutting off and almost completely surrounding the two Egyptian armies opposing them, touching off near panic in Cairo and deep concern in Moscow. The Soviet threat to intervene, which touched off the most serious superpower crisis since 1962, was designed to stop the Israeli advance by putting pressure on the United States to restrain its client. An effective cease-fire put an end to the crisis and left moot the question of what Moscow would have done had Israel resisted American appeals to halt its offensive on the Egyptian front (George, 1979; Blechman and Hart, 1982; Garthoff, 1985; Sagan, 1985; Kissinger, 1982).

The other danger that third parties pose stems from the proliferation of nuclear weapons. In a superpower crisis, especially one focused on Europe, the British and French nuclear arsenals must also be taken into account. In the Far East there is China to contend with. Very little is publicly known about the alert procedures of any of these powers or about the circumstances in which they would bring their strategic forces up to wartime readiness. Nor do we know how the Soviet Union would respond to force generation by any of them.

Britain is, from the perspective of crisis stability, probably the least worrisome of the three countries. Its strategic forces consist of aircraft- and submarine-based missiles. Submarines are under relatively little pressure to launch immediately because their commanders expect them to survive the initial round of a nuclear war. However, their communication links to national command authorities are extremely vulnerable, giving rise to the same kind of problems we encountered in the case of U.S. submarine force. This vulnerability could generate pressures for preemption. There is also the danger of mistaken retaliation. Britain is replacing its aging fleet of Poseidons with Ohio-class boats, each of which will carry twenty-four MIRVed missiles. As most of these warheads will continue to be targeted against Soviet cities, just one mishap probably will prompt full-scale reprisal. Soviet leaders, if they were still alive, would not necessarily know that it was a British rather than an American SSBN that had attacked them. The United States could end up paying a horrendous price for an allied mistake, which makes it imperative that we learn more about the British command and control system and its susceptibilities to malfunction (Baylis, 1977; Freedman, 1980; Sigal, 1983; Malone, 1984; Bowie and Platt, 1984; Arkin and Fieldhouse, 1985).

France poses a different kind of problem. The *force de dissuasion* includes nuclear-capable aircraft as well as submarine- and land-based missiles. The missiles are deployed in underground silos on the Plateau d'Albion, where they are vulnerable to attack from Soviet theater and intercontinental missiles. They are scheduled to be replaced by less vulnerable, mobile missiles sometime in the 1990s. The short flight time of the Soviet SS-20, and the even shorter flight time of follow-on missile systems that could be launched from East Germany or Czechoslovakia, puts pressure on the French to develop some option along the lines of launch on warning or launch under attack. A hair trigger of this kind is highly destabilizing for all the reasons discussed in the previous chapter. Crisis stability would be better served by a different strategy: ride out an attack, rely instead on the retaliatory power of the more survivable submarine force to deter the Soviet Union from attacking the land-based missile force (Sigal, 1983; Laird, 1983, 1984; Yost, 1984–85a, 1986).

British forces are integrated into NATO but can still be used independently, as the war in the Falklands demonstrated. It is difficult, however, to conceive of a scenario in which the British government would contemplate unilateral use of nuclear weapons against the Soviet Union. France's forces are independent of NATO but presumably would not be used unless the territorial integrity of France were directly threatened (Harrison, 1981; Yost, 1984–85b). By then, NATO might already have made a decision to go nuclear. The more important consideration for our purposes is the nature of French alerting procedures and the circumstances in which the French would bring nuclear forces, strategic and tactical, up to higher states of readiness. If France were to go to a higher state of alert than the United States or alerted its forces earlier, it could make a Soviet-American crisis centered in Europe much more difficult to resolve.

Even less is known about Chinese nuclear policies and alert procedures, which constitute another possible source of instability (Treverton, 1980; Segal, 1981, 1985; Wang, 1984). China is not an American ally, nor are Chinese and American security policies coordinated. A Chinese nuclear alert would still prompt some kind of Soviet response, and certain circumstances might even tempt the Soviets to launch a preemptive attack. A Soviet strike against the Chinese, even just a counteralert, would prompt the United States to raise its own state of military readiness. Extreme risk lies in the possibility of setting in motion a spiral of escalating interactions between the alert and response systems of the two superpowers.

Soviet and American strategic forces thus remain vulnerable not only to each other but also to the forces and policies of third parties. So many uncertainties surround the consequences of the interaction of superpower strategic forces that we cannot with confidence render any kind of judgment about the risks that various levels of alert entail. But we can be certain that the existence of third-party nuclear forces makes those risks greater than they would otherwise be.

Conclusions

Crises, this chapter has shown, could lead to unintended nuclear war in several different ways. Most disturbing of all in this regard is the link they reveal between preemption and loss of control. For the most important means of protecting against the one makes the other more likely.

Because there are no observable differences between military preparations for defensive purposes and those for offensive purposes, both superpowers, to be on the safe side, generally assume the worst about adversarial intentions. Such assumptions could easily lead them to carry out military preparations in response to any strategic alert by their adversary. By doing so, they reduce their vulnerability to preemption and thereby their adversary's incentive for striking first. However, high levels of alert risk accidental war because of all the difficulties involved in controlling alerted forces in a crisis. Thus military preparations that began as a purely defensive response to a threatening situation could provoke a cycle of reaction and counterreaction that could end up triggering an unintended nuclear war.

As if this were not bad enough, there is the complicating factor of third parties. The United States has only one nuclear adversary: the Soviet Union. By contrast, the Soviet Union is targeted with nuclear weapons by China, Britain, France, and possibly Israel as well. A crisis in the Far East, the Middle East, or Europe could therefore entail nuclear alerts by other countries in addition to the superpowers. Such alerts could provoke a superpower alert. The greater vulnerability of third-party nuclear forces, and their command and control, constitutes another important source of crisis instability. Finally, these forces are likely to be even more accident-prone when alerted because they lack many of the safeguards or redundant communication links that characterize superpower command and control.

The policy lesson of this chapter is clear: it is imperative that the superpowers do their best to refrain from nuclear alerts. But the American defense establishment still conceives of nuclear alerts as an effective means of demonstrating resolve. The misplaced belief in the political value of alerts constitutes an important and correctible source of crisis instability.

References

Abel, E. *The Missile Crisis.* Philadelphia: Lippincott, 1966.

Allison, G. T. *Essence of Decision: Explaining the Cuban Missile Crisis.* Boston: Little, Brown, 1971.

Arkin, W. M., and Fieldhouse, R. W. *Nuclear Battlefields.* Cambridge, Mass.: Ballinger, 1985.

Bagley, W. H. *Sea Power and Western Security: The Next Decade.* Adelphi Paper, no. 139. London: International Institute of Strategic Studies, 1977.

Ball, D. "Nuclear War at Sea." *International Security,* 1985–86, *10,* 3–31.

Ball, D. "The Soviet Strategic Command, Control, Communications and Intelligence (C³I) System." In *C³I Handbook.* Palo Alto, Calif.: EW Communications, 1986.

Barnett, C. *The Swordbearers: Supreme Command in the First World War.* Bloomington: Indiana University Press, 1975.

Barron, J. *KGB: The Secret Work of Soviet Secret Agents.* Pleasantville, N.Y.: Reader's Digest, 1974.

Baylis, J. *British Defence in a Changing World.* London: Croom Helm, 1977.

Berman, R. P., and Baker, J. C. *Soviet Strategic Forces: Requirements and Responses.* Washington, D.C.: Brookings Institution, 1982.

Blair, B. G. *Strategic Command and Control: Redefining the Nuclear Threat.* Washington, D.C.: Brookings Institution, 1985.

Blechman, B. M., and Hart, D. M. "The Political Utility of Nuclear Weapons: The 1973 Middle East Crisis." *International Security,* 1982, *7,* 132–156.

Bowie, C. J., and Platt, A. *British Nuclear Policymaking.* Santa Monica, Calif.: Rand, 1984.

Bracken, P. *The Command and Control of Nuclear Forces.* New Haven, Conn.: Yale University Press, 1983.

Breemer, J. S. "The Soviet Navy's SSBN Bastions: Evidence, Inference, and Alternative Scenarios." *Journal of the Royal United Services Institute,* 1985, *130,* 18–26.

Carter, A. B., Steinbruner, J. D., and Zraket, C. A. (eds.). *Managing Nuclear Operations.* Washington, D.C.: Brookings Institution, 1987.

Cockburn, A. *The Threat: Inside the Soviet Military Machine.* New York: Random House, 1983.

Congressional Research Service. *Authority to Order the Use of Nuclear Weapons.* Washington, D.C.: Congressional Research Service, 1975.

Ford, D. *The Button: The Pentagon's Strategic Command and Control System.* New York: Simon & Schuster, 1985.

Freedman, L. *Britain and Nuclear Weapons.* London: Macmillan, 1980.

Garthoff, R. L. *Détente and Confrontation: American-Soviet Relations from Nixon to Reagan.* Washington, D.C.: Brookings Institution, 1985.

Gelb, L. "Keeping an Eye on Russia." *New York,* Nov. 29, 1981, pp. 31ff.

George, A. L. "The Arab-Israeli War of October 1973: Origins and Impact." In A. L. George, *Managing U.S.-Soviet Rivalry: Problems of Crisis Prevention.* Boulder, Colo.: Westview, 1983.

Halloran, R. "Military's Message System Is Overloaded, Officers Say." *New York Times,* Nov. 25, 1985, p. 17.

Harrison, M. M. *The Reluctant Ally: France and Atlantic Security.* Baltimore, Md.: Johns Hopkins University Press, 1981.

Hart, G., and Goldwater, B. *Recent False Alerts from the Nation's Missile Attack Warning System.* Report to the Senate Committee on Armed Services. Washington, D.C.: U.S. Government Printing Office, 1980.

Heider, F. *The Psychology of Interpersonal Relations.* New York: Wiley, 1958.

Jervis, R. *Perception and Misperception in International Politics.* Princeton, N.J.: Princeton University Press, 1976.

Johnson, N. L. *The Soviet Year in Space: 1983*. Colorado Springs, Colo.: Brown Teledyne Engineering, 1984.

Jones, E. E., and others. *Attribution: Perceiving the Causes of Behavior*. Morristown, N.J.: General Learning Systems, 1971.

Kennedy, R. F. *Thirteen Days: A Memoir of the Cuban Crisis*. New York: Norton, 1969.

Kissinger, H. *Years of Upheaval*. Boston: Little, Brown, 1982.

Laird, R. F. *French Nuclear Forces in the 1980s and 1990s*. Alexandria, Va.: Center for Naval Analysis, 1983.

Laird, R. F. "The French Strategic Dilemma." *Orbis*, 1984, *28*, 307–328.

Lebow, R. N. *Nuclear Crisis Management: A Dangerous Illusion*. Ithaca, N.Y.: Cornell University Press, 1987.

Lin, H. "The Development of Software for Ballistic Missile Defense." *Scientific American*, 1985, *253*, 46–53.

Los Angeles Times, Oct. 14, 1984, p. 28.

Malone, P. *The British Nuclear Deterrent*. New York: St. Martin's Press, 1984.

Medvedev, Z. A. *Nuclear Disaster in the Urals*. (G. Saunders, trans.) New York: Norton, 1979.

Meyer, S. M. "Space and Soviet Military Planning." In W. Durch (ed.), *National Interests and the Military Use of Space*. Cambridge, Mass.: Ballinger, 1984.

Meyer, S. M. "Soviet Perspectives on the Paths to Nuclear War." In G. T. Allison, A. Carnesale, and J. S. Nye, Jr. (eds.), *Hawks, Doves, and Owls: An Agenda for Avoiding Nuclear War*. New York: Norton, 1985.

Michotte, A. E. *The Perception of Causality*. New York: Basic Books, 1963.

New York Times, May 25, 1975a, p. 42.

New York Times, July 6, 1975b, pp. 1, 26.

New York Times, Jan. 20, 1976, pp. 1, 4.

New York Times, Nov. 4, 1977, p. A9.

New York Times, Nov. 11, 1979a, p. 30.

New York Times, Dec. 16, 1979b, p. 25.

New York Times, June 18, 1980a, p. A16.

New York Times, June 23, 1980b, p. 58.

Penkovskiy, O. *The Penskovskiy Papers*. New York: Doubleday, 1965.

Perrow, C. *Normal Accidents: Living with High Risk Technologies*. New York: Basic Books, 1984.

President's Commission on the Accident at Three Mile Island. *The Need for Change: The Legacy of TMI*. Washington, D.C.: U.S. Government Printing Office, 1979.

Prokhanov, A. "Yadernyy Shchit." ["Nuclear Shield."] *Literaturnaya Gazeta*, 1982, *46*, 10.

Roderick, H., and Magnusson, U. (eds.). *Avoiding Inadvertent War: Crisis Management*. Austin: Lyndon B. Johnson School of Public Affairs, University of Texas, 1983.

Ross, L. "The Intuitive Psychologist and His Shortcomings: Distortions in the Attribution Process." In L. Berkowitz (ed.), *Cognitive Theories in Social Psychology*. Orlando, Fla.: Academic Press, 1978.

Sagan, S. D. "Nuclear Alerts and Crisis Management." *International Security*, 1985, *9*, 99–139.

Schlesinger, A. M., Jr. *A Thousand Days: John F. Kennedy in the White House*. Boston: Houghton Mifflin, 1965.

Segal, G. "China's Nuclear Posture for the 1980s." *Survival*, 1981, *23*, 11–18.

Segal, G. *Defending China*. New York: Oxford University Press, 1985.

Sigal, L. V. "No First Use and NATO's Nuclear Policy." In J. D. Steinbruner and L. V. Sigal (eds.), *Alliance Security: NATO and the No-First-Use Question*. Washington, D.C.: Brookings Institution, 1983.

Snyder, J. *The Ideology of the Offensive: Military Decision Making and the Disasters of 1914*. Ithaca, N.Y.: Cornell University Press, 1984.

Stanford, P. "Who Pushes the Button?" *Parade*, Mar. 28, 1976.

Steinbruner, J. "Nuclear Decapitation." *Foreign Policy*, 1981–82 (45), 16–28.

Stern, P. C., and Aronson, E. (eds.). *Energy Use: The Human Dimension*. New York: W. H. Freeman, 1984.

Stratton, W., Stillman, D., Barr, S., and Agnew, H. M. "Are Portions of the Urals Really Contaminated?" *Science*, 1979, *206*, 423–425.

Tate, R. "Worldwide C³I and Telecommunications." In *Seminar on Command, Control, Communication, and Intelligence*. Cambridge, Mass.: Program on Information Resources Policy, Harvard University, 1980.

Trabalka, J. R., and others. *Analysis of the 1957–58 Soviet Nuclear Accident*. Report ORNL-5613. Oak Ridge, Tenn.: Oak Ridge National Laboratory, 1979.

Treverton, G. "China's Nuclear Forces and the Stability of Soviet-American Deterrence." In *The Future of Strategic Deterrence*. Pt. 1: *Papers from the IISS 21st Annual Conference*. Adelphi Paper, no. 160. London: International Institute of Strategic Studies, 1980.

U.S. Congress, House. Subcommittee on International Security and Scientific Affairs. *Nuclear Weapons: Preserving Responsible Control*. 94th Cong., 2nd sess., 1976.

U.S. Congress, House. *Failures of the North American Aerospace Defense Command's Attack Warning System*. Hearings before a Subcommittee of the Committee on Government Operations, 97th Cong., 1st sess., 1981.

U.S. Department of Defense. *Annual Report of the Secretary of Defense for Fiscal Year 1979*. Washington, D.C.: U.S. Government Printing Office, 1978.

U.S. Department of Defense. *Soviet Military Power*. Washington, D.C.: U.S. Government Printing Office, 1984.

U.S. General Accounting Office. *NORAD's Missile Warning System: What Went Wrong?* Washington, D.C.: U.S. Government Printing Office, 1981.

U.S. News and World Report, Oct. 5, 1964.

Vershinin, K. "The Influence of Scientific Technical Progress on the Development of the Air Force and Its Strategy in the Post War Period." *Military Thought*, 1966, *5*, 36–44.

Vershinin, K. "The Development of the Operational Art of the Air Force." *Military Thought*, 1967, *6*, 1–13.

Wang, R. S. "China's Evolving Strategic Doctrine." *Asian Survey*, 1984, *24*, 1040–1055.

Watkins, J. D. "The Maritime Strategy." In *The Maritime Strategy*.

Suppl. *Proceedings of the U.S. Naval Institute*, Washington, D.C., Jan. 1986, p. 13.

Weick, K. E. "A Stress Analysis of Future Battlefields." In J. G. Hunt and J. D. Blair (eds.), *Leadership on the Future Battlefield.* Washington, D.C.: Pergamon Brassey's, 1985.

Weick, K. E. "Organizational Culture as a Source of High Reliability." *California Management Review*, 1987, *29* (2), 112–127.

Williamson, O. E. *The Economics of Discretionary Behavior: Managerial Objectives in a Theory of the Firm.* Englewood Cliffs, N.J.: Prentice-Hall, 1964.

Williamson, O. E. *Corporate Control and Business Behavior: An Inquiry into the Effects of Organization Form on Enterprise Behavior.* Englewood Cliffs, N.J.: Prentice-Hall, 1970.

Yost, D. S. *France's Deterrent Posture and Security in Europe.* Pt. 1: *Capabilities and Doctrine.* Adelphi Paper, no. 194. London: International Institute of Strategic Studies, 1984–85a.

Yost, D. S. *France's Deterrent Posture and Security in Europe.* Pt. 2: *Strategic and Arms Control Implications.* Adelphi Paper, no. 195. London: International Institute of Strategic Studies, 1984–85b.

Yost, D. S. "French Nuclear Targeting." In D. Ball and J. Richelson (eds.), *Strategic Nuclear Targeting.* Ithaca, N.Y.: Cornell University Press, 1986.

Chapter 11

Conclusion

The Analogy of Organizations as Nation-States

Mayer N. Zald

Analogical theorizing has its advantages and disadvantages. To the extent that an analogy is strong, it makes sense to use well-developed concepts and tools from one domain to explore similar but less well studied aspects of another. On the other hand, if the analogy is weak or if there are fundamental differences between the domains of analysis, working back and forth, as we have, may be only a dilettante's game—cute, but not substantial. Thirty and forty years ago, general systems theorists argued for the cross-level analysis of all living systems with a single set of concepts. "From cell to society" was their battle cry. That approach has not fulfilled their hopes because it tended to ignore the emergent properties and complexities of each successive level of biosocial organization. On the other hand, we believe that there are large gains to be had from cross-level analysis and integration when the differences and similarities between levels are closely analyzed and respected.

We have argued that there is substantial coherence to the analogy between nations and organizations (Chapter Two). Although there are real differences between nations and organizations and between interorganizational relations and international relations, the similarities are strong enough that we have felt confident of the usefulness of our venture. For example, even though the absence of a sovereign in international relations is a fundamental difference, leading conflict in international relations to be infinitely more perilous than conflict in interorganizational relations, there is a substantial variation in the range and structure of conflict and interdependency among organizations as among nations.

Moreover, differences should not be assumed or exaggerated. It may well be that although conflict is more perilous in international relations, the stability of international alliances and of national interests over long periods of time allows more trusting relations to develop in some areas of international relations than in interorganizational relations. One should not assume that international relations are inherently and invariably more conflictual. In short, as long as the limits of the analogy are respected, as we believe we have respected them, it ought to be possible to work back and forth between organizations and nations.

Moreover, there is a practical aspect to using organizations as analogs to nations. Trial-and-error learning and learning by doing carry unacceptable risks in some aspects of international relations. Learning about international relations by studying and experimenting with interorganizational relations gives a broader scope for thinking about the life-and-death issues of social systems. Organizational extinction and recombination occur every day, without the costs to mortality and freedom found in wars.

It might be argued that the analogy works because both interorganizational relations and international relations are specifications of a more abstract level of analysis, the analysis of social interaction and interdependence. In this sense, game-theoretic and social-interactional concepts comprehend both organizational interaction and national interaction. There is something to be said for this point of view, and our discussions of impression management (Chapter Seven), of alternative game strategies (Chapter Nine), and of de-escalation (Chapter Five) draw as much on concepts of interpersonal relations and decision making as they do on organizational research per se. Organizational interaction and international action both deal with the interaction of individuals, albeit bounded by social system role requirements. Thus, general concepts of social interaction are of considerable utility.

However, there are similarities between the problems of interaction among organizations and among nations that are not revealed in the

analysis of social interaction in general. Both nations and organizations can be analyzed as social systems in themselves. In both, there
exist internal constituencies. Thus, the management of external interdependencies almost always ramifies into the internal life of the
system. Foreign affairs and negotiations have consequences for the
fate of many communities, organizations, and groups within the nation. Competition and cooperation between organizations have consequences for stockholders, managers, and employees at different
locations within organizations. Principal-agent problems come into
view in interorganizational and international relations. They are ab-
sent in more general analyses of interaction that do not focus upon
the interaction of social systems.

Several other features of nations have clearer parallels in organizations than in other kinds of social systems (for example, small
groups, communities) or in social interaction more generally. In
both nations and organizations, there are clear authority systems
and gradations of power. In both, ideologies are used to justify
policy choices. In both, rewards and penalties over members are
substantial and often explicit. Thus, as long as the differences are
kept in mind, analogical theorizing and research between these two
levels of analysis ought to be fruitful.

The constituency parallel has been particularly important to our
work, and several chapters in this volume have used it: Chapter
Two, which deals with joint ventures and contracts, discusses constituency problems from the point of view of delegated agents and
their relations to principals. Chapter Four shows how bureaucratic
and organizational interests within the United States contributed to
the escalation of the arms race; and Chapter Seven, which analyzes
issues of impression management, uses the meeting of Gorbachev
and Reagan at Reykjavik to show how the conduct of international
negotiation ramifies into public opinion and politics in the participating nations.

The choice of topics for the chapters in this volume reflects our
commitment to exploring the strong analogy between organizations
and nations. We asked the question "How does thinking about the
problems of international security change if we consider parallel
issues in organizational analysis and social interaction?" The chapter titles indicate the substantive areas to which this question has

led us, and each chapter can be considered an attempt to answer that basic question as it applies to a specific topic.

A good example is provided by the chapter on negotiations (Chapter Six) by Leonard Greenhalgh and Roderick Kramer. Both authors have done experimental and organizational analyses of negotiation processes, and both have noticed that deterrence theory seems to require no negotiation. In contrast to distributive and integrative bargaining, deterrence in principle requires only the ability to impose costly sanctions. Yet negotiation in international relations has continued within the context of deterrence. Greenhalgh and Kramer have therefore confronted the question of how to expand the theory of negotiation to include the context of deterrence—mutually assured destruction. We believe that the resulting chapter is important both for students of negotiation and for experts on international relations. The issue of deterrence emerged as principle and policy at the international rather than the organizational level, and the authors deal explicitly with international issues. Certain aspects of negotiation in organizations are thrown into sharp relief, however, by their analysis. The benefits of cross-level analysis accrue to both levels.

A different example of how our answers to the question of organizational-international parallelism developed can be seen in Chapter Five on de-escalation. As we thought about problems of conflict and conflict resolution, we were struck by a great imbalance in the literature—much work on polarization, conflict spirals, and escalation; much less on de-escalation, especially de-escalation by the voluntary actions of the antagonists themselves. The imbalance is greatest in the research literature of international relations, which deals extensively with escalation toward war. Research on organizations has been more concerned with the resolution of conflict, but almost always through the intervention of third parties, either as consultants or as the designers of experiments. Chapter Five, by Kahn and Kramer, begins to redress these imbalances.

All the chapters of this book reflect our shared professional interest in the study of human organizations. The book began, however, out of our concerns as citizens and our desire to contribute to the attainment of a more stable and peaceful world. We have not attempted to develop an explicit agenda of reform, on the assumption that such political tasks are best left to the political process. The chapters differ in the degree to which action implications are made explicit, with the differences shaped more by the state of research than the preferences of authors. Chapter Eight, by Irving Janis, is perhaps the most directly advisory. Janis's model of decision making is applied to past international crises and then used as a source of suggestions for managing crises in the future.

One task for the future is to develop similar links between research and action in the domains addressed by other chapters. Other tasks involve the extension of the nation-organization analogy to further aspects of international relations. For example, consider the potential usefulness of network theory to international relations. Mathematical and theoretical developments have made it possible for organizational analysts to model the forces that shape interactions among organizations. Much has been learned about how interlocking directorates and resource interdependence shape the economic and political behavior of organizations (Burt, 1983; Mizruchi, 1989). The possibility of applying network models and methods of analysis to international alliances already exists, and it is full of promise (Guilarte, 1990).

Other possibilities are being generated by changes in international affairs, which have begun to outpace if not confound the predictions and explanations of experts. This project began at a time when the cold war seemed firmly in place. It is completed at a time when many analysts tell us that the cold war is over, and at least one influential article envisions a period of such stability as to constitute "the end of ideological contest in international relations" (Fukuyama, 1989). We believe, however, that the welcome movement toward more open and peaceful relations among nations brings international and organizational issues more closely together.

The scheduled emergence of the European Community constitutes a massive transformation of the complex interrelationships of many nations, a transformation that acknowledges their interdependence and signals their intention to manage the interdependence. International organizations are the necessary vehicle for such management (Chapter Two), and the analysis of federations, of joint ventures, and of procedures for collective decision making will be increasingly important elements on the international agenda.

The reduction of anarchical relations is what organization means, and organizational theory and research have much to contribute to this great task at the international level, as they have much to learn from international scholarship and experience. We conclude our book with the hope that scholars in both fields, international and organizational, will be moved to enlarge the work that we have begun.

References

Burt, R. S. *Corporate Profits and Cooperation: Networks of Market Constraints and Directorate Ties in the American Economy.* Orlando, Fla.: Academic Press, 1983.

Fukuyama, F. "The End of History?" *The National Interest,* 1989, *16,* 3–18.

Guilarte, M. "The Delegitimation of the Colonial System After World War II." Unpublished doctoral dissertation, Columbia University, 1990.

Mizruchi, M. S. "Similarity of Political Behavior Among Large American Corporations." *American Journal of Sociology,* 1989, *35* (2), 401–424.

Name Index

Subject Index